Frontiers in Pension Finance

In memory of Dirk Witteveen,
who ushered pension supervision into a new era

Frontiers in Pension Finance

Edited by

Dirk Broeders

De Nederlandsche Bank, the Netherlands

Sylvester Eijffinger

Tilburg University, RSM Erasmus University and Netspar, the Netherlands

Aerdt Houben

De Nederlandsche Bank, the Netherlands and IOPS

Edward Elgar

Cheltenham, UK • Northampton, MA, USA

Published by
Edward Elgar Publishing Limited
Glensanda House
Montpellier Parade
Cheltenham
Glos GL50 1UA
UK

Edward Elgar Publishing, Inc.
William Pratt House
9 Dewey Court
Northampton
Massachusetts 01060
USA

A catalogue record for this book
is available from the British Library

Library of Congress Cataloguing in Publication Data

Frontiers in pension finance / edited by Dirk Broeders, Sylvester
Eijffinger, and Aerdt Houben.
    p. cm.
    Includes bibliographical references and index.
    1. Pensions—Finance. 2. Pensions—Management. 3. Pension
trusts—Management. I. Broeders, Dirk, 1969– II. Eijffinger, Sylvester C. W.
III. Houben, Aerdt C. F. J.
    HD7091.F85 2008
    658.3'253—dc22

2007039447

ISBN 978 1 84720 660 2 (cased)

Printed and bound in Great Britain by MPG Books Ltd, Bodmin, Cornwall

Contents

Figures

Tables

Contributors

The following persons have contributed to this book. This list mentions their most important affiliations, but is not exhaustive in the latter respect.

Keith Ambachtsheer is Director of the Rotman International Centre for Pension Management (ICPM) and Adjunct Professor of Finance at the Rotman School of Management, University of Toronto

John Ashcroft is Former President of the International Organisation of Pension Supervisors (IOPS) and Head of Strategy at the Pensions Regulator, United Kingdom

Solange Berstein is Superintendent of Pension Fund Administrators in Chile

Henrik Bjerre-Nielsen is Director General of Finanstilsynet (the Danish FSA)

David Blake is Professor of Pension Economics and Director of the Pensions Institute at Cass Business School, London

Zvi Bodie is the Norman and Adele Barron Professor of Management at Boston University

Axel Börsch-Supan is Director of the Mannheim Research Institute for the Economics of Aging (MEA), and Professor of Economics at the University of Mannheim

Lans Bovenberg is Scientific Director of Netspar, and Professor of Economics at Tilburg University

Dirk Broeders is Senior Economist at the Supervisory Strategy Department of De Nederlandsche Bank (DNB) and organizer of this conference on behalf of DNB

Gregory Brunner is Financial Sector Specialist, Financial Markets for the Social Safety Net in the Finance and Private Sector Development Vice Presidency at the World Bank

Ismail Düzgün is Research Assistant at the Mannheim Research Institute for the Economics of Aging (MEA)

Sylvester Eijffinger is Professor of Financial Economics at Tilburg University, Professor of European Financial Integration at RSM Erasmus University Rotterdam, and organizer of this conference on behalf of Netspar

Jon Exley is an actuary with over 20 years of pensions experience

Jeremy Gold is Proprietor of Jeremy Gold Pensions which provides pension finance consulting to sponsors of defined benefit pension plans

Richard Hinz is Pension Policy Adviser in the Social Protection Team of the Human Development Network at the World Bank

Roy Hoevenaars is Senior Portfolio Manager at ABP Investments

Aerdt Houben is Head of the Supervisory Strategy Department of De Nederlandsche Bank (DNB), and chairman of the Technical Committee of the International Organisation of Pension Supervisors (IOPS), and organizer of this conference on behalf of DNB and IOPS

Ross Jones is President of the International Organisation of Pension Supervisors (IOPS) and Deputy Chairman of the Australia Prudential Regulation Authority (APRA) and Associate Professor at the School of Finance and Economics at the University of Technology, Sydney

Klaas Knot is Division Director of Supervisory Policy at De Nederlandsche Bank and Professor of Money and Banking at the University of Groningen

Kees Koedijk is Professor of Financial Management at the RSM Erasmus University Rotterdam and Professor of Finance at Maastricht University

Raimond Maurer is Professor of Finance at the Goethe University, Frankfurt am Main, Germany

Olivia Mitchell is Professor of Insurance and Risk Management at the Wharton School of the University of Pennsylivania and Executive Director of the Pension Research Council

Roderick Molenaar is Senior Researcher at ABP Investments

Theo Nijman is Scientific Director of Netspar, and Professor of Investment Theory at Tilburg University

Lucas Papademos is Vice-President of the European Central Bank

Ambrogio Rinaldi is Central Director of the Commissione di Vigilanza sui Fondi Pensione (COVIP, Italy) and chairman of the OECD Working Party on Private Pensions

Roberto Rocha is Manager of the Financial Policy Development Unit, Financial Sector Vice-Presidency at the World Bank

Ralph Rogalla is Research Assistant at the Goethe University, Frankfurt am Main, Germany

Peter Schotman is Vice-Dean of the Faculty of Economics and Business Adminstration of Maastricht University, and Professor of Empirical Finance at Maastricht University

Tom Steenkamp is Chief Investment Officer, allocation and research, Member of the Board at ABP Investments, and Professor of Investments at the VU University Amsterdam

Coen Teulings is Director of the Netherlands Bureau for Economic Policy Analysis (CPB), and Professor of Economics at the University of Amsterdam

Matthias Weiss is Vice Director of the Mannheim Research Institute for the Economics of Aging (MEA), University of Mannheim

Nout Wellink is the President of De Nederlandsche Bank, and Chairman of the Basel Committee on Banking Supervision

Dirk Witteveen was the Executive Director of De Nederlandsche Bank and chairman of the Joint Forum

Preface

Economists are clamouring for reforms to global pension systems. They stress the need for restructuring from different angles. The driving motive is the upcoming demographic change in many countries. Looking ahead, the aging process will challenge the financing of pension benefits, reaching a climax in the 2030s when babyboom generations will have retired. As pension expenditures rise relative to the tax and premium bases from which they are financed, pay-as-you-go pension systems will become unsustainable. This is the first angle on pension reform. To secure a durable pension structure, many countries need to shift, at least in part, to pre-funding their pension commitments. The earlier this measure is taken, the easier. Incentives for greater labour market participation and lifespan education will also alleviate the impact of the demographic shift.

A second angle is the need to cope with the financial implications of greater reliance on pre-funding. As accumulated pension savings rise in relation to economic production, fluctuations in asset values and discount rates will have an increasing impact on balance sheets and, via numerous transmission channels, on domestic income and expenditure. How best to handle the associated mismatch risks between assets and liabilities depends on preferences and points of departure. In this context, the influence of pension fund regulation and supervision will rise markedly. Thus, designing judicious regulatory and supervisory policies becomes crucial.

Beyond this, a third angle relates to financial education. Recent years have seen a major change in the distribution of pension risks, away from companies and pension entities and towards households. At the same time, evidence points to shortcomings in the capacity and willingness of households to understand and shoulder these risks. Thus, strides need to be made in increasing pension risk awareness and in tailoring default options that coach individuals towards adequate premia levels and appropriate investment portfolios.

Substantial progress has been made in recent years to address these issues. For instance, broad consensus has emerged on measuring assets and liabilities in a market-consistent fashion. At the same time, financial innovation and information technology have increased the scope for efficient risk sharing and hedging. Together with tightened governance requirements, improved risk assessments have buttressed the financial soundness of pension entities, and communication requirements surrounding an individual's prospective pension benefits are being stepped up. But much remains to be done.

This is the backdrop to this book. It provides state-of-the-art analyses of the financial, institutional and supervisory dimensions of pensions. More specifically, it debates sustainable solutions to the key issues arising from population aging, provides guidance for pension plan design and stimulates the development of best practices in risk management and pension fund governance. In that respect this book is of interest not only to policy makers, supervisory officials and academics, but to all those with a broader interest in pension issues.

The contributions in this book stem from a conference entitled 'Frontiers in Pension Finance and Pension Reform' jointly organized by De Nederlandsche Bank (DNB), the Network for Studies on Pensions, Aging and Retirement (Netspar) and the International Organisation of Pension Supervisors (IOPS) on 22–23 March 2007. At this conference, pension experts from across the world gathered in Amsterdam to explore the prime challenges of pension design. This generated a pack of innovative chapters and cutting-edge discussions. These contributions have been brought together in this book, to push the frontiers further for a wide audience.

Nout Wellink
President of De Nederlandsche Bank

Acknowledgements

This book is based on the proceedings of the international conference 'Frontiers in pension finance and reform', which was held in The Hotel Grand, Amsterdam, the Netherlands on 22–23 March 2007.

The contributions to this book are written in a personal capacity. The views expressed are those of the authors, and do not necessarily represent those of the organizations to which they are affiliated. The responsibility for the contents of the chapters and discussions is entirely with the authors themselves. The editors express their gratitude to all the contributors to this book and thank De Nederlandsche Bank (DNB), the Network for Studies on Pensions, Aging and Retirement (Netspar) and the International Organisation of Pension Supervisors (IOPS) for financial support.

We are indebted to the following persons for their kind assistance with the organization of the conference: Marenne de Lange van Bergen, Isabella Ciocca, Loek van Dalen, Sylvia van Drogenbroek, Lenie Laurijssen, Robert Mosch, Mirjam van der Poel, Margreet Punt, Fiona Stewart, Jacqueline Valiente-Martinez and Tim Willems.

Dirk Broeders, Sylvester Eijffinger, Aerdt Houben

1. An introduction to frontiers in pension finance

Dirk Broeders, Sylvester Eijffinger and Aerdt Houben

1.1 INTRODUCTION

All over the world, pension systems are being transformed, for several reasons. To begin with, over the next decades, societies will come up against the combined consequence of increased life expectancy and lower fertility rates, making pay-as-you-go pension systems difficult to sustain. Secondly, the 'perfect storm' in the period 2000–2002 highlighted the vulnerability of funded pension systems to adverse financial market developments and showed that funded pension provisions need to be flexible to cope with such shocks. In the third place, many companies have opted to rid themselves of the residual risk of their pension plans, and have shifted it to individuals who may be considered less qualified to manage financial risks.

At the same time, these challenges are met with breakthroughs in pension finance and a better understanding of the many facets of the way pension systems work. Traditional pension paradigms are being revised in tune with an increasing awareness of the implications of an aging society for both labour and financial markets. Financial market integration, innovations in financial instruments and advances in information technology are enhancing the possibilities for efficient risk management. Meanwhile, pension regulation is aiming to align these developments with those in risk management and disclosure. Improved risk assessment, transparency and governance consequently add, not just to the financial soundness of individual institutions, but also to the resilience of the global financial system.

All this raises important questions which were discussed during the conference, 'Frontiers in pension finance and reform'. Three main topics passed in review: (i) recent developments in pension finance and actuarial science, (ii) the institutional design of pension systems, and (iii) international dynamics in pension governance and supervision. These themes are introduced in the next sections.

1.2 RECENT DEVELOPMENTS IN PENSION FINANCE AND ACTUARIAL SCIENCE

In pension finance, a key role is played by the amalgamation of finance and actuarial science, as a direct result of the fact that pension risks have both a financial and an actuarial component. Pension risks arise when pension financing offers insufficient guarantees that the envisaged benefits will be available. This may be due to replacement rate inadequacy at retirement, social security cuts, the risk of outliving one's savings, investment risk and inflation risk (Bodie, 1990).

Pension financing is up against such uncertainties and pension fund trustees need to have a clear and consistent understanding of these risks. Accordingly, assets and liabilities are increasingly disclosed on a mark-to-market basis. This facilitates professional risk management with modern financial market instruments. It also enhances market discipline and transparency.

However, both Jon Exley and Jeremy Gold argue in this book that market valuation principles can also be used to demonstrate that, in a perfect (Modigliani–Miller) world, financial risk management does not create value. A key issue in this respect is that pension schemes generally contain implicit options which transfer value from one stakeholder to another. For instance, if shareholders have a claim to a potential surplus in the company pension fund, it may be tempting to increase the risk profile of this fund's assets to increase the value of this claim, thereby lowering the value for the fund's beneficiaries. In other words, embedded options potentially misalign the interests of shareholders and employees. Exley thus states that any justification for pension provision will favour simple transparent and non-contingent defined benefit pension plans rather than the complex benefit schemes with embedded options of various forms which are commonly observed.

Furthermore, one can argue that the world is imperfect and that second-order effects may play an important role in deriving optimal solutions. Gold reasons in Chapter 3 that, in many Anglo-Saxon countries, returns on bonds owned by corporations and individuals are more highly taxed than those on stocks while, for pension plans, stock and bond returns are treated equally. On this assumption, he claims that it is optimal to establish net negative market (beta) exposure in defined benefit pension plans; this challenges conventional wisdom.

1.3 INSTITUTIONAL DESIGN OF PENSION SYSTEMS

After this theoretical background, let us take a look at the design of pension systems. Reviewing the current structures of pension systems in the western world, one immediately sees that they are predominantly pay-as-you-go systems (see, for example, Table 10.1 in this book).

The current predominance of these schemes can be attributed largely to a single historical reason. As prosperity increased after the Second World War, policy makers began to address the financial position of the elderly. It appeared that many workers had not been able to save sufficiently for their old age. As this caused an immediate and urgent need for some form of old age income provision, many governments decided to instal pay-as-you-go schemes, which become active immediately, rather than funded systems which take effect only after one generation has saved up enough retirement capital. Post-war retirees consequently received a windfall gain as they had not contributed to the pay-as-you-go system during their working lives, but still got to enjoy a full benefit during retirement.

The current pay-as-you-go systems, however, now find themselves under considerable pressure, as aging increases the number of benefit recipients relative to the number of active contributors. Moreover, as most economies are dynamically efficient, the rate of return on a funded system, that is, the interest rate, is higher than the implicit rate of return on a pay-as-you-go system, which equals the economic growth rate (Aaron, 1966). For these two reasons alone, numerous authors have pleaded for (partial or gradual) conversion of existing pay-as-you-go systems into funded ones.

However, the earlier discussed windfall gain for the first generation has an important drawback: owing to the resulting Ponzi game nature of a pay-as-you-go system, the current reform issue is not to be trifled with. After all, the currently working generation contributes to the pay-as-you-go system in the belief that they too will eventually receive a pay-as-you-go benefit from the same system. They are thus accumulating an implicit claim on the subsequent generation. To be politically feasible, any reform scenario should therefore take these claims seriously by solving the problem of who is going to bear the transitional burden.

A number of authors (see, for example, Breyer (1989) and Verbon (1989)) have shown, however, that, whatever option is chosen, the (partial or gradual) replacement of pay-as-you-go by funding cannot be organized in a Pareto-improving way. Nevertheless, reforms seem necessary. In this context, the contribution of Raimond Maurer, Olivia Mitchell and Ralph Rogalla in this book sheds an interesting light on reform possibilities for the current pay-as-you-go pension system for civil servants in the German federal state of Hesse. Their analysis assesses the impact of introducing a supplementary tax-sponsored pension fund whose contributions are invested in capital markets and are used to relieve the public budget of a part of future pension payments.

Whereas the regular focus in the aging literature is often on the consequences for the public budget, the contribution of Axel Börsch-Supan, Ismail Düzgün and Matthias Weiss to this book takes a different angle. They focus on the consequences of aging for labour productivity, which has hardly received attention in the literature so far. The productivity of older workers will be an increasing determinant of total labour productivity. The authors come up with two remarkable conclusions. First, it seems that the loss of productivity as employees get older is compensated by the gain in experience. Secondly, they find evidence against the generally accepted hypothesis that work teams perform better when consisting of a mix of young and older workers. Communication within the team seems to be important; younger workers seem to put the elderly under strain, thereby reducing their performance.

Finally, akin to the funding decision is the issue of the optimal design and implementation of a pension contract. The contribution of David Blake deals with this topic. He focuses on the optimal design of defined contribution schemes and provides evidence that the current UK private pension plans are poorly designed. The main point in this chapter is that the commission charges for selling these plans are front-loaded. By contrast, Blake argues that the best way of delivering value in the pension industry is to have charging structures that are simple, fully transparent, performance-related and non-front loaded.

1.4 INTERNATIONAL DYNAMICS IN PENSION GOVERNANCE AND SUPERVISION

Pre-funded pension systems already play an important role in today's economy. According to the OECD Global Pension Statistics, the weighted average of pension fund assets relative to GDP was 88 per cent in 2005, compared to only 29 per cent in 1987. Given the projected further aging of populations and the increasing need for pre-funding in pension finance, the ratio of total pension assets to GDP is projected to rise even further in the coming years. This means that pension funds are also likely to have an increasing influence on financial markets. Today, aggregate pension fund assets represent more than 20 per cent of the domestic equity and 10 per cent of the domestic bond market capitalizations in the G10 countries (Visco, 2005). As these percentages are likely to go up further, aging may also contribute to the deepening of financial markets, as well as to a stronger role for capital market intermediation (Blommestein, 2001).

Pension funds thus play a far greater role in today's economy, but not only on a macro level. Pension funds also have an important role as financial intermediaries, helping individuals to save for old age and to protect the value of their pensions (Boeri et al., 2006). The stakes for effective supervision have consequently increased considerably. Indeed, the regulation and supervision of pension funds are essential from both the macro and the micro perspective. They should primarily be aimed at guaranteeing a certain benefit level, at reasonable cost without straining financial stability. In this light, the contributions of Gregory Brunner, Richard Hinz and Roberto Rocha, Keith Ambachtsheer, Zvi Bodie and Lans Bovenberg to this book are relevant. Brunner et al. plead for a wider introduction of risk-based supervisory models, arguing that these are better aligned with the needs of efficient capital market operation. The authors arrived at this conclusion after systematically reviewing risk-based supervisory models in Australia, Denmark, Mexico and the Netherlands.

Ambachtsheer subsequently argues that pension providers which deal effectively with agency issues and practise good governance will create more value for their beneficiaries. He shows that US mutual fund participants suffer at least a 1 per cent net return loss per annum on their retirement savings, relative to participants in a pension fund. Bodie argues that, apart from adequate returns, guarantees are also essential to retirement planning, as they are readily understandable for consumers, and therefore reduce the need for costly financial education. His chapter concentrates on methods to manage pension guarantees so as to minimize the cost of shortfall.

Bovenberg takes a broader stance. He argues that an optimal pension contract should be flexible: it should be a defined contribution when participants are young and possess relatively high human capital with which to absorb shocks, while it should gradually be transformed into a defined benefit contract as the participant depletes his stock of human capital over the course of his life. Furthermore, Bovenberg pleads for stand-alone pension funds, arguing that these are an attractive third way between some continental European pay-as-you-go schemes and Anglo-Saxon defined contribution schemes. Moreover, with stand-alone pension funds, companies no longer have a claim to a possible surplus in the fund, so that conflicts of interest between shareholders and pension fund participants (as noted by Exley and Gold) are ruled out.

1.5   GENERAL CONCLUSIONS

The previous sections show that the contributions collected in this volume cover a wide range of topics central to the ongoing debate on pensions. Overall, the common goal is to improve the efficiency and resilience of pension systems. Both are crucial to the sustainability of adequate old age provisions, as well as to stable financial developments. Clearly, these are dynamic issues as pension systems worldwide have to cope with three major challenges.

The first challenge is to quantify and deal with risks in pension funding. The 'perfect storm' at the beginning of this decade is an excellent example underpinning the importance of adequate pricing and, with that, anticipating pension risks. Pension funds should be encouraged to find a market-oriented optimum in terms of risk, return and transparency. In combination with a movement from rule- to principle-based regulation and supervision, as John Ashcroft pointed out during the panel discussion (see Chapter 12), these measures should help bolster the resilience of the pension system to developments such as those at the turn of the century. But this is not the final stage. The pension industry is constantly changing, mainly owing to internationalization, innovative investment methods and increased competition from, among others, insurance companies. Another issue, specifically related to the latter, is the question whether or not the supervision of pension funds and insurance companies should be harmonized, as advocated by Henrik Bjerre-Nielsen during the panel discussion.

The second challenge is to address the implications of the transfer of pension risks to households. As pension savings rise and companies seek to shield their exposure to financial risks, defined contribution schemes are on the rise all over the world. This involves a massive transfer of risks to households that are often less capable of managing those risks. Lusardi and Mitchell (2005) find that fewer than one-fifth of Americans believe they engage in successful retirement planning. It seems therefore that people need assistance in securing adequate personal pension benefits. Financial innovation, progress in information technology and life-cycle saving as well as progress in investment theory can provide benefit plans that are more in line with the preferences of individuals. To achieve all this, it is necessary to improve transparency through more timely and easy-to-understand customer information, as underscored by Dirk Witteveen during the panel discussion.

The third challenge is to find pragmatic solutions to the economic challenges of aging. Over the next few decades, societies will be forced to deal with the combined effect of increased life expectancy and lower fertility rates, as well as the labour market withdrawal of the baby boom generation.

The challenge lies in ensuring greater, larger and more productive participation in the labour force.

As Lucas Papademos argues, this will have a significant economic impact in many different areas. While aging will have significant implications for economic growth, real interest rates and financial markets, Papademos states that the consequences of aging do not require any changes to the monetary policy framework or to the ECB's focus on price stability. However, it is essential to monitor and analyse carefully the way in which demographic forces, associated financial market developments and pertinent reforms affect the monetary transmission mechanism over time. Furthermore, for governments, the problems associated with aging do require timely policy actions to keep public finances sustainable. Papademos concludes that there is an urgent need to continue to implement appropriate reforms. We hope these conference proceedings will add to this sense of urgency and stimulate a pragmatic approach to reform based on a combination of theoretical and practical considerations.

REFERENCES

Aaron, H. (1966), 'The social insurance paradox', *The Canadian Journal of Economics and Political Science*, **32**(3), 371–4.

Blommestein, H. (2001), 'Ageing, pension reform, and financial market implications in the OECD area', CeRP Working Paper No. 9, Turin (Italy).

Bodie, Z. (1990), 'Pensions as retirement income insurance', *Journal of Economic Literature*, **28**(1), 28–49.

Boeri, Tito, A. Lans Bovenberg, Benoît Coeuré and Andrew W. Roberts (2006), 'Dealing with the New Giants: Rethinking the Role of Pension Funds', Geneva Reports on the World Economy, 8.

Breyer, F. (1989), 'On the intergenerational Pareto efficiency of pay-as-you-go financed pension systems', *Journal of Institutional and Theoretical Economics*, **145**, 643–58.

Lusardi, A., and O.S. Mitchell (2005), 'Financial literacy and planning: implications for retirement wellbeing', DNB Working Paper, No. 78.

Verbon, Harrie A.A. (1989), 'Conversion policies for public pension plans in a small open economy', in Björn A. Gustafsson and N. Anders Klevmarken (eds), *The Political Economy of Social Security*, Amsterdam: Elsevier, pp. 83–95.

Visco, I. (2005), 'Ageing and pension system reform: implications for financial markets and economic policies', a report prepared at the request of the Deputies of the Group of Ten.

2. Are market values fair?

Jon Exley

2.1 THE PRACTICAL APPLICATION AND THE PHILOSOPHY OF FAIR VALUES

Both the regulation and accounting of corporate pension plans in Europe have increasingly adopted the principle of 'fair value' or market valuation of assets and liabilities. Market valuation is not necessarily the obvious choice for such applications. For example, the market valuation of corporate pension obligations for accounting purposes is inconsistent with the current valuation of other forms of corporate debt obligation at book value. Furthermore, for regulatory purposes it can be argued that a strictly rule-based valuation based on tightly prescribed assumptions provides a more objective and less costly (in terms of the costs of carrying out the necessary valuations and monitoring the results) basis for regulatory supervision when compared with the more principle-based market valuation.

However, this market valuation approach towards both accounting and regulation of corporate pension funds is consistent with a wider drive towards the 'fair value' approach in the supervision of financial institutions in banking. Furthermore, accounting has increasingly moved towards the recognition of market values: for example, in the case of derivative contracts, even if the traditional debt and equity components of balance sheets remain at book value.

This use of fair values for corporate pension plan accounting and regulation has had two significant consequences. First, the accounted cost of pension schemes and the required company contributions driven by regulation have both risen significantly, particularly as market interest rates have fallen; secondly, the volatility of pension fund assets and liabilities has had a significant impact on company balance sheets. Both of these consequences have been a driver for company managers seeking to curtail and modify the provision of traditional corporate defined benefit pension schemes.

In this chapter I introduce the concept of a bid and an offer valuation for pension benefits from the perspective of the various stakeholders and advance the proposition that application of such market valuation principles to pension schemes suggests limited scope for existing arrangements to add economic value. The response of corporate managers to the disciplines imposed by market value or fair value accounting is thus consistent with these conclusions.

2.2 THE LAW OF ONE PRICE

Regardless of the motivations of regulators or accounting bodies, the key economic principle behind the application of market (or 'fair') valuation of corporate pension contracts is the Law of One Price. Assuming that a market satisfies this law is significantly weaker than assuming any form of market efficiency. In other words, markets can be inefficient (meaning that there are many opportunities for investors to derive abnormally high risk-adjusted returns by adopting particular investment policies) while still obeying the Law of One Price.

All that is required for the Law of One Price to hold is that identical cash flows have the same price and value, regardless of the legal structure delivering the cash flows. For example, if $1 of equities is held in a unit trust and the payouts from this unit trust holding are identical to the payouts that one would obtain from holding the same $1 equities directly, then they both have a price – and fair value – of $1.

Of course, in this extreme form, the Law of One Price is of limited use – it is unlikely that we will ever be comparing two absolutely identical sets of cash flows when applying this law to pension funds. For example, the payments from a unit trust will probably never be *exactly* the same as the payments from holding the same underlying assets directly: there may be expenses and various transaction costs and possibly taxation effects to take into account.

The need to allow for these latter sorts of issues means that, although efficient markets are not a central assumption behind fair values, a version of the efficient market theory is required as a subsidiary assumption to fill in some gaps in practical applications. In other words, if two sets of cash flows only differ owing to some minor discrepancies, then we need some way of pricing these discrepancies (or a reason to justify ignoring them).

A good example of this in the context of a classical application of efficient markets would be to assert that, if the discrepancies are 'non-systematic', then we can apply the same value to both cash flows, provided that the discrepancies have zero expectation. On the other hand, if residual risks have a systematic component, then we need to use an asset-pricing model (and associated model assumptions) to derive a reasonable adjustment to a fair value derived using the law of one price. However, it is important to

stress that it is usually only at the margins that we will need to make adjustments based on such models. In general, the basic valuation of most
pension liabilities by reference to easily recognizable comparables is relatively straightforward.

2.3 VALUE TO SHAREHOLDER ASSOCIATED WITH PROVIDING SIMPLE DEFINED BENEFITS

We can now explore some of the consequences of applying our fair value
principle (the Law of One Price) to corporate pensions. Let us look first
from the perspective of the shareholder of a company offering a straightforward defined benefit pension scheme to employees backed by a pension
fund.

We consider first an idealized example where the pension fund benefits are
tightly prescribed, not dependent on survivorship, non-discretionary and,
furthermore, suppose regulation requires the pension promise to be fully
funded (on a market valuation basis) so that the benefit promise is highly
secure (akin to collateralization or asset backing of a financial contract).

If we suppose that the shareholder is entitled to receive any balance of
the pension fund assets remaining after paying out the benefit, then the economic liability to the shareholder is the same as if he had a short (sold) position in a treasury bond (since the ability to default is practically eliminated)
and a long position in the pension fund assets. In other words, the shareholder can replicate exactly the same economic market exposure by selling
a treasury bond and buying whatever assets are held by the fund.

However, there is now one very subtle nuance to the use of the Law of
One Price to *value* the shareholder's position (rather than more weakly
asserting the equivalence of the asset exposures to the short and long exposures described). This subtlety derives from the fact that we can (or do,
implicitly) assume that the shareholder's exposure to the pension liability
and the assets in the fund is marginal relative to his total asset and liability
exposure.

By way of extreme counter example, if the shareholder's only (or principal) asset was shares in this single company (and for some reason he was
prevented from diversifying) and the pension fund was large in relation to
this company, then it is possible for the pension fund assets to be worth less
or more to the individual than their market value since, if the assets are
in equities, he may not want to hold a large exposure to equities and
may prefer cash, or he may actually want to hold a more diversified equity
holding via the pension fund. However, in normal circumstances, we can
assume indifference between all choices of marginal reallocation of assets

and liabilities at market value from the perspective of a well diversified, utility-maximizing shareholder.

At this stage we can also relax a number of our strong conditions on benefit design without losing the essence of the argument that our shareholder is concerned only with fair values. First, if demographic risks are introduced into the pension promise then either these are non-systematic and diversifiable from the shareholder perspective or they are systematic and can be replicated by holding shares in an insurance companies, or reinsurers, writing the relevant type of business. Secondly, discretionary benefits contingent on asset returns (for example) or the ability to default in certain circumstances create valuation complexity but the same valuation principles apply to the extent that the option characteristics can be replicated with other financial assets. We discuss such benefits in more detail later.

Ironically, although market accounting has been a significant motivation for the change in the behaviour of company managers, the shareholder is potentially indifferent as to the basis on which these liabilities are reported and on which pension provision is regulated (except to the extent that it influences the ability to default or the extent to which discretionary benefits are awarded). In principle, as long as the shareholder has enough information to value the liability himself (at fair value) he should not care what value is reported, apart from the costs involved in the shareholder using this information to provide his own estimates of fair values.

However, to the extent that agents make decisions on behalf of the shareholder using market values as a consequence of accounting and regulation, I argue that these decisions are more likely to be aligned with the interests of the shareholder. Crucially, for our utility-maximizing and fully diversified shareholder, only one such company management decision is relevant. This is the decision as to which form of benefit design and asset allocation maximizes economic value defined as the saving in cash wage W that would otherwise need to be paid in lieu of the pension benefit, less the fair value of the benefit V, less the associated administration costs A. In other words, from the shareholder perspective: value added (destroyed) = $W - (V + A)$.

The shareholder is indifferent to asset allocation or benefit design except to the extent that it affects value added.

2.4 VALUE TO EMPLOYEE ASSOCIATED WITH SIMPLE DEFINED BENEFITS

As noted above, the real subtlety of the use of fair values from the perspective of a shareholder is that the validity of the measure of value rests on the shareholder being indifferent to marginal reallocation of his asset and liability exposures. Once we accept this assumption we are led easily to the conclusion that this market value, or fair value, of the benefit promise (versus the additional cash wages otherwise required) is actually the *only* issue of relevance to the shareholder. However, it is clear that this crucial condition is less likely to be met for typical employees receiving pension benefits in lieu of cash wages.

An idealized employee concerned only with the value of the pension benefit being provided would need to satisfy a number of very strong conditions when compared with the equivalent criteria for a shareholder. Essentially, either (a) the pension benefit would need to be small in relation to the employee's total financial and non-financial asset exposure, or (b) the employee would need to have access to costless financial instruments that allowed him either to go long or 'short' of the financial risk exposures associated with the pension benefit.

We will disregard the first as an unlikely situation for most employees in view of the level of employer pension provision typically provided, although we do emphasize that pension assets are rarely the only asset of individuals. In particular, in a wider context it is not only necessary to recognize other savings assets but also to recognize housing and mortgage exposures as well as human capital in the form of both training and family, such as investment in children and obligations to parents.

Accordingly we will focus on the second situation and recognize that in reality employees face transaction costs in buying or selling these exposures. We can then characterize upper and lower bounds on the value added by pension arrangements effectively in terms of a bid and an offer spread around 'fair value' V as defined from the shareholder perspective. If the employee values the pension benefit at offer, then value has been added by the provision of pension benefits in lieu of cash salary, provided that the offer-mid spread exceeds the costs of corporate provision. Value has been destroyed if he values at bid as we cross not only the bid-mid spread but also the costs of corporate provision A. The extent of the value creation or destruction depends on the size of the bid-mid or offer-mid spread.

2.5　COMPONENTS OF 'OFFER' AND 'BID' SPREADS TO MID FOR SIMPLE DEFINED BENEFIT PENSIONS

A clear upper bound on the offer value that an employee might place on a corporate pension benefit (and hence forgo salary up to this level) is provided by the offer price of retail products R delivering the same or similar benefits, since the employee could take cash in lieu and buy the product at the retail value. In other words: economic value added $< R - (V + A)$. For example, a highly secure final salary pension benefit without any discretion in the benefit can be replicated by the purchase of non-profit deferred annuities.

If we suppose that there is demand for this product (this being the assumption underlying an offer valuation by employees) then we might suppose that this offer value provides investors in the insurance company with some return on capital invested after allowing for costs. It is unlikely that a corporate pension provider would see lower ongoing administration costs than a high-volume retail provider, although it is possible that the regulatory costs are higher for an insurance company (if one supposes that regulatory costs have no associated equivalent value to customers). However, it is possible that the 'cost of sales' could be lower for a corporate, in terms both of the capital investment required to build a franchise that competes in the retail market and of the ongoing costs of servicing a sales force.

The above argument needs to be pursued with care, though. It is difficult to argue that 'sales costs' are a pure deadweight cost in a market economy. In particular, the sales process ensures that customers have a choice and, for the most part, buy goods that they want to buy. In terms of our presentation here, this is equivalent to ensuring that retail customers are on the 'offer' side of our equation of value added. It is quite possible, by contrast, that a large number of employees given a pension in lieu of salary will be on the 'bid' side of our equation.

On the bid side, we must measure the cost to an employee of selling unwanted pension benefits. For relatively simple financial contracts many individuals do in fact have some scope to reduce unwanted exposure. For example, an employee given a simple defined benefit pension in lieu of salary can take out a larger mortgage or pay down a mortgage more slowly. Whilst like for like cost comparison is not straightforward, the retail cost loadings in mortgages are probably not dissimilar to the loadings in annuity policies, giving us roughly a symmetrical bid–offer spread for a simple defined benefit pension.

As noted earlier, there is, however, an in-built asymmetry to our equation of value even if the bid–offer spread is symmetrical: the administration costs A of providing the unwanted pension are in addition to the transaction costs T associated with the employee shorting this exposure. In other words, for simple, defined benefit pensions replicable with non-profit deferred annuities: $-T <$ Value added $- A < R - V$.

In terms of whether most individuals would be on the offer or bid side of this equation, it is perhaps worth noting that there are far more individuals with mortgages (a proxy short of the pension benefit) than there are individuals who direct their own savings towards non-profit deferred annuities.

2.6   COMPLEX CONTINGENT (CONDITIONAL) FORMS OF DEFINED BENEFIT PENSION

We now go on to discuss more complex pension benefits that cannot easily be replicated. It is worth saying that creation of a form of corporate pension benefit which cannot easily be replicated does not automatically push our equation of value in favour of value added. A necessary condition is that the contract is also in demand and possibly a contract does not exist elsewhere (and cannot be replicated) precisely because it is not demanded. In this situation the provision of such benefits can destroy significant value as they are not only unwanted but the exposure is also potentially difficult to short.

The first case to consider is a hybrid corporate pension arrangement that can be expressed as a simple linear combination of a defined benefit (which can be valued as a bond as discussed above) plus the returns on a defined contribution 'pot' belonging to the member. This type of structure in fact has clear and unambiguous value to all parties. The defined benefit element has a relatively clear equation of value added (as described above) and the defined contribution pot has a value to the employee (give or take the effect of transaction costs and expenses) equal to its current market value, with no contingent liability to the sponsor regardless of the asset allocation of this pot.

The situation is, however, different if we consider more complex, non-linear, linkage between the assets of a pension fund and its liabilities. For example, suppose that the benefits are subject to price indexation only if the fund achieves certain returns. If this type of contract is fully specified then it can be represented as an asset to employees equivalent to an index-linked bond *less* the value of a put option on the fund held by the shareholder. Equivalently, as a liability the shareholders of the company are short of this bond but long of the put option asset.

2.7   VALUE TO SHAREHOLDER ASSOCIATED WITH PROVIDING COMPLEX DEFINED BENEFITS

Once again from our economic framework we conclude that sharing financial risks in complex forms of defined benefit pension is generally of no value to the shareholder. If we are looking at marginal parts of the shareholder's total portfolio then this indifference to risk exposure is axiomatic. From this shareholder's perspective the worst aspect of these conditional or contingent pay-out structures is the likely imprecision in the link between the pension fund returns and the contingent liabilities. This makes the fair value of the contract difficult to estimate with any accuracy. Misvaluation of the contract could potentially result in the shareholder misvaluing the shares in a particular company owing to misspecified employment costs. I should make a sharp distinction here between the costs of imprecision in the contract and the potential benefits of a flexible contract. A pension contract does not have to be inflexible – it can be subject to frequent renegotiation if this flexibility enhances overall value to both parties – but imprecision in the rules and conditions under which the benefits are provided (imprecision in the contract terms) destroys value. Put another way, flexible contracts are potentially valuable but there needs to be precision as to the terms of the contract, including precision in the areas that are or are not flexible and open to renegotiation.

Arguably the costs of this misvaluation are relatively small if different shareholders make different judgments of value on a non-systematic basis. In this case the value destroyed by the imprecise contract is similar to the costs associated with any other poor accounting or lack of disclosure. However, the presence of options in these structures opens the possibility of systematic misvaluation to the extent that the nature of a contingent payout which has not been properly defined will take a large amount of data to uncover – and may only be uncovered in extreme events. The analogy here is the difference between a company making profits from an undisclosed long equity position compared with a company making profits from writing an undisclosed deep out of the money put option: the scope for investors given simple accounting information such as cash profits systematically to misvalue the latter company is far greater than in the former case. Systematic misvaluation could result in significant misallocation of capital away from efficiently managed companies (or whole economies if the practice is widespread) in favour of inefficiently managed companies (or economies).

However, whether the misvaluation is non-systematic or systematic it is apparent that this uncertainty in the fair value of a contingent contract must represents a cost (and never a benefit) to the shareholder – we refer to the costs of misvaluation borne by the shareholder as XS, so that, for a complex form of benefit, economic value added $= W - (V + A + XS)$.

An important further issue to address in the context of such contracts is, however, whether there is any gain to the shareholder from the inability of the employee to understand the value of the pension benefit. If the design of complex forms of contingent payment can result in employees systematically over-estimating the value of the benefit being provided by their employer then this would provide some support from the shareholder perspective for these forms of pension benefit design.

However, we exclude this from the overall equation of economic value added by this type of pension design since we argue that there is a net destruction of economic welfare in such circumstances. Employees could work for lower total compensation than otherwise for a prolonged period reflecting the difficulty of valuing a deep out of the money contingent put held against them. This would simply represent only a transfer of wealth from labour to shareholders and not creation of value. Furthermore, the same corporate finance theory that explains the limits on the benefits to shareholders from asset substitution would also suggest that the ultimate response of employees to such practice would be to apply punitive discounts to corporate pensions in their personal valuation of the benefits. Arguably defaults by some corporate pension funds have had precisely this effect.

2.8   VALUE TO EMPLOYEE ASSOCIATED WITH PROVIDING COMPLEX DEFINED BENEFITS

From the employees' perspective, the destruction of value created by complex forms of contingent contract is far more apparent since not only are there frictional costs associated with the inability of the employee to value the contract but this contract also forms a large proportion of his wealth and it has unknown (or difficult to establish) risk characteristics.

This latter issue potentially results in additional costs associated with employees holding suboptimal personal portfolios even in situations where the employee has the ability to create exposures in his non-pension portfolio to offset or supplement the financial asset risk exposures created by the contract.

2.9   COMPONENTS OF 'OFFER-MID SPREADS' AND 'BID-MID SPREADS' FOR COMPLEX DEFINED BENEFITS

Furthermore we can also, as before, look at the potential maximum offer value that an employee could place on the underlying contract and the bid value that would represent the costs of shorting unwanted exposure.

Ironically, we argue that, once contingent pension indexation contracts are stripped of the costs of imprecise or uncertain payoff, as already discussed, the remaining contracts can often be replicated (to within the precision likely to be required by a retail investor) relatively easily by the purchase of straightforward option contracts. Although retail investors generally pay significant transaction costs on these types of product, it is worth noting (as stressed earlier) that some of these sales and regulatory costs are associated with explaining the contracts to the individual and ensuring that it meets his requirements. Thus, although the retail cost R of such products may show a more significant premium to fair value when compared with simpler products, we are arguably overstating the upper bound on the economic value added. However, we will include the costs to the employee of lack of information in the systematic and non-systematic costs XE borne by the employee due to the lack of precision in the contract. Once again I emphasize here that we are talking about the costs of an imprecise contract rather than the potential benefits of a flexible contract.

Finally, on the bid side we need to estimate the costs to an employee of shorting unwanted exposure to these types of contract, assuming that we know what the contract involves. For example, whereas we argued that it may be possible for many employees to short unwanted exposure to a simple bond (via mortgage borrowing, for example) it is far less easy for an employee to take a short position in a complicated contingent claim on the equity market. Indeed we argue that it is much more costly for an employee to short this unwanted exposure to a contingent claim than to obtain proxy exposure in long form through retail products. Nevertheless we use the same parameter T to denote these transaction costs. Thus we have for contingent or conditional pension benefits: $-T <$ Value added $+ A + XS - XE < R - V$. In other words, in order for such a contract to add value it not only has to be wanted by the employee (to hit the offer side of the above inequality) but it also has to overcome all of the systematic and non-systematic costs associated with the inability of the shareholder to value the contract and the inability of the employee both to value and to incorporate the complex structure within an optimized personal asset portfolio, in addition to the administration costs.

2.10 A SPECIAL CASE OF CONTINGENT OR CONDITIONAL PENSION BENEFITS: EMPLOYER DEFAULT RISK

Finally, we consider a special case of contingent benefits where the payout is linked to the credit of the sponsoring employer. This introduces no new issues from the perspective of the shareholder since the option to default (subject to the difficulty of obtaining good information on the value of this option) forms part of the shareholder's portfolio and can be valued at the margin in the same way as any other short position in a debt obligation.

However, from the employee perspective, we will almost certainly find that the employee values exposure to the default risk of his employer on the bid side: few employees would seek to acquire additional exposure to the risk of their employer through their pension savings. Furthermore, in terms of the bid value itself, employees will generally have limited ability to short their personal exposure to the fortunes of their employer and thus the value placed on a benefit with this attached risk can be valued by the employee at a significant discount to the fair value. Thus constructing a pension benefit which gives employees significant exposure to the risk of default by a single employer appears to be a highly inefficient means of reducing the economic cost of a pension benefit. The reduction in the value of the benefit to the employee arising from this risk seems to far outweigh the cost reductions to shareholders in a fair value framework.

We can incorporate this effect into our final equation of value added by assuming the reduction in cost to the employer from the option to default is D whilst an employee will value this loss as λD (where $\lambda > 1$). Hence our equation of value becomes:

$$-T < \text{Value added} + A + XS + XE + (\lambda - 1)D < R - V.$$

2.11   CONCLUSIONS

The economic principles behind the use of such fair values are very simple: we find traded assets that replicate the same cash flows in order to value a financial contract. This approach relies most heavily on the Law of One Price – our key principle – and we only need to assume regular or efficient markets in the valuation of discrepancies between tradable assets and the contract in question. However, the philosophy behind the use of fair values is more subtle. If we delve into the rationale for the law of one price we find ourselves looking at the position of the end shareholder and the employee as the two counterparties to a transaction that can in principle add or destroy value, and I have developed an analysis of pension provision in a fair value context in terms of bid and offer values to the relevant stakeholders within which any value enhancement (or destruction) is constrained.

This analysis throws up a number of well established principles in market economics: costs associated with not meeting individuals' personal preferences, frictional costs associated with imprecision and mis-valuation of contracts by both parties and aversion to non-diversifiable risks such as employer default. This in turn leads us to the conclusion that it is by no means easy to establish the source of the value added by corporate pension provision when it is analysed using standard principles of economic valuation. Furthermore, to the extent that justification for pension provision might exist, this supports simple transparent and non-contingent defined benefit provision rather than complex contingent benefits with embedded written put options of various forms. This conclusion appears to be at odds with the widespread provision of corporate defined benefits that are not only complex and contingent on asset returns but also often subject to the risk of default by the employer providing the benefit.

These conclusions represent wholly personal views and are in no way representative of my employer or of the UK actuarial profession.

Discussion of 'Are market values fair?'

Peter Schotman

FAIR VALUE FOR THE PENSION PLAN PARTICIPANTS

Jon Exley addresses more than just the title question 'Are market values fair?' The real issue raised in the paper is whether pension plans add value and, if so, for whom: firms or participants in the plan? When fair value is treated as synonymous with market value, the net balance position of a pension fund is the same as a replicating portfolio of financial instruments. If it is as simple as that, a straightforward finance argument, the law of one price implies that the pension plan does not create value.

Of course, the argument only holds under the assumptions of perfect and complete financial markets and the absence of other externalities like agency costs. The paper thus discusses the imperfections and concludes that costs perhaps outweigh the benefits such that, on balance, defined benefit (DB) pension plans do not create value.

As a discussant I will stress the benefits of pension funds and the costs of private arrangements.

1. One of the strongest arguments in favour of pension funds with DB plans is that they enable intergenerational risk sharing. Intergenerational risk sharing is valuable. Gollier (2007) estimates the certainty equivalent value of defined benefit over defined contribution at 1.1 per cent per year. Even limited defined benefit arrangements with solvency constraints imposed by a supervisor add value relative to a pure individual defined contribution.

2. Pension funds show better investment returns than mutual funds. Evidence in Bauer, Frehen, Lum and Otten (2006) indicates that mutual funds underperform pension funds by about 2.5 per cent per year. They attribute the difference to misalignment of interests. In a related study, Campbell (2006) argues that private financial intermediaries do not have incentives to offer the right products. Retail

products are often unnecessarily opaque and offer the institutions the opportunity to earn premium returns on the less sophisticated customers.

3. From behavioural studies we have learned that individuals make very bad investment decisions. The large literature on 401(k) pension plans in the US and the more recent experience with the Swedish premium pension provide ample evidence (see, for example, Cronqvist and Thaler, 2004; Agnew, 2006). Moreover, many households are not waiting for more choice (Iyengar, Jiang and Huberman, 2003). A further literature documents that many individuals also lack the financial knowledge to make sound decisions about retirement planning (Lusardi and Mitchell, 2006). All these arguments would favour a pension plan with at least a well-defined default option without too much compromising individual preferences (Choi, Laibson, Madrian and Metrick, 2003).

4. Pension funds help in completing the markets by removing liquidity constraints of individuals. Individuals would like equity exposure when they are young, but are usually unable to invest in stocks as they lack the financial capital and cannot borrow against future labour income.

5. Fair value is not always well-defined for claims that are not easily replicated by financial instruments. Examples of incomplete markets are wage-indexed defined benefit pensions, where wage-index-linked bonds do not exist. Other examples are illiquid assets such as direct real estate, for which many pension funds claim they have an edge as long-term investors.

6. The main obstacle in applying rigorous corporate finance arguments about the value added is the incomplete pension contract: who owns the fund surplus? The incomplete contract can be seen as a cost, as Jon Exley argues, but it is not clear how big that cost is.

7. Not included in the analysis are taxes. Taxes will affect value calculations for pension funds (see, for example, Tepper, 1981).

Implicit in the discussion so far is that pension plans are mainly of the defined benefit type. Pure defined benefit pension plans, however, are under pressure. Hybrid arrangements reduce the benefits of intergenerational risk sharing, but do not undermine the costs and behavioural economics arguments. Ultimately all benefits must be weighed against the costs of some government paternalism and reduced choice for participants. Although not all elements have yet a quantifiable cost or benefit, it seems that on balance pension funds do provide value for their participants.

REFERENCES

Agnew, J.R. (2006), 'Do behavioral biases vary across individuals? Evidence from individual level 401(k) data', *Journal of Financial and Quantitative Analysis*, **41**(4), 939–62.

Bauer, R., R. Frehen, R. Lum and R. Otten (2006), 'Economies of scale, lack of skill or misalignment of interest? A study on pension and mutual fund performance', LIFE working paper, University of Maastricht.

Campbell, J.Y. (2006), 'Household finance', *Journal of Finance*, **61**(4), 1553–604.

Choi, J.J., D. Laibson, B. Madrian and A. Metrick (2003), 'Optimal defaults', *American Economic Review*, **93**(2), 180–85.

Cronqvist, H. and R.H. Thaler (2004), 'Design choices in privatized social-security systems: learning from the Swedish experience', *American Economic Review*, **94**(2), 424–8.

Gollier, C., (2007), 'Intergenerational risk-sharing and risk-taking of a pension fund', IDEI working paper.

Iyengar, Sheena S., Wei Jiang and Gur Huberman (2003), 'How much choice is too much? Contributions to 401(k) retirement plans', in Olivia S. Mitchell and Stephen P. Utkus (eds), *Pension Design and Structure: New Lessons from Behavioural Finance*, Oxford: Oxford University Press.

Lusardi, A. and O.S. Mitchell (2007), 'Financial literacy and retirement, preparedness: evidence and implications for financial education', *Business Economics*, **42**(1), 35–45.

Tepper, I. (1981), 'Taxation and corporate pension policy', *Journal of Finance*, **36**(1), 1–13.

3. The intersection of pensions and enterprise risk management

Jeremy Gold

3.1 INTRODUCTION

For most of the last 40 years, corporate defined benefit pension plan assets have been managed to balance risk versus reward in more or less the same way that a risk-averse individual would do with his own portfolio. Recently liability cognizant strategies have been developed, but these also attempt to balance risks and rewards.

Pension plans are not individuals; they, much like their widely-held corporate sponsors, are pass-through institutions. The economics of such entities are found in the corporate finance literature rather than in the literature of portfolio choice. The corporate finance (and thus the pension finance) objective is economic value added rather than return for risk.

Enterprise risk management is a corporate finance activity too and its goal should also be value added rather than return for risk. The intersection of enterprise risk management and pension finance leads to a value-based discipline with two startling results: first, widely-held corporations can increase shareholder value by hedging away their own systematic risk (for example, CAPM β); secondly, very many corporate defined benefit pension plans should define their liabilities and manage their assets to develop a net short equity exposure (negative β).

3.1.1 Portfolio Management versus Modern Corporate Finance

Defined benefit (DB) plan investing and much of today's practice of enterprise risk management (ERM) suffer from the same weakness. Managers and consultants present each as a trade-off between risk and reward, implying some optimal balance. This is a legacy deriving from a failure to distinguish between two major branches of financial economics:

- the portfolio management branch,[1] applying to investment by individuals modelled as risk-averse expected utility maximizers; and

- the modern corporate finance branch,[2] applying to institutions which pass their performance through to individual investors; such institutions are modelled as value maximizers.

The Fisher (1930) Separation Theorem shows that these are different, but compatible, roles: value-maximizing firms best serve the needs of expected-utility-maximizing individual investors.

Defined benefit investing and ERM properly belong to the latter branch. In practice, and in their language, they are almost always treated as belonging to the former. We will not dwell on why this is how things are but will, instead, look at how ERM and DB plan management might operate and cooperate as corporate finance disciplines. ERM may be broadly divided into financial and operational risk management, where the latter may be broken down into a variety of subcategories. Financial risk management often refers to capital structure and hedging decisions – areas that may be considered to be two sides of the same coin (Shimpi, 2004). We will deal primarily with financial risk management, although some of the same principles can be applied to real project management and operational risk.

Section 2 briefly looks at the history of risk and DB plan management. Section 3 develops the corporate finance (economic value added) approach to risk management and DB asset allocation. Section 4 shows that many corporations can increase shareholder value by eliminating their own market exposure (for example, CAPM β) and how the pension plan can leverage these gains. Section 5 concludes.

3.2 HISTORY

3.2.1 Risk Management

Certainly human beings have made great gains from taking risk and have surely experienced much pain as well. In a very basic sense, risk management amounts to pursuing some risky endeavours and avoiding others; the 'management' is in the choosing. Individuals seem to balance risks and opportunities in very personal ways, implying idiosyncratic preferences for risks and potential rewards.

Corporate risk management, in practice, seems to follow from the individual. Companies and their managers may be characterized as more or less risk-tolerant, with risk aversions and appetites spread across a continuum from Caspar Milquetoast to Evel Knievel, from the highly prudent New York Life to the bet-it-all game plan of the next Yahoo wannabe.

Individual attitudes towards risk are the essence of utility theory, a basic building block of modern economics; corporate attitudes towards risk are more problematical for economists. Whose risk tolerance shall the corporation serve? Is there an objective corporate utility function?

Financial economics describes individual risk takers, especially investors, in terms of risk preferences and utility functions; we say that individuals are expected utility maximizers. We then say, however, that corporations are value maximizers. Individuals are modelled as balancing risks and rewards in order to maximize utility while corporations accept the market price for risk and seek to maximize value, without regard for the risk preferences of their investors. As Fisher (1930) demonstrates, this is a compatible separation of duties. A widely held corporation that based decisions on non-market prices for risk – reflecting its 'own' risk aversion or appetite – would not maximize value and would ill serve its investors' efforts to maximize utility.

Nonetheless, in practice, we hear of corporations with risk appetites, risk tolerances and risk budgets, feeding these into quantitative models of enterprise risk management. Do these models misrepresent corporate duties and badly serve their investors? Often, the simple answer is 'yes'. Subjective risk management can signify the ascendance of managers' private interests over the welfare of investors. But it is also true that risk management, which may appear merely to reflect the risk tolerances and aversions of managers, can protect and increase investor value. This is discussed further in Section 3.3.3.2.1. The use of sloppy language and concomitant sloppy thinking about risk is especially rampant in the corporate management of defined benefit pension plans. Cleaning up the language of risk management (substituting the value-oriented analysis offered by modern corporate finance) could go a long way towards reconciling the academic and the practical. It would also discipline the practice and the practitioners in valuable ways.[3]

3.2.2 Pension Risk Management

Ask any pension manager in the last 50 years: 'Are you managing risk?' and the answer would be 'yes'. In 1955, we would have been told, 'Our plan is insured by the great XYZ insurance company'. In 1965, we would be told, 'We are no longer insured, we are now investing in equities for their long-term high returns; diversification allows us to minimize risk; Harry Markowitz (1952) showed us how to diversify, have you heard about the efficient frontier?' In 1975, we would learn 'Our risk management is even more diversified and we are better able to tell which of our asset managers are adding value after adjusting for risk; Bill Sharpe (1964) showed us how to measure risk (β) and performance (α); have you heard of the Capital Asset Pricing Model (CAPM)?'

By 1985, 'We continue to diversify because we believe in equities for the long run, but we have immunized some of our liabilities using long dura-tion bond portfolios; this allows us to insist that our actuaries raise their discount rate and lower our liabilities; matching some of the liabilities lowers our risk, so we can increase our allocation to equities; Marty Leibowitz (1986) at Salomon Brothers showed us how; have you read his research reports?'

1995: 'Our strong commitment to equities has really paid off, we think our surplus (assets less liabilities) gives us two benefits: no contributions today and a large enough risk buffer to weather almost any market down-turn; do you have any hot stocks to recommend? You know, hi-tech with a great eyeballs-to-burn-rate ratio'.

And today, 'We weathered quite a storm from 2000 to 2002 and are paying even more attention to risk than ever; we have added high α invest-ments including hedge funds (those hedge fund managers are expensive, but wow), private equity and absolute return strategies; we manage our inter-est rate risk using derivative overlays; this liability-driven investing (LDI) strategy protects us against another perfect storm and we use portable α to get the excess returns we need for the long run; yep, we are managing risk and generating real performance'.

3.2.3   Integration of ERM and Pensions Today

Efforts to apply ERM to DB pension plans focus on plan risk: the mis-match between plan assets and liabilities. There is often a tacit assumption that a mismatch wherein the assets have a higher expected return than the liabilities (for example, equity investments to fund bond-like liabilities) is desirable as long as the risk is not too large to manage. A comparison of the size of the corporation to the size of the plan may be invoked to demon-strate that mismatching in a relatively small plan will not be too risky for the plan sponsor. Similarly, reference may be made to a risk budget, sug-gesting that the plan can take mismatch risk within limits defined at the sponsor level.

This kind of approach might be useful if the basic mismatch were gen-erating shareholder value that could not be achieved by the shareholders themselves. In most cases, however, quite the opposite is true; Tepper (1981) and Black (1980) show that, in a transparent environment with a tax regime found in many nations,[4] DB plan equity investments destroy shareholder value. There should be no risk budget for value-destroying activities.

3.3 THE CORPORATE FINANCE APPROACH TO RISK AND DB ASSET MANAGEMENT

3.3.1 Why not to Manage Risk and DB Asset Allocation

Financial risk management comprises capital structure, hedging and insurance decisions. Under the Modigliani–Miller (1958) conditions (no taxes, no contracting cost, no financial distress cost, no relationship between financing choices and investment decisions), financial risk management adds no value:[5]

- Systematic risk: by definition, this is risk that must end up in investor hands no matter how much they may diversify. Because each investor chooses how much risk to bear, systematic risk ends up being borne by those most willing to hold it at the lowest market-clearing price.
- Idiosyncratic risk: although firms can shed idiosyncratic risk (for example, by buying insurance), diversified investors (who also invest in the insurance sector) end up on both sides of the trade, losing transaction costs along the way.

Defined benefit plan assets are traded in the same markets as well. Any decisions made to allocate such assets may be offset by diversified shareholders in their own portfolios. Note that operational risk management can add value: consider the chief risk officer who picks a banana peel off the shop floor and disposes of it cheaply. His action adds value; his decision does not depend on his or his investors' risk preference, appetite or aversion.

3.3.2 Why to Manage Risk and DB Asset Allocation

If markets where risk is perfectly priced and traded make financial risk management and DB asset allocation unnecessary, we must look to market imperfections:

- Black (1980) and Tepper (1981) show that tax effects should influence DB plan asset allocation. In tax regimes where some assets (e.g. bonds) are more heavily taxed than others (e.g. equities) and where DB plans are tax sheltered, investor wealth can be increased by investing DB plans in highly taxable assets.[6]
- Smith and Stulz (1985) explore several exceptions to the perfect model, each of which leads to a value-based rationale for corporate risk management (hedging): taxes, contracting costs and financial distress. In each case, the exception leads to a convex cost for

unhedged risk and, as elaborated on below, a net value gain when hedging cost is low.

3.3.3   Managing Risk in a Corporate Finance Framework

Why do corporations take risks? Folk wisdom has it that you must take risks in order to earn rewards. Although this is generally true, it puts the cart before the horse. Under the value paradigm espoused by modern corporate finance, firms pursue rewards by undertaking projects offering positive net present value (NPV); inevitably risks come along with each project.

Maximizing firm value is an ex-ante activity occurring at time zero when decisions are made with respect to the projects to be undertaken, the financing of those projects, and risk management via hedging and insurance. Suppose a project requires a single cash investment at time zero which leads to a single uncertain cash outflow (proceeds) at time one. Additions to firm value are measured by discounting the proceeds and subtracting the investment. This discount must reflect the uncertainty of the proceeds. There are two levels of discount:

- By reference to the capital markets, we will value the uncertain proceeds in accordance with an asset pricing model. To preserve generality, we posit a 'pricing kernel'[7] such that the market value of the proceeds is equal to the expectation of the kernel-weighted cash flows. For convenience, we will also use some of the language (e.g. β) of the very much more restricted CAPM.
- We will also examine the internal firm cost that derives from the uncertainty of the proceeds. Consistent with the 'E' in ERM, we will consider the portfolio of contemporaneous projects of the firm.[8] We will consider this aggregate portfolio in conjunction with taxes, contracting and financial distress costs in order to determine a second level of discount for risk. This discount will also have to be assessed ex ante in order for it to guide corporate risk management decisions.

Investor value consists of the discounted proceeds from the project portfolio (I will refer to this as 'level one' value) less the level two cost of firm risk.[9] Although the market discount of project outcomes (level one) reflects risks, this is not the arena for risk management. The pricing kernel will ignore firm-specific (idiosyncratic) risks and will charge the minimum price for systematic risk. Consistent with the 'Why not to manage risk . . .' section above, if transaction costs are nil or ignored, level one value is unaffected by market transactions.

All financial risk management activity will have to be designed to minimize the indirect (level two) cost of firm risk. Interestingly, despite the internal nature of level two, it is these costs that can be affected by otherwise value-neutral market activities.[10]

3.3.3.1 Risk retention/disposal

Under the prevailing risk-versus-reward framework, we would ask whether each marginal risk that remains (after accounting for cross-hedging in the enterprise portfolio) should be taken in light of corporate risk appetite or aversion. The question, 'Is this risk worth taking?' or, for a proposed new project, 'Is this marginal addition to our risk portfolio worth taking?' would be answered in utilitarian terms. The modern corporate finance framework, however, would rephrase the question as 'Which is more valuable: retaining this risk in the enterprise risk portfolio or disposing of it in the marketplace (for example, by insuring or hedging)?' The cost of disposition is determined outside of the firm; the cost of retention must be determined internally.

Because the 'retain' versus 'dispose' decision is properly made at the portfolio level, we have a sequencing problem. The retention cost of risk needs to be determined as the marginal cost in the enterprise portfolio context. Thus the projects that will constitute the portfolio must already be chosen. In order for the projects to be chosen, however, we need to know their NPV. But the NPV must be discounted for the cost of risk. There are two ways out of this box. In theory, the entire set of decisions is undertaken simultaneously. Each possible project and risk can be considered with a tentative decision as to whether disposal or retention leads to more value. Then the portfolio of projects and risks is optimized to maximize value over the set of decision variables which includes a vector of project weights and a matrix of retain-versus-dispose decisions. In practice, the problem is usually simpler: a new project is considered against a backdrop of existing projects. In this context, the marginal cost of risk retention is more easily determined as the project, if undertaken, will retain or dispose of the marginal contribution it makes to the enterprise risk portfolio – choosing the cheaper approach.

3.3.3.2 The convex risk penalty model

We develop the level two cost of risk in a model where the secondary cost that follows a negative shock to level one value is always absolutely greater than the secondary benefit that follows a positive shock of equal magnitude.

3.3.3.2.1 Binary variation of outcomes In the simplest case, let us assume two equally likely outcomes. The level one value of the bad outcome is $750 million below expectation and the good outcome is $750 million above.

What can we say about the indirect (level two) costs or benefits that ensue? Some of these indirect effects will be cash, others will have an impact on intangibles, such as franchise value. The corporate finance and risk management literature offers several reasons why the indirect damage will exceed any indirect benefits (that is, why the level two cost will be convex). Smith and Stulz (1985) begin with a convex tax schedule that charges a higher rate as corporate income increases. Taxes might, for example, increase by $200 million when the outcome is positive but decline by only $125 million when negative. Smith and Stulz's second example identifies the deadweight costs of bankruptcy which are more likely to be incurred when project returns are shocked to the downside. The literature often uses the term 'financial distress' as a generalization of the increased likelihood of incurring bankruptcy costs. Froot, Scharfstein and Stein (1993) identify two threats to franchise value: when internally generated cash is less than expected, the firm must abandon otherwise positive NPV projects and/or finance the projects in the face of higher external capital costs. When a company chooses its projects based on NPV, the least positive projects are abandoned first and the 'cost' of abandonment increases thereafter. The NPV-ordered project opportunity set is concave and thus the abandonment cost is convex. Borrowing costs increase with weakened credit and with the amount borrowed, and so this second threat implies a convex cost as well.[11]

We can get similar implications with even a single measure of financial distress (such as deadweight bankruptcy cost) that either occurs or does not in accordance with a probability distribution of level one results. As shown by Almeida and Philippon (2007), if the distribution of outcomes is positively correlated with the market via the pricing kernel (or, more simply, project outcomes exhibit positive CAPM β), financial distress will be more likely to occur in bad times (when prices in the capital markets are down) than in good, and thus should be priced ex ante using a below-risk-free discount rate.

Smith and Stulz (1985) add a third example based on the personal risk aversion of corporate managers. One might be tempted to look upon any ensuing risk management as an example of misbehaviour, an agency cost created by managers serving their own interests before those of their shareholders. But this need not be the case. Suppose that we (the readers and the author) are acting as a board of directors on behalf of our fellow shareholders and that we are simultaneously developing risk management strategy and managerial compensation policy. We solve a classic principal–agent problem which endogenizes a risk-reducing hedge and a managerial incentive compensation scheme. Our managers demand more if compensation is risky and less if it is certain. Because we want to tie future compensation to future shareholder value, our managers will carry substantial project risk. To the extent that project risk may be reduced, our ex ante compensation may be lowered, that is, compensation cost increases with project outcome variation.

3.3.3.2.2   Convex risk penalty   The common thread in the literature is the observation that there is a convex penalty for risk which may be estimated ex ante so that a decision may be made whether or not to hedge. The risk penalty illustrated in Figure 3.1 is a function of possible variations in project outcomes. For convenience, I have shown a zero penalty for project outcomes that meet or exceed expectations.[12]

Suppose, as shown in Figure 3.2, that there are two equally likely outcomes with ex ante values $750 million above and below expected. If the inferior result occurs, we estimate $34 million in secondary cost attributable to the causes outlined in the literature. One interpretation would be that financial distress reduces franchise value by this ex ante amount. Under these circumstances, the expected financial distress cost is $17 million, as shown in Figure 3.3.

3.3.3.2.3   Hedging   We next suppose (Figure 3.4) that a hedge may be effected at a cost of $4 million which will eliminate the plus or minus $750 million uncertainty and thus the potential $34 million risk penalty. The decision to hedge adds $13 million in shareholder value. Thus, by reducing level two costs, risk management adds value that is independent of risk preferences or tolerances.

In Figure 3.5, we suppose a project-outcome distribution that is normal, rather than binary. From now on we will integrate, rather than sum, in order to compute the expected risk penalty.[13] In Figure 3.6, we suppose that the expected penalty is $20 million. If, as illustrated in Figure 3.7, we can find hedges that sharply lower the distribution variance, we will be able to reduce the level two cost by more than the cost of the hedge, thus generating shareholder value.

Many of the uncertainties in project outcomes may depend on variables for which market hedges exist: interest rates, energy and other commodity prices, foreign exchange rates and general equity exposure (β). Hedging transactions in these variables can usually be implemented at very low cost, which in Figure 3.8 we will treat as cost-free. Only the most efficient market hedges come close to this ideal.[14]

3.4   SHORTING THE MARKET

The cheap hedges discussed above have generally been aimed at well-defined narrow exposures such as interest rates, energy and currency. For

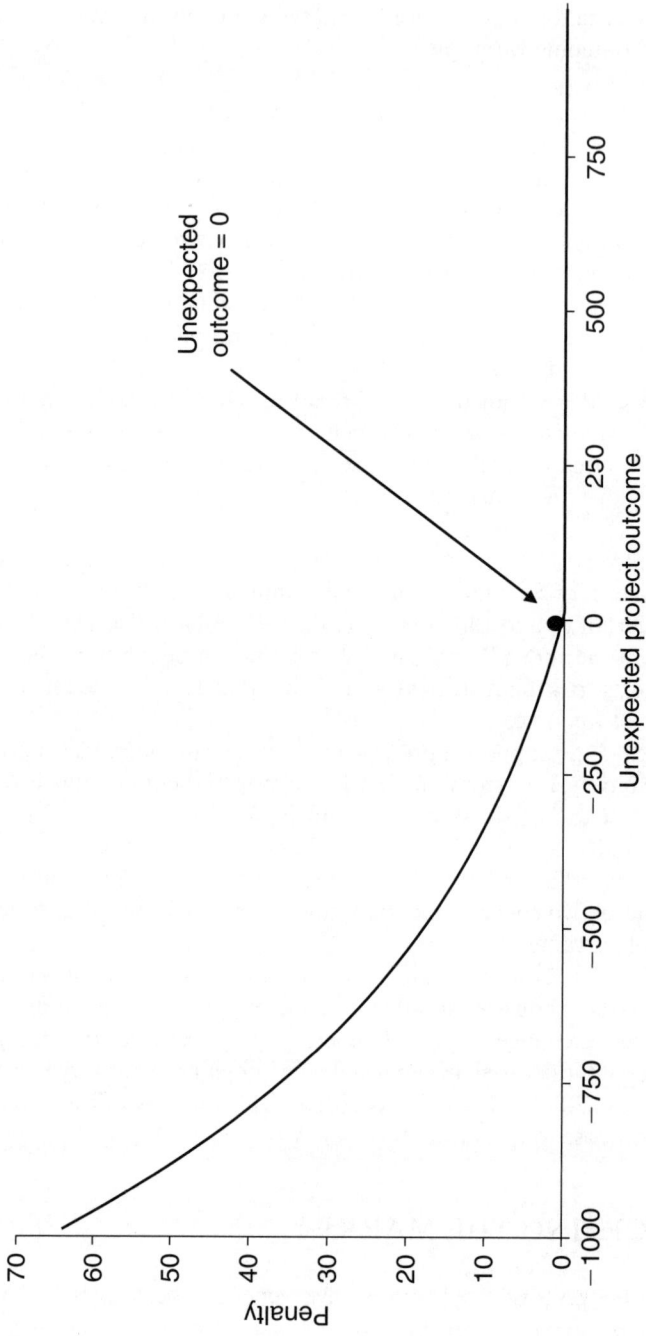

Figure 3.1 Convex risk penalty ($ millions)

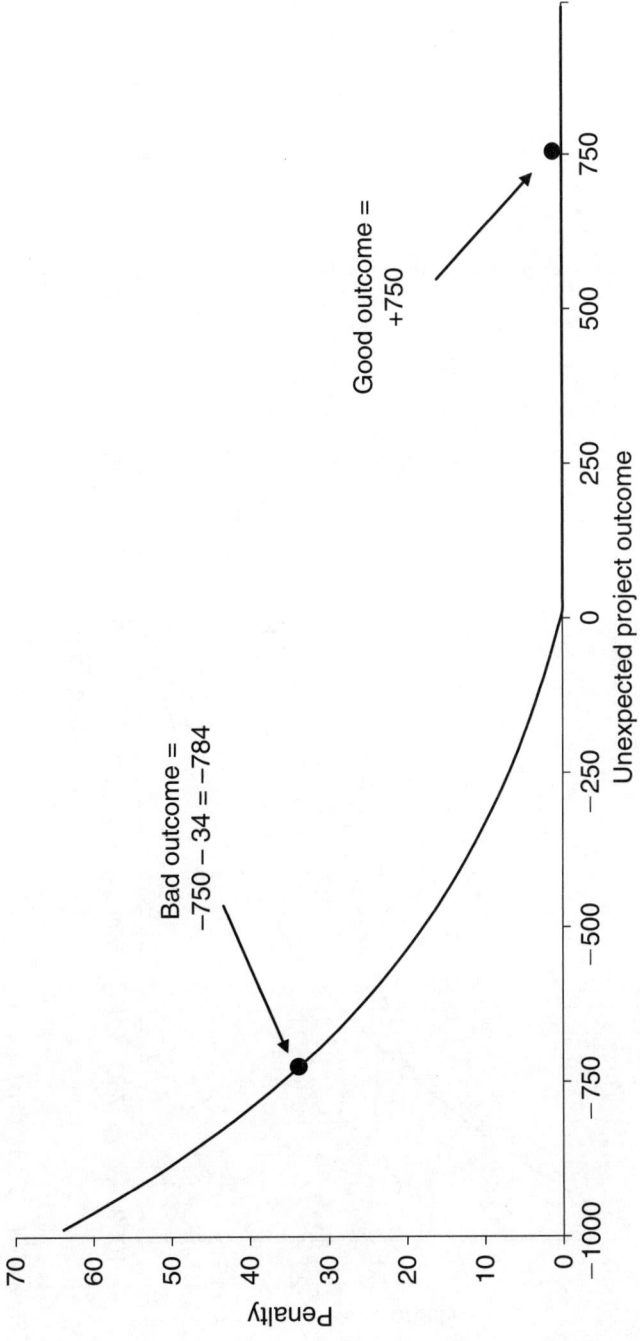

Figure 3.2 Binary outcomes (+750/−750)

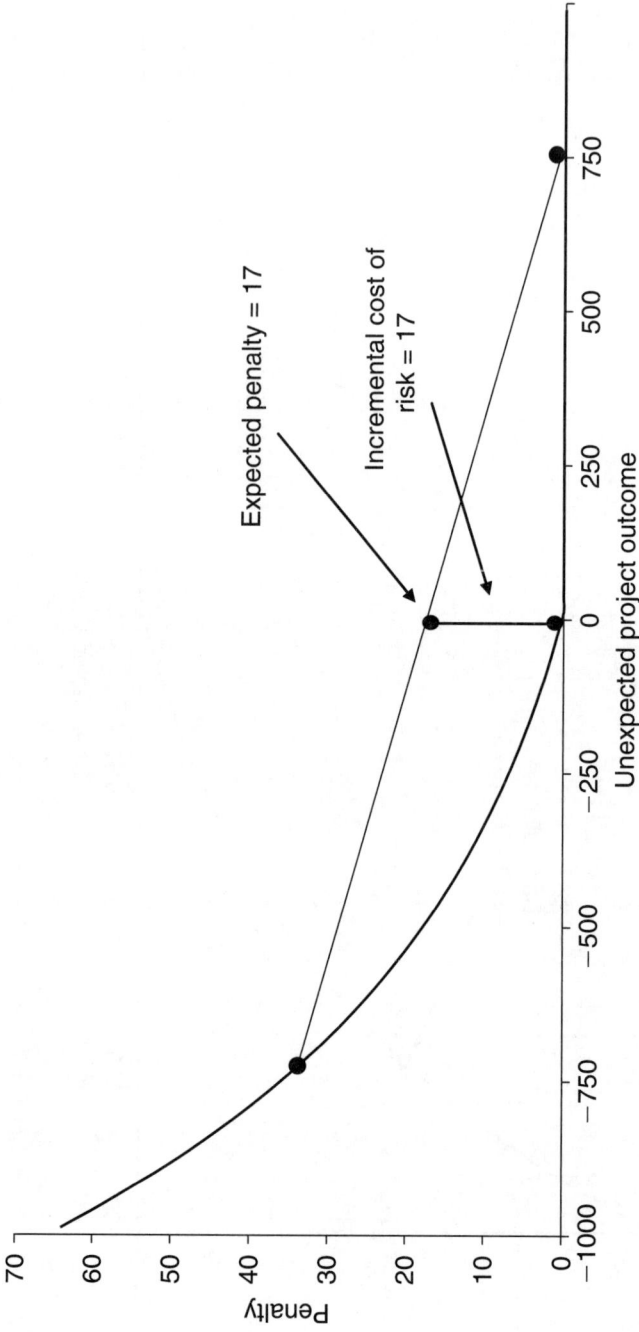

Figure 3.3 Cost of risk

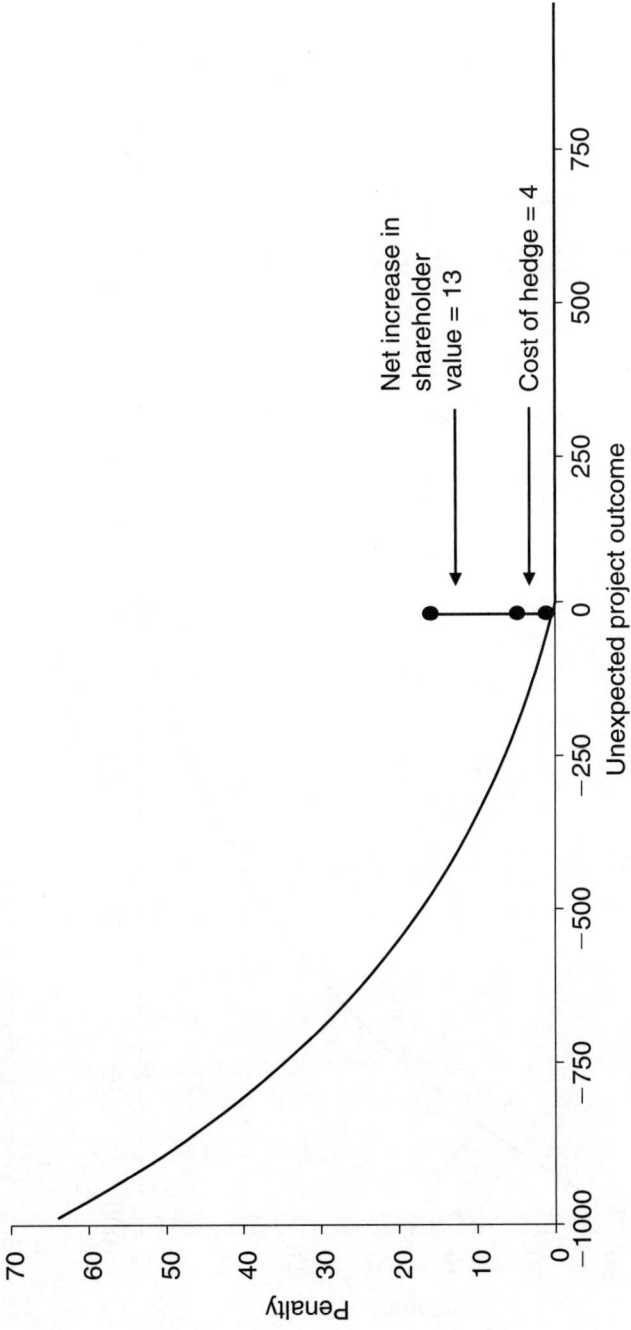

Figure 3.4 Cost of risk (hedged)

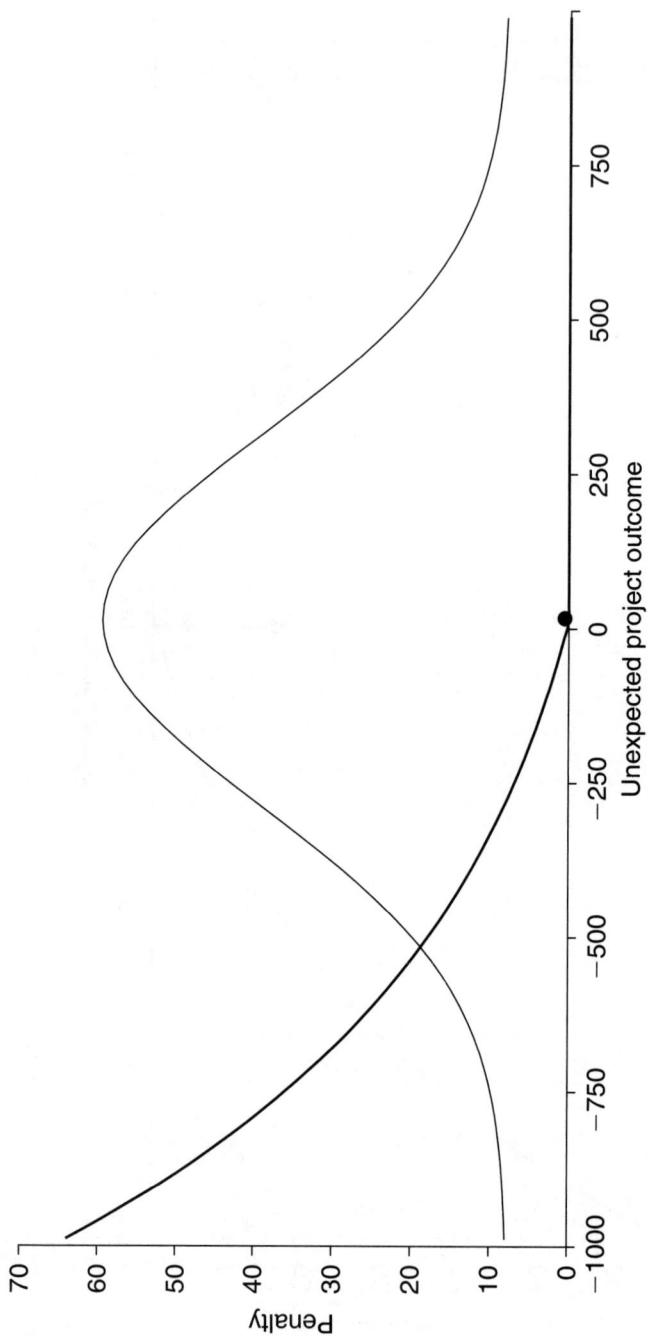

Figure 3.5 Symmetric distribution (normal)

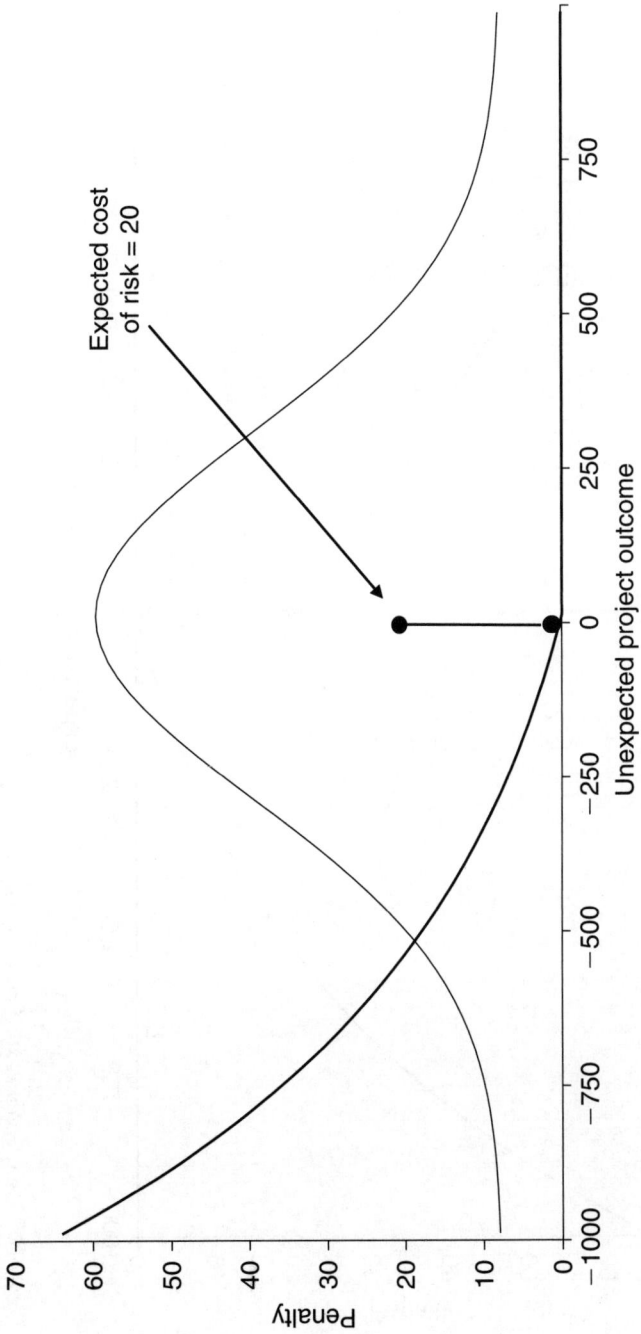

Figure 3.6   Expected cost of risk

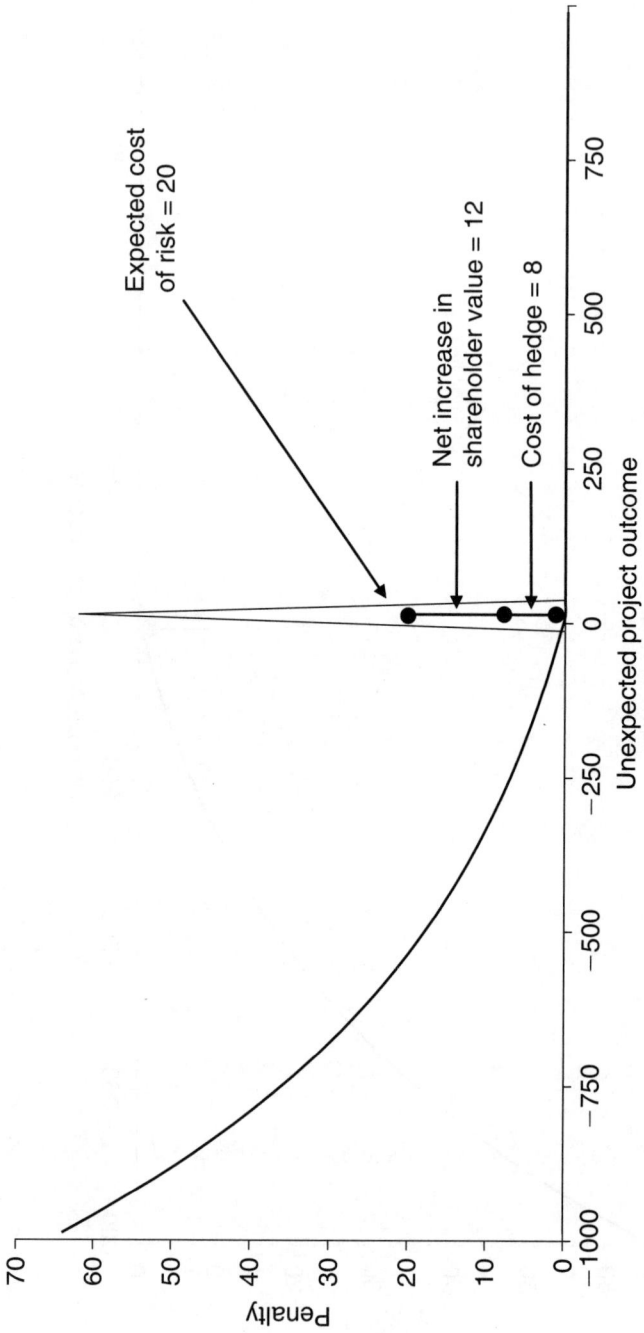

Figure 3.7   Expected cost of risk (hedged)

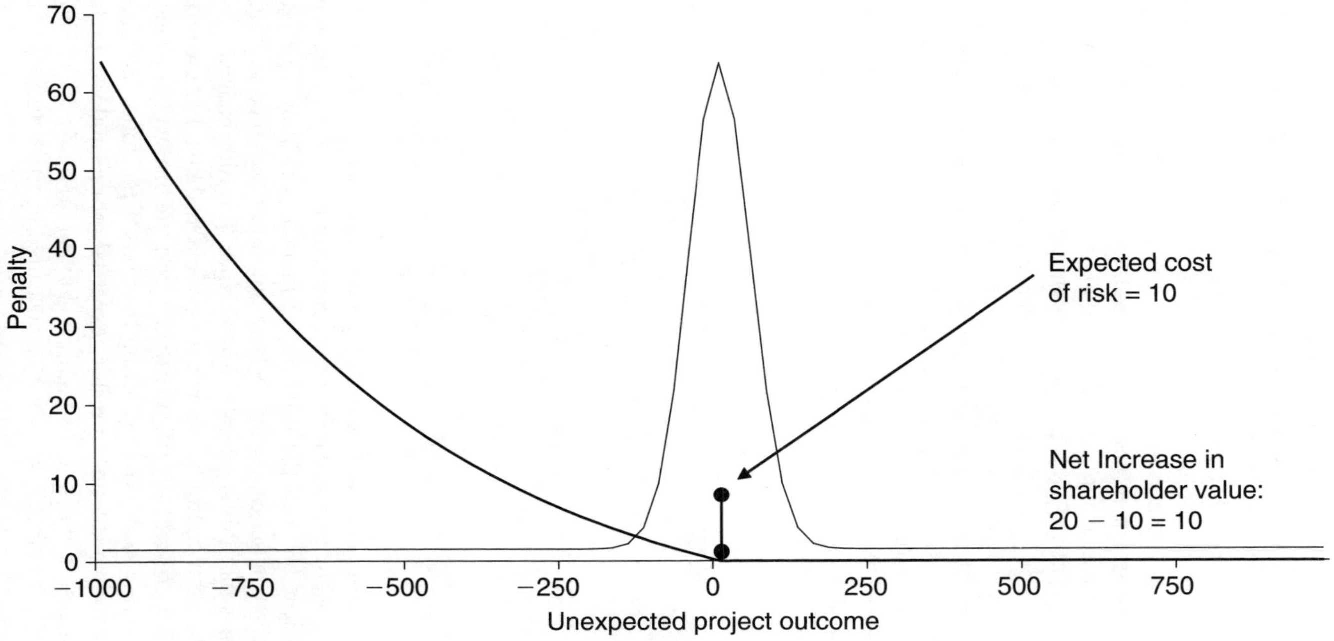

Penalty
70
60
50
40
30
20
10
0
−1000
−750
−500
−250
0
250
500
750
Unexpected project outcome
Expected cost of risk = 10
Net Increase in shareholder value: 20 − 10 = 10

Figure 3.8 Expected cost of risk (reduced by costless hedging)

such narrow exposures, the relationship between the hedging instrument and the exposure will be quite tight and the hedges will contract the range of project outcomes.

The goal, however, is ex ante reduction of the variance of project outcomes and therefore a broader hedge with the same statistical implication can be just as effective at increasing investor value. Most publicly traded companies engage in projects whose outcomes correlate positively with states of the world as represented by broad market indices; in short, their projects have positive β. It is this property that underlies the observation by Almeida and Philippon (2007) that financial distress has negative β: it is inherited from the positive project β of the company.

Suppose we hedge our project β.[15] We wish to determine how much to hedge when project outcomes, with an ex ante investment value of $1 million, are normally distributed with variance σ_p^2 and β equal to b. We will hedge this portfolio by shorting $$c$ million of the market portfolio.[16] We are looking for the value of c that will minimize the variance of the firm's hedged project portfolio, using:

$$Var^{uh} = \sigma_p^2$$

$$Var^h = \sigma_p^2 + c^2\sigma_m^2 - 2c\rho_{pm}\sigma_p\sigma_m$$

$$\rho_{pm} = b\frac{\sigma_m}{\sigma_p}$$

$$Var^h = \sigma_p^2 + c^2\sigma_m^2 - 2cb\sigma_m^2$$

$$\frac{\partial Var^h}{\partial c} = 2c\sigma_m^2 - 2b\sigma_m^2$$

$$\frac{\partial^2 Var^h}{\partial c^2} = 2\sigma_m^2 > 0$$

$$\frac{\partial Var^h}{\partial c} = 0 \Rightarrow c = b,$$

where Var^{uh} and Var^h represent the project variance without and with hedging; σ_m^2 is the variance of the market portfolio; and ρ_{pm} is the correlation coefficient between the project and market portfolios. The positive second derivative indicates that we have minimized variance and the final implication is that this is achieved when project β is fully hedged.

Notice that β need not be positive for optimal hedging. For the rare firm with negative project β, c will be negative and the firm will implement its hedge by buying rather than shorting the market portfolio. Shareholders may adjust their portfolios to restore expected returns and risk by taking the opposite hedge position, generally by buying the market portfolio. The net gain for shareholders will then be measured by the reduction in deadweight (level two) financial distress cost.

3.4.1 The Concave Zone

Figure 3.9 differs from Figure 3.1 for unexpected project losses greater than $750 million. Figure 3.9 reflects a limit on the convexity that can be postulated for the risk penalty of a limited liability corporation. At some point bad project outcomes consume all the value (tangible and intangible) held by the corporation. Although a firm financed entirely by equity investors might destroy all of its value along a convex curve, it is more realistic to assume that diminishing franchise value and a sharing of damage with other parties (lenders, guarantors, suppliers and the rest) will create a concave penalty zone, as shown on the left side of Figure 3.9.

This shape is consistent with models of approaching bankruptcy (for example, Merton, 1974) where control remains with shareholders whose ownership interest becomes manifestly option-like. Sharpe (1976) identifies a similar optionality in the context of defined benefit plans guaranteed by the US Pension Benefit Guaranty Corporation (PBGC). A company whose forward prospects are dire may find that the bulk of its likely project outcomes will fall in the concave zone, as shown in Figure 3.10.

Such companies increase shareholder value by increasing the riskiness of their underlying projects, playing a 'heads our shareholders win, tails somebody else loses' game. For these companies, prospective level two costs have become negative. Such companies might be advised to forgo hedging and take every gamble. It is interesting to note that one very solid US airline has substantially hedged its fuel costs in recent years while its more troubled sisters have generally taken their chances (Carter et al., 2006).

3.4.2 The Pension Gambit

Using common assumptions about transparency and investor diversification and rationality, Tepper (1981) and Black (1980) show that investor value increases when corporate defined benefit plans sell equities and buy bonds. They rely on tax rules in many countries where (1) bond returns are more highly taxed than stock returns in taxable accounts, and (2) special tax rules treat pension plan stock and bond returns identically. Using Modigliani–Miller-style arguments and taking advantage of this differential tax treatment, they conclude that shareholders (Tepper) or the corporations themselves (Black) can reproduce the investment risk (β) and expected equity premiums while reducing taxes in their own accounts.

Twenty-five years after publication, the lessons of Tepper and Black have yet to achieve significant traction with practitioners. The emergence of liability-driven investments and impending changes to plan accounting rules suggest that the future may be different from the past. Gold (2005)

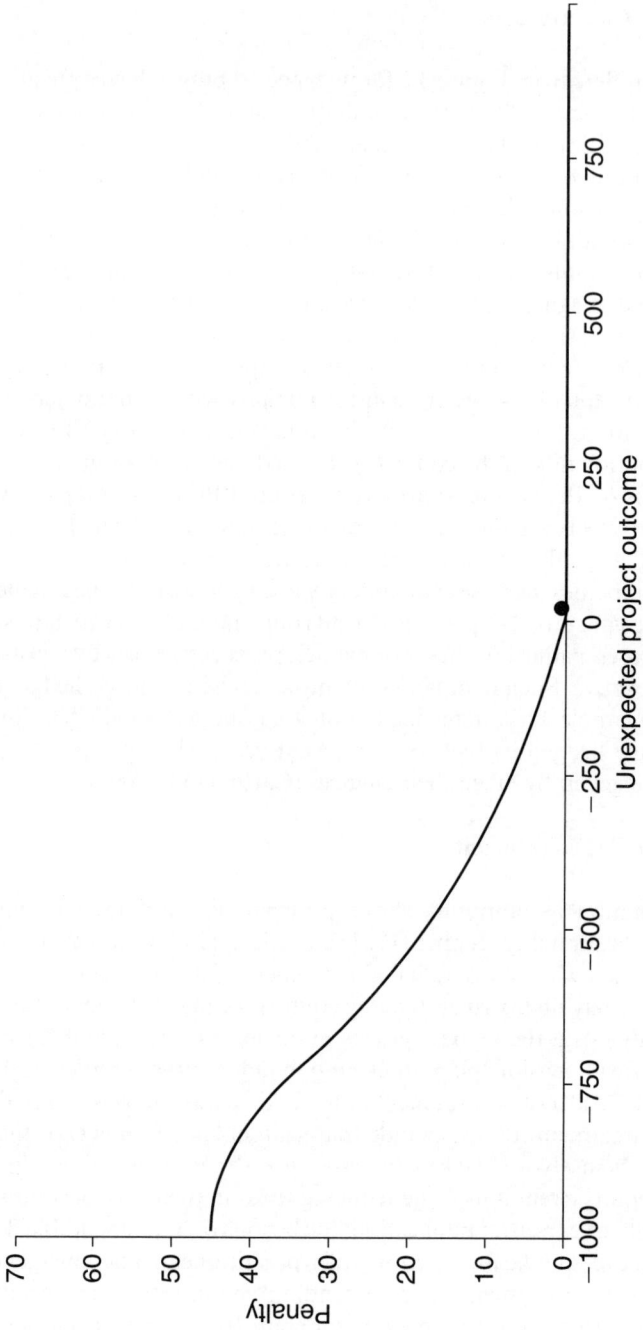

Figure 3.9 Concave zone ($ millions)

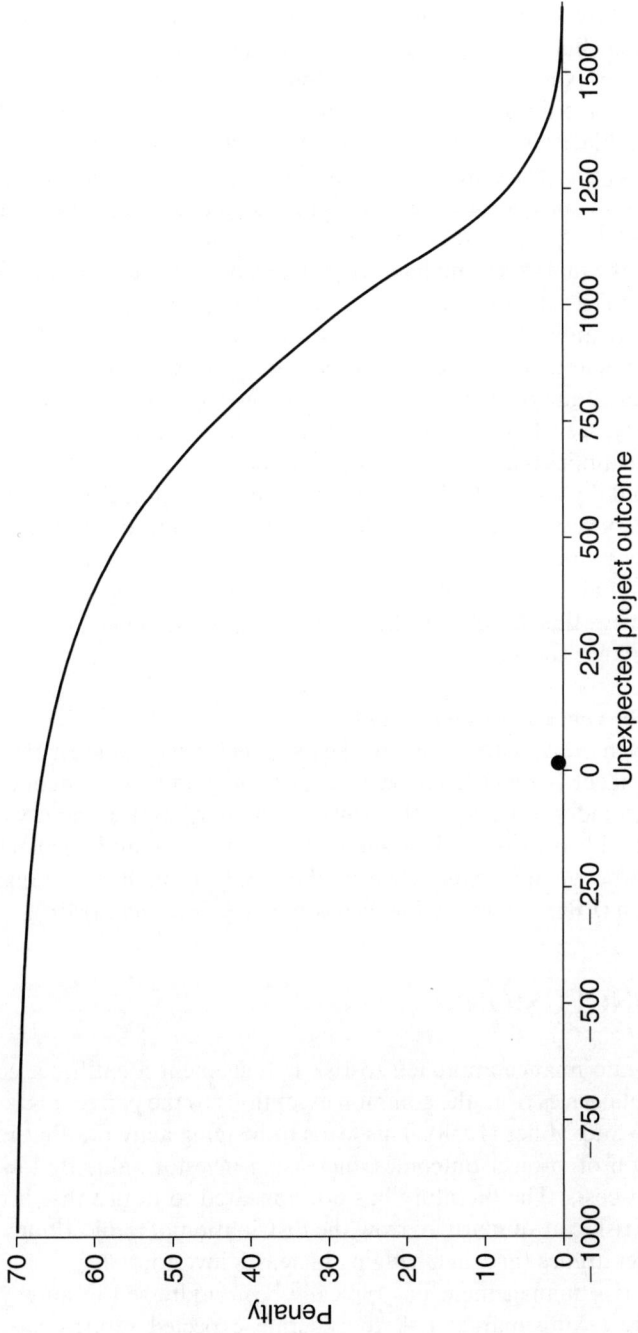

Figure 3.10 Concave zone ($ millions)

argues that the prevailing accounting treatment[17] creates spurious financial reporting benefits from equity investments that stand as a barrier to economic value maximization via β reduction.

When the liabilities of the plans are modelled as zero-β cash flows, Tepper and Black maximize value and minimize mismatch risk by setting pension asset β to zero. Gold (2001) extends Tepper and Black in a model where the sponsor chooses the asset β and defines the liability β each in the range [0,1]. Under these circumstances, shareholder value is maximized when asset β equals zero and liability β equals one. There is nothing magic about the [0,1] limitation and after-tax level one value continues to grow as the net (asset minus liability) β decreases. But any non-zero net β implies mismatch risk and we have seen that risk can cause level two costs.

For the great majority of companies that have positive β project portfolios, we have seen that shorting β actually reduces level two cost. Gold (2001) then implies that such firms should not only hedge away their project β but should do so by establishing a net negative pension β position. This layers two sources of economic value enhancement on top of each other. Overall risk reduction lowers level two cost and the net negative β in the pension plan adds tax benefits. Those companies with negative project β cannot achieve this double benefit and should acquire their long β hedges on their balance sheets.

3.4.2.1   The concave pension gambit

A company in the concave zone can take risks, including β, almost anywhere but we can identify two reasons why the pension plan may be a good location: (1) the 'independence' of the pension plan may limit the ability of the sponsor's creditors to invoke leverage-limiting covenants; and (2) plan losses may be borne by guarantors such as the US Pension Benefit Guaranty Corporation (PBGC) and the UK Pension Protection Fund (PPF).

3.5   CONCLUSIONS

The corporate finance approach to risk management identifies a convex penalty that derives from the common exceptions to the perfect markets of Modigliani and Miller (1958). This leads to hedging activities that reduce the variation of project outcomes, increasing investor value by lowering deadweight costs. The literature has not appeared to notice that hedging systematic risk can similarly narrow the distribution of project outcomes. This chapter argues that such hedging increases investor value.

Pension risk management has typically been addressed in an environment where taking market risk to generate expected returns has been assumed to add value. Thus risk reduction has generally been perceived as a restriction on this return-seeking activity. The potential to add value by eliminating market risk, identified 25 years ago by Tepper (1981) and Black (1980), has not been widely embraced. Recent concerns about pension risk have revived some interest in their work, but little action. This chapter argues for an extension of Tepper and Black to establish net negative market exposures in defined benefit pension plans under tax regimes common in Anglo-Saxon nations.

Hedging systematic risk increases investor value and using defined benefit pension plans to do so can add a second layer of value. The reluctance of defined benefit plan sponsors to reduce equity exposure is strong and persistent. For numerous reasons, plan sponsors are exceedingly unlikely to follow this course. It is therefore presumptuous of me to point out that an interesting piece of follow-up research might begin with the equilibrium question: what if every sponsor wanted to short their own market exposure? Who would hold systematic risk and what equity risk premium would be required?

ACKNOWLEDGEMENTS

I wish to thank the following for their comments on earlier drafts: Lawrence N. Bader, Tony Day, Theo Nijman, Michael W. Peskin, Prakash Shimpi, Sven Sinclair and Andrew L. Turner.

NOTES

1. E.g. Markowitz (1952), Sharpe (1964).
2. E.g. Modigliani and Miller (1958), Stiglitz (1969), Jensen and Meckling (1976).
3. Nocco and Stulz (2006) bridge the language of risk management and corporate finance, translating concepts like 'risk appetite' into objective measures based on the deadweight cost of financial distress.
4. Where (1) the effective tax rate on bond returns is higher than that on equity returns for investments held in taxable individual accounts; and (2) tax rates are identical for these two asset types held in a pension plan. This is common in Anglo-Saxon countries.
5. Doherty (2000).
6. Exley (2005) points out that this is not a net gain in equilibrium but represents a benefit to investors at the expense of taxpayers.
7. Also called 'the state price deflator' or 'the stochastic discount factor'.
8. This implies that project risks that are less than perfectly correlated will offset each other – an internal hedge that may reduce the corporate demand for external hedging or insurance. We proceed as though the entire portfolio were a single project subject to net risks after taking account of these cross-hedges.
9. It may be convenient, but not necessary, to think of the first level of valuation as being entirely cash-based and the second to reflect the impact on a firm's franchise value (its ability to find and finance value-added projects in subsequent periods).

10. Although we are continuing with an essentially financial risk management story, we can, as an aside, note that some operational risks may be eliminated from the risk portfolio at negative cost: that is, the effort to eliminate the risk is less costly than any price to hedge or insure it. The example of the shop floor banana fits in this category. We can consider this to be a project choice activity: the project with the banana peel on the floor has a lower NPV than the project without the banana peel and so the latter is chosen.
11. Faced with convex costs, value-oriented decision makers will mimic the behaviour of risk-averse investors. This can give credence to the idea that the firm itself is risk-averse.
12. The penalty value for the expected outcome could be positive or negative and the curve need not be linear at any point. The only necessary quality of the penalty is its convexity.
13. This suggests further research into the combination of risk penalty shapes and outcome distributions that result in positive and negative level two costs.
14. Insurances and private contracts will be less efficient. Asymmetric insurances and options may also change the distribution providing shareholder gains in exchange for premiums. Under the Smith and Stulz (1985) tax model, this may introduce additional costs.
15. We will hedge the residual β after narrower hedges have been implemented.
16. This may be implemented using various tools such as swaps and futures contracts.
17. FAS 87 in the US, CICA 3461 in Canada, FRS 17 in the UK, and IAS 19 internationally credit immediate earnings for expected returns on risky assets, smoothing actual return deviations over time.

REFERENCES

Almeida, H. and T. Philippon (2007), 'The risk-adjusted cost of financial distress', forthcoming in *Journal of Finance*.
Black, F. (1980), 'The tax consequences of long-run pension policy', *Financial Analysts Journal*, **36**(4), 21–8.
Carter, D.A., D.A. Rogers and B.J. Simkins (2006), 'Hedging and value in the US airline industry', *Journal of Applied Corporate Finance*, **18**(4), 21–33.
Doherty, Neil A. (2000), *Integrated Risk Management: Techniques and Strategies for Reducing Risk*, New York: McGraw-Hill, pp. 193–4.
Exley, C.J. (2005), 'Pension funds and the UK economy', *North American Actuarial Journal*, **9**(1), 73–87.
Froot, K.A., D.S. Scharfstein and J.C. Stein (1993), 'Risk management: coordinating corporate investment and financing policies', *Journal of Finance*, **48**(4), 1629–58.
Gold, J. (2001), 'The Shareholder-Optimal Design of Cash Balance Pension Plans', The Pension Research Council, Working Paper, 2001–07.
Gold, J. (2005), 'Accounting/actuarial bias enables equity investment by defined benefit pension plans', *North American Actuarial Journal*, **9**(3), 1–21.
Jensen, M.C. and W.H. Meckling (1976), 'Theory of the firm: managerial behavior, agency costs and ownership structure', *Journal of Financial Economics*, **3**(4), 305–60.
Leibowitz, M.L. (1986), 'Total portfolio duration: a new perspective on asset allocation', *Financial Analysts Journal*, **42**(5), 18–29.
Markowitz, H. (1952), 'Portfolio selection', *Journal of Finance*, **7**(1), 77–91.
Merton, R.C. (1974), 'On the pricing of corporate debt: the risk structure of interest rates', *Journal of Finance*, **29**(2), 449–70.

Modigliani, F. and M.H. Miller (1958), 'The cost of capital, corporation finance and the theory of the firm', *American Economic Review*, **48**(3), 261–97.

Nocco, B.W. and R.M. Stulz (2006), 'Enterprise risk management: theory and practice', *Journal of Applied Corporate Finance*, **18**(4), 8–20.

Sharpe, W.F. (1964), 'Capital asset prices: a theory of market equilibrium under conditions of risk', *Journal of Finance*, **19**(3), 425–42.

Sharpe, W.F. (1976), 'Corporate pension funding policy', *Journal of Financial Economics*, **3**(3), 183–93.

Shimpi, P. (2004), 'Leverage and the cost of capital in the insurative model', working paper.

Smith, C.W. and R.M. Stulz (1985), 'The determinants of firms' hedging policies', *Journal of Financial and Quantitative Analysis*, **20**(4), 391–405.

Stiglitz, J.E. (1969), 'A re-examination of the Modigliani–Miller theorem', *American Economic Review*, **59**(5), 784–93.

Tepper, I. (1981), 'Taxation and corporate pension policy', *Journal of Finance*, **36**(1), 1–13.

Discussion of 'The intersection of pensions and enterprise risk management'

Theo Nijman

Gold's chapter reaches a thought-provoking policy recommendation: pension funds should short equities. This recommendation is orthogonal to conventional wisdom which states that pension funds should take long positions in equity and should use developments such as Liability Driven Investments (LDI) to balance risk and return. Other strands in the literature even argue in detail how the long position in equities that the fund is to take depends on the age composition of the fund (see, for example, Bovenberg et al., 2007, for a recent survey). In this discussion I will first of all summarize the standard recommendation and subsequently analyse the difference in assumptions which makes Gold's findings so drastically different.

The main motivation for the recommendation that pension funds should tailor their investments to their liabilities is discontinuity risk. Through adequate balancing of risk and return, pension funds can ensure that the risk of becoming underfunded and the magnitude of the underfunding do not get too large. This is crucial, because pension funds have given guarantees to participants and need sufficient funds to meet these promises in all future scenarios. Underfunding due to poor returns on risky investment can to some extent be solved through additional contributions of the sponsor or the participants in the fund. But additional contributions of the sponsor are not assured in the case of discontinuity, that is, if this sponsor can go bankrupt. Likewise, if the additional contributions are to be paid by current participants in the scheme, discontinuity can be an issue because participants can avoid fulfilling their contract: they can reduce their labour supply and/or leave the sector or firm and work elsewhere.

The main motivation for the recommendation that pension funds should be long in equities is that human capital is almost riskless and that, to earn the risk premium on total wealth, a substantial fraction of financial wealth is to be invested in risky assets. This is even more true for young participants where the ratio of financial wealth to total wealth is the smallest. The important underlying assumption is that not just the value of the pension entitlement matters for the individual, but the risk characteristics as well. The assumption is that agents cannot or do not unwind the position imposed on them by collective pension funds. The recent literature on behavioural finance and financial literacy has often been put forward to support this assumption (see, for example, Munnell and Sunden, 2004; Rooij et al., 2007). The potential conflict of interest between the participants in the fund and the sponsor is usually not analysed in this literature.

Gold takes a very different starting point. He starts from the corporate finance literature and assumes that financial markets are transparent and frictionless and that agents are fully rational. As a consequence, nothing but the market value of the claim offered by the pension fund is relevant. In the simplest setting, where no frictions exist within the firm either, the risk taking of the sponsor and pension fund is irrelevant, as in the well-known Modigliani–Miller theorem in corporate finance. In line with the more recent corporate finance literature, risk taking is then made relevant by considering the cost of financial distress and progressive taxation rules. In this setting, risks are to be reduced by the firm. This can be done by shorting equities, because almost all projects undertaken by the firm will perform better in prosperous economic conditions. This recommendation is supported by the well-known reasoning of Tepper (1981) and Black (1980) that pension investment should overweight bonds if bonds are taxed more heavily than stocks in taxable accounts. This conclusion can be turned around only if the firm is in the concave zone of the risk penalty curve, where more risk taking is rewarded. This will be the case, for example, if the firm benefits heavily from the fact that the value of the put options that are written by pension guarantee funds such as the PBGC and the PPF increase with the level of risk taking, while the contribution to these guarantee funds is not affected. In such cases long positions in equities are value maximizing.

Gold concentrates on the convex part of the risk penalty curve where a short position in equities in the pension fund is value maximizing. The assumption is that firms cannot default and will provide additional funding if the returns on the assets of the pension fund are low. Discontinuity risk is ignored. Moreover, it is assumed that the reduced equity holding of the pension fund will be compensated by rational unconstrained individuals who take additional equity risk in their other assets. Note that, if the value of the other assets is small relative to pension wealth, the required equity exposure can easily exceed unity. Implicitly, therefore, the assumption is made that individuals can borrow to invest in equities and /or use derivatives to lever their other assets.

In summary, the contribution by Gold is thought provoking because it questions common wisdom. The analysis is, moreover, correct given the assumptions made and nicely introduces findings from the corporate finance literature in the literature on pension management. In my personal view, though, the assumption that individuals cannot and do not unwind the decision made by their pension fund is more realistic than the assumption that only market values matter. Under these assumptions common wisdom survives.

ADDITIONAL REFERENCES

Bovenberg, A.L., R.S.J. Koijen, T.E. Nijman and C.N. Teulings (2007), 'Saving and investing over the life cycle and the role of collective', Netspar Panel Paper.
Munnell, Alicia and Annika Sunden (2004), 'Coming up short: the challenge of 401(k) plans', Washington: The Brookings Institution.
Van Rooij, M., H. Prast and C. Kool (2007), 'Risk return preferences in the pension domain: are people able to choose', *Journal of Public Economics* **91**, 701–22.

4. The victory of hope over angst? Funding, asset allocation and risk taking in German public sector pension reform

Raimond Maurer, Olivia Mitchell and Ralph Rogalla

4.1 INTRODUCTION

Public employee pension systems throughout the developed world have traditionally been of the pay-as-you-go (PAYGO) defined benefit (DB) variety, where pensioner payments are financed by taxes (contributions) levied on the working generation. But as the number of retirees rises relative to the working-age group, such systems have begun to face financial distress. This trend has been exacerbated in many countries, among them Germany, by high unemployment rates producing further deterioration of the contribution base. In the long run, public sector pension benefits will have to be cut or contributions increased, if the systems are to be maintained.

An alternative path sometimes offered to ease the crunch of paying for public employee pensions is to move toward funding: here, plan assets are gradually built up, invested, and enhanced returns devoted to partly defray civil servants' pension costs. In this study, we evaluate the impact of introducing partial pre-funding, paired with a strategic investment policy for the German federal state of Hesse. The analysis assesses the impact of introducing a supplementary tax-sponsored pension fund whose contributions are invested in the capital market and used to relieve the state budget from (some) pension payments. Our model determines the expectation and the Conditional Value-at-Risk of economic pension costs using a stochastic simulation process for pension plan assets. This approach simultaneously determines the optimal contribution rate and asset allocation that controls the expected economic costs of providing the promised pensions, while at the same time controlling investment risk. Specifically, we offer answers to the following questions:

1. How can the plan be designed to control cash-flow shortfall risk, so as to mitigate the potential burden borne by future generations of taxpayers?
2. What is the optimal asset allocation for this fund as it is built up, to generate a maximum return while simultaneously restricting capital market and liability risk?
3. What are reasonable combinations of annual contribution rates and asset allocation to a state-managed pension fund, which will limit costs of providing promised public sector pensions?

We anticipate that this research will interest several sorts of policy maker groups. First, focusing on the German case, the state and Federal governments should find it relevant, as these entities face considerable public sector pension liabilities. Secondly, our findings will also be of interest to other European countries, as most have substantial underfunded defined benefit plans for civil servants.

In what follows, we first offer a brief description of the structure of civil servant pensions in Germany, focusing on their benefit formulas, their financing, and the resulting current as well as future plan obligations for taxpayers. Next, we turn to an analysis of the actuarial status of the Hesse civil servants' pension plan and evaluate how much would have to be contributed to fund this plan in a non-stochastic context. Subsequently we evaluate the asset-liability and decision-making process from the viewpoint of the plan sponsor, to determine sensible plan asset allocation behaviour. A final section summarizes findings and implications.

4.2   CIVIL SERVANT PENSIONS IN GERMANY

Whereas civil servant pensions are relatively well-funded in the United States (Mitchell et al., 2001), the same is not the case in Germany. There, most civil servants have been promised an unfunded, non-contributory, tax-sponsored DB pension with benefits which are a function of salary and service. Over time, politicians and employees have gradually become aware of the cost of public pensions, particularly as the population has aged, and a few small reforms have been implemented to date. In 1996, for instance, the German state of Rhineland-Palatinate launched a financing fund for newly hired civil servants to cope with the increasing burden of future pension payments. The state currently pays 20–30 per cent of covered payroll for active civil servants into that fund. No doubt owing to politicians' risk aversion, the fund's investment portfolio has thus far been restricted to government bonds, thereby neglecting the opportunity to improve returns by investing in equity markets. Accordingly, while first steps toward funding German civil servants pensions have been taken, no public pension plan is fully funded and investment patterns in the few cases where the plans have assets are extraordinarily conservative.

4.2.1 Public Sector Pension Parameters

It is widely recognized that a pension plan represents a long-term contract between an employer and the plan participants. That is, workers give up current salary in exchange for future retirement benefits, either directly through salary deferral, or indirectly through forgone earnings (Husted and Mitchell, 2001). From the perspective of an employer, the structure of a retirement plan and its overall generosity can be an important means of attracting, recruiting and retaining valued employees. Particularly when an employer must invest in specific training for the employee to do his job, it is in his interest to restrict worker mobility once trained so as to maximize returns on this investment (McGill et al., 2005). In this sense, traditional DB pensions have been recognized as suitable for workers in lifetime jobs (and less appropriate for mobile workers).

Originating in the Middle Ages, the German civil service system with its rights and duties was initially codified in the Allgemeines Preussisches Landrecht of 1794, an early Prussian constitution, and, with some adaptations, the system is still in force today (Gillis, 1968). As in many other countries, a German civil servant traditionally commits his lifetime to public sector tasks. This civil servant is then promised a retirement annuity that depends on his age at retirement, his years of service in the public sector and his final salary. In exchange for a non-contributory plan, civil servants 'pay' indirectly by having significantly lower gross earnings than other public sector workers with comparable credentials.[1] Civil servants are also not included in the national social security system,[2] nor covered by supplementary occupational pensions; rather, each state has a DB pension plan specific to that state.[3] As public employees are not covered by social security, they receive higher retirement benefits than their private sector counterparts who tend to receive both social security and occupational pension benefits (Heubeck and Rürup, 2000).

In recent years, however, German public pension plan generosity has begun to be curtailed substantially. Until 1991, for instance, the DB pension formula provided accruals according to a non-linear function. Thus, for service upto 10 years, the replacement rate was 35 per cent of final salary; for an additional 15 years of service, benefits rose by 2 per cent per year. After 25 years of service, benefit accruals increased at only 1 per cent annually, resulting in a maximum replacement rate of 75 per cent of final salary after 35 years of service. Then, in 1992, the benefit formula was transformed into a strictly linear function: benefit accrual was set at 1.875 per cent of final salary per year of service, so that the traditional 75 per cent replacement rate would be paid only after 40 years of service (rather than after 35 years, as previously). In 2003, new legislation again brought benefit cuts for civil servant pensions. Over time, annual pension accruals will be gradually reduced to 1.79375 per cent of final salary, providing retiring civil servants with a maximum replacement rate of 71.75 per cent after 40 years of service. Current pensioners will also be affected in that their usual post-retirement benefit increases will be slightly reduced. After eight rounds of pension increases, their nominal replacement rate will have declined to (a maximum of) 71.75 per cent (although the nominal pension benefit will have increased to some extent).

The standard retirement age for civil servants is currently 65, although early retirement is possible at age 63; for early retirement, a discount factor of 0.3 percentage points per month of early retirement is applied. Because police work and fire fighting are physically demanding occupations, retirement benefits for public safety workers typically allow retirement at earlier ages, in part to maintain a younger workforce.[4] If an active or retired civil servant dies, the spouse is entitled to a survivorship benefit of 55 per cent (formerly 60 per cent) of the deceased civil servant's pension (in addition, orphans receive 20 per cent and half-orphans 12 per cent).

From the employee's perspective, the relatively more generous civil servant pension is partial compensation for their inflexibility and non-portability. For instance, if a civil servant were to leave his job for the private sector, he would forgo a substantial part of his accrued pension benefits, losing over half of his pension accruals.[5] It is clear that this creates a strong disincentive for older civil servants to leave their public sector jobs.

4.2.2   Key Aspects of Hesse's Civil Servant Pension System

To illustrate the opportunities and risks of reform, we turn to an assessment of the civil servant pension offered to public workers employed by the German federal state of Hesse, one of 16 states that form the Federal Republic of Germany. Located in the southwestern centre of Germany, Hesse's population of 6.1 million represents almost 8 per cent of Germany's 83 million residents. Hesse's economic heart is the Rhine-Main area located around the 650 000 inhabitant city of Frankfurt, which is the centre of the German financial and banking industry, domicile of Europe's second most important stock exchange and one of the world's largest airports. With a GDP of €204 billion, Hesse contributes about 9 per cent to the German GDP.[6] As Hesse was part of the former West

Germany, its population of civil servants may be seen as rather representative of the approximately 1.5 million active (about 4.5 per cent of German workforce) and 900 000 retired civil servants in Germany as a whole.[7]

The data set on which our study is based was provided by the Hessian statistical office. It contains anonymized demographic and economic data on virtually all active and retired civil servants in Hesse as of the beginning of 2004, including their age, sex, marital status, line of service (for active civil servants), and salary/pension payments.[8] In addition, to derive civil servant-specific mortality tables, we have sampled data on the number of living retirees at the beginning of each year as well as the number of those deceased each year for the period 1994–2004, by age and sex. Descriptive statistics on our sample appear in Table 4.1.

The overall number of active civil servants in our sample for 2004 is 104 919, of which 45 per cent are female. Salary payments to this work group amounted to an annual €4.26 billion or 33 per cent of Hesse's annual state tax revenues. The higher service level includes mostly university professors and high school teachers, of which 37 per cent are female and the average age is 47.7 years; annual salary levels average €46 000. Some 61 per cent of the sample is in the upper service level, which includes police inspectors and elementary and junior high school teachers. As many teachers are female, women make up 49.3 per cent of employees in this group. With an average age of 45.6 years, these civil servants receive an average salary of €38 000. The middle service level employs 11 609 workers, for example, in lower police service, 38.4 per cent of which are female. On average, these civil

Table 4.1   Summary statistics for civil servant and retiree pension obligations

	Number	Female (%)	Avg. salary/ pension	Avg. age
Active civil servants by service level	104 919	44.5	€39 000	44.7
Higher	28 946	37.0	€46 000	47.7
Upper	63 843	49.3	€38 000	45.6
Middle	11 609	38.4	€31 000	40.3
Lower	503	12.5	€26 000	43.7
Pensioners by origin of claim	60 418	47.2	€29 000	71.8
Retired civil servants	43 065	28.0	€33 000	69.6
Surviving dependants	17 353	95.0	€18 000	77.3

Note: Authors' calculations using data provided by the State of Hesse for 2004.

servants are 40.3 years old and earn €31 000 per year. The lower service level is on average 43.7 years old and earns an average annual income of €26 000.

Turning to retirees, pension payments for those in our sample amount to an overall €1.76 billion or 14 per cent of Hesse's annual tax revenues. In total, the number of pensioners is 60 418, of which 71 per cent represent retired civil servants; the remaining 17 353 pensioners are surviving dependants. Most of the retired civil servants (72 per cent) are male, but 95 per cent of the dependants are female. Male retired civil servants are on average 70 years old and receive an average annual pension of €34 500, whereas female retired civil servants average 68.6 years of age with an average annual pension of €30 500. Among surviving dependants, females are on average 77.7 years old and earn an annual average pension income of €18 500, while their male counterparts are only 68.8 years on average and receive mean dependants benefits of €15 500 per year.

4.3 VALUING THE PUBLIC PENSION IN A NON-STOCHASTIC FRAMEWORK

Next we turn to an analysis of the actuarial status of the Hesse civil servants' pension plan. In this section, we evaluate how much would have to be contributed to fund this plan in a non-stochastic context, which of course requires an actuarial evaluation of the plan's liabilities. In this section, accordingly, we combine information about the benefit formulas and anticipated retirement ages with demographic and economic assumptions. Specifically, we project how and when participants will leave active association with the plan and how long benefits will be paid after retirement. These assumptions must include anticipated mortality and disability rates, probabilities of retirement, and regular as well as survivor benefits. In what follows, we discuss these assumptions in detail for the civil servants covered by pensions in the state of Hesse.

4.3.1 Mortality Patterns

German civil servants generally tend to enjoy lower mortality rates than the general population (apart from police and other special service units). For this reason, it is essential to derive mortality tables specific to this group, yet the state government does not currently maintain these. We therefore derive the relevant mortality tables using standard actuarial methods and personnel statistics provided by the Hessian statistical office. To this end, for each year from 1994 to 2004, we sampled the numbers $l_{x,t}$ of active and retired civil servants by sex which were alive at age x at the beginning of the respective year t, and out of this cohort we compute the number $d_{x,t}$ of those who died before reaching year $t + 1$. By dividing the aggregate number of deaths by the aggregate number of lives covered, we derive the raw rate of mortality $\hat{q}_{x,1999}$ of a person aged x around the year 1999 (Wolfsdorf, 1997, pp. 50ff., DAV, 2004, p. 76):

$$\hat{q}_{x,1999} = \frac{\sum_{t=1994}^{2004} d_{x,t}}{\sum_{t=1994}^{2004} l_{x,t}}. \tag{4.1}$$

To smooth erratic changes in mortality rates because of the small samples taken, we employ the well-established method of Whittaker (1923) and Henderson (1924) to obtain graduated rates of mortality $q_{x,1999}$:

$$\min_{q_i} \sum_{i=0}^{T} x_i(\hat{q}_i - q_i)^2 + g\sum_{i=0}^{T-3}(\Delta^3\hat{q}_i)^2, \tag{4.2}$$

where x_i represents the size of the number of observations for cohort i relative to the overall sample size, g balances the goodness-of-fit versus the level of smoothness, with $g = 0$ resulting in a perfect fit of raw and graduated mortality rates, and Δ represents the difference operator (Joseph, 1952, p. 99).

On analysing the mortality rates thus derived, it turns out that, for ages 60 to 80, the results are quite close to the annuitant mortality rates published by the German Association of Actuaries (DAV, 2004), supporting the notion that civil servants live longer than the average population (see Figure 4.1).[9] We make use of this result when estimating mortality rates for those above the age of 80. Here, the usual approach would be to specify a law of mortality (for example, Gompertz-Makeham), calibrate it based on empirical observations, and then extrapolate mortality rates for the very old (Milbrodt and Helbig, 1999). Owing to the limited number of observations in our sample, we instead use annuitant mortality rates for over age 80.

To account for future mortality improvements, we incorporate an exponential trend function to project future mortality rates based on those of 1999 (DAV, 2004, p. 38):

$$q_{x,t} = q_{x,1999} \cdot \exp(-F(x) \cdot (t - 1999)). \tag{4.3}$$

For the age-depending trend factor $F(x)$ we also rely on data provided by the German Association of Actuaries, using its unadjusted mid-term trend function (Zieltrend 2. Ordnung) (see DAV, 2004, pp. 56ff.). Employing this

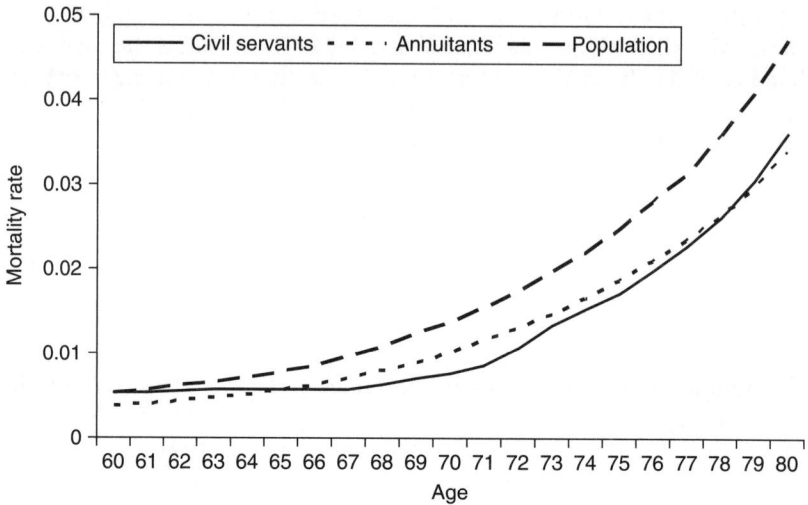

Notes: Authors' compilation of mortality rates for female Hessian civil servants; annuitants' mortality rates as derived by the German Association of Actuaries (DAV, 2004); population mortality rates as stated by the German Federal Statistical Office (mortality table 2003/2005).

Figure 4.1   A comparison of mortality rates for civil servants, the total population and annuitants

trend function, the rate of mortality of a female civil servant aged 65 will decrease by 40 per cent until the year 2030.

4.3.2   Population Dynamics

When analysing the transition to a funded pension system, it is necessary, not only to account for current employees, but also to recognize that new employees will be hired in the future. Projecting civil service employment far into the future is, of course, quite complex, and a complete character-ization of all possible evolutionary paths of the future workforce is not the primary focus of this study. We therefore take a simple yet sensible approach to describe the development of the future workforce, drawing on the current active population as a base. We forecast the evolution of age and salary for every existing civil servant, assuming constant marital status over time. When a position becomes vacant, we assign to that job a new civil servant with a 50 per cent chance of being male or female, abstracting from promotion from within. The new worker's age is assigned as the average age of new hires, accounting for average time spent on position-related

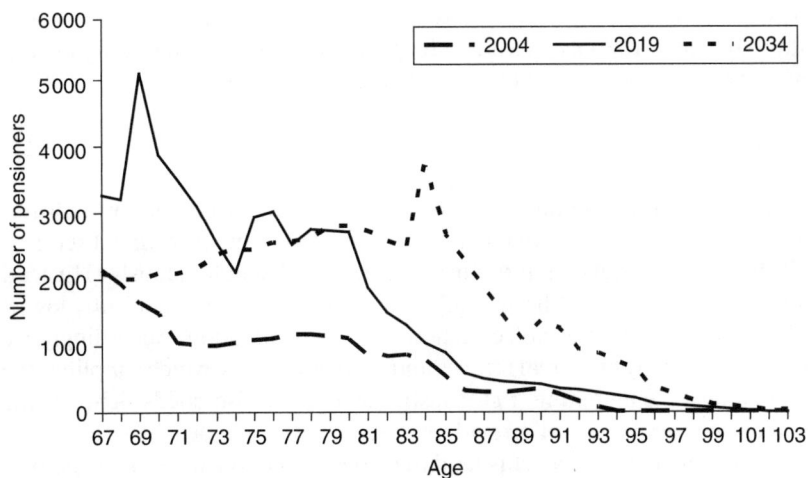

Note: Authors' calculations using data provided by the State of Hesse.

Figure 4.2   Projected age distribution of old-age pensioners

education or other types of public service that will be credited as pension-able years in civil service. The worker's salary is assigned as the age-related remuneration for this position and marital status is that of the previous position holder.

Employee turnover other than retirement can be assumed to be of minor significance. While there might be some fluctuation within the group of assistant professors that leave civil service after not receiving tenure and who start a career in the private sector, most state employees remain in service once they become full civil servants.[10] We therefore do not account for employee turnover and instead assume that civil servants remain in service until retirement age. This latter is set at 67, anticipating that the latest changes to public pension regulations (that is, the increase in regular retirement age from 65 to 67) is also required for civil servants. It is fur-thermore assumed that all civil servants reach this age with certainty and remain active until then.[11]

Retired civil servants are not modelled individually; rather, they are rep-resented by the expected cash flows that result from the indexed life annu-ities they receive according to the civil service pension benefit formula based on service years and final salary. For workers with a spouse, these annuities are indexed joint-and-survivor annuities where we assume that both partners are of same age and opposite sexes. Figure 4.2 shows the pro-jected age distribution for old-age pensioners over the next 30 years. As can be seen, the number of retirees and their average age is projected to rise substantially over the next decades. In particular, we find that a significant number of civil servants will retire from 2017 onwards.

4.3.3 Economic Assumptions

The three central economic factors that have a major impact on the valuation of a pension plan are inflation, salary growth and investment returns; all these are interrelated and must be considered simultaneously (Hustead and Mitchell, 2001). Although inflation in the Euro zone is currently low, it is still important for pension cash flows and their valuation. Accordingly, we base all our analysis on real returns and financial values, which simplifies the modelling by eliminating a stochastic factor and also sheds light on the actual economic cost of providing real civil servant pensions, as salary increases and pension benefits tend to be tied to the consumer price index.[12] We therefore assume that salaries and pensions are at least increased with inflation, that is, the minimum growth rate of real wages is zero. (Below we also report an alternative set of results using a real wage growth rates of 1 per cent, to explore further how these salary assumptions affect results.)

Assumptions on investment returns are crucial as they influence the rate at which pension liabilities should be discounted. Because of their long-term character, pension liabilities have a long duration and therefore are sensitive to the discount rate selected. On the choice of the discount rate there is an ongoing debate, which Blake (2006, p. 77) defines as the difference between an actuarial versus an economic valuation of pension liabilities. Traditionally, actuaries choose the discount rate which reflects a reasonable projected expected return of the asset backing the pension liabilities. If the pension assets are partly invested in equities, the discount rate includes also an equity risk premium, which is, from an ex ante perspective, not realized. By contrast, many economists argue that the relevant number for discounting future pension payments is the riskless rate of interest rate reflecting the financing cost of the plan sponsor. In what follows, we follow the latter approach and discount liabilities at the real rate on (quasi-) risk-free long-term government bonds. Our economic rationale is that this rate reflects the state's financing costs. We assume that this real risk-free interest rate is in the base case 3 per cent.[13] To check for the interest rate sensitivity of our analysis, we also explore results with a real interest rate of 1.5 per cent.

4.3.4 Implied Pension Debt for Current Civil Servants

Our primary focus in this chapter is to show how one can structure and fund public employee pension promises in the future. Nevertheless, it is worth

Table 4.2   Implied pension debt for current pensioners and workers

Disc. Rate		Current pensioners		PBO active workers		Future accumulations	
		Salary/pension Increase p.a.		Salary/pension Increase p.a.		Salary/pension Increase p.a.	
		0%	1%	0%	1%	0%	1%
		(1)	(2)	(3)	(4)	(5)	(6)
		Panel 1:total (billion €)					
(1)	1.5%	28.41	31.90	28.52	37.43	20.70	30.41
(2)	3%	24.30	26.97	19.63	25.21	12.14	17.36
		Panel 2: as % of explicit public debt					
(3)	1.5%	96.5	108.3	96.9	127.1	70.3	103.3
(4)	3%	82.6	91.6	66.7	85.6	41.2	59.0

Note: Authors' calculations using data provided by the State of Hesse for 2004.

knowing how large already-accrued pension claims might be. Table 4.2 summarizes both the implied pension debt for retired civil servants currently receiving old age and survivor benefits, and active workers' accrued pension liabilities (as of 2004), as well as future projected benefits. We offer these for two alternative discount rates and real rates of salary and pension increases.

Panel 1 of the table reports pension liabilities in terms of billions of 2004 €, while Panel 2 relates the liabilities to the official level of state indebtedness. Pension debt is referred to as 'implied' in the table, as it is not formally reported as explicit government debt. The results show that explicit state debt is greatly understated by omission of the civil servant pension obligations. For instance, for the base case with a discount rate of 3 per cent and zero real pension increases (Row 2, Column 1), the pension liability to current pensioners totals €24.3 billion, or 82.6 per cent of the official €29.44 billion Hessian Government debt reported in 2004. For active workers, we calculate the projected benefit obligation (PBO) defined as (Milevsky, 2006, p. 173):

$$PBO = \sum_i \frac{1.79375 \cdot \tau_i \cdot S_{67,i} \cdot \bar{a}_{67,i}}{(1+r)^{67-Age_i}}, \tag{4.4}$$

where (for each civil servant i of Age_i) τ_i is the current number of service years in 2004, $S_{67,i}$ is the (expected) salary at retirement age 67, $\bar{a}_{67,i}$ is the immediate pension annuity factor, and r is the discount rate. While there is an ongoing debate about whether the PBO in general is an adequate measure for DB pension liabilities (c.f. Bodie, 1990; Mittelstaedt and

Regier, 1993; Gold, 2004), we argue that employing the PBO is appropriate for German civil servants' pension liabilities. In addition to the inflation-related pay rises discussed above and promotions to higher-paid positions, which we do not include in this study, civil servants' salaries increase deter-ministically with age. As there is no turnover in the workforce, using the accumulated benefit obligation (ABO) and therefore neglecting these pay increases would understate the already-accrued liabilities.

With the same economic assumptions, pension liabilities for current workers amount to €19.63 billion, or 66.7 per cent of the official debt (rows 2 and 4, column 3). Here we see that the implied pension debt for retired and currently active civil servants to date – representing already-accrued benefits – adds up to €43.9 billion, a figure that is almost 150 per cent of explicit state debt (adding the values in rows 2 and 4, columns 1 and 3). Not surprisingly, if the discount rate were cut to 1.5 per cent holding real wages and benefits constant, accrued pension obligations would grow by €13 billion, or by almost 30 per cent.

As civil servant turnover is virtually negligible, it is safe to assume that nearly all workers retire from the system in the future. For this reason, columns 5–6 of Table 4.2 show what new liabilities would result if the current system were kept in place for active civil servants; in other words, this represents future pension accumulations owing to the replacement rate increasing over time. With no salary increases and an interest rate of 3 per cent, these future pension accruals can be valued at €12.1 billion or 41 per cent of debt outstanding (rows 2 and 4, column 5). For active workers, then, the pension promise (both past and future) amounts to about €31.8 billion, or about 108 per cent of current explicit debt (adding columns 3 and 5 in rows 2 and 4, respectively); to this, the state's total obligation to retirees must be added, amounting to a total of 190 per cent of explicit debt (adding columns 1, 3, and 5, Row 4). In other words, the total obligation for both active and retired civil servants amounts to almost twice the current explicit state government debt.

This is of course a lower-bound estimate, as non-zero real salary increases are anticipated by most civil servants. If salaries were to rise in real terms by a single percentage point per year, this would elevate the expected present value of public pension commitments to a staggering €69.5 billion, or 236 per cent of explicit debt (adding columns 2, 4, and 6, rows 2 and 4, respectively). On the assumption that already-retired indi-viduals' pensions might be financed separately, in what follows below we focus only on active workers; scheduled benefit formulas maintained into the future would cost €42.6 billion, or 145 per cent of explicit debt if workers receive 1 per cent real annual salary growth. (Using a 1.5 per cent discount rate boosts unfunded liabilities for current workers to €67.8

billion, and the unfunded unrecognized debt to 230 per cent of recognized state debt.)

4.3.5 Funding Future Civil Servants' Pension Benefits

Moving to fund the public DB pension plan requires that assets be built up and invested in the pension fund. Accordingly, a key responsibility of the plan sponsor is to figure out pension liability patterns, and then to specify how much must be contributed to pay for those liabilities. In other words, one must assign in a systematic and consistent manner the expected cost of pension accruals as each year of service passes which gives rise to that cost. One way to make this assignment or cost allocation is termed the *actuarial cost method*, which assigns to each fiscal or plan year the actuarial present value of the costs assumed to have accrued in that year, or the so-called 'normal cost', on the view that actuarial assumptions are realized. Since civil servant pension benefits in Hesse are determined as a percentage of final salary times years of service, we use the aggregate level percentage of payroll method to determine the normal cost. This means that the total projected cost allocated to the plan is expressed as a percentage of active members' payroll (McGill et al., 2005). Accordingly, we calculate the actuarial present value of future pension accruals based on future salary and service over the next 50 years (2004 to 2053), starting with our initial population, and evolve it through time given the dynamics presented above. As of 2053, we conduct a discontinuance valuation, although of course this calculation could be extended further into the future quite naturally. The ratio of present value of pension liabilities to the present value of salary payments may be interpreted as the deterministic yearly contribution rate as a percentage of active civil servants' covered payroll needed to fund pension promises.[14]

In what follows, we assume that these contributions are paid by the state (that is, the employer) at the beginning of each year and the returns on invested asset are determined by a fixed (that is, non-stochastic) interest rate. In this case, contributions, in conjunction with the return on invested assets, would have to be sufficient to finance promised pension payments. Results are summarized in Table 4.3 for the 3 per cent discount rate and zero salary/benefit growth rate, along with the two alternatives we focused on above, namely, a 1.5 per cent discount rate and 1 per cent real salary/pension growth. The first four columns of Table 4.3 show the present value of current workers' projected pension liabilities and salaries for various rates of annual increase, while columns 5 and 6 report the ratio of the present value of pension costs to salaries on a contribution basis.

Focusing as a benchmark on the results with the 3 per cent discount rate and no real salary or pension increases, the present value of future pension

*Table 4.3 Projected benefit obligations (PBO) and contribution rates:
deterministic model*

	Disc. Rate	PV pension liabilities (in €bn)		PV salaries (in €bn)		PV pensions/PV salaries (%)	
		Salary/pension Increase p.a.		Salary/pension Increase p.a.		Salary/pension Increase p.a.	
		0% (1)	1% (2)	0% (3)	1% (4)	0% (5)	1% (6)
(1)	1.5%	44.8	79.8	149.3	186.6	30.0	42.8
(2)	3%	20.8	34.6	111.5	135.3	18.7	25.6

Note: Authors' calculations using data provided by the State of Hesse for 2004.

liabilities incurred until 2053 amounts to €20.8 billion (row 2, column 1), while salary payments over the same horizon have a present value of €111.5 billion (row 2, column 3). Accordingly, the ratio of present values and therefore the average required contribution rate is 18.7 per cent of payroll each year into the future (row 2, column 5). If real salaries and pensions instead were to rise by 1 per cent per year, the implied contribution rate would be closer to 26 per cent of payroll every year. Not surprisingly, the results are also sensitive to the discount rate, since, when a lower discount rate is applied, this increases both the present value of pension liabilities and salary payments. But since pension liabilities are of longer duration than salary payments, contribution rates rise when discount rates fall. If the discount rate were 1.5 per cent, for instance, contribution rates would vary between 30 and 42.8 per cent, while they range between 18.7 and 25.6 per cent for the 3 per cent interest rate. Inasmuch as the contribution rate of 18.7 per cent of payroll per year amount corresponds rather well to the contribution rates adopted to enhance the funding in Rhineland-Palatinate's new civil servant plan, we shall use this contribution target below in our further analysis.

4.4 STOCHASTIC INVESTMENT RETURNS AND PENSION PLAN FUNDING

A major concern of plan sponsors running a DB plan is the inherent uncertainty of the capital market returns earned on assets backing the pension liabilities. On the one hand, good investment performance can help the plan sponsor meet his benefit promises and reduce required contribution. On the other hand, if assets fall short of plan liabilities, supplementary contributions by the plan sponsor might be required to fill the gap. The gap itself, of course, may be used as a funding target for plan liabilities specified in a solvency plan. Also crucial is the plan's asset allocation policy, namely how it weights the portfolio in terms of equity and bonds, as this influences the DB pension system's risk and return profile. In what follows, we evaluate the asset-liability and decision-making process from the viewpoint of the plan sponsor, to determine a sensible plan asset allocation.

4.4.1 The Pension Manager's Objectives and Asset/Liability Modelling

Let us assume that the objective of moving to a funded DB pension scheme is to minimize the worst-case total cost of running the plan over a future long-term time horizon.[15] In our case, the actuarial projection of plan liabilities uses a year-by-year PBO valuation over a 50-year horizon with mortality rates and populations dynamics described in the previous section. In this framework, at the beginning of every period t, the sponsor endows the pension plan with funds in the form of regular contributions RC_t, determined by a fixed contribution rate CR related to the salary payments of active civil servants in t. Pension payments due at time t are made out of the fund, and remaining plan assets are invested in the capital markets.

At the end of every period, the plan's funding situation is scrutinized. If the funding ratio, defined as the ratio of current plan assets to the current projected benefit obligation, were to drop below 90 per cent, then a solvency rule requires supplementary contributions SC_t must be made to the plan, so as to return to a funding ratio of 100 per cent. If the funding ratio ever exceeds 120 per cent, the rate of regular contributions (CR) can be reduced by 50 per cent. The plan sponsor will benefit from a contribution holiday (that is, $RC = 0$) when the funding ratio rises above 150 per cent. Depending on the scenario under investigation, the plan sponsor may be able to withdraw excess funds when the funding ratio exceeds 180 per cent. After 50 years, the plan is assumed to be terminated by a (hypothetical) hard freeze; that is, at that time, all accrued liabilities are transferred to a private insurer, together with assets to fund them.

The aim of the investment policy is to generate a sufficiently high return that helps reduce overall pension plan costs, while at the same time controlling for capital market fluctuations that might result in substantial worst-case risks. In our model, the investment universe comprises two broad asset classes: a global equity index fund and a European government bond index fund. By assuming that the state invests only in index funds, we can ensure that the state cannot systematically influence prices. The stochastic and dynamics of the evolution portfolio's value over time are governed by a multiplicative random walk with drift. The serially independent and identically normal distributed one-period log-returns are given by:

$$R_{P,t} = \mu_P + \sigma_P Z_t, \tag{4.5}$$

where $Z_t \sim N(0,1)$. Under the assumption of a static asset allocation over time, the portfolio is continuously rebalanced to maintain the original investment weights. In this case, the expected portfolio log-return μ_P and the portfolio return standard deviation σ_P can be derived as (Feldstein et al., 2001):

$$\sigma_P^2 = x^2\sigma_E^2 + (1-x)^2\sigma_B^2 + 2x(1-x)\sigma_E\sigma_B\rho_{E,B},$$
$$\mu_P = x(\mu_E + 0.5\sigma_E^2) + (1-x)(\mu_B + 0.5\sigma_B^2) - 0.5\sigma_P^2, \tag{4.6}$$

where x represents the weight of equities in the portfolio, μ_E (μ_B) is the expected log-return, σ_E (σ_B) the return standard deviation of equities (bonds) and $\rho_{E,B}$ the coefficient of correlation between both asset classes.

The asset model parameters we employ for the simulation are given in Table 4.4. For equities, these are estimated from the MSCI World Equities total return index (1974–2003). For bonds, our estimates are based on the JP Morgan European Government Bonds total return index (1988–2003), which we augment with the REXP German Government Bonds total return index for the period 1974–1987 owing to unavailability of the former. All index data are provided by DataStream. To incorporate estimation risk in the critical estimation of expected asset returns, we increase the estimated return standard deviations by the standard errors of the mean return estimations (Barry, 1974; Klein and Bawa, 1976; this corresponds to the two-step estimation procedure used in Feldstein et al., 2001). Financial integration in Europe, the creation of the European Monetary Union, and the accompanying Maastricht convergence criteria, have reduced interest rates in the Euro zone, leading to lower expected future returns on

Table 4.4   Simulation model parameters for stochastic asset case

	Expected log return	Standard deviation	Correlations	
			Global equities	European bonds
Global equities	7.1%	20.2%	1	
European bonds	4.5%	6.7%	0.14	1

Note: Authors' calculations.

European government bonds. We therefore reduce the historically estimated return expectation for the European bonds by 1 per cent. Finally, we
subtract the equivalent of 30 basis points from the annual portfolio return
to reflect administrative expenses.

The optimal investment and contribution policy for the partially funded
public plan is obtained from running a Monte Carlo simulation with 10 000
iterations over the 50-year projection horizon. To identify the optimal investment and contribution policy for the pension plan, we assume that the objective of the plan sponsor is to minimize the worst-case cost of running the
plan.[16] Accordingly, we specify the probability distribution of the stochastic
present value of total pension cost *TPC* and identify the asset allocation and
regular contribution rate fixed at the beginning of the projection horizon[17]
that minimizes the Conditional Value at Risk at the 5 per cent level.

More formally, total pension costs are calculated as the sum of regular
contributions RC_t and supplementary contributions SC_t made by the plan
sponsor in period t. Depending on the set-up, these plan costs may or may
not be reduced by the withdrawals W_t of excess funds. All payments into or
withdrawals from the plan are discounted at the fixed real interest rate r,
reflecting the government's financing cost. Thus the optimization problem
is specified by:

$$\min_x CVaR_{5\%}\left(TPC = \sum_{t=0}^{T} \frac{RC_t + SC_t(1 + \xi_1) - W_t(1 - \xi_2)}{(1 + r)^t} \right). \quad (4.7)$$

The Conditional Value at Risk (CVaR) at the α per cent confidence level is
defined as the expected total pension cost under the condition that its realization is greater than the Value at Risk (VaR) for that level, that is:

$$CVaR_{\alpha\%}(TPC) = E(TPC|TCP > VaR_{\alpha\%}(TPC)) \quad (4.8)$$

CVaR has significant advantages as a measure of risk over the commonly
used VaR measure, defined as $P(TPC > VaR_\alpha) = \alpha$; that is, the costs that
will not be exceeded with a given probability of $(1-\alpha)$ per cent. First, CVaR
not only concentrates on a specified percentile of a loss distribution, but it
also accounts for the extent of the loss in the distributional tails beyond this
percentile. Therefore, the Conditional Value at Risk is a coherent risk
measure with respect to the axioms developed by Artzner et al. (1997,
1999). Second, from the perspective of numerical portfolios optimization,
CVaR is better behaved than VaR because of its convexity with respect to
decision variables (Rockafellar and Uryasev, 2002).

In principle, pension benefits ought to be financed by the regular contributions to the plan so that supplementary contributions should be required

only as a last resort (for example, in case of a severe capital market down-turn). If a plan sponsor must be forced to make supplementary contributions often, this indicates that the rate of regular contributions is likely to be insufficient. To encourage adequate regular contributions, we therefore introduce a penalty for supplementary contributions represented by the parameter ξ_1. This is structured such that, to finance an asset shortfall of €1, the sum of $(1+\xi_1)$ euros must be accounted for as a plan cost. At the same time, it seems reasonable to restrict the pension plan from being used as a 'hedge fund' investment account that can become hugely overfunded (which might happen if the sponsor were to short government bonds to create excess revenues by cashing in on the equity premium). For this reason, we levy a withdrawal penalty on the state pension plan of ξ_2, so withdrawing €1 from the plan means only $(1-\xi_2)$ euros are credited. The term ξ can also be interpreted as the cost of additional financing, and it therefore counters a common perception that public funds paid into the civil servant pension plan are 'free' money.

4.4.2 Optimal Pension Fund Asset Allocation with a Fixed Contribution Rate

Next we draw on our results above to derive the optimal asset allocation for plan assets when the contribution rate is fixed at a given ratio of projected benefit obligation to the present value of projected future salaries. Table 4.5 summarizes the results for the same real discount rate of 3 per cent, no real salary or pension increases, and a 20 per cent penalty factor for supplementary contributions ξ_1 and withdrawals ξ_2. The fixed contribution rate is set at 18.7 per cent since, in Table 4.3, this resulted in a deterministic PBO of €20.82 billion; this is a useful benchmark against which we can measure the risk/return profile of various investment strategies.

Key findings are provided for three asset allocation policies, namely a 100 per cent bond portfolio, a 100 per cent equity portfolio, and the endogenously determined optimal portfolio which minimizes the CVaR. Results reported in Panel 1 of Table 4.5 display the related portfolio weights in equity and bond investments assuming a static asset allocation (rows 1 and 2), the expected present value of total pension costs (row 3), and the 5 per cent Conditional Value at Risk (row 4). Panel 2 contains, for the same investment policies, the expectation and the 5 per cent Conditional Value at Risk of discounted supplementary contributions (rows 5 and 6), as well as the discounted final-period withdrawals credited to the objective function (rows 7 and 8). Additionally, two ways to dispose of pension surplus are modelled. Columns 1–3 permit the pension manager to withdraw plan assets exceeding 180 per cent of the PBO (reduced by the penalty factor);

Table 4.5 *Risk of alternative asset allocation patterns for active workers, assuming fixed contribution rate*

Fixed contribution rate: 18.7% Deterministic PBO: €20.82 bn Real discount rate: 3%	Withdrawals credited			Withdrawals NOT credited		
	100% Bonds (1)	100% Equities (2)	Cost min. Asset mix (3)	100% Bonds (4)	100% Equities (5)	Cost min. Asset mix (6)
Panel 1						
(1) Equity weight	0%	100%	30%	0%	100%	24%
(2) Bond weight	100%	0%	70%	100%	0%	76%
(3) Expected pension costs (€bn)	11.74	−12.90	3.03	17.60	15.04	14.96
(4) 5%-CVaR pension costs (€bn)	23.92	28.74	19.70	25.50	35.56	22.70
Panel 2						
(5) Exp. Suppl. Contributions (€bn)	1.18	6.61	0.79	1.18	6.61	0.70
(6) 5%-CVaR Suppl. Contrib. (€bn)	5.95	21.97	4.94	5.95	21.97	4.50
(7) Exp. Withdrawals (€bn)	5.93	32.30	11.80	0.00	0.00	0.00
(8) 5%-CVaR Withdrawals (€bn)	0.18	4.35	1.28	0.00	0.00	0.00

Notes: Authors' calculations using data provided by the State of Hesse. Contribution rate in % of salaries, real salary/pension increase 0%. Supplementary contributions required in case of funding ratio (i.e. *fund assets/PBO*) below 90% to restore funding ratio of 100%. Contribution rate reduced by 50% (100%) in case of funding ratio above 120% (150%). Withdrawal of funds in excess of 180% of liabilities. Opportunity costs of supplementary contributions addressed by accounting for an agio of $\xi_1 = 20\%$. Withdrawals credited to objective function in case *Withdrawals credited* ($\xi_2 = 20\%$), lost in case *Withdrawals NOT credited* ($\xi_2 = 100\%$).

these would be credited to the objective function as reducing pension costs. By contrast, in columns 4–6, the excess assets are not credited, that is, $\xi_2 = 100$ per cent which reduces the plan manager's incentive to overendow the pension fund by leaning on the excess of the equity premium over the assumed discount rate.

Before evaluating the optimal asset investment policy, we assess two polar cases, namely a 100 per cent bond investment case, and a 100 per cent equity case. When the fund is fully invested in bonds, total expected pension costs for active employees come to €11.74 billion (row 3, column 1) and the CVaR is valued at €23.92 billion or about €2.1 billion higher than the deterministic PBO benchmark (row 4, column 1). On top of regular pension contributions, taxpayers must anticipate making another €1.18 billion in supplementary contributions, with a 5 per cent CVaR of this amount about five times that, at €5.95 billion (rows 5 and 6, column 1). When expected withdrawals can be credited, albeit with a penalty, the managers can anticipate a value of almost €6 billion, while virtually no funds will be withdrawn in the worst case (rows 7 and 8, column 1).

By comparison, if the plan were to invest fully in equity (which we recognize is highly unlikely in the case of a public pension), there is enormous upside as well as downside potential. For instance, the expected value of withdrawals comes to an impressive €32.3 billion (row 7, column 2), resulting in a negative expected total pension costs of −€12.9 billion (row 3, column 2). What this means is that 'on average', after a start-up phase, the plan manager could expect to have contribution holidays if he invested the entire fund in equities, and withdrawals would be sufficient to recover more monies than were paid into the plan. However, this impressive upside potential comes at the price of substantially enhanced capital market risk that could easily drive the funding situation to unacceptable levels. The CVaR of supplementary contributions comes to €21.97 billion (column 2, row 6), leading to a CVaR of total pension costs of €28.74 billion (column 2, row 4), which substantially exceeds the expected costs calculated under the deterministic PBO benchmark.

In column 3 we depict the optimal investment strategy given the contribution rate, which in rows 1 and 2 consists of 30 per cent equities and 70 per cent bonds. This lowers expected pension costs for active employees to only €3.03 billion (row 3, column 3), much lower than the €20.82 billion benchmark of required funding in the deterministic case. This low level of costs can be attributed to the considerable expected benefit of investing in the capital market. The fund is paid 18.7 per cent of payroll from the outset for each active employee, but actual pension cash flows are initially small. Accordingly, a pension fund invested 30 per cent in equities and 70 per cent in bonds yields an expected gross return of 6.24 per cent per year, which is double the 3 per cent threshold for which the benchmark contribution rate of 18.7 per cent was derived. With a return volatility of 8.17 per cent, the pension fund faces rather moderate capital market risk and, as a result, the plan would be expected to accumulate considerable assets rather quickly. The possibility of contribution holidays as well as withdrawals steadily increases through time, while the risk of supplementary contributions required by the solvency rule diminishes. Compared with the deterministic case with a present value of payments or PBO of €20.82 billion, this funding and investment policy mix reduces expected costs substantially. The worst case exposure is also well-controlled. For instance, the 5 per cent Conditional Value at Risk of total pension costs (that is, average costs in the 5 per cent worst cases) only comes to €19.7 billion (row 4, column 3), well below the benchmark. Expected supplementary contributions are also rather low, with a present value of €790 million (row 5, column 3) and in the worst case – again represented by the 5 per cent Conditional Value at Risk – they amount to €4.94 billion, roughly 25 per cent of the deterministic PBO (row 6, column 3). Giving managers credit for withdrawals can offer major cost-cutting potential for the plan. In the worst-case scenario, plan withdrawals would be only €1.28 billion, but in expectation they amount to €11.8 billion (rows 7 and 8, column 3).

If excess withdrawals are not credited to the account, managerial incentives to overendow the plan are greatly reduced. Here, the only incentive for risking supplementary contributions caused by underfunding is the opportunity to enjoy reduced contribution rates or even contribution holidays if the funding ratio should exceed 180 per cent. Columns 4–6 of Table 4.5 show that expected pension costs and the CVaR amounts now exceed comparable values in columns 1–2 when either extreme investment strategy is selected, while the supplementary contributions are the same. By contrast, the optimal investment strategy now requires that only 24 per cent of the funds must be held in equities (row 1, column 6), which is 6 percentage points less than when withdrawals are credited. Clearly, having a capped upside potential makes return-driven investment less attractive. At the same time, not rewarding risk taking curtails worries about having to make supplementary contributions. The impact on total plan costs given the optimal investment strategy can again be seen in Panel 1. If withdrawals are not credited, the worst-case costs rise to an overall €22.7 billion (row 4, column 6) with expected plan costs of €14.96 billion (row 3, column 6). This is an increase of almost €12 billion compared to the case where withdrawals are permitted, roughly the value of expected withdrawals if they are allowed.

In sum, allowing the public pension plan partially to prefund benefits and engage in an optimal investment policy could be expected to mitigate the economic cost of providing the pension promise, while at the same time minimizing the consequences of capital market volatility.

4.4.3 Simultaneously Optimizing Contribution Rates and Pension Fund Asset Allocation

In the case of public pension plans, it is often thought that current policy makers might prefer relatively low contribution rates to hold the line on current fiscal expenditures. On the other hand, if regular contributions are too low, this could require high future supplementary contributions if the plan becomes underfunded. Accordingly, a balance must be found across these interests. Therefore we next analyse how changes in the contribution rates might affect key pension outcomes, in addition to asset allocation.

Given a contribution rate of 18.7 per cent, we showed above that the optimal asset allocation is 30 per cent in equities and 70 per cent in bonds when pension asset withdrawals are credited to the plan manager's objective function. We also show that the worst-case total pension costs measured by the 5 per cent CVaR are €19.7 billion, compared to the deterministic PBO of €20.82 billion (at the benchmark discount rate of 3 per cent). Yet there is some room for the pension plan manager to tap the full risk budget, if he can change both the asset allocation and the regular contribution rate. Accordingly, in what follows, we seek the optimal combination of a fixed contribution rate and asset allocation which fully bails out the given risk budget specified by the deterministic PBO.

To obtain this solution, we vary the equity weights and the contribution rate (between 0 and 18.7 per cent) to identify the equity/contribution pair that provides an overall worst-case pension cost equal to the PBO. From a formal perspective, we use the same objective function as equation (4.7) but we optimize over the investment weight in equities x as well as the rate of regular contributions CR:

$$CVaR_{x,CR}^{5\%}\left(TPC = \sum_{t=0}^{T}\frac{RC_t + SC_t(1+\xi_1) - W_t(1-\xi_2)}{(1+r)^t}\right) = PBO. \quad (4.9)$$

Results are depicted in Figure 4.3, assuming a 3 per cent discount rate and permitting final-period excess funds to be credited. Here we observe the structural interrelation between the rate of regular contributions (CR) and the optimal equity exposure for a given risk budget measured by the 5 per cent Conditional Value at Risk of total pension costs. Specifically, we present the 'Iso-CVaR' curve for a value of €20.82 billion in the space spanned by the fraction in equity and the regular contribution rate. This curve is U-shaped. This means the pension plan manager can reduce

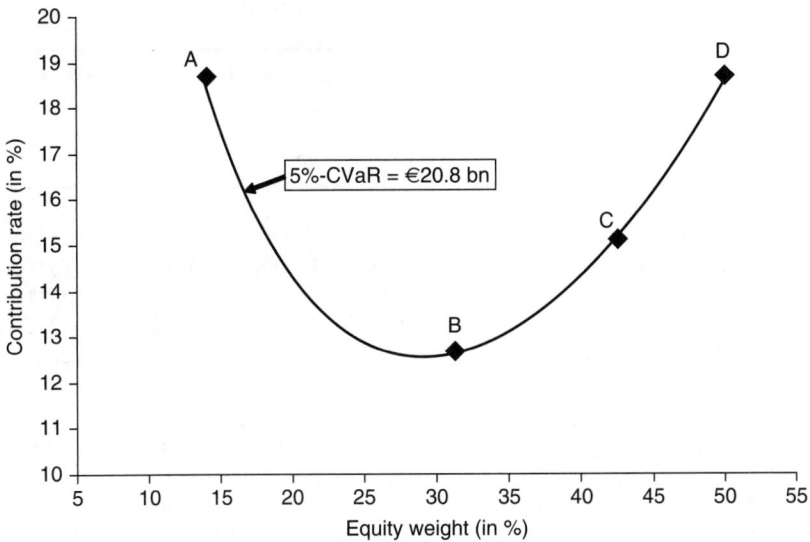

Note: Authors' calculations using data provided by the State of Hesse.

Figure 4.3   Iso-CVaR curve of total pension costs

regular payments up to a minimum level of about 12.7 per cent when simultaneously choosing an equity exposure of about 32 per cent (Point B in Figure 4.3). If a higher regular contribution rate is preferred, the equity exposure can either be reduced or increased. For example, a contribution rate of 18.7 per cent is consistent with the predetermined PBO risk budget for either an equity weight of about 14 per cent (Point A) or 50 per cent (Point D). This can be explained as follows: a portfolio heavier in equity is expected to generate relatively higher returns, which offers the opportunity of future contributions holidays and possible withdrawals. Yet the relatively high volatility of asset returns might also cause pension asset shortfalls, leading to a relatively high risk of supplementary contributions that naturally offsets the possibility of contribution holidays and withdrawals. By contrast, a more bond-oriented investment policy provides more stable expected investment returns over time, and therefore a relatively low risk of supplementary contributions. On the other hand, future taxpayers will have little chance to cut plan financing costs.

For more insight into these interrelations, we analyse four specific combinations of contribution rates and equity weights depicted in Figure 4.3, namely the minimum return volatility combination (Point A), the minimum regular contribution combination (Point B), the maximum return

Table 4.6   Asset allocation and regular contributions for given risk budget

	Deterministic PBO: €20.82 bn Real discount rate: 3%	Min. return volatility (1)	Minimum reg. contr. (2)	Intermediate (3)	Maximum return (4)
	Panel 1				
(1)	Contribution rate	18.70%	12.70%	15.00%	18.70%
(2)	Equity weight	14.00%	32.00%	43.00%	50.00%
(3)	Bond weight	86.00%	68.00%	57.00%	50.00%
(4)	Expected pension costs (€bn)	7.63	3.98	0.46	−2.23
(5)	5%-CVaR pension costs (€bn)	20.80	20.80	20.80	20.80
	Panel 2				
(6)	Exp. suppl. contributions (€bn)	0.71	3.67	2.77	1.45
(7)	5%-CVaR suppl. contrib. (€bn)	4.37	10.27	9.70	7.83
(8)	Exp. withdrawals (€bn)	8.31	10.54	13.91	16.88
(9)	5%-CVaR withdrawals (€bn)	0.84	0.51	0.92	1.62

Notes: Authors' calculations using data provided by the State of Hesse. Contribution rate in % of salaries, real salary/pension increase 0%. Supplementary contributions required in case of funding ratio (i.e. *fund assets/PBO*) below 90% to restore funding ratio of 100%. Contribution rate reduced by 50% (100%) in case of funding ratio above 120% (150%). Withdrawal of funds in excess of 180% of liabilities. Opportunity costs of supplementary contributions addressed by accounting for an agio of $\xi_1 = 20\%$. Withdrawals credited to objective function ($\xi_2 = 20\%$).

combination (point D) and an intermediate setting (point C). Table 4.6 summarizes the results. Consistent with our objective function (Formula 4.9), all strategies have similar worst-case pension costs of €20.8 billion equal to the deterministic PBO benchmark (row 5). On the other hand, the different funding and investment policies generate substantial differences with regard to the risk of supplementary contributions and the opportunities for possible withdrawals. Starting with an 18.7 per cent contribution, and a 14 per cent equity weight (the minimum return volatility case in column 1), the risk of supplementary contributions is low as a result of sufficient regular funding and stable investment returns over time. Supplementary contributions amount to only €710 million in expectation, and €4.37 billion in the worst case (rows 6 and 7, column 1). This, however, comes at the price of meagre possible withdrawals (rows 8 and 9) and a lower chance of contribution holidays.

Next we examine what would happen if the hope was to make only a minimum regular contribution – an option that might be favoured by politicians with a relatively near-term time horizon. Column 2 sets the contribution rate at only 12.7 per cent and then invests 32 per cent of the fund assets in equities (rows 1 and 2); the results show that this approach leads to considerably higher risks for future generations, compared with the better funded case. For instance, the worst-case supplementary contributions required to offset possible underfunding amount to €10.27 billion (row 7), which is more than twice the sum of the minimum volatility case (column 1). Worst-case supplementary contributions are about 25 per cent higher, compared to the maximum return case (column 4), while at the same time expected withdrawals only amount to about 60 per cent (row 8).

Alternatively, we examine the results from maintaining a regular contribution rate of 18.7 per cent but increasing the equity exposure to 50 per cent (column 4). Naturally this results in a quite different risk/return profile for future generations. Here, the worst-case supplementary contributions almost double the benchmark, rising from €4.37 to €7.83 billion (row 7, columns 1 versus 4). Of course this tactic does offer future taxpayers a respectable chance of participating in the capital markets and profiting from contribution holidays. As can be seen from row 8, the expected present value of withdrawals under this high equity scenario comes to €16.88 billion (column 4), which is more than twice the amount in the minimum return volatility case.

Column 3 shows an intermediate case, which seeks to balance the interest of both groups. Here current taxpayers only have to pay regular contributions of 15 per cent, and the portfolio is held 43 per cent in equities. This allows future generations to benefit from possible contribution holidays and withdrawals, while providing an acceptable level of risk of supplementary contributions resulting from underfunding.

4.4.4 Further Results

To verify the robustness of our results, we have repeated the analyses for a variety of other parameter settings. Reducing the discount rate from 3 to 1.5 per cent and cutting expected asset returns by the same 1.5 per cent results in a deterministic PBO of €44.8 billion and a corresponding contribution rate of 30 per cent (Table 4.3, row 1, columns 1 and 5). Based on these and crediting fund withdrawals, the optimal equity weight comes to 26 per cent with expected total pension costs of €18.47 billion. Worst-case pension costs exceed the deterministic PBO by only €1.7 billion, or 4 per cent.

Increasing the penalty factors for supplementary contributions and withdrawals to $\xi_1 = \xi_2 = 0.5$ also leads to an optimal equity weight of 26 per cent. Expected and worst-case pension costs increase from €3.03 billion and €19.7 billion (Table 4.5, column 3, rows 3 and 4) to €8.42 billion and €21.44 billion, respectively.

Allowing for contribution holidays already to be taken when the funding
ratio exceeds 120 per cent and postponing the withdrawal of excess funds
until the final period results in expected pension costs of €2.49 billion and
€19.6 billion in the worst case. This requires 29 per cent of plan funds being
held in equities and 71 per cent in bonds.

4.5 CONCLUSIONS

As in many other nations, German civil servants are covered by unfunded
defined benefit pensions. This substantial underfunding represents a commensurate liability that is not, to date, recognized as explicit taxpayer
obligations. For the German state of Hesse, we have conservatively estimated this liability for current pensioners of €24 billion in present value,
and amounts already accrued by current workers add another €20 billion
(with a discount rate of 3 per cent and zero real salary/pension increases).
The total of €44 billion is massive, amounting to almost 150 per cent of
explicit state debt. When we then also account for future pension accruals
for active workers under current formulas, new obligations can be valued
at €12 billion or an additional 41 per cent of outstanding debt. In other
words, the total obligation of €56 billion for both active and retired civil
servants amounts to almost twice the current explicit state government
debt. A 1 per cent rise in salaries and benefits elevates the expected present
value of public pension commitments to a staggering €70 billion, or 236 per
cent of explicit debt.

Next we analyse ways to move to a better funded pension plan for Hesse's
civil servants, narrowing the focus to active employees (on the assumption
that already-retired workers' benefits would have to be paid from other
sources). We show that annual contribution rates of around 19 per cent of
payroll would be consistent with a traditional actuarial valuation (assuming a discount rate of 3 per cent). Given this, we study alternative investment policies using a stochastic asset/liability framework that minimizes
the expected economic costs of providing the promised pensions, while at
the same time controlling possibly adverse capital market outcomes. We
illustrate that the optimal pension fund investment strategy given this contribution rate consists of 30 per cent equities and 70 per cent in bonds. It is
interesting that this is virtually identical to the 31/69 stock/bond allocation
for US public sector pension plans in 2007 (Wilshire Consulting, 2007).
Compared with the deterministic case, this funding and investment policy
mix reduces expected costs substantially, and the worst-case exposure is
also well controlled. Finally, we show that the pension plan manager can
better tap the risk budget if he is allowed to alter both his asset allocation

and the plan's regular contribution rate. In one interesting case, current tax-payers are asked to pay regular contributions of only 15 per cent, and the portfolio is held 43 per cent in equities. This allows future generations to benefit from possible contribution holidays and withdrawals, while providing an acceptable level of risk of supplementary contributions resulting from underfunding.

Our research should be of broad interest to employees as well as taxpayers, insofar as many civil servant pensions in Europe are underfunded or even totally unfunded. For the German case, it would be useful to assess all state and Federal Government public sector pension liabilities following methodology such as that presented here. Furthermore, we have shown that, under plausible assumptions, as the shortfalls are gradually funded, the assets could be sensibly invested to reduce expected burdens on future workers and retirees. In ongoing work, we are evaluating additional aspects of the optimal investment scenario.

NOTES

1. For example, a single research assistant aged 30 with no children, employed under private law at a university, earns an annual gross salary of about €41 000. If that person is promoted to the rank of assistant professor, he will then be employed under civil servant rules, and his gross salary will shrink to about €39 000.
2. Civil servants are also exempt from unemployment insurance and the state pays a certain fraction of health expenses of civil servants and their families (ranging from 50 to 85 per cent, depending on family status and number of children); see Börsch-Supan and Wilke (2003).
3. While each state has its own pension plan, the benefit structure for civil servant pensions is nearly equal across the different states in Germany.
4. Another pathway to retirement for civil servants is disability, which we do not focus on in the present study. Disability payments are based on final salary and the replacement rate accrued until being disabled, reduced by 0.3 percentage points per month before age 63 (not to exceed 10.8 per cent). If disabled while on duty, payments are based on the salary projected to regular retirement. Subject to the regular maximum replacement rate, the civil servant is additionally credited one-third of the regular accrual he would have received up to the age of 60; the replacement rate is then increased by 20 per cent. Altogether, the disability pension comes to at least two-thirds but cannot exceed 71.75 per cent of the relevant salary.
5. In this instance, the state will pay to the social security programme an amount equal to the forgone employer contributions to social security for that employee.
6. All data provided by the German Federal Statistical Office and the Hessian Statistical Office (2006).
7. These numbers include only federal and state civil servants, but not the approximately 200 000 active and 500 000 retired civil servants who worked for former state-owned (but now privatized) enterprises, such as the German national railway and federal mail (Bundesministerium des Innern, 2005).
8. For reasons of anonymity, information on top-level civil servants as well as judges and state attorneys were omitted. Smaller cohorts, such as those within the lower service level, were grouped into larger units.

9. Specifically, the mortality table we employ is the DAV 2006 R, Aggregattafel 2. Ordnung (see DAV, 2004, pp. 53ff.).
10. This is due to the fact that the pension benefits are not particularly portable when a civil servant moves to the private sector. As a result, observed low turnover is in line with the general aim of a generous DB-pension plan, that is, to retain public sector employees in their jobs.
11. Provisions for early retirement and disability benefits, as well as dependants' benefits due to death in service, are therefore neglected.
12. Federal law stipulates that salaries as well as pensions are adjusted for changes in the general economic and financial circumstances, which mainly means changes in consumer prices. Cost of living adjustments are not explicitly guaranteed on an annual basis, but in the past salaries and pensions have kept pace with inflation and they may even rise in real terms thanks to rises in real average incomes outside the public sector.
13. The difference between the average nominal par yield of long-term German Government bonds and the average inflation rate for the post-WWII period is about 4 per cent. Inflation protected bonds in the Eurozone currently yield about 2 per cent. This market is currently not well developed for government bonds (especially those with long durations) which supports the assumption of a real interest rate of 3 per cent.
14. To be clear, here we set aside the pension obligation already accrued by retirees, on the presumption that these will have to be handled with some other financing mechanism.
15. As described previously, we set aside benefits already promised to today's retirees as well as those accrued by currently active civil servants.
16. See also Albrecht et al. (2006).
17. We deliberately do not consider a strategy whereby the investment weights and contribution rates are optimized dynamically over time, for example by using a dynamic optimization framework. While from a theoretical vantage point this might yield better results, here we argue that political decision-makers may be unable to implement this in practice.

REFERENCES

Albrecht, Peter, Joachim Coche, Raimond Maurer and Ralph Rogalla (2006), 'Understanding and allocating investment risks in a hybrid pension plan', in David Blitzstein, Olivia S. Mitchell and Stephen P. Utkus (eds), *Restructuring Retirement Risks*, Oxford: Oxford University Press, pp. 204–25.
Artzner, P., F. Delbaen, J. Eber and D. Heath (1997), 'Thinking coherently', *Risk*, **10**(11), 68–72.
Artzner, P., F. Delbaen, J. Eber and D. Heath (1999), 'Coherent measures of risk', *Mathematical Finance*, **9**(3), 203–28.
Barry, C.B. (1974), 'Portfolio analysis under uncertain means, variances, and covariances', *Journal of Finance*, **29**(2), 515–22.
Blake, David (2006), *Pension Finance*, Chichester: Wiley.
Bodie, Z. (1990), 'The ABO, the PBO and pension investment policy', *Financial Analysts Journal*, **46**(5), 27–34.
Börsch-Supan, A. and C.B. Wilke (2003), 'The German public pension system: how it was, how it will be', MRRC Working Paper 2004-41, Michigan Retirement Research Center.
Bundesministerium des Innern (2005), *Dritter Versorgungsbericht der Bundesregierung*, Berlin.
Deutsche Aktuarsvereinigung DAV (2004), *Herleitung der DAV-Sterbetafel 2004, R für Rentenversicherungen*, Köln.

Feldstein, Martin, Elena Ranguelova and Andrew A. Samwick (2001), 'The transition to investment-based social security when portfolio returns and capital profitability are uncertain', in John M. Campbell and Martin Feldstein (eds), *Risk Aspects of Investment-Based Social Security Reform*, Chicago: University of Chicago Press, pp. 41–81.

Gillis, J.R. (1968), 'Aristocracy and bureaucracy in nineteenth-century Prussia', *Past and Present*, **41**, 105–29.

Gold, J. (2003), 'Periodic cost of employee benefits', presented at *The Great Controversy: Current Pension Accrual Practice in Light of Financial Economics Symposium*, Vancouver.

Henderson, R. (1924), 'A new method of graduation', *Transactions of the Actuarial Society of America*, **25**, 29–40.

Heubeck, K. and B. Rürup (2000), *Finanzierung der Altersversorgung des öffentlichen Dienstes*, Frankfurt: Peter Lang Verlag.

Hustead, Edwin C. and Olivia S. Mitchell (2001), 'Public sector pension plans', in Olivia S. Mitchell and Edwin C. Hustead (eds), *Pensions in the Public Sector*, Philadelphia: University of Pennsylvania Press, pp. 3–10.

Joseph, A.W. (1952), 'The Whittaker–Henderson method of graduation', *Journal of the Institute of Actuaries*, **78**, 99–114.

Klein, R. and V. Bawa (1976), 'The effect of estimation risk on optimal portfolio choice', *Journal of Financial Economics*, **3**, 215–31.

McGill, Dan M., Kyle N. Brown, John J. Haley and Sylvester J. Schieber (2005), *Fundamentals of Private Pensions*, Oxford: Oxford University Press.

Milbrodt, Hartmut and Manfred Helbig (1999), *Mathematische Methoden der Personenversicherung*, Berlin: de Gruyter.

Milevsky, Moshe A. (2006), *The Calculus of Retirement Income*, Cambridge: Cambridge University Press.

Mitchell, Olivia S., David McCarthy, Stanley C. Wisniewski and Paul Zorn (2001), 'Developments in state and local pension plans', in Olivia S. Mitchell and Edwin C. Hustead (eds), *Pensions in the Public Sector*, Philadelphia: University of Pennsylvania Press, pp. 11–40.

Mittelstaedt, H.F. and Ph.R. Regier (1993), 'The market response to pension plan terminations', *The Accounting Review*, **68**(1), 1–27.

Rockafellar, R.T. and S. Uryasev (2002), 'Conditional value-at-risk for general loss distributions', *Journal of Banking and Finance*, **26**(7), 1443–71.

Whittaker, E.T. (1923), 'On a new method of graduation', *Proceedings of the Edinburgh Mathematical Society*, **41**, 63–75.

Wilshire Consulting (2007), *Wilshire Report on State Retirement Systems: Funding Levels and Asset Allocation*, Wilshire, CA.

Wolfsdorf, Kurt (1997), *Versicherungsmathematik – Teil 1: Personenversicherung*, Stuttgart: Teubner.

Discussion of 'The victory of hope over angst? Funding, asset allocation and risk taking in German public sector pension reform'

Tom Steenkamp, Roy Hoevenaars and Roderick Molenaar

The chapter by Maurer, Mitchell and Rogalla addresses three main topics. First, it roughly sketches the history and describes the characteristics of civil servant pensions in Germany and the Federal State of Hesse. Main characteristics are pension payments based on final salary and years of service and a tax-sponsored pay-as-you-go financing system. What is remarkable is the severe penalty for job mobility: more than 50 per cent of pension benefits is lost when civil servants take a job in the private sector. Secondly, the authors introduce a pension fund partly to finance future pension payments. This pension fund only finances new accrued benefits and leaves current accrued benefit obligations aside. The average contribution rate is determined by the cost of yearly accrued benefits as a percentage of total wages. Furthermore, there is a contribution rate 'ladder' that depends on the funding ratio of the pension fund. The contribution rates are invested in a combination of stocks and bonds. To define the liabilities for the pension fund, mortality tables are constructed and a simple model of population dynamics is assumed. These dynamics ultimately lead to a steady state and it should be of interest to the reader what the characteristics of the liabilities are (for example duration, average age profile) in this steady state. Thirdly, the authors try to determine, with a stochastic simulation model, an optimal asset allocation given the (average) contribution rate or simultaneously to determine asset allocation and contribution rate, given the risk budget. The horizon of the study is 50 years; after that, the fund is terminated and assets and liabilities are transferred to a private insurer. Pension liabilities are discounted at a fixed real rate of interest, in the base scenario 3 per cent. Liabilities are always fully indexed against inflation. The objective function of the pension fund is to minimize the conditional value at risk at the 5 per cent level in terms of the present value of the total plan cost.

We consider this document a clear policy paper. As an exercise in public finance it gives the German policy maker interesting and valuable insights into the trade-offs for the (proposed) German pension reform. From an academic perspective, however, there are some serious shortcomings in this study. The study could benefit from better founded assumptions, such as the chosen objective function and the economic assumptions. The authors should also show the results from a sensitivity analysis of the most important variables and parameters.

Our general remarks and critiques include the following:

- *Risk sharing*: The content of the proposed 'pension reform' in the chapter is rather limited: a capital-funded scheme with a specific contribution rate ladder. We acknowledge the fact that the chapter should be focused, but it is worthwhile to mention at least other options for pension reform. Pension reform could also consider the discussion on risk sharing, particularly in situations where the solvency position is under pressure. This relates pension reform to discussions about intergenerational solidarity. A transparent and explicit pension contract on risk sharing between the current and future participants seems a necessary condition for the long-term sustainability of the pension deal. Furthermore, a mature fund benefits more from indexation cuts than additional contributions. Since the chapter already applies a contribution rate ladder, it might be interesting to extend the risk sharing with an indexation ladder. Furthermore, the chapter could refer to the discussion in academic literature and Netspar papers with respect to optimal pension contracts and risk-sharing arrangements.
- *Objective function*: Although the objective function leads to clear policy conclusions, we doubt whether the outcome can be interpreted as 'the expected present value of total pension costs'. Since the future payoffs from contributions and final wealth are inherently uncertain (and subject to equity and bond risk), they should be discounted by a stochastic discount rate instead of a fixed discount rate. Furthermore, the choice of this function is not very well founded in the chapter (is this the behaviour of politicians?). The objective function solely focuses on the downside risks and does not take explicitly into account the averages and risks. Finally – in our view – optimal decisions cannot be derived by value functions but need a utility function. The final trade-off for the government is the trade-off between expected pension costs and the volatility in those costs.

- *Asset liability management*: This study is not really an exercise in asset and liability management. In the current approach there is no direct link between assets and liabilities due to the fixed discount rate. In our opinion the ALM analysis would improve by using stochastic interest rates. This would make the asset liability perspective more explicit and in line with the fair value frameworks (such as the Financial Assessment Framework in the Dutch Pension Act). The liabilities then move more consistently with the stochastic bond returns, and this opens the discussion on the duration mismatch policy and interest rate hedging. Furthermore, inflation hedging qualities are not explicitly emphasized in the investment policy. Both interest rate and inflation hedging qualities should be addressed explicitly for the evaluation of liability-driven investment strategies.
- *Long-term investing*: Since the horizon is 50 years, it might be interesting to include recent findings in the academic literature on long-term investing. The authors take a simple I.I.D. model for the stochastic process of investment returns. It is well-documented that risks are horizon-dependent (instead of the fixed 20.2 per cent equity volatility and 0.15 equity–bond correlation).[1] The inclusion of human capital or an analysis based on the total balance sheet of the government could give additional results as well.

NOTE

1. See e.g. Campbell, Chan and Viceira (2003).

REFERENCES

Campbell, J.Y., Y.L. Chan and L.M. Viceira (2003), 'A multivariate model of strategic asset allocation', *Journal of Financial Economics*, **67**(1), 41–80.

5. Labour productivity in an aging society

Axel Börsch-Supan, Ismail Düzgün and Matthias Weiss[1]

5.1 INTRODUCTION

The productivity of the labour force is an important, if not the most important, driver of our living standard. With relatively stable populations and capital inputs over recent decades, the increase in labour productivity has clearly been the single-largest contribution to economic growth in the developed world. Population aging will increase this importance even more since the relative size of the labour force will decline. With a declining quantity of labour, future growth will have to be generated from the quality of labour.

At the same time, the proportion of the workforce aged 55 or over will more than double between now and 2035, rising from approximately 12 per cent to almost a quarter of all employees. There are two reasons for this. The first is the dominance of the baby boom generation, which is now entering their 50s. This dominance is exacerbated by a second trend, namely the increase in retirement age currently introduced in many countries in order to stabilize public and private pension schemes. Labour productivity of older works will therefore be an increasing component of total labour productivity.

For both reasons, there is an increasing academic and practical interest in understanding the relation between age and the productivity of employees. While various disciplines have studied this relationship, findings so far have been very different, often contradictory. Our sober summary of the literature is simply that we know very little about the effect of age on labour productivity. This lack of knowledge is in stark contrast to the prevailing prejudice that older workers are less productive. Indeed, still to date the human resources policy generally adopted by companies aims at lowering the age of the workforce through early retirement models – a policy that is bolstered by the statutory rules of the public pension systems.

This chapter's purpose is to shed more light on the relationships between age and productivity at work. After setting up the conceptual framework, it begins by providing a brief summary of the research to date. We claim that a large part of the contradicting results is due to methodological differences. Some existing studies measure the productivity of individuals. We contend that, in a modern society where division of labour is optimized, labour productivity is as much a result of the interactions between younger and older employees as it is of the isolated performance of an individual worker.

Other studies compare labour productivity at the company level. This is much more in the spirit of modern production organization. We contend, however, that comparing companies that produce very different products with respect to their age structures is often meaningless because it is close to impossible to standardize output. Hence, productivity differences measured at the company level may be artifacts due to less than perfectly standardized outputs.

This chapter therefore presents empirical results using a new approach to measuring productivity which works on the middle ground between single individuals and entire companies, namely work teams which produce a standardized product. The chapter is also intended to shift somewhat the focus in the aging debate. Public debates have primarily focused on the consequences for the pay-as-you-go social security systems: pensions, health and long-term care. These social support systems are indeed under considerable pressure because the number of beneficiaries is rising whilst, at the same time, the number of contributors is falling. However, even before the baby boomers retire and their pensions have to be financed by the much smaller younger generation (around the years 2015–2035), the age composition of the labour force will dramatically change, as described above, possibly endangering growth and living standards, and thus indirectly, yet again, the financing of social security schemes. Since these structural changes are happening right now, labour productivity-enhancing policies need to be addressed right now as well.

Finally, while this chapter is written by economists and focuses on the economics of labour productivity, we would also like to stress the psychological aspects. There is much damage done by the prejudice that older workers are less productive and should be removed from the labour force as soon as the pension regulations permit, if indeed that prejudice lacks justification. One of the areas where people gain a feeling of self-worth and a reason for living is from the perception that they are needed at their place of work and make a contribution to value creation.

5.2 CONCEPTUAL FRAMEWORK

Our framework of thinking is guided by two countervailing developments over the life cycle. On the one hand, studies in the fields of medicine,

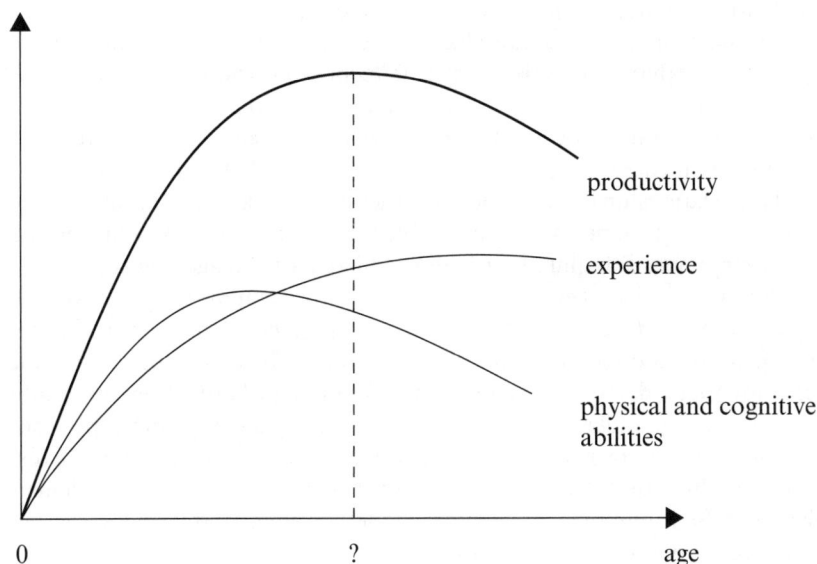

Figure 5.1   Productivity over the life cycle (schematic)

psychology and gerontology have clearly shown that physical and cognitive skills deteriorate with age (see Skirbekk, 2004, for a survey of the literature). On the other hand, however, there is evidence from sociology and psychology to indicate that the experience gained with age leads to an increase in productivity up to a certain age. Figure 5.1 illustrates this concept. The core question is at what age the first development dominates the second. While it seems inescapable that this will happen eventually, it is obviously very important to know whether this age is, on average, more likely to be 45 or 60, in particular as far as labour market policies are concerned.

While Figure 5.1 symbolizes the average worker, we know that there is a huge variation across individuals. Some of this variation may be due to genetic predisposition, childhood experiences or other factors that are, at this point in life, beyond our influence. Others, such as further education or workplace design and organization, are not. Our second key question regards the determinants of an earlier or later peak of productivity.

This relates to our understanding of labour productivity. In a modern society where the division of labour is one domain of optimization, productivity at work is due less to an individual person and is more likely to be achieved in cooperation with work colleagues. Our framework presupposes that the contribution made by older employees to creating value (experience, wisdom, a balanced approach during conflicts, contribution to the working atmosphere and so on) is more likely to reveal itself in the overall result of a team effort than in an isolated measurement of individual cognition or the ability of an individual to cope with the workload. The significance of this is that measurements of an individual's work productivity are less relevant than the influence of the average age of a team on that team's productivity and the relationship between the age structure of a team and the labour productivity. For instance, it is conceivable that the right mix of younger and older employees is required for high productivity in all age brackets.

Our empirical framework therefore puts more emphasis on the composition of work teams (age composition, experience composition, gender composition and so on) than individual traits. The contribution to value creation that is demonstrated in the team has to date hardly been taken into account. If the older workers' contribution is precisely giving experience and so on to younger workers, conventional productivity estimates are distorted in disfavour of the older employees. Such a distortion is problematical because it reinforces the 'deficit model' of aging and wrongly justifies staff reductions among older workers.

5.3   LESSONS FROM OCCUPATIONAL MEDICINE

Cognitive ability and muscle strength are easy to measure. Accordingly, occupational medicine has collected a large body of evidence on these biological markers. The response of the human body at work and the maximum amount of oxygen that can be absorbed is decisive for physical performance. The maximum amount of oxygen that can be absorbed increases up to the age of around 20 to 25 and after that it decreases (Ilmarinen, 1999). This signifies that, after the age of 25, the amount of oxygen available to a person gradually reduces, which in turn means that it is a natural process for physical fitness to deteriorate after the age of 25.

A relationship with biological processes exists in the case of mental and physical functional capacities such as the ability of a person to carry out various tasks that require intellectual and other forms of mental effort. Medical research has produced a host of evidence that the performance of the entire human system for processing information degenerates. A deterioration in the accuracy of assessments and the speed of perception of signals that act on a person from outside are among the most important changes (Ilmarinen and Tempel, 2002).

There are, however, distinct differences between people in the same age group that cannot be attributed to genetic influences alone but appear also to be linked to environmental conditions at the workplace and other socio-economic and socio-psychological conditions.

5.4 LESSONS FROM GERONTOLOGY AND SOCIOLOGY

The many gerontological, geronto-sociological and geronto-psychological studies also stress multicausality: a great number of factors play a role in performance as individuals age. Skills such as agility, powers of deduction, coordination of cognitive processes and accuracy degenerate with age. These skills are termed 'fluid intelligence'. In contrast, skills such as general knowledge, experience and understanding of language – called 'crystallized intelligence' – increase with age (Weinert, 1992; Maercker, 1992).

Moreover, state of health and socio-economic status are often linked to fluid and crystallized intelligence, as are the social and geographical environment and the educational history (Lehr, 2000). This explains a great deal of the large heterogeneity observed in work performance. Accounting for this, studies on work performance show that there are no discernible differences between older and younger workers (Staudinger and Baltes, 1996; Staudinger, 1999). Farr, Tesluk and Klein (1998) as well as Maier (1998) invalidate another frequent prejudice. According to their empirical research, older employees are just as creative, willing to make decisions and motivated as younger employees.

5.5 LESSONS FROM ERGONOMICS

Ergonomic studies stress that the key aspect determining performance is not age, but the working conditions under which people have to perform. This primarily relates to a workplace design that is appropriate for the age of the person concerned by implementing very simple changes such as raising the height of a table, or similar modifications (Huber, 2002). Such measures can prevent illnesses and maintain good performance with age.

Other aspects are to retire gradually through individual arrangements appropriate for the phase of a person's working life or to maximize the benefits of a mix of age groups where the intention is to blend wisdom and experience with new knowledge and new ideas. Management and training appropriate for the age of the employee has a considerable influence on satisfaction with work and consequently also work performance (Tuomi and Ilmarinen, 1999; Ilmarinen and Tempel, 2002). Last but not least, measures to promote good health play an important role. These measures include, for instance, selective changes to duty rosters, stress management programmes, health check-ups and therapeutic exercise programmes, which have been shown to improve performance at work and reduce absences from work (Ell, 1995).

As has already been emphasized, age-related variations in performance are not uniform but vary strongly from individual to individual. There is little evidence to substantiate what is termed the deficit hypothesis of aging, that is, a 'natural' degeneration in skills determined by age. Ergonomic studies on work performance show that no across-the-board difference in performance can be ascertained between older and younger people (Koller and Plath, 2000; Kruse, 2000; Morschhäuser, 2002; Petrenz, 1999).

5.6   LESSONS FROM ECONOMICS

Economic studies which examine value creation at company level find differing – often even contradictory – results on the relationship between age and work productivity (Hellerstein and Neumark, 1995; Hellerstein, Neumark and Troske, 1999; for a survey, see Skirbekk, 2004). Partially, this appears to be due to the fact that these studies relate to highly aggregated productivity measures which are difficult to interpret because they aggregate very different products into comparable value units. Other studies project aggregated productivity assuming the existence of extreme scenarios, which differ in relation to the development of productivity in old age. The results show that the effects of age on productivity are not decisive for aggregated productivity (Boockmann and Steiner, 2000; Börsch-Supan, 2002).

Another set of studies has investigated salaries as a measure of productivity since economic theory equates wages with marginal productivity. Kotlikoff and Wise (1989) pioneered this approach, investigating salaries at a large insurance company. When looking at the salaries of employees in sales, a reversed U-shaped curve is found, similar to Figure 5.1. Salaries in the clerical lines of business exhibited a steadily increasing trend with age. Both findings are subject to the general critique that salaries and wages do not have much in common with actual productivity but with the seniority principle: earnings are indexed to age for various incentive-related reasons (cf. Lazear, 1995), most pronounced, for example, in public services.

5.7   OUR OWN EMPIRICAL RESEARCH

Our own study measures productivity in work teams. We evaluate extensive company data from DaimlerChrysler AG's Wörth truck plant in a multivariate analysis that links quality data with personnel data. Unit of observation is a shift (eight hours) of a work team, consisting of about 12 workers on average, usually ranging from 10 to 15. Our data set has about 50 000 of such observations, carried out in 2003 and 2004.

We took great care in using a measure of labour productivity that is not confounded by product heterogeneity. As production in this plant takes the form of team work on an assembly line, both output of production (a standard set of trucks) and speed of production (the speed with which the assembly line moves) are perfectly standardized: all work teams produce the same product at the same speed. The only difference is the number of errors which are made in assembling the trucks. Such errors are recorded electronically at what are termed 'quality gates'. They are then assigned to the responsible work teams.

In addition to the number of errors, we also use information on their severity. We ran our analyses with and without using these severity weights, without discernible differences. This is an interesting finding in itself, on which we will comment later. The error data are matched with the personnel data. These data include in anonymized form the characteristics of the employees who made up the team on this specific day. It should be stressed that the daily characteristics of the teams vary considerably, giving us the necessary variation for our statistical analyses. The personnel data include the age, sex, educational status and nationality of the team members as well as how long they have worked for the company.

We generate our results by plotting the number of errors (vertical axis) against the average age, the average experience, and other characteristics of the work team (horizontal axis). Each characteristic is shown in isolation, holding all other characteristics artificially constant. In technical terms, we employ a multivariate regression using three flexible smoothing approaches for the variable on the horizontal axis. Age, for instance, is grouped ('age dummies'), expressed as a third-order polynomial, or as a set of linear splines. It should be stressed again that the horizontal axis does not represent individual workers but entire work teams.

5.8   RESULTS I: AGE AND EXPERIENCE

Figure 5.2 depicts the pure age effect: that is, investigating the average age of work teams in artificial isolation from all other characteristics, such as experience or educational attainment. In concrete terms, experience (that is, length of service at this plant) is normalized to be zero. Comparing two points on the horizontal axis hence means that, for example, we juxtapose a work team that has an average age of 48 with a work team that has an

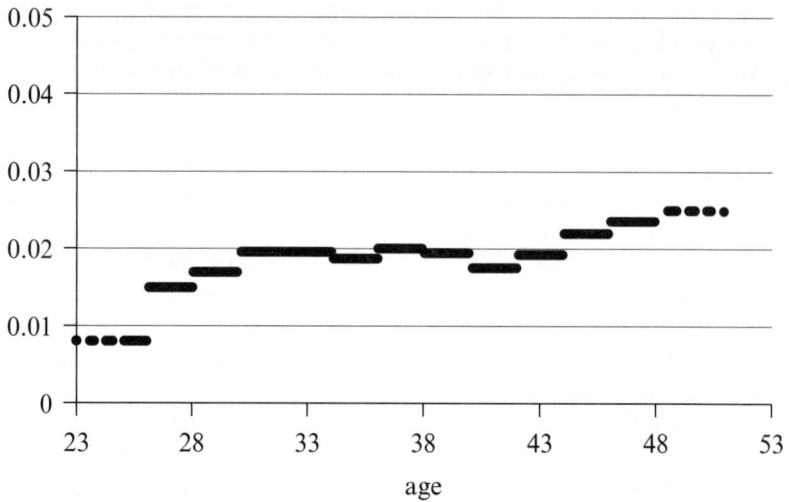

Source: own calculations.

*Figure 5.2   Number of errors by average age of work team members,
holding average experience constant*

average age of 23. Neither team has any experience. Figure 5.2 shows
clearly that the older team makes considerably more errors than the much
younger team. We are tempted to conclude that labour productivity falls as
the typical worker in the team grows older.

In contrast, the effect of experience is positive: see Figure 5.3. This means
that experience, measured as the number of years spent at this assembly
plant, has a positive influence on work productivity, now holding age constant. For instance, a work team employed by the plant for an average of 25
years which has the same age as a work team with zero years of experience
with the plant would make less than half of the errors of the inexperienced
team.

It is, however, impossible to gain experience: without aging at the same
time, and vice versa. Hence, both Figure 5.2 and Figure 5.3 are pure thought
experiments that isolate two mechanisms which always work together in the
real world. What we actually observe in reality is the combined effect, that
is, the effects of age and experience at the same time. This is depicted in
Figure 5.4, which shows that productivity is basically decoupled from the
average age of the work teams. Teams of every average age are about equally
productive. The effects of age and experience practically cancel each other
out; the apparent differences are not statistically significant.

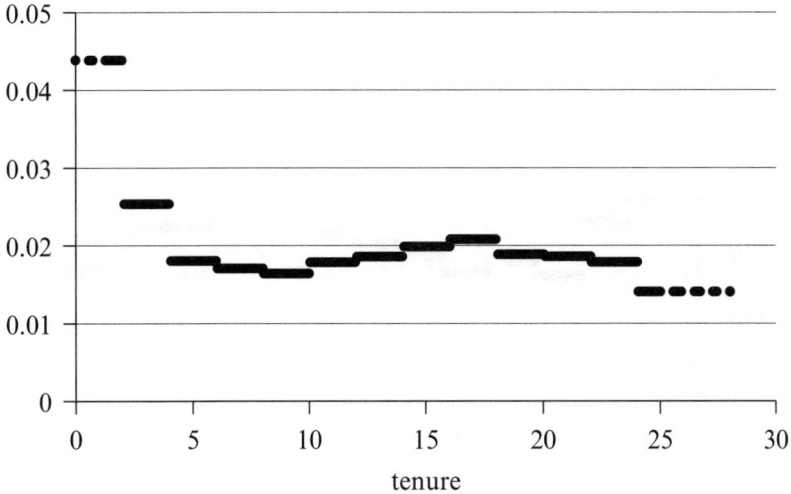

Source: own calculations.

Figure 5.3 *Errors by average years of experience with the plant, holding age constant*

5.9 RESULTS II: THE COMPOSITION OF TEAMS

So far we have looked at the average age and experience of work teams. Teams with the same average age, however, may have very different composition. At one extreme, all members will have exactly the same age. Age-related heterogeneity is zero. At the other extreme, all ages are equally represented, from very young to very old. For our purposes, we define the degree of age-related heterogeneity as one, if all 10-year age groups (15–25 years, 25–35 years, and so on to 55–65 years) are represented equally in the team.

Figure 5.5 shows that the labour productivity of mixed-age teams decreases with age-related heterogeneity, holding all other measured influencing variables such as heterogeneity, gender and the rest constant. This is a surprising result in the face of the very popular hypothesis that 'old and young work best together' because they 'balance innovation with experience'. In this assembly plant, this is not the case.

We have calculated various specifications of age-related heterogeneity to establish the robustness of our results. All specifications have produced similar results. Mixed-age teams make considerably more errors and are therefore less productive than teams with a homogeneous age structure.

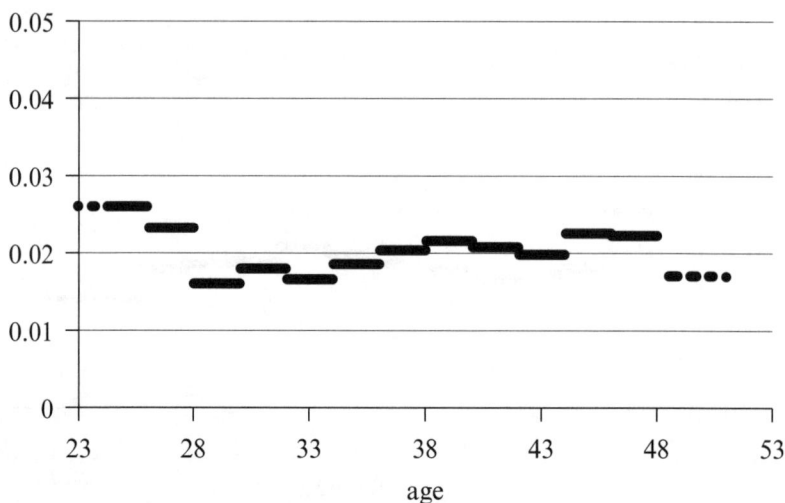

Source: own calculations.

Figure 5.4   Combined effect of age and experience

Experience-related heterogeneity did not exhibit statistically significant effects on labour productivity. While the majority of workers in the plant are male (96.3 per cent), the presence of women in a work team increased labour productivity if the average age was relatively high; for younger teams, the reverse happens. The mix of nationalities (mainly German, French and Turkish) has no statistically discernible influence.

5.10   CONCLUSIONS AND OUTLOOK

This chapter has studied the relationship between the age composition of work teams and their productivity. We began with a brief survey of the literature. While there are contradictory results, one common theme is the stress on the heterogeneity of life-cycle profiles of labour productivity. There is no such thing as a scientific law that older workers systematically perform worse.

We now explore a unique data set that combines data on errors occurring in the production process of a large car manufacturer with detailed information on the personal characteristics of workers responsible for the errors. This set-up is ideally suited for our topic, for two reasons: it provides a standardized environment for our study, and it collects data on the level

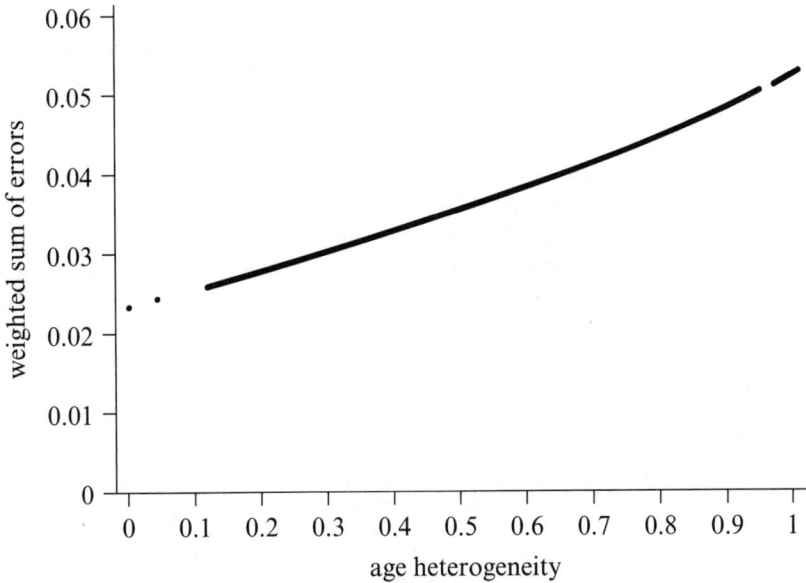

Note: Where the degree of age heterogeneity is 1, all age groups (15–25 years, 25–35 years, etc. to 55–65 years) are represented equally in the team. In contrast, with 0 all members of the team belong to the same age group.

Figure 5.5   Errors by degree of age-related heterogeneity

of work teams rather than the extremes typically found in the literature, namely individual workers or entire companies.

Our results may come as a surprise since they run against two common prejudices. First, we do not find evidence that productivity declines in the age range of typical older workers; secondly, we are able to test the prevalent hypothesis regarding the effect of teams' age structure on their performance: good performance requires a mix of young (fit, flexible) and old (experienced) workers. We find strong evidence against this hypothesis.

Our results hold in this assembly line factory of trucks in Germany. It is therefore a case study rather than a study of the universal truth. We think, however, that in service industries our results will be more, rather than less, likely to hold, since experience counts more and fitness less than at the assembly line. Another caveat concerns sample selectivity. We observe those older workers who are still in the factory. Less productive workers may have taken early retirement on the various generous schemes available in Germany, often encouraged by the plant management. Such selectivity will bias our results against finding declining labour productivity. While this argument is well taken, there is also the opposite effect: employees who still work on the assembly line are a negative selection in terms of labour productivity since they would otherwise have made a career in supervisory positions. Preliminary evidence (see Börsch-Supan, Düzgün and Weiss, 2007) shows that these effects cancel each other out, with the second effect appearing slightly greater than the first.

In future research, we will investigate this sample selectivity further, and we plan to perform similar studies in other sectors, including the service sector.

NOTE

1. This chapter is a first summary of a research project partially funded by the Hans Böckler Foundation. We are grateful for this financial support. We also thank Melanie Gräsle and Verena Arendt who did an excellent job in preparing the data. Finally, we wish to express our special thanks to the Wörth truck plant of DaimlerChrysler AG. It would not have been possible to carry out this project without the superb support we received from our contacts in the Human Resources, Production and Quality Management Departments as well as from the plant management and Works Council. For methodological details and a systematic literature review the reader is referred to the accompanying scientific paper.

REFERENCES

Boockmann Bernhard and Viktor Steiner (2000), 'Gesellschaftliche Alterung, Humankapital und Produktivität', in Frankfurter Institut, Stiftung Marktwirtschaft und Politik (ed.), *Prosperität in einer alternden Gesellschaft*, Bad Homburg: Stiftung Marktwirtschaft, pp. 107–36.
Börsch-Supan, Axel (2002), 'Kann die Finanz- und Sozialpolitik die Auswirkungen der Bevölkerungsalterung auf den Arbeitsmarkt lindern?', in Bernd Genser (ed.), *Finanzpolitik und Arbeitsmärkte, Schriften des Vereins für Socialpolitik, Gesellschaft für Wirtschafts- und Sozialwissenschaften*, N. F. vol. 289, Berlin: Duncher & Humblot.
Börsch-Supan, A., I. Düzgün und M. Weiss (2007), 'Productivity and the age composition of work teams: evidence from the assembly line', MEA-Discussion Paper, http://www.mea.uni-mannheim.de/publications.
Ell, Werner (1995), 'Arbeitszeitverkürzung zur Belastungsreduzierung älterer Arbeitnehmer im öffentlichen Personennahverkehr – 10 Jahre Erfahrungen aus den Interventionsmaßnahmen in den Verkehrsbetrieben in Nürnberg', in Rudolf Karazman, Irene Kloimüller and Norbert Winker (eds), *Alt erfahren und gesund. Betriebliche Gesundheitsförderung für älterwerdende Arbeitnehmer*, Gamburg: Conrad, pp. 160–70.
Farr, James L., Paul E. Tesluk and Stephanie R. Klein (1998), 'Organizational structure of the workplace and the older worker', in K. Warner Schaie and Carmi Schooler (eds), *Impact of Work on Older Adults*, New York: Springer, pp. 143–85.

Hellerstein, J.K. and D. Neumark (1995), 'Are earnings profiles steeper than productivity profiles? Evidence from Israeli firm-level data', *Journal of Human Resources*, **30**(1), 89–112.

Hellerstein, J.K., D. Neumark and K.R. Troske (1999), 'Wages, productivity and worker characteristics: evidence from plant level production function and wage equations', *Journal of Labor Economics*, **17**(3), 409–46.

Huber, Achim (2002), *Strategien zur alternsgerechten Gestaltung von Gruppenarbeit – Gesundheitsförderung und Qualifizierung*, Booklet Series: Demographie und Erwerbsarbeit, Stuttgart: Fraunhofer.

Ilmarinen, J. (1999), 'Ageing workers in the European Union – status and promotion of work ability, employability and employment', Working Paper, Helsinki.

Ilmarinen, J. and J. Tempel (2002), 'Arbeitsfähigkeit 2010 – Was können wir tun, damit Sie gesund bleiben?', Working Paper, Hamburg.

Koller, B. and H.-E. Plath (2000), 'Qualifikation und Qualifizierung älterer Arbeitnehmer', *Mitteilungen aus der Arbeitsmarkt- und Berufsforschung*, **33**(1), 112–25.

Kotlikoff, Laurence J. and David A. Wise (1989), 'Employee retirement and a firm's pension plan', in David A. Wise (ed.), *The Economics of Aging*, Chicago: University of Chicago Press, pp. 279–334.

Kruse, A. (2000), 'Psychologische Beiträge zur Leistungsfähigkeit im mittleren und höheren Erwachsenenalter – eine ressourcenorientierte Perspektive', in C. von Rothkirch (ed.), *Altern und Arbeit: Herausforderung für Wirtschaft und Gesellschaft*, Berlin: Edition Sigma.

Lazear, Edward P. (1995), *Personnel Economics*, Cambridge, Mass.: MIT Press.

Lehr, Ursula (2000), *Psychologie des Alterns*, Wiebelsheim: Quelle & Meyer.

Maercker, A. (1992), 'Weisheit im Alter', *Münchener Medizinische Wochenschrift*, **134**(33), 518–22.

Maier, G. (1998), 'Formen des Erlebens der Arbeitssituation: ein Beitrag zur Innovationsfähigkeit älterer Arbeitnehmer', *Zeitschrift für Gerontologie*, **31**(2), 127–37.

Morschhäuser, Martina (2002), 'Betriebliche Gesundheitsförderung angesichts des demographischen Wandels', in Martina Morschhäuser (ed.), *Demographie und Erwerbsarbeit. Gesund bis zur Rente. Konzepte gesundheits- und alternsgerechter Arbeits- und Personalpolitik*, Stuttgart: Fraunhofer.

Petrenz, Johannes (1999), 'Alter und berufliches Leistungsvermögen', in Max Gussone, Achim Huber, Martina Morschhäuser and Johannes Petrenz (eds), *Ältere Arbeitnehmer. Alter und Erwerbsarbeit in rechtlicher, arbeits- und sozialwissenschaftlicher Sicht*, Frankfurt: Bund-Verlag.

Skirbekk, Vegard (2004), 'Age and individual productivity: a literature survey', in Gustav Feichtinger (ed.), *Vienna Yearbook of Population Research*, Vienna: Verlag der Österreichischen Akademie der Wissenschaften.

Staudinger, U.M. (1999), 'Older and wiser? Integration results on the relationship between age and wisdom-related performance', *International Journal of Behavioral Development*, **23**(3), 641–64.

Staudinger, U.M. and P.B. Baltes (1996), 'Weisheit als Gegenstand psychologischer Forschung', *Psychologische Rundschau*, **47**(2), 57–77.

Tuomi, Kaija and Juhani Ilmarinen (1999), 'Work, lifestyle, health and work ability among ageing municipal workers in 1981–1992', in Juhani Ilmarinen and Veikko Louhevaara (eds), *Finn-age – Respect for the ageing: action programme*

to promote health, work ability and well-being of aging workers in 1990–96, Finnish
Institute of Occupational Health, People and work, Helsinki, Research Reports
26, 220–32.
Weinert, Franz E. (1992), 'Altern in psychologischer Perspektive', in Paul B. Baltes
and Jurgen Mittelstrass (eds), *Zukunft des Alterns und gesellschaftliche
Entwicklung*, Berlin, New York: De Garuyter, pp. 180–203.

Discussion of 'Labour productivity in an aging society'

Klaas Knot

1 OVERVIEW

The chapter by Börsch-Supan, Düzgün and Weiss investigates the impact of workers' age on labour productivity. Therefore it uses productivity observations of car assembly teams with a diversity of composition in, among other things, age. The authors have a huge and unique data set of a German car manufacturer at hand, so that this study contributes substantially to the literature on this topic. The results show that age lowers productivity as a consequence of reduced fitness, but that experience fully compensates for that, so that, remarkably, the 'net effect' of age is virtually neutral. In addition, the composition of the teams appears to be important: teams with workers of similar age are significantly more productive than teams with (strongly) varying ages. This is quite surprising as one might expect that a mixture of experienced and old with vital and young workers would be optimal. All in all, it is a very relevant chapter, which I have read with great interest. It contains a clear presentation of an original approach to unique data, and provides convincing and robust results.

2 COMMENT

As often is the case with this type of studies, it is difficult to generalize the results. First, this is a particular assembly line, so that results do not necessarily hold for all other types of production, particularly not for office work and the service industry. Note that many service industry jobs depend strongly on information technology, so that human capital in that sector tends to depreciate more rapidly. Hence, the value of experience is often more limited than in the manufacturing industry. Secondly, productivity may not coincide fully with 'avoiding errors in the production' as assumed in the chapter. Avoiding errors as a proxy of productivity is the more inaccurate, since the speed of the assembly line can be varied, so that a trade-off exists between productivity and avoiding errors.

In the remainder of this comment I expand on the discussion of the first conclusion. The chapter does not provide a direct link to pensions. However, the major suggestion of this study is that, from an economic point of view, not necessarily supported by the employees, we might delay retirement as older workers remain productive and, further, in that case we could pay them accordingly. In that light, I consider the fact that this chapter studies the current age composition of the workers as a practical shortcoming. After all, elderly people in the critical years from age 55 to 65 are heavily underrepresented, as is made clear in Figure 5.2. Hence, the results suffer from so-called 'selection bias': less productive or less motivated workers have higher chances of becoming unemployed or disabled, so that the remaining workers constitute an above-normal productive selection. This might explain the remarkable outcome of a flat level of productivity over age classes.

This uniform distribution of productivity across all ages is indeed quite remarkable. It raises the question of what would happen if classes with older workers were to be included in the analyses. (Note that the future retirement age for Germany has recently been set at 68 years.) Would productivity remain flat also for the additional groups? In any case, one expects a fall in productivity after a certain age limit, as the fall in vitality will cancel out experience. In this light an alternative and maybe a more interesting research approach for thinking about pension reform would be to provide the optimal (average) retirement age, for instance, based on an age-dependent decline in productivity (if any): if productivity falls below a critical threshold, the related income (or productivity) becomes 'insufficient'. As this study, however, suggests that productivity remains equal over the age profile, a more extensive data set would be necessary to obtain this building block for such retirement-age theory.

6. It is all back to front: critical issues in the design of defined contribution pension plans

David Blake[1]

6.1 INTRODUCTION

If a defined contribution (DC) pension plan is well designed, it will be a single, integrated financial product that delivers at reasonable cost to the plan member a pension that provides a high degree of retirement income security. This pension will provide an adequate replacement income for the remaining life of the plan member (and possibly also his or her partner) and removes the risk that the member outlives his or her resources. A well-designed plan will therefore be designed from back to front, that is, from desired output to required inputs. A well-designed plan will also ensure that, at each stage in the delivery process, appropriate incentives are given to those delivering key services.

There are six critical issues in the design of DC plans: charges, lapses, investment strategy, investment performance, fund annuitization and provider incentives. This chapter examines how well Personal Pension Plans (PPPs) deal with these issues. PPPs are the the main type of individual DC plan operating in the UK. They were introduced in 1988 by the Thatcher government (Social Security Act 1986) to increase labour market flexibility by improving pension portability. Workers were allowed to leave their employer's occupational plan and start a PPP which could be transferred with them when they changed jobs.[2] We end by offering suggestions about how the design of individual DC plans can be improved.

6.2 CHARGES[3]

Charges are needed to pay for key services such as plan administration and fund management as well as provider profit, but the higher the charges, the lower the accumulated fund value at the retirement date and the lower the subsequent pension. At the same time, any particular charging structure has implications for the incentives offered to those delivering such key services.

An important problem facing plan members is not only that plan charges can be substantial, but also that charging structures can be complex and disguised and this provides a potential source of confusion.[4] Furthermore, these charging structures generally incorporate substantial front-loaded elements which can be detrimental for members, since they have the effect of tying them to potentially inefficient providers who, in consequence, have little incentive to improve their efficiency. Also front-loaded charges involve significant penalties for those plan members who exit early from plans, and, according to industry average estimates for the UK, around 84 per cent of plan members drop out of 25-year plans prior to maturity.[5]

It is important to understand both the nature of charges and also how those charges are reported.

6.2.1 Types of Charges

Pension plan charges can be levied on a number of bases:

1. Charges based on contributions:
   - entry charges, either related to or independent of contributions,
   - regular (periodic) charges, either related to or independent of contributions.
2. Charges based on asset values:
   - regular charges based on interim value,
   - exit charge based on redemption (that is, terminal, transfer or paid-up) value.

If charges are extracted prior to the delivery of the service to which they relate, they are said to be *front-loaded*; if they are extracted afterwards, they are said to be *back-loaded*. Front-loaded charges do not tend to provide the best incentive for providers to deliver good service.

To illustrate the effects of these charges on fund value, we define the following terms:

V_T Redemption value of the fund at period T.

V_t Value of the fund at the end of period t; t will take the value 0 at the start of the plan and T at the end of the last period of contribution.

g_t Realized growth rate in the fund's value achieved by the fund manager in period t.

C_t Contribution made in period t. We assume that contributions are made at the beginning of each period and that contributions grow at an annual rate of e per cent (for example, the rate of growth might reflect the growth rate in national average earnings). Thus $C_t = C_{t-1}(1 + e_{t-1})$, where $e_0 = 0$.

M_t Policy fee for the period. This is assumed to be uprated at the rate of i per cent per annum (for example, i might be related to the rate of change in the consumer price index). Thus $M_t = M_{t-1}(1 + i_{t-1})$, where $i_0 = 0$.

f Fund management fee (expressed as a proportion). This is assumed to be paid annually on the fee date and to be proportionate to the value of the fund at that date.

a Allocation of contributions to units, adjusted for levies on any capital units and any loyalty bonuses (expressed as a proportion).

s Bid–offer spread on contributions (expressed as a proportion).

x_t Redemption fee payable either at maturity (when $t = T$) or when the plan is transferred or converted to paid-up status (when $t < T$).

F_0 Policy set-up fee, paid at the start of the plan.

Z_0 Annuitized value of any set-up fee (e.g. the independent financial adviser's (IFA's) fee).

The value of the fund in period t is then given by the following iterative equation:

$$V_t = \{V_{t-1} + a(1 - s)C_{t-1}(1 + e_{t-1})$$
$$- M_{t-1}(1 + i_{t-1})\}(1 - f)(1 + g_t)(1 - x_t) - Z_0, \qquad (6.1)$$

which can also be expressed as:

$$V_t = \sum_{m=1}^{t} \left[\left\{ Ca(1 - s) \prod_{k=0}^{m-1} (1 + e_k) - M \prod_{k=0}^{m-1} (1 + i_k) \right\} \right.$$
$$\left. \times (1 - f)^{t-m+1} \prod_{k=1}^{t-m+1} (1 + g_k) \right] (1 - x_t) - Z_0. \qquad (6.2)$$

In this equation, C represents the amount contributed by the plan member (which is uprated annually by e_t), while the g_t terms represent the realized returns achieved by the fund manager. *All other terms are related to charges.*

6.2.2   Reduction in Yield

The complexity of equation (6.2) means that there is no simple summary measure for the impact of charges. The conventional approach is to calculate the reduction in yield (RiY) resulting from the charges.

Suppose that g is the geometric mean of the g_t terms, then the RiY is defined as the difference between the geometric mean return (g) achieved by the plan in question and the plan's *effective yield* (g'), which is equal to the yield on a hypothetical zero-load plan (that is, one for which $a = 1$, $s = 0$, $M = 0$, $f = 0$, $x = 0$, $Z_0 = 0$) with the same gross contributions and having the same terminal value as the plan in question. Hence, g' is the solution to the following equation:

$$V_t = \sum_{m=1}^{t}\left[\left\{C\prod_{k=0}^{m-1}(1+e_k)\right\}(1+g')^{t-m+1}\right],\qquad(6.3)$$

where V_t is defined as in (6.1) or (6.2). The reduction in yield is calculated as:

$$RiY = g - g'.\qquad(6.4)$$

The higher the charges, the lower will be the net contributions invested; hence, the lower will be g' and the larger will be the reduction in yield.

The value of a particular fund at the end of a particular investment horizon will be affected both by the charges it imposes and by the *realized* growth rate, g_t, in assets achieved over the investment horizon. However, since the realized returns are not known until the end of the investment horizon, the UK financial regulator (the Financial Services Authority) requires that funds disclose their RiY, based on a standard *assumed* or *projected* growth rate (that is, calculations are required in which the growth rate g is *assumed* to be the same both for each year of the investment horizon and for all funds).

Table 6.1 illustrates both charges and reductions in yield for a regular premium PPP paying £200 per month as reported in the October 1998 *Money Management* survey when the FSA's standard assumed investment rate was 9 per cent per annum. The table shows that, for a five-year investment horizon, the best fund had a RiY of 1.26 per cent (equivalent to 3.1 per cent of the terminal fund value), while the worst fund had a RiY of 8.47 per cent (equivalent to 19.2 per cent of fund value). For 25-year plans, the RiY lay in the range 0.68–2.16 per cent and averaged 1.39 per cent, implying charges that average 19 per cent of fund value and rise to as high as 28 per cent. As a result of these high charges, the UK Government introduced a new low-cost individual DC plan in 2001 called a Stakeholder Pension Plan (SPP). SPPs originally had a maximum RiY of 1 per cent (equivalent to 13.7 per cent of fund value) and allow penalty-free transfers of assets between plans. However, they are not popular with pension plan providers who do not actively promote them and as a consequence very few of them

*Table 6.1   Charges and reduction in yield in personal pension plans
         (percentages)*

	5 years	10 years	15 years	20 years	25 years
Charges as a percentage of fund value					
Best overall[a]	3.1	4.1	7.2	8.5	9.8
Best commission loaded fund	4.0	4.1	7.4	8.9	10.6
Industry average	11.6	13.0	14.8	17.7	19.0
Worst fund	19.2	22.0	24.6	28.2	27.8
Reduction in yield (%)					
Best overall[a]	1.26	0.79	0.90	0.76	0.68
Best commission loaded fund	1.63	0.79	0.92	0.80	0.73
Industry average	4.91	2.65	1.93	1.68	1.39
Worst fund	8.47	4.76	3.43	2.88	2.16

Notes: Regular premium personal pension plan (£200/month); [a] lower of best commission-loaded and best commission-free.

Source: *Money Management* (October 1998).

have been sold. Under pressure from the pensions industry, the government increased the charge cap in 2005 to 1.5 per cent for the first 10 years, but even this has not been sufficient for the providers to begin actively promoting SPPs.

6.2.3   Reduction in Contributions

An even more striking way of reporting charges is the *reduction in contributions (RiC)*. This is defined as the difference between the gross contributions (*C*) into a plan and the plan's *effective contributions (C')*, as a proportion of gross contributions. Effective contributions are equal to the contributions into a hypothetical zero-load plan with the same average return and with the same terminal value as the plan in question. The effective contribution is therefore the value of *C'* which solves the following equation:

$$V_t = \sum_{m=1}^{t} \left[\left\{ C' \prod_{k=0}^{m-1} (1 + e_k) \right\} (1 + g)^{t-m+1} \right], \qquad (6.5)$$

where V_t is defined as in (6.1) or (6.2). The reduction in contributions is calculated as:

$$RiC = (C - C')/C. \qquad (6.6)$$

Since the left-hand sides of equations (6.3) and (6.5) are identical, the right-hand sides must equal each other, which implies that the RiC is related to the gross and effective yields as follows:

$$RiC = 1 - \left[\sum_{m=1}^{t}\left\{\prod_{k=0}^{m-1}(1+e_k)\right\}(1+g')^{t-m+1}\right] \div$$

$$\left[\sum_{m=1}^{t}\left\{\prod_{k=0}^{m-1}(1+e_k)\right\}(1+g)^{t-m+1}\right]. \qquad (6.7)$$

If there is no inflation uprating, then this reduces to the following approximation:

$$RiC \approx t \times RiY/2. \qquad (6.8)$$

Table 6.2 presents calculations of the RiY and RiC for a PPP with regular premiums of £200 per month and a typical charging structure. The first panel of the table shows that, as a result of a combination of the front-loading of charges and the effects of compounding, the effective yield on the fund rises with term to maturity and, as a consequence, the RiY falls with term from 5.7 per cent for a five-year plan to 1.7 per cent for a 25-year plan. However, although the RiY falls with term, it does not fall sufficiently rapidly to compensate for the effects of compounding and so the RiC rises with term (see (6.8)). The RiC is 13.4 per cent for a five-year plan and 23.2 per cent for a 25-year plan, marginally more than the tax relief on pension plans currently available to a basic rate taxpayer in the UK (i.e., 20 per cent). Similarly, the total compounded charge as a percentage of terminal fund value rises from 15.4 per cent to 30.2 per cent. Even the new SPPs, with their original maximum charge of 1 per cent of fund value, imply a RiC of 13.6 per cent over a 25-year investment horizon.

6.2.4   Frequently Changing and Disguised Charging Structures

An examination of *Money Management*'s annual *Personal Pensions* publications[6] reveals that funds change their charging structures on a regular basis. This makes it very difficult to compare funds over time and raises the question as to whether particular charging structures and changes to them are used to conceal the impact of costs, and thereby confuse the plan member.

One illustration of this relates to the treatment of paid-up plans (or PUPs), highlighted by Slade (1999). When plan holders move to a new pension plan, they have the choice of taking a transfer value with them or leaving their assets in the original plan, which is then converted into a

Table 6.2   Reduction in yield and reduction in contributions for a typical plan (percentages)

	5 years	10 years	15 years	20 years	25 years
Ignoring plan lapses					
Effective yield (*g*)	3.3	5.8	6.6	7.0	7.3
Reduction in yield (*RiY*)	5.7	3.2	2.4	2.0	1.7
Reduction in contributions (*RiC*)	13.4	15.5	17.9	20.5	23.2
Total compounded charges as a percentage of terminal fund value	15.4	18.4	21.8	25.7	30.2
Adjusting for plan lapses					
Effective yield (*g*)	−18.3	−11.9	−9.6	−8.3	−7.4
Reduction in yield (*LARiY*)	27.3	20.9	18.6	17.3	16.4
Reduction in contributions (*LARiC*)	50.2	64.6	74.9	82.3	87.6
Total compounded charges as a percentage of terminal fund value	20.1	27.3	38.5	54.9	78.7

Note: Regular premium personal pension plan (£200/month) with the following assumptions:

Charging structure:

Component	Symbol	Value
Allocation	*a*	95%
Bid–offer spread	*s*	5%
Fund management fee	*f*	0.75%
Policy fee	*M*	£3 p.m.
Uprating factor for policy fee	*i*	4.5% p.a.

Other assumptions:

Return	*g*	9% p.a.
Lapse rate in year 1	q_1	13.4%
Lapse rate in year 2	q_2	13.4%
Lapse rate in year 3	q_3	14.0%
Lapse rate in year 4	q_4	12.0%
Lapse rate from year 5	q_{5+}	6.5% p.a.

PUP: the assets cannot be liquidated prior to retirement. At present, only 15 per cent of plan holders take transfer values; the rest leave PUPs with the original provider. The regulator requires that pension plans disclose only transfer values and full maturity values. There is no obligation to quote PUP maturity values, and few providers do so.

There is clearly a trade-off between high transfer values and high full maturity values: plans with front-loaded charges will quote low transfer values and high maturity values relative to plans with level charges. Different providers compete on the basis of the transfer and full maturity values that they quote. However, PUP maturity values, which, in principle, should be related to transfer values, can turn out to be poor value for money, because the original providers can continue to extract charges similar to those that they would have done had the plan remained active. For example, Slade discusses the case of a particular insurance company which quotes the highest transfer value amongst 12 leading providers, but ranks twelfth for its PUP maturity value quote. It appears that some plans quote high transfer values to attract business, knowing that only 15 per cent of those plan members not going to full term are likely to take transfers, while the remaining 85 per cent end up with low PUP maturity values.

Another example of hidden charges comes from a survey of European fund management fees by Towers Perrin (1998): some fund managers do not report their full set of charges. The three key charges are for asset management, broking (that is, transaction execution) and custody. There are also charges for reporting, accounting and performance measurement.

Some fund managers report the asset management fee (as some proportion of the value of the net assets under management) only *after* deducting the broking and custody fee. Some fund managers justify this on the grounds that both the portfolio transactions and the safe keeping are conducted by a third party independent of the fund manager, typically the global custodian. Other fund managers operate full 'clean fees' (that is, report full charges, including third party fees which are merely passed through to the client). Yet other fund managers add a commission to third party fees before passing them through. In some cases, however, the broker or custodian is related to the fund manager (for example, is part of the same investment banking group) and, in such cases, it is more difficult to assess charges appropriately.

The lack of transparency can also lead to incentive problems. Brokerage fees are related to turnover which provides an incentive to churn (that is, overtrade) the portfolio; this is especially so if the transactions are executed by an in-house broker and the brokerage fee is hidden from the client. Some fund managers, in contrast, use discount brokers to reduce the cost to the client. Some clients impose turnover limits to reduce costs. However, the most effective means of keeping charges down is complete fee transparency and full disclosure for each fund management function and benchmark-related performance measurement (where the impact of hidden fees is exposed through poor performance).

In summary, we find that charging structures in PPPs are generally complex and disguised and this leads to customer confusion. Consumers are not able to compare charges across plans easily, which means that competitive forces do not operate effectively. As a consequence, charges tend to be very high and this reduces the net terminal value of the fund available for paying pensions.

6.3 LAPSES

6.3.1 The Impact of Low Persistency on Charges

A regular premium pension plan involves a substantial commitment of time and resources by both the plan's sponsor and its members if the desired objectives are to be achieved. Any significant front-loading of charges in plans means that members suffer a substantial loss if their contributions lapse prematurely. As the Personal Investment Authority (the predecessor to the Financial Services Authority) argues, 'if investors buy policies on the basis of good advice, they would not normally be expected to cancel premiums to their policies unless forced to do so by unexpected changes in their personal circumstances. This means that persistency is a powerful indicator of the quality of the selling process' (1998, p. 3). The PIA defines persistency as 'the proportion of investors who continue to pay regular contributions to their personal policies, or who do not surrender their single premium policy' (p. 3).

Table 6.3 shows that persistency rates (that is, the percentage of policies that have not lapsed) after four years of membership are between 57 per cent and 68 per cent. The persistency rate is higher for plans arranged by independent financial advisers than by company representatives, suggesting that

Table 6.3 Persistency rates for regular premium personal pension plans (percentages)

	Company representatives: after				Independent financial advisers: after			
	1 Year	2 Years	3 Years	4 Years	1 Year	2 Years	3 Years	4 Years
1993	84.1	72.3	63.6	56.7	91.5	83.3	76.6	70.5
1994	83.7	72.8	64.4		91.3	82.1	74.5	
1995	85.5	75.0			90.8	81.6		
1996	86.6				90.2			

Source: PIA (1998, Table 1).

108   *Frontiers in pension finance*

the clients of the former are generally more satisfied with their policies than those of the latter. However, the one-year rates indicate a small improvement in the persistency rate of plans arranged by company representatives since 1993 and a small decline in that for plans arranged by IFAs. Nevertheless, although only four years of data are available, the table suggests that very few personal pension plan members are likely to maintain their membership of the plan long enough to build up an adequate pension.

The PIA regards these persistency rates as 'disturbing' (p. 10) and offers a number of explanations: members were missold pensions which were either unsuitable or too expensive; regular premium plans might be unsuitable for those with irregular earnings or uncertain long-term employment; a change of employment may lead to a member joining an occupational plan and abandoning their personal one; adverse general economic conditions could worsen persistency rates. The PIA also offers suggestions as to why the IFAs are more successful than company representatives. First, IFAs tend to advise clients on higher incomes, who are more likely to continue contributing; secondly, plans chosen by an IFA are likely to be from a wider range of policies than those offered by representatives of any single company, leading to a greater likelihood of the plan matching closely the particular needs of the client.

6.3.2   Reduction in Yield and Reduction in Contributions, Accounting for Plan Lapses

It is possible to incorporate the effect of plan lapses in the calculation of the *RiY*. If we define q_t as the lapse rate in period t for a particular provider, the expected value of a fund becomes:

$$V_t^* = \sum_{m=1}^{t} \left[\prod_{k=1}^{m} (1-q_k) \left\{ Ca(1-s) \prod_{k=0}^{m-1} (1+e_k) - M \prod_{k=0}^{m-1} (1+i_k) \right\} \right.$$
$$\left. \times (1-f)^{t-m+1}(1+g)^{t-m+1} \right] (1-x_t) - Z_0 \tag{6.9}$$

and the *lapse-adjusted reduction in yield* (*LARiY*) experienced by that provider's plan holders will depend on the effective yield (g^*) that solves:

$$V_t^* = \sum_{m=1}^{t} \left[\left\{ C \prod_{k=0}^{m-1} (1+e_k) \right\} (1+g^*)^{t-m+1} \right], \tag{6.10}$$

where V_t^* is defined as in (6.9) and the product of the m terms in $(1-q_k)$ measures the persistency rate over m periods. In the calculations below, we assume lapse rates for the first four years based on FSA data for company representatives, namely 13.4 per cent, 13.4 per cent, 14 per cent and 12 per cent (see Table 6.3), and then project forward from year 4 at the industry average annual lapse rate of 6.5 per cent. The industry average persistency rate over 25 years was estimated to be just 16 per cent.

These expressions indicate that the *LARiY* rises with higher average takes and falls with higher persistency. The latter result follows because the take at maturity is much higher than in earlier years, since the terminal bonus awarded in the final year is a very high proportion of the total value of the fund. So strong persistency means that lower *LARiY*s are needed to achieve the same average take. In other words, the effect of positive lapse rates is to increase the *LARiY* relative to the *RiY* since g^* is lower than g'.

The *lapse-adjusted reduction in contributions* (*LARiC*) is found by substituting the effective yield (g^*) from equation (6.10) into equation (6.7) in place of g'. The second panel of Table 6.2 shows the *LARiY* and *LARiC*. Lapses have a remarkable impact on charging measures: the likelihood of maintaining contributions for 25 years is so low for the average plan member that the effective contribution over this period is just 12p for every £1 of premium paid.

In summary, we find that high lapses can lead to pensions that are very poor value for the money invested. Some may argue that low persistency is a matter for the plan member alone and clearly there are many individuals who do not have the commitment to maintain contributions for the full term of the plan. But low persistency is as much an indicator of a bad product that was initially missold and subsequently followed by poor after-sales service.

6.4 INVESTMENT STRATEGY

With DC plans, the size of the pension depends critically on the level of net contributions. It also depends on the investment strategy pursued. There is a trade-off between the planned level of contributions and the investment strategy. The more conservative the investment strategy, the lower the anticipated return on investments and the higher the planned level of contributions the accruing fund will require in order to deliver a particular pension level in retirement. But there is another trade-off between investment strategy and risk. The less conservative the strategy, the greater the asset risk and the more volatile the contribution pattern if a desired pension target is to be achieved. There is also a bigger risk that the target pension will fail to be achieved. Risks are all-important in DC plans because they are borne entirely by plan members. Particularly critical are the risks faced right at the moment of retirement: as forced sellers of assets and forced buyers of life annuities, pension plan members are typically subject to potentially substantial investment risk (manifesting itself in the form of low asset values), interest rate risk (manifesting itself in the form of low interest rates and hence annuity rates) and longevity risk (manifesting itself in the form of higher future survival probabilities that again lower annuity rates) all on the same day.

6.4.1 The Nature of Risk in DC Plans

Because DC plans, unlike defined benefit (DB) plans, involve no promises about the size of the pension, they involve no risk to the plan provider. The risk of ending up with a low pension falls entirely on the plan member. A natural measure of this risk is the risk of falling short of the pension available from a fully-funded DB plan, that is, one with planned contributions and an investment strategy that are sufficient to build up a fund of the size needed to deliver a target pension in full. We therefore need to look more closely at how a DB plan works.

Figure 6.1 shows that the present value of the DC pension on the retirement date depends entirely on the value of the fund's assets on that date. Figure 6.2 shows that the present value of the DB target pension (L) is independent of the value of the fund's assets. Figure 6.3 shows that the DB pension can be replicated using an implicit long put option (*Put*) and an implicit short call option ($-Call$) on the underlying assets of the fund (A), both with the same exercise price (L) which equals the present value of the DB target pension payments at the member's retirement age. The put option is held by the plan member and written by the plan sponsor, while the call option is written by the member and held by the sponsor. On the retirement date of the member, which coincides with the expiry date of the options, if one of the options is in-the-money, it will be exercised. If the value of the fund's assets is less than the exercise price, so that the plan is showing an actuarial deficit, the member will exercise his or her put option against the sponsor who will then be required to make a deficiency payment ($L-A$). If, on the other hand, the value of the assets exceeds the exercise price, so that the plan is showing an actuarial surplus, the sponsor will exercise his or her call option against the member and recover the surplus ($A-L$). This implies that a DB plan is, in effect, a risk-free investment from the member's viewpoint: DB plan members end up with the same pension whatever the value of the underlying assets.

It is clear from this how DB and DC plans are related. A DC plan is invested only in the underlying financial assets. A DB plan is invested in a portfolio containing the underlying assets (and so is, in part, a DC plan) *plus* a put option *minus* a call option on these assets:

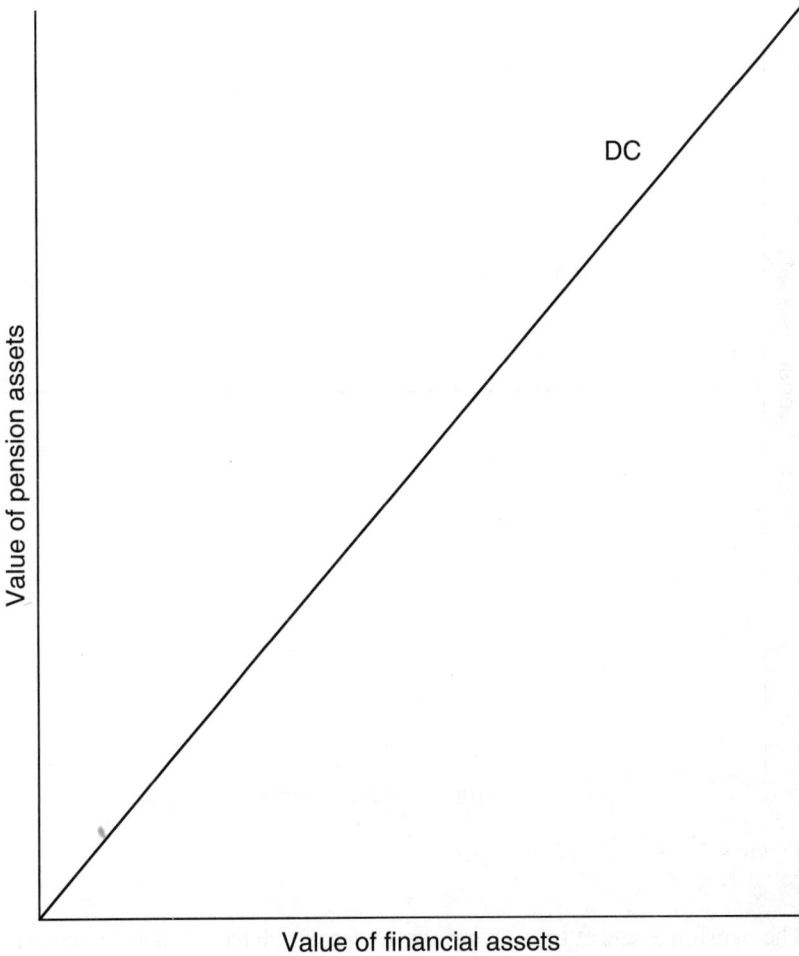

Figure 6.1   A defined contribution pension plan

$$DB = L$$
$$= A + Put - Call$$
$$= DC + Put - Call. \qquad (6.11)$$

The actuarial surplus at time t (S_t) with a DB plan is defined as the difference between pension assets (A_t) and liabilities (L_t):

$$S_t = A_t - L_t. \qquad (6.12)$$

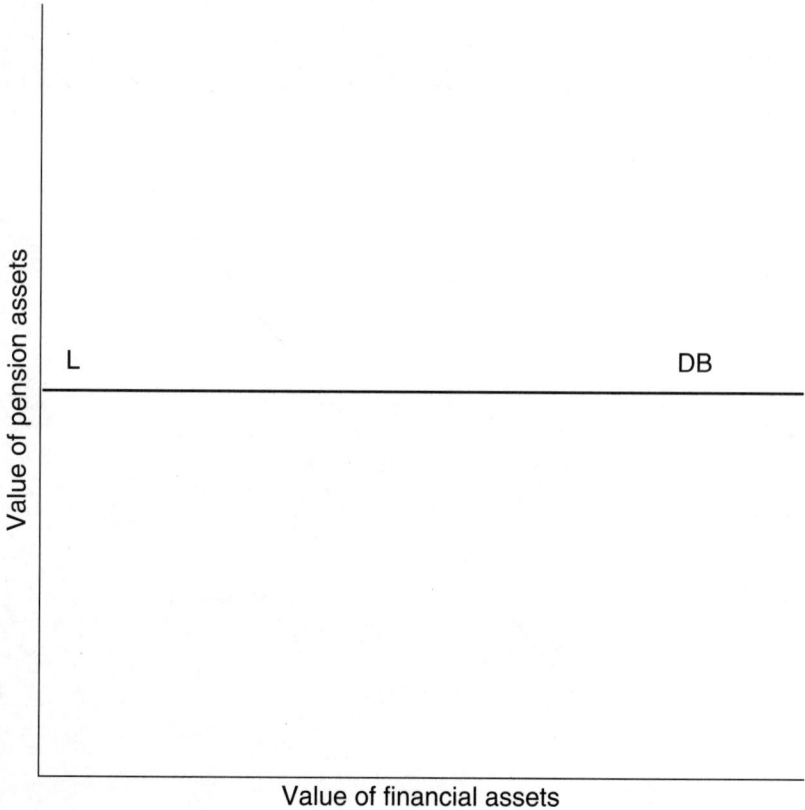

Figure 6.2   A defined benefit pension plan

The pension assets at time t comprise the accumulated financial assets *plus* the present value of the promised future contributions into the plan. The pension liabilities at time t are equal to the present value of the expected future pension payments from the plan.

Surplus risk (also called shortfall risk) at time t (σ_{St}^2) is given by the variance (that is, volatility) of S_t in (6.12):

$$\sigma_{St}^2 = \sigma_{At}^2 + \sigma_{Lt}^2 - 2\sigma_{At}\sigma_{Lt}\rho_{AL}$$
$$= (\sigma_{At} - \sigma_{Lt})^2 \text{ if } \rho_{AL} = 1. \tag{6.13}$$

It depends on the volatility of asset values (σ_{At}^2), the volatility of pension liabilities (σ_{Lt}^2) and the correlation (ρ_{AL}) between asset values and pension liabilities. The main sources of these volatilities are uncertainties

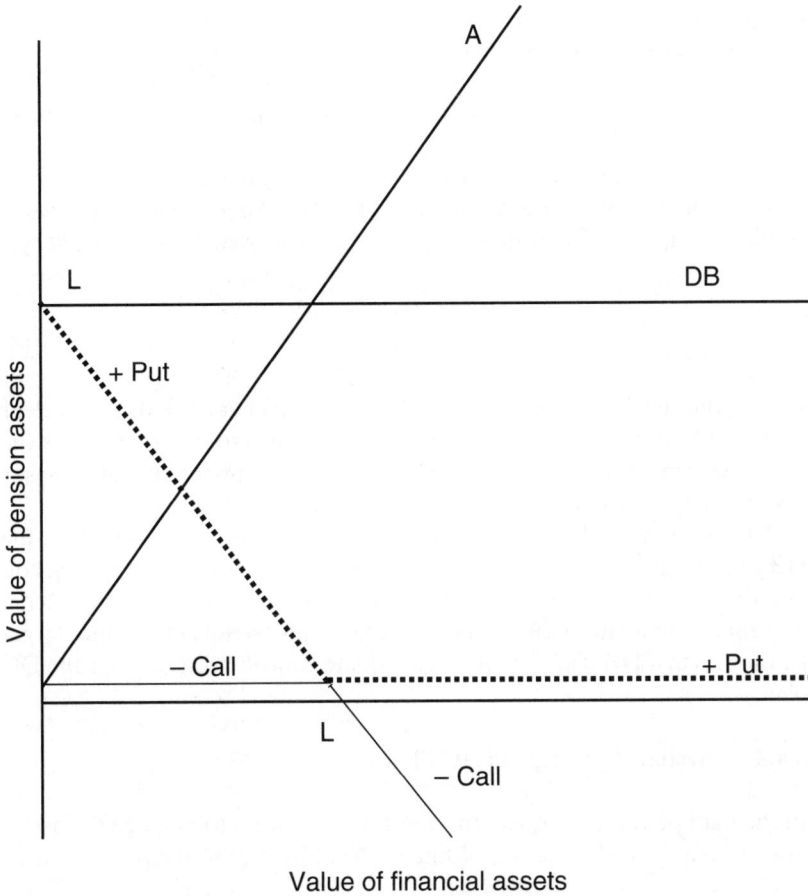

Figure 6.3   The option composition of a defined benefit pension plan

concerning future investment yields, real earnings (that is, productivity) growth rates and inflation rates. This is because investment yields determine the rate at which contributions into the pension fund accumulate over time, the growth rate in real earnings determines the size of both contributions into the plan and the pension liability at the retirement date, and the inflation rate determines the growth rate of pensions during retirement.

Equation (6.11) involves Fisher–Margrabe exchange options.[7] These are a variant of the more familiar Black–Scholes options which recognize that the options in equation (6.11), if exercised, exchange risky assets at an exercise price that is indexed to the uncertain value of the pension liabilities, in contrast with the standard model where the exercise price is constant. The value of the call option is given by:

$$Call_t = N_1(\sigma_{St}^2)A_t - N_2(\sigma_{St}^2)L_t, \tag{6.14}$$

where $N_1(\cdot)$ are cumulative normal distribution functions of σ_{St}^2 (amongst other variables) which lie between zero and unity, taking the latter value when surplus risk is zero. The value of the put option is given by put–call parity:

$$\begin{aligned} Put_t &= Call_t + L_t - A_t \\ &= Call_t - S_t \end{aligned} \tag{6.15}$$

If both the surplus and surplus risk are maintained at zero, then it is clear from (6.14) and (6.15) that the call and put have zero value. If this is the case, they can be issued by, respectively, the plan member and plan sponsor free of charge since they will never be exercised.

Returning to (6.11), it follows that, if these conditions are satisfied, the DB and DC plans are equivalent in the sense of delivering the same pension in retirement. In other words, it is possible to manage a DC plan in such a way that it generates (with a high degree of probability) the same target pension as in a DB plan, so long as adequate contributions go into the DC plan.

6.4.2 Investment Strategy in DC Plans

In the light of these observations, there are two ways to manage the assets in a DC plan, which differ according to the objectives of the plan member.

6.4.2.1 Maximizing risk-adjusted expected value

The simplest investment strategy is to choose a particular contribution level into the fund and then select an investment strategy that maximizes the risk-adjusted expected terminal value ($\overline{A}_T^{RA}$) of the accumulating fund. This is defined as the expected terminal value of the pension assets ($\overline{A}_T$) net of a risk penalty, which is proportional to the product of the fund risk (as measured by the terminal variance of the fund's assets (σ_{AT}^2)) and the degree of risk aversion of the plan member (R_A):

$$\overline{A}_T^{RA} = \overline{A}_T - 0.5R_A\sigma_{AT}^2. \tag{6.16}$$

The lower the degree of risk aversion, the greater the risk that can be borne by the plan's assets and hence the greater the expected value of the pension fund at the retirement date. It is possible to increase the expected value of the pension assets by taking on more risk (that is, increasing the terminal volatility of the fund's assets measured from the start date of the plan), but if too much additional risk is taken on, $\overline{A}_T^{RA}$ will fall, especially if R_A is high. The risk penalty measures the cost for a given individual of taking on more asset risk. $\overline{A}_T$ is set equal to the value of the pension assets needed to deliver the target pension in retirement. The contribution level is fixed at the beginning of the plan and does not change in the light of intermediate investment outcomes. Similarly, the investment strategy does not change over the life of the plan. In other words, there is no feedback control with this particular investment strategy.

Individual DC plans are provided by financial institutions such as insurance companies, banks, building societies, unit trusts (that is, open-ended mutual funds) and investment trusts (that is, close-ended mutual funds) and open-ended investment companies (OEICs). The plan provider will offer the member a choice of investment vehicle in which the pension assets will accumulate, ranging from low risk (such as a deposit administration plan), through medium risk (such as an endowment policy investing in a managed fund with an insurance company) to high risk (such as a unit-linked plan). The deposit administration plan is aimed at a plan member with a very high degree of risk aversion, while the unit-linked plan is aimed at a plan member with a low degree of risk aversion. However, it is arguable whether low-yielding deposits are a suitable investment vehicle for long-horizon investment programmes such as pension plans. Other asset categories, such as equities, offer much higher returns over the long term. Investing in deposit administration plans or bonds has been described as a strategy of 'reckless conservatism'.

Once a plan member has selected a particular type of plan, the fund manager's task is to choose the asset allocation (between T-bills or 'cash',[8] bonds and equities) that maximizes the value of $\overline{A}_T^{RA}$ in (6.16).[9] The resulting asset allocation is said to be myopic, that is, equivalent to that which will be determined in a single-period portfolio choice model (see, for example, Campbell and Viceira, 2002, ch. 2). Table 6.4 illustrates some different possible outcomes. Individuals with very high degrees of risk aversion (35 is the average for households in the UK as estimated in Blake, 1996) will choose very conservative investment strategies with a weighting above 90 per cent in low yielding T-bills. For a typical contribution rate in the UK (10 per cent of earnings, divided evenly between the member and his employer) this will generate a pension in retirement after 40 years of membership in the plan of less than 40 per cent of that available from a fully funded final salary plan, namely two-thirds of final salary:[10] it is only just over 30 per cent for a woman because of her greater anticipated longevity.[11]

Table 6.4 *Maximizing risk-adjusted expected value*

Risk aversion (R_A)	35	35	35	35	35	35	35	35
	Male	Female	Male	Female	Male	Female	Male	Female
Net contribution rate (%)	10.0	10.0	15.0	15.0	20.0	20.0	24.75	29.85
Asset allocation (%):								
T-bills	92.69	92.69	92.69	92.69	92.69	92.69	92.69	92.29
Bonds	4.22	4.22	4.22	4.22	4.22	4.22	4.22	3.20
Equities	3.09	3.09	3.09	3.09	3.09	3.09	3.09	4.51
Financial assets:								
Return (%)	1.56	1.56	1.56	1.56	1.56	1.56	1.56	1.68
Risk (%)	4.04	4.04	4.04	4.04	4.04	4.04	4.04	4.04
Liabilities:								
Growth rate (%)	2.09	2.09	2.09	2.09	2.09	2.09	2.09	2.09
Risk (%)	2.06	2.06	2.06	2.06	2.06	2.06	2.06	2.06
Corrn. with assets (%)	17.99	17.99	17.99	17.99	17.99	17.99	17.99	18.24
Pension (% of target pen.)	39.74	32.75	59.94	49.40	80.37	66.25	100.00	100.00
Terminal fund risk (%)	120.35	99.20	143.52	118.30	167.88	138.38	191.91	180.11
Call (% of liabilities)	31.79	25.64	42.27	33.56	53.89	42.38	66.27	63.22
Put (% of liabilities)	92.06	92.89	82.34	84.16	73.52	76.14	66.27	63.22

Risk aversion (R_A)	8	8	8	8	1.5	1.5	1.0	1.0
	Male	Female	Male	Female	Male	Female	Male	Female
Net contribution rate (%)	10.0	10.0	21.89	25.66	8.69	9.49	7.15	7.82
Asset allocation (%):								
T-bills	92.00	92.00	85.12	81.83	0.00	0.00	0.00	0.00
Bonds	2.45	2.45	5.19	7.17	56.19	52.55	45.62	37.74
Equities	5.56	5.56	9.69	11.00	43.81	47.45	54.38	62.26

Financial assets:								
Return (%)	1.77	1.77	2.27	2.44	6.64	6.83	7.20	7.61
Risk (%)	4.04	4.04	4.19	4.31	11.15	11.58	12.50	13.69
Liabilities:								
Growth rate (%)	2.09	2.09	2.09	2.09	2.09	2.09	2.09	2.09
Risk (%)	2.06	2.06	2.06	2.06	2.06	2.06	2.06	2.06
Corrn. with assets (%)	18.43	18.43	19.73	19.77	20.06	19.56	16.99	14.06
Pension (% of target pen.)	41.34	34.08	100.00	100.00	100.00	100.00	100.00	100.00
Terminal fund risk (%)	171.00	140.94	148.73	92.13	304.97	303.11	324.65	364.03
Call (% of liabilities)	38.90	31.88	54.29	35.49	84.50	87.04	89.54	93.12
Put (% of liabilities)	97.56	97.80	54.29	35.49	84.50	87.04	89.54	93.12

It takes net contributions (after charges) of 25 per cent of male earnings and 30 per cent of female earnings into a DC plan to generate the same expected pension as a DB plan. High net worth individuals have a coefficient of risk aversion of around eight, but this still involves a very high weighting in T-bills and hence very high contribution rates are still needed to achieve a reasonable pension. As the coefficient of risk aversion falls, the weighting in equities rises: at 1.5, the weighting is still below 50 per cent. At unity (the risk aversion level typical of institutional investors), we begin to observe similar asset allocations to those of mature occupational pension plans in the UK, namely 60 per cent in equities and 40 per cent in bonds, and the target pension can be achieved with net contributions of below 8 per cent of earnings.

The table also shows the terminal fund risk (σ_{AT}). This is very high even for conservative investment strategies and it rises with the level of equity risk assumed, confirming the trade-offs outlined above between contribution rates, investment strategy and asset risk.

Figure 6.4 and 6.5 illustrate, using information in Table 6.4, some possible distributions of the terminal fund values as a proportion of that from a fully funded DB plan offering an index-linked pension of two-thirds of final salary. Figure 6.4 shows the distribution based on 1000 monte carlo simulations in the case of a male with $R_A = 35$ and contributing 10 per cent of earnings into a plan. The investment strategy is a very conservative one and this has two discernible effects: the average pension is very low (only 20 per cent of final salary) and so is the dispersion of the pension, with a semi-interquartile range of just five percentage points. Figure 6.5, in contrast, shows the wide dispersion of possible outcomes from the high risk–high return asset allocation chosen by a male with $R_A = 1$. It is possible to achieve on average the same pension as that from a DB plan with contributions of 7.15 per cent of earnings, and there is a 23 per cent chance of doing better than this. But this means that there is a 77 per cent chance of getting less than the DB pension and, in particular, there is a 44 per cent chance of ending up with a pension of less than 25 per cent of the DB pension.

Figure 6.6 shows that this dispersion can be reduced by adopting a 'deterministic lifestyle' (or age phasing) investment strategy. This is a commonly used investment strategy in DC plans intended to reduce the volatility of the pension fund's value as the retirement date approaches.[12] With this strategy, the contributions are initially invested entirely in equities, but the assets are systematically switched over to bonds and/or T-bills over a pre-set period (such as five years) leading up to the retirement date. If the switch is to T-bills, Table 6.4 shows that there is only a 7 per cent chance of getting less than 25 per cent of the DB pension, but only an 11 per cent

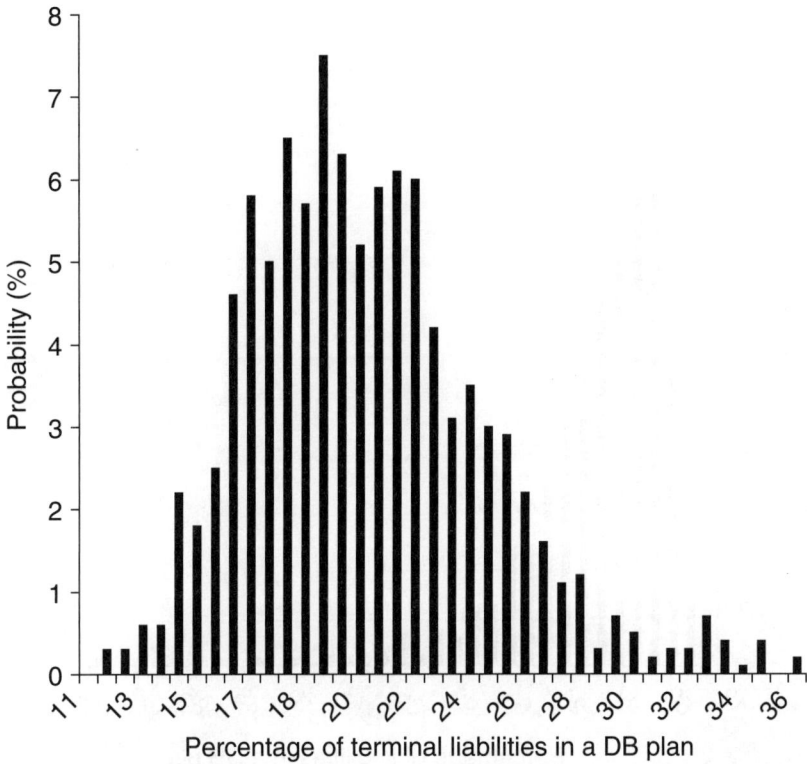

Y-axis label: Probability (%)
X-axis label: Percentage of terminal liabilities in a DB plan

Note: For 40 years, contributions of 10% of male earnings are made into a pension plan and the portfolio is invested 92.69% in T-bills, 4.22% in bonds and 3.09% in equities and has a mean real return of 1.56% and a standard deviation of 4.04%. The properties of the distribution of terminal values (as a percentage of terminal liabilities) from 1000 monte carlo simulations are as follows:

Probability	25%	Mode	Median	Mean	25%
Percentage of terminal liabilities	<17	20	20	20	>22

Figure 6.4   Frequency distribution of terminal fund values: a low-risk, low-return asset allocation

chance of getting more than 100 per cent. However, the cost in terms of a lower average pension is quite substantial: the average pension falls from 100 per cent to 63 per cent of the DB pension.

6.4.2.2   Minimizing the contribution rate and surplus risk

Suppose, instead, the plan member's objective is to target specifically a particular pension level, as happens in a DB pension plan, such as two-thirds

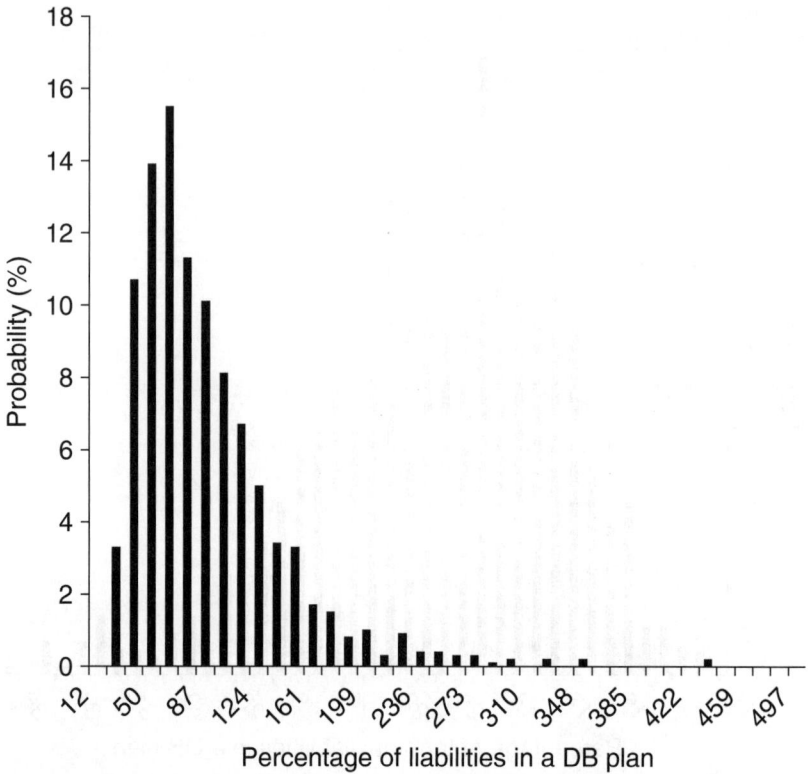

Note: For 40 years, contributions of 7.15% of male earnings are made into a pension plan and the portfolio is invested 45.62% in bonds and 54.38% in equities and has a mean real return of 7.2% and a standard deviation of 12.5%. The properties of the distribution of terminal values (as a percentage of terminal liabilities) from 1000 monte carlo simulations are as follows:

Probability	44%	Mode	Median	Mean	23%
Percentage of terminal liabilities	<25	52	66	100	>100

Figure 6.5   Frequency distribution of terminal fund values: high-risk, high-return asset allocation

of final salary. The DC plan can now be thought of as having 'pension liabilities', which equal the expected present value of the target pension payments between retirement and death. The appropriate investment management strategy is asset-liability management (also called surplus risk management or shortfall risk management). This involves constructing a portfolio of financial assets that minimizes the cost (in terms of planned contributions) of matching pension liabilities in two key respects: size and

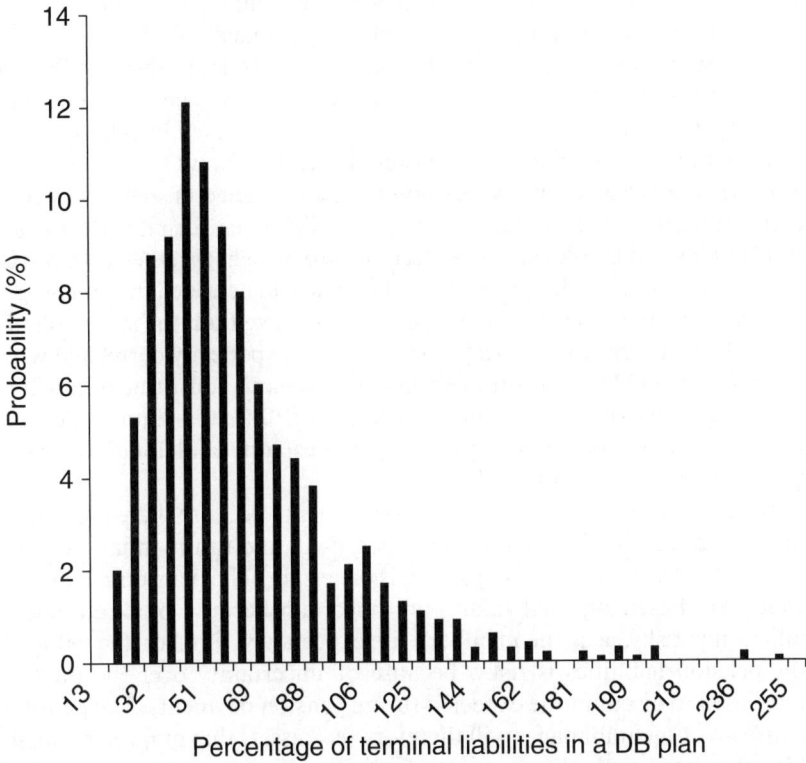

Note: For 40 years, contributions of 7.15% of male earnings are made into a pension plan and for the first 35 years, the portfolio is invested 45.62% in bonds and 54.38% in equities and has a mean real return of 7.2% and a standard deviation of 12.5%; for the final five years, the fund is switched linearly into T-bills with a mean real return of 1.28% and a standard deviation of 4.04%. The properties of the distribution of terminal values from 1000 monte carlo simulations are as follows:

Probability	7%	Mode	Median	Mean	11%
Percentage of terminal liabilities	<25	44	48	63	>100

Figure 6.6   *Frequency distribution of terminal fund values: deterministic lifestyle asset allocation*

volatility. Formally, the fund manager's objective is to minimize each period the following loss function of the contribution rate and surplus risk:

$$\psi_t = \lambda C_t^2 + \sigma_{St}^2, \tag{6.17}$$

subject to the condition that the surplus (6.12) is always zero.[13] This is a dynamic programming problem with the contribution rate into the fund and the asset allocation as the control variables, and the trade-off between these variables is measured by the weighting parameter (λ).[14]

If pension plans are always fully funded, so that assets are always sufficient to meet liabilities in full (implying $A_t = L_t$ at all times), then it is clear from (6.12) that the surplus will always be zero. This is achieved by adjusting the contribution rate into the fund to ensure that (6.12) always holds.

Further, if the assets in the pension fund are selected in such a way that their aggregate volatility matches that of the liabilities, then it is clear from (6.13) that surplus risk can be reduced to zero, which, together with $S = 0$, implies that the implicit options in the DB plan can be issued free of charge. This requires the assets in the pension fund to have both the same volatility as the pension liabilities ($\sigma_{At}^2 = \sigma_{Lt}^2$) and to be perfectly correlated with them ($\rho_{AL} = 1$). This, in turn, requires the assets to constitute a liability-matching or liability-immunizing portfolio (LIP), that is, a portfolio that immunizes the productivity, inflation, interest rate and longevity risks embodied in the pension liabilities.

A plan member's future labour income is risky because there are uncertainties concerning future productivity growth and future inflation. This means that the member's final salary is uncertain. The pension payments, which are based on final salary, are uncertain because post-retirement inflation is risky, as is the member's life expectancy. Further, the value of the pension liabilities is risky, because of uncertainty over the interest rates used to discount the expected future pension payments. The pension plan's investment manager will therefore seek assets that are, where possible, correlated with shocks to productivity, inflation, interest rates and longevity. In practice, financial assets do not exist which are perfectly correlated with these shocks; that is, a perfect LIP cannot be constructed using existing financial assets. Nevertheless, the objective of asset-liability management is to construct a portfolio of assets whose returns are as highly correlated with changes in the value of the pension liabilities as possible.

Table 6.5 shows the required contribution rates into the plan to maintain the surplus at zero. They depend on the level of the trade-off parameter λ. From (6.17), it is clear that the higher the λ, the greater the penalty from having high contributions, and therefore the greater the weighting in higher returning but also more risky equities. For $\lambda = 1$, the minimum contribution rate for men is 10.58 per cent of earnings and the optimal asset allocation is 6.76 per cent in T-bills, 59.31 per cent in bonds and 33.94 per cent in equities. For $\lambda = 1000$, the optimal male contribution rate is 5.44 per cent and the optimal asset mix is 25.38 per cent in bonds and 74.62 per cent in equities. Tables 6.4 and 6.5 also show that the highest correlation between assets and liabilities is of the

Table 6.5 Minimizing the contribution rate and surplus risk

Weighting parameter (λ)	1 Male	1 Female	10 Male	10 Female	100 Male	100 Female	1000 Male	1000 Female
Net contribution rate (%)	10.58	10.87	10.07	10.73	8.83	10.30	5.44	6.42
Asset allocation (%):								
T-bills	6.76	4.06	3.14	3.78	2.46	2.10	0.00	0.00
Bonds	59.31	50.41	53.45	50.01	47.94	46.44	25.38	24.13
Equities	33.94	45.53	43.40	46.20	49.60	51.46	74.62	75.87
Financial assets:								
Return (%)	5.58	6.27	5.79	6.33	6.34	6.50	8.28	8.39
Risk (%)	11.30	13.26	12.94	13.38	14.16	14.54	18.00	18.19
Liabilities:								
Growth rate (%)	2.09	2.09	2.09	2.09	2.09	2.09	2.09	2.09
Risk (%)	2.06	2.06	2.06	2.06	2.06	2.06	2.06	2.06
Corrn. with assets (%)	9.34	5.08	5.51	5.55	3.25	3.35	1.71	1.95
Pension (% of target pension)	100.00	100.00	100.00	100.00	100.00	100.00	100.00	100.00
Terminal surplus risk (%)	266.75	328.12	303.32	331.69	342.28	360.92	476.39	489.63
Call (ratio of liabilities, %)	81.77	89.91	87.06	90.28	91.30	92.89	98.28	98.56
Put (ratio of liabilities, %)	81.77	89.91	87.06	90.28	91.30	92.89	98.28	98.56

order of 20 per cent, well below the perfect positive correlation needed for $\sigma_{St}^2 = 0$.

One important implication of this is that, while it is possible in practice to maintain an equality between the values of the implicit put and call options, it is not possible in practice to reduce this value to zero. Table 6.5 shows that, if the listed asset allocations are maintained for the whole investment horizon, the terminal surplus risk measured at the starting date of the plan will be very high. This leads to the call and put options taking values approaching 100 per cent of the value of the liabilities. Clearly no one would be prepared to buy these options separately, but, in combination, they provide a zero-cost option strategy that fully hedges the asset risk in the portfolio of assets, so long as the plan is fully funded. However, the absence of a market in long-term options means that in practice the reported asset allocations would not be maintained for the full investment horizon. What in practice tends to happen is that fund managers adopt the deterministic lifestyle investment strategy mentioned in the previous section. This is the only practical way of reducing the surplus risk and dealing with the problem of being a forced seller of volatile financial assets as the retirement date approaches.

In summary, we find that the investment strategy is another critical ingredient of the pension plan, and that it involves a complex set of trade-offs between contributions, asset allocation and asset risk. Conservative investment strategies will either lead to low pensions or require high compensating contribution rates. In contrast, a heavy equity component to the asset allocation will raise both the expected return on the portfolio and its risk: the first factor will have the effect of lowering the required contribution rate, while the second will raise surplus risk unless more conservative investment strategies are adopted as the retirement date approaches or the plan member is prepared to make additional contributions in the period just before retirement in the case where a deficiency emerges. These trade-offs are not well explained to plan members and, given the very high degree of risk aversion demonstrated by most of them, they will typically choose conservative investment strategies unsuited to a long-term investment horizon. Furthermore, none of the investment strategies discussed above specifically hedges interest rate (and annuity) risk on the retirement date: the main purpose of the deterministic life-styling strategy, for example, is to reduce exposure to equity risk on the retirement date. There is, in short, a complete disconnection in DC plans between the investment strategies of the accumulation and decumulation stages. But plan providers will be little concerned by any of this, since they have no contractual obligation to deliver a particular fund size on the retirement date.

6.5   INVESTMENT PERFORMANCE

Investment performance is critical to the size of the pension in the case of a DC plan. Even if the general investment strategy is suitable, the particular assets chosen by the fund manager can underperform and members of DC plans can find themselves locked into a poorly performing fund, facing very high costs of transferring to a better performing fund. In addition, the type of funds in which members invest can and do close down and then the assets have to be transferred to a different fund. In this section, we examine the investment performance of the two main classes of fund in which pension contributions are invested: unit-linked funds and managed funds.

6.5.1   The Investment Performance of Unit-linked Funds

The anticipated return from a high-risk investment is greater than from a low-risk investment, but there can be wide differences in realized returns, even for plans investing in the same risk class. Blake and Timmermann (1998) conducted a study of the investment performance of unit trusts (open-ended mutual funds) in the UK, one of the key investment vehicles for DC plans.[15] Table 6.6 shows the distribution of returns generated by unit trusts operating in the four largest sectors. These figures indicate enormous differences in performance, especially over the long life of a pension plan. For example, the 4.1 percentage point per annum difference between

Table 6.6   *Distribution of returns generated by UK unit-linked funds, 1972–95*

Sector	Top quartile	Median	Bottom quartile	Ratio of fund sizes
UK Equity Growth	16.0	13.6	11.9	3.2
UK Equity General	14.3	13.4	13.1	1.4
UK Equity Income	15.4	14.0	12.4	2.3
UK Smaller Companies	18.7	15.5	12.8	5.3

Note: The first three columns are averages measured in percentages per annum for the sample period 1972–95; the last column gives the ratio of fund sizes after 40 years, based on the top and bottom quartile returns. The formula is (assuming the same contribution stream):

$$\frac{(1+g_T)^T - 1}{g_T} \div \frac{(1+g_B)^T - 1}{g_B},$$

where $g_T = 0.160$, $g_B = 0.119$ and $T = 40$, etc.

Source: Blake and Timmermann (1998) and Lunde, Timmermann and Blake (1999).

the best and worst performing unit trusts in the UK Equity Growth sector leads, over a 40-year investment horizon, to the accumulated fund in the top quartile being a factor of 3.2 times larger than the accumulated fund in the bottom quartile for the same pattern of contributions. The 5.9 percentage point per annum difference between the best and worst performing unit trusts in the UK Smaller Companies sector leads to an even larger fund size ratio after 40 years, of 5.3.[16]

This suggests that DC plan members can find themselves trapped in poorly performing funds. But should it not be the case in an efficient capital market that systematically underperforming funds fail to survive and are taken over by more efficient fund managers? Lunde, Timmermann and Blake (1999) investigated this possibility. They found that underperforming trusts are eventually merged with more successful trusts, but that on average it takes some time for this to occur. Figure 6.7 shows the distribution of durations across the whole unit trust industry of trusts that were eventually wound up or merged. The modal duration is 4.25 years (51 months), but the average duration is about 16 years. Across the whole unit trust industry, the average return on funds that survived the whole period was 13.7 per cent per annum, while the average return on funds that were wound up or merged during the period was 11.3 per cent per annum. This implies that a typical DC plan member might find themself locked into an underperforming trust that is eventually wound up or merged into a more successful fund, experiencing an underperformance of 2.4 per cent p.a., over a 16-year period. This translates into a fund value that is 19 per cent lower after 16 years than a fund that is not wound up or merged. So it seems that, in practice, PPP members cannot rely on the markets to provide them with a painless way of extricating them from an underperforming fund. They have to do it themselves, paying up to one-quarter of the value of their accumulated fund in transfer costs.[17]

6.5.2   The Investment Performance of Managed Funds

The investment performance of managed funds between 1986 and 1994 has been investigated in Blake, Lehmann and Timmermann (BLT) (1999, 2002).[18] While the average or median performance has been very good over the sample period, the median return conceals a wide distribution of performance. This can be seen from Table 6.7, which shows the cross-sectional distribution of returns realized by the pension funds in the sample over the period 1986–94 in the most important individual asset classes as well as for the total portfolio. The semi-interquartile range is quite tight, below two percentage points for most asset classes, and only just over one percentage point for the total portfolio return. This suggests evidence of a possible

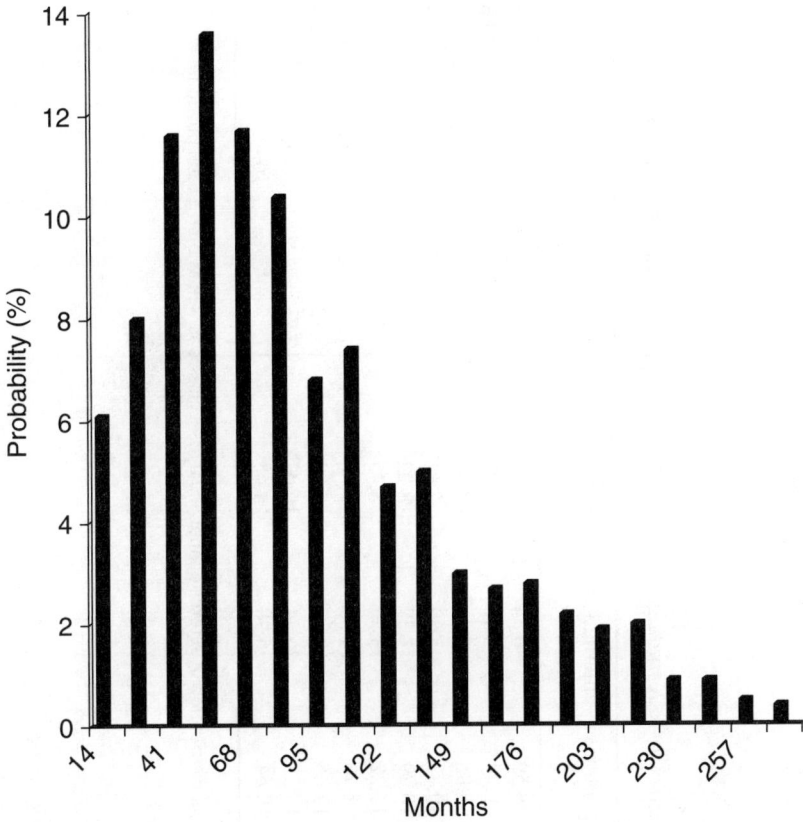

Note: The diagram shows the distribution of the lifetimes in months of the 973 unit trusts which were wound up or merged during sample period 1972–75.

Source: Lunde, Timmermann and Blake (1999, Table 1).

Figure 6.7 Frequency distribution of durations of UK unit trusts from inception

herding effect in the behaviour of pension fund managers, which can be explained by the fact that the reputation of fund managers is based on their *relative* performance against each other.[19] Nevertheless, the difference between the best and worst performing funds is very great, as the last row of Table 6.7 indicates.

Table 6.8 shows how well UK pension funds have performed in comparison with other participants in the market. The fourth column reveals that the average UK pension fund underperformed the market average by 0.45

Table 6.7   Fractiles of total returns by asset class for UK managed funds, 1986–94, average annualized percentages

	UK equities	International equities	UK bonds	International bonds	UK index bonds	Cash/other inv'mnts	UK property	Total
Minimum	8.59	4.42	6.59	–0.64	5.59	2.67	3.05	7.22
5%	11.43	8.59	9.44	2.18	7.20	5.46	5.07	10.60
10%	11.85	9.03	9.95	7.56	7.81	7.60	6.58	10.96
25%	12.44	9.64	10.43	8.30	7.91	8.97	8.03	11.47
50%	13.13	10.65	10.79	11.37	8.22	10.25	8.75	12.06
75%	13.93	11.76	11.22	13.37	8.45	11.72	9.99	12.59
90%	14.81	12.52	11.70	14.55	8.80	14.20	10.84	13.13
95%	15.46	13.14	12.05	18.15	8.89	16.13	11.36	13.39
Max	17.39	14.68	17.23	26.34	10.07	19.73	13.53	15.03
Max–Min	8.80	10.26	10.64	26.98	4.48	17.06	10.48	7.81

Note: The table shows the fractiles of the cross-sectional distribution of returns on individual asset classes as well as on the total portfolio.

Source: Blake, Lehmann and Timmermann (1998, Table 1).

Table 6.8   Performance of UK managed funds in comparison with the market, 1986–94 (percentages)

	Average portfolio weight (%)	Average market return (%)	Average pension fund return (%)	Average out-performance (%)	Percentage out-performers
UK equities	53.7	13.30	12.97	−0.33	44.8
International equities	19.5	11.11	11.23	0.12	39.8
UK bonds	7.6	10.35	10.76	0.41	77.3
International bonds	2.2	8.64	10.03	1.39	68.8
UK index bonds	2.7	8.22	8.12	−0.10	51.7
Cash/other investments	4.5	9.90	9.01	−0.89	59.5
UK property	8.9	9.00	9.52	0.52	39.1
Total		12.18	11.73	−0.45	42.8

Note: International property is excluded since no market index was available.

Source: Blake, Lehmann and Timmermann (1999, Table 2).

per cent per annum; and this is before the fund manager's fee is taken into account. Further, only 42.8 per cent of funds outperform the market average. The main explanation for this is the relative underperformance in UK equities, the largest single category with an average portfolio weighting of 54 per cent over the sample period; the average underperformance is −0.33 per cent per annum and only 44.8 per cent of UK occupational pension funds beat the average return on UK equities. To be sure, relative performance is better in other asset categories, especially UK and international bonds, but the portfolio weights in these asset categories are not large enough to counteract the relative underperformance in UK equities.

Tables 6.7 and 6.8 together indicate how close the majority of the pension funds are to generating the average market return. The median fund generated an average total return of 12.06 per cent per annum, just 12 basis points short of the average market return, and 80 per cent of the funds are within one percentage point of the average market return. This suggests that, despite their claim to be active fund managers, the vast majority of UK pension fund managers are not only herding together, they are also closet index matchers.[20]

The final result concerns the abilities of UK pension fund managers in active fund management; that is, in their attempts to beat the market in

Frontiers in pension finance

comparison with a passive buy and hold strategy. The most important task of managed fund managers is to establish and maintain the strategic asset allocation. This is essentially a 'passive' fund management strategy. However, fund managers claim that they can 'add value' through the 'active' management of their fund's assets. There are two aspects to active management: security selection (also known as stock selection) and market timing (also known as tactical asset allocation). Security selection involves the search for undervalued securities (that is, it involves the reallocation of funds within asset categories) and market timing involves the search for undervalued sectors (involving the reallocation of funds between sectors or asset categories).

BLT decomposed the average total return (12.034 per cent p.a.) generated by fund managers into the following components (see appendix):

Component	Percentage
Strategic asset allocation	99.47
Security selection	2.68
Market timing	−1.64
Other	−0.51
Total	100.00

They found that 99.47 per cent of the total return generated by UK fund managers can be explained by the passive strategic asset allocation. In terms of active components, the average pension fund was unsuccessful at market timing, generating a negative contribution to the total return of −1.64 per cent. The average pension fund was, however, more successful in security selection, making a positive contribution to the total return of 2.68 per cent. But the overall contribution of active fund management was just over 1 per cent of the total return (or about 12 basis points p.a.), which is *less than the annual fee that active fund managers charge* (which range between 20 basis points for a £500m fund to 75 basis points for a £10m fund).[21]

In summary, we find that, although investment performance is another critical determinant of the size of the pension in retirement, there is little evidence that fund managers as a group can systematically deliver superior investment performance over long investment horizons from active fund management.[22] There is, however, strong evidence of both herding and closet index matching. There are also problems with assessing investment performance. First, the performance of fund managers seems to be so highly concentrated around the peer-group median that performance rankings are uninformative, because very small changes in performance of only a few basis points by a particular fund manager would produce very considerable changes in the rankings, without indicating any substantive change in the skill of the fund manager. Equally, the small numbers of managers at the extremes of the distribution have such wide differences in performance between themselves that even quite major changes in performance by one of these managers would result in no change in the rankings. This suggests that a fund manager's current ranking is likely to provide a very poor indicator of both absolute and relative future performance. Secondly, the benchmark return against which fund managers are to be judged must be interpreted with considerable caution. To illustrate, one of the key benchmarks is the peer-group benchmark, but the peer group does not remain constant over time, as some managers will drop out (that is, fail to survive) while other new ones will join. This makes it difficult to construct a consistent time series for the benchmark. In the case of some performance measurement services, the information on non-surviving funds is actually removed from their database. Since the non-surviving funds will generally have had poor performance prior to their demise, their deletion from the database will raise the average benchmark performance[23] and make the remaining funds appear to have worse performance relative to the now biased benchmark than is actually the case. Blake and Timmermann (1998) estimated the resulting survivorship bias to be approximately 0.8 per cent per annum.[24] It is difficult to avoid the conclusion that most PPP members would be better off by investing in passive index funds and paying the much lower fund management fees that passive managers charge.

6.6 FUND ANNUITIZATION

Eventually, and certainly by age 75, in the UK, the full value of the assets owing to the plan member must be liquidated and the proceeds used to purchase a life annuity. Generally, some of the proceeds can be taken as a cash lump sum. In many countries, such as the US, Japan, Germany and Australia, there is no formal requirement to take an annuity: the entire proceeds from the DC plan can be taken as a lump sum. But unless the plan member uses the lump sum to buy an annuity at some stage, he or she bears another type of risk, namely longevity risk, the risk of outliving one's resources.[25]

DC plans will only be considered a success if they can deliver adequate life-long pensions in retirement. But there is a major impediment to the provision of decent pensions during the retirement phase itself, namely the annuity market. The principal vehicle for delivering DC pensions is an annuity purchased from a life assurance company. Even in economies with well-developed annuity markets, the market for immediate annuities is highly concentrated with, for example, only around 10 serious providers at any one time from a potential market of more than 200 authorized life companies in the UK.[26] In this section, we review the problems facing annuity providers.

6.6.1 The Problems Faced by Annuitants and Annuity Providers

There are a number of problems facing both annuitants and annuity providers. First, there is interest rate risk. Annuity rates vary substantially over the interest rate cycle. They are related to the yields on government bonds of the same expected term. Since historically the yields on long-term government bonds have varied by up to 150 per cent over the cycle,[27] we can expect annuity rates to vary by the same order of magnitude. Secondly, there is inflation risk, the risk faced by those purchasing level annuities that unanticipated high inflation rapidly reduces the real value of the pension.

Thirdly, there is an adverse selection bias associated with longevity risk. This is the risk that only individuals who believe that they are likely to live longer than the average for the population of the same age will voluntarily choose to purchase annuities. Individuals have a good idea, on the basis of both their own personal medical and family histories, whether they are likely to experience lighter or heavier mortality. Insurance companies do not have access to this information with the same degree of reliability. There is therefore an *informational asymmetry* between the insurance company offering the annuity and the prospective annuity purchaser. The insurance company is not able to differentiate between prospective purchasers who will experience heavier mortality (and so make a profit for the insurance company) and those who will experience lighter mortality (and hence make a loss for the insurance company); however, it realizes that those most likely to purchase annuities will come from the latter group rather than the former group. To hedge this risk, the insurance company will base its annuity rates on the 'select group' that is most likely to purchase annuities. Annuities will therefore be poor value for money for members of the first group.

Fourthly, mortality rates tend to improve over time and there can be severe financial consequences if insurance companies underestimate mortality improvements. Mortality forecasts errors of 15–20 per cent over 10-year horizons are not uncommon[28] and some insurance companies in the UK have underestimated the average life expectancy of their pool of annuitants by up to two years.[29]

Fifthly, there is reinvestment risk. This is the risk faced by annuity providers that there are insufficient long-maturing matching assets (especially government bonds) available to provide the annuity payments, with the consequence that the proceeds from maturing assets may have to be reinvested on less favourable terms.

Table 6.9 shows that insurance companies impose charges of between 10 and 20 per cent of the fund value to cover the risks that they face. It is possible to decompose the charges on annuities extracted by life companies into the following components using estimates derived by Finkelstein and Poterba (2002, hereafter FP): a component arising from the selection risk associated with the type of people who purchase annuities, a component arising from the additional risk associated with the type of people who purchase annuities in the voluntary market, a component arising from escalation risk, and a component that covers administration costs and profit to the insurance company. It is also possible to identify a size effect, an age effect and a sex effect.

The basis for FP's analysis is the *money's worth of an annuity* which is defined as the ratio of the expected present value (*EPV*) to the premium, where the *EPV* is defined as:

$$EPV = \sum_{t=1}^{T} \frac{Y(1+\pi)^t P_t}{\prod_{k=1}^{t} (1+r_k)} \times 100, \qquad (6.18)$$

where:

$Y =$ Nominal initial annuity payment,
$\pi =$ Escalation factor (zero for level annuity),
$r_k =$ Nominal spot yield for year k derived from the government bond spot yield curve,
$T =$ Maximum length of pension based on the assumption that no one lives beyond age 112, and
$P_t =$ Probability that the annuitant survives t years.

FP derive estimates of (6.18) based on three different sets of single-life mortality tables: the population mortality tables provided by the UK Government Actuary's Department, and the mortality tables for voluntary and compulsory annuitants provided by the Institute of Actuaries. The latter two sets of tables are the IM80 and IF80 tables for voluntary purchase male and female life annuities and the PM80 and PF80 tables for the compulsory purchase male and female life annuities that must be bought when someone retires from a PPP. These tables are based on the mortality experience of these two select groups during the period 1979–82 and have been adjusted to account for mortality improvements since that period.

Table 6.9   Decomposition of charges in annuities with £10 000 purchase price

	Level		Escalating at 5%	
	Compulsory	Voluntary	Compulsory	Voluntary
Male aged 65				
Initial annuity payment (£)	879.70	844.40	550.20	522.90
Total implied charge (%)[a]	10.3	13.5	14.2	19.6
composed of:				
volunteer premium (%)[b]	—	4.2	—	6.5
escalation premium (%)[c]	—	—	2.2	2.3
selection premium (%)[d]	4.7	4.6	6.4	6.1
administration cost and profit[e]	5.6	4.7	5.6	4.7
Size premium:[g]				
£10 000 to £50 000	−1.3	NA	NA	NA
£50 000 to £100 000	0.2	NA	NA	NA
Male aged 70				
Initial annuity payment (£)	1036.10	992.80	703.70	670.40
Total implied charge (%)[a]	13.1	16.3	17.1	21.4
composed of:				
volunteer premium (%)[b]	—	6.6	—	8.9
escalation premium (%)[c]	—	—	2.6	1.6
selection premium (%)[d]	4.7	4.6	6.1	5.8
administration cost and profit[e]	8.4	5.1	8.4	5.1
Age premium[f]	0.0	2.4	0.1	1.4
Size premium:[g]				
£10 000 to £50 000	−0.6	NA	NA	NA
£50 000 to £100 000	0.3	NA	NA	NA
Female aged 65				
Initial annuity payment (£)	768.50	727.60	445.4	420.3
Total implied charge (%)[a]	9.9	14.7	14.1	20.7
composed of:				
volunteer premium (%)[b]	—	3.2	—	4.7
escalation premium (%)[c]	—	—	3.1	3.5
selection premium (%)[d]	1.9	1.9	3.0	2.9
administration cost and profit[e]	8.0	9.6	8.0	9.6
Size premium:[g]				
£10 000 to £50 000	−1.4	NA	NA	NA
£50 000 to £100 000	0.5	NA	NA	NA

Table 6.9   (continued)

	Level		Escalating at 5%	
	Compulsory	Voluntary	Compulsory	Voluntary
Female aged 70				
Initial annuity payment (£)	885.20	843.50	560.80	532.10
Total implied charge (%)[a]	12.7	16.7	17.2	22.4
composed of:				
volunteer premium (%)[b]	—	4.5	—	5.9
escalation premium (%)[c]	—	—	3.4	3.4
selection premium (%)[d]	1.8	1.8	2.9	2.7
administration cost and profit[e]	10.9	10.4	10.9	10.4
Age premium[f]	−0.1	1.2	0.2	0.9
Size premium:[g]				
£10 000 to £50 000	−1.0	NA	NA	NA
£50 000 to £100 000	0.6	NA	NA	NA

Notes:
[a]   The difference between an actuarially fair annuity (100%) and the money's worth of the annuity using the population mortality table (e.g. 100–89.7 for the level compulsory annuity for a 65-year-old male).
[b]   For voluntary annuities only, the difference between the money's worth of the annuity using the voluntary mortality table and the money's worth using the compulsory mortality table (e.g. 95.3–91.1 for the level voluntary annuity for a 65-year-old male).
[c]   For escalating annuities only, the difference between the money's worths of the level and escalating annuities, both evaluated using the own-market mortality table (e.g. 94.2–92.2 for the compulsory annuity for a 65-year-old male).
[d]   The difference between the money's worth of the annuity using the own-market mortality table and the money's worth using the population mortality table (e.g. 94.4–89.7 for the level compulsory annuity for a 65-year-old male).
[e]   The difference between the total implied charge and the sum of the volunteer, escalation and selection premiums.
[f]   The difference between the sums of the volunteer, escalation and selection premiums at age 70 and 65.
[g]   The difference in money's worth between the lower and higher valued annuities, both evaluated using population mortality tables (e.g. 89.7–91.0 for the £10 000 and £50 000 annuities for a 65-year-old male).

Source: Author's calculations based on the averages from a sample of nine insurance companies reported in Tables 2, 7 and 12 of Finkelstein and Poterba (2002).

If an annuity is fairly priced, its money's worth should be 100 per cent. In practice, though, it will be less than this because of the charge components outlined above. FP use data provided by Moneyfacts and Annuity Direct for November 1998: they analyse the money's worth of an immediate single-life annuity with monthly payments and a premium of £10 000. Their decomposition is presented in Table 6.9.

Take, for example, the case of a 65-year-old male and a level annuity. This pays £879.70 in the compulsory purchase market and £844.40 in the voluntary open market, the difference reflecting the greater life expectancy of those who purchase annuities on a voluntary basis over those who are required to do so as part of their pension plan (we denote this component of charges the 'volunteer premium'). The total implied charge is 10.3 per cent of the purchase price in the compulsory market and 13.5 per cent in the voluntary market. This is found as follows: calculate (6.18) using the population mortality table with $Y = £879.70$ for the compulsory annuity and £844.40 for the voluntary annuity and divide this by the purchase price (£10 000) to give the money's worth, which is then subtracted from 100 per cent. Using population mortality data to calculate (6.18) is equivalent to assuming the longevity experience of a typical member of the population as a whole.

If, using population mortality, the money's worth is below 100 per cent, this implies that there are additional longevity risks associated with the select group of the population who purchase annuities. We quantify these additional risks as follows. The 'selection premium' covers the additional longevity risk of someone who purchases an annuity in comparison with a typical member of the population at large of the same sex and age. The selection premium associated with compulsory annuities is 4.7 per cent: it is measured as the difference in money's worths calculated using (6.18) based on compulsory mortality tables and (6.18) based on population mortality tables. So even though members of PPPs have no choice about whether or not to buy an annuity, they, as a group, experience sufficiently lighter mortality than the population as a whole, that insurance companies need to charge 65-year-old men a premium of 4.7 per cent to cover this additional risk. The selection premium with voluntary annuities is, at 4.6 per cent, of a similar order of magnitude.

Since those who buy annuities voluntarily experience even lighter mortality than PPP members, insurance companies charge such purchasers an additional volunteer premium. This is calculated as the difference between the money's worth in the voluntary market using the voluntary mortality table and the money's worth in the voluntary market using the compulsory mortality table. For a 65-year-old male, the volunteer premium is 4.2 per cent.

The table also reports evidence of a size effect in annuity provision and two countervailing influences are apparent. The first is a scale effect: the cost of administering an annuity is independent of its size, so that insurance companies should be willing to pass scale economies on to high-valued plan members. The table shows that this happens, although evidence is only available on compulsory level annuities: the charge is 1.3 percentage points lower for a 65-year-old man when the purchase price is £50 000 than when it is £10 000. The second effect is a wealth effect: richer people tend to live longer than poorer people, and this should be reflected in a higher longevity premium. This effect begins to dominate the scale effect on annuities over £50 000: there is a small increase in charges of 0.2 percentage points as the plan size rises from £50 000 to £100 000.

We can assess the importance of the age effect by comparing these results with those relating to a male aged 70. There are two factors to consider: an older man has on average fewer remaining years of life than a younger man, but, because he has survived to a greater age than the younger man he has greater total life expectancy. The first factor will result in a higher annuity for the older man than for the younger man, but this will be partly counteracted by the second factor: the risk that an annuitant will live a very long time increases with the age at which he purchases the annuity. The second panel of the table shows that a 70-year-old man receives an annuity that is 18 per cent higher than that for a 65-year-old man in both the compulsory and voluntary level markets. However, the total charges for the 70-year-old are nearly three percentage points higher in each market. The selection premium remains the same in both markets, but the volunteer premium is 2.4 percentage points higher. We can interpret the figure of 2.4 per cent as the 'age premium' and note that, in the case of 65-year-old men, the age premium is present only in the voluntary market, not the compulsory market. A size effect is also present, although the orders of magnitude differ slightly in comparison with the 65-year-old male.

The final effect that we can identify is a sex effect: women tend to live longer than men and this is reflected in the size of the annuity they are offered for a given premium. A 65-year-old women receives a level annuity that is 13–14 per cent lower than that of a 65-year old man, while a 70-year-old woman receives broadly the same annuity as a 65-year-old man. The level and pattern of charges differs, however. The total charge for men is generally higher than for women in the compulsory market, but lower in the voluntary market. Both the selection and volunteer premiums are lower for women than for men. There is a positive age premium in the voluntary market, but at 1.2 per cent it is only half that for men, while in the compulsory market, the age premium is negative (-0.1 per cent): the age premium is the difference between the sums of the volunteer, selection and escalation premiums at age

70 and 65 years, respectively. The wealth component of the size effect is larger for women than for men (0.5 compared with 0.2 at age 65 and 0.6 compared with 0.3 at age 70).

The initial annuity payment with a 5 per cent escalating annuity is 37 per cent lower than for a level annuity for a 65-year-old man in the compulsory market and 38 per cent lower in the voluntary market. It takes six years for the escalating annuity to catch up with the level annuity and 13 years before the total cash payments under the two policies are equalized. In the case of a 65-year-old woman, the initial payment from the escalating annuity is 42 per cent lower for both the compulsory and voluntary markets. It takes around seven years for the two cash amounts to equalize and a further eight years before the total cash payments equalize.

The total implied charge is higher for escalating annuities than for level annuities. This is because both the volunteer and selection premiums are higher and there is an additional 'escalation premium' to take into account. The escalation premium covers a type of longevity risk that arises from the backloading of payments with escalating annuities: if the annuitant lives longer than anticipated, the additional payments will be rising with the escalating annuity but remain constant with the level annuity. It is calculated as the difference between the money's worths of the level and escalating annuities, each evaluated using own-market mortality tables. The escalation premium varies between 1.6 and 2.6 per cent for men and between 3.1 and 3.5 per cent for women.

To illustrate in the case of a 65-year-old man, the volunteer premium is 6.5 per cent with the escalating annuity and 4.2 per cent with the level annuity. The selection premium is 6.4 per cent compared with 4.7 per cent in the compulsory market and 6.1 per cent compared with 4.6 per cent in the voluntary market. In comparison, with a 65-year-old woman, the volunteer premium is 4.7 per cent with the escalating annuity and 3.2 per cent with the level annuity. The selection premium is 3.0 per cent compared with 1.9 per cent in the compulsory market and 2.9 per cent compared with 1.9 per cent in the voluntary market. The age premium is smaller for both men and women in the compulsory market (at 0.1 per cent and 0.2 per cent, respectively) than in the voluntary market (at 1.4 per cent and 0.9 per cent, respectively).

The allowance for administration costs and profit is calculated as the difference between the total implied charge and the sum of the volunteer, escalation and selection premiums. We find that compulsory annuities are generally more profitable than voluntary annuities, reflecting the fact that the compulsory market is a captive one, that female annuities are more profitable than male annuities and that the profit margin rises with age, especially in the compulsory market.

6.6.2 How Annuitants and Insurance Companies Currently Deal with these Problems

Insurance companies use the government (and high grade corporate) bond market to protect themselves against both interest rate and inflation risk arising *after* the annuity is purchased. When an insurance company sells a level annuity, it uses the proceeds to buy a fixed-income government bond of the same expected term as the annuity (typically 15–17 years) and then makes the annuity payments from the coupon payments received on the bond. Similarly, when an insurance company sells an indexed annuity, it buys an index-linked bond of the same expected term as the annuity; few if any insurance companies would take the risk of selling indexed annuities with expected maturities beyond that of the most distant trading indexed-linked government bond, although the emergence of an inflation swaps market is beginning to change this.

But annuitants themselves remain exposed to interest and inflation risk. If a DC plan member retires during an interest rate trough (as happened during the late 1990s and early 2000s in the UK, for example), he or she can end up with a very low pension. Similarly, if a 65-year-male old annuitant chooses a 5 per cent escalating annuity, he will receive an initial cash sum that is about 37 per cent lower than a level annuity, and it would take six years for the escalating annuity to exceed the level annuity. Since retired people also tend to underestimate how long they will continue to live,[30] most prefer to buy a level annuity and thereby retain the inflation risk. In 1995, as a result of falling interest rates, the UK Government was pressed into allowing income drawdown (also known as systematic withdrawal): it became possible to delay the drawing of an annuity until annuity rates improved (or until the age of 75) and in the interim take an income from the fund which remained fully invested.

So insurance companies use the financial markets (in particular they make use of financial instruments issued by the government, namely fixed-income and index-linked bonds) to hedge the interest and inflation rate risks that they face from the date that the annuity is purchased. But the interest rate risk up to the date of retirement is borne by the future annuitant, and the inflation risk after the retirement date is also borne by the annuitant unless he or she is willing to forgo a substantial cash sum at the start of retirement as a consequence of purchasing an indexed annuity. The longevity risk and the risk associated with underestimating improvements in mortality appear to be shared between insurance companies and annuitants: despite adding substantial cost loadings of 10–20 per cent to cover these risks, most insurance companies in the UK do not actively seek annuity business.

In summary, we find that annuities form the weak tail in DC pension provision. Not only do they involve substantial charges to cover longevity risk, some key risks, such as interest rate risk, are borne directly by the annuitant himself (as the forced purchaser of an annuity on the retirement date unless income drawdown is used) and the insurance industry has been particularly unimaginative in designing products that hedge such predictable risks.

6.7   IMPROVING THE DESIGN OF DC PENSION PLANS

If we add together the 30 per cent of fund value accounted for by charges during the accumulation stage for a typical plan (see Table 6.2) with the 10–20 per cent charge on annuities (see Table 6.9), we arrive at a figure for lifetime pension charges of between 40 and 50 per cent of the total fund size. That is an extraordinarily high proportion and is likely to lead to DC plans eventually falling into disrepute if it cannot be reduced. Apart from charges, there are also problems with lapses, investment strategy, investment performance, fund annuitization and provider incentives. There are also market failures which the government could help ameliorate. In this section, we examine ways of dealing with these issues, some of which are interrelated.

6.7.1   Charges, Investment Performance and Incentives

High charges and poor investment performance can both separately and together lead to the plan member having a low fund to annuitize on the retirement date. However, some people have argued that some of these factors can be offsetting. For example, one argument often put forward by pension professionals is that high charges can be justified by good investment performance. One provider's charges might be higher than another's because it has employed better (and more expensive) fund managers, but if this is more than matched by superior investment performance, then the net benefit to the customer could still be positive.

There are problems with this argument. The findings above suggest that there is a limit to how much superior performance could compensate for very high charges: a *RiY* of 20 per cent as a result of high charges, for example, is likely to swamp any realistic degree of superior performance that could be achieved. In addition, as Table 6.7 showed, the bulk of funds generate returns that are very close to each other. The difference between the best and worst funds is indeed large, but the difference between the fifth and ninety-fifth percentile of funds is quite small. As we have already argued, this means that most rankings will be very sensitive to small variations in market conditions and these variations in rankings will be economically insignificant. It is therefore very unlikely that any measure of expected superior performance would be sufficiently robust to differentiate clearly between two middle-ranked firms.

However, the greatest difficulty with this argument is that it would require estimates of *expected* superior performance (that is, alpha) over the remaining investment horizon of the plan, rather than *past* superior performance. Unfortunately, there is no way in which expected performance can be reliably estimated. Modern finance theory (as well as the empirical evidence reported above) suggests that, in an efficient financial system, it is impossible to achieve consistently superior net investment performance. While there may be differences in the academic literature about the degree of financial market efficiency at the margin, there is no academic support for the proposition that an institutional investor is able to obtain consistently superior investment performance over extended periods of time, after taking into account risk and transactions (that is, research and trading) costs. Similarly, while in any given period, some investors will perform better than the average and others will perform worse, there is nothing in the academic literature to suggest that any outperformance will persist over any extended period.

Table 6.10 provides empirical evidence that is consistent with this theoretical view. It shows the consistency of performance for each of three non-overlapping five-year periods achieved by a large number of UK managed

Table 6.10 *Consistency of managed funds' investment performance (percentages)*

Years above average	Total fund				UK equities				Chance
	1980–84	1985–89	1992–96	Mean	1980–84	1985–89	1992–96	Mean	
5	3	3	5	4	2	5	5	4	3
4	25	18	17	20	14	18	21	18	16
3	26	28	28	27	35	26	28	30	31
2	25	34	35	34	31	27	24	30	31
1	15	14	13	11	15	18	15	13	16
0	6	3	2	4	3	6	5	5	3

Notes: The table shows the percentage of firms achieving the given number of years of above average performance during each five-year period. The final column shows the percentages that would be expected if fund performance was purely random.

Source: CAPS *General Reports*, 1985, 1989, 1996.

funds. The table reveals that, across all three periods, only 4 per cent of funds managed to achieve consistently above-average performance in each of the five years, while another 4 per cent of funds underperformed in each of the five years. About half the funds had superior performance in three or more years and about half had below-average performance in three or more years. Comparing these figures with those in the final column confirms that this distribution is almost exactly what would be expected if above- (or below-) average performance arose entirely by chance in each year. This pattern is found consistently in each of the three five-year periods and is not affected by whether the investments considered are UK equities or more broadly based portfolios. Similar results have been found for UK unit trusts for periods in excess of three years.

Other studies did find some evidence that consistency of performance was possible, particularly in the top and bottom quartiles, but only over very short horizons. For example, Blake, Lehmann and Timmermann (1999) found that, in the case of managed pension funds, UK equity managers in the top quartile of performance in one year had a 37 per cent chance of being in the top quartile the following year, rather than the 25 per cent that would have been expected if relative performance arose purely by chance. Similarly, there was a 32 per cent chance of the UK equity managers in the bottom quartile for one year being in the bottom quartile the following year. There was also evidence of consistency in performance in the top and bottom quartiles for cash/other investments, with probabilities of remaining in these quartiles the following year of 35 per cent in each case. However, there was no evidence of consistency in performance for any other asset category or for the portfolio as a whole. Nor was there evidence of any consistency in performance over longer horizons than one year in any asset category or for the whole portfolio. Lunde, Timmermann and Blake (1999) found similar results for unit trusts: for example, a unit trust specializing in UK equity which was in the top quartile in one year had a 33 per cent chance of remaining in the top quartile the following year, while there was a 36 per cent chance of a trust remaining in the bottom quartile for two consecutive years. Thus the evidence is consistent with the suggestion that so-called 'hot hands' in investment performance is a very short-term phenomenon and that fund managers are unable to produce superior performance over extended periods.[31][32]

The evidence in Section 5 above does, however, allow the rather limited suggestion that *gross* superior performance is possible, but *only* at the expense of matching higher investment costs.[33] Furthermore, the academic argument behind this view that *net* returns to investors will be the same whether or not they engage in costly research is powerful[34] and implies that assuming that particular funds will outperform (net of risk and transactions costs) in the future, even if they have outperformed temporarily in the past, could not be justified.

So, if there is no relationship between the level of charges and performance, there seems to be little alternative but to keep charges low. The best way of achieving this is for the regulatory authority to cap charges and to allow penalty-free transfers between plans, thereby forcing economies of scale on plan providers. This is what the UK Government introduced for Stakeholder Pension Plans in 2001 and what the UK Pensions Commission has proposed and the UK Government has accepted for the new system of Personal Accounts for low-income workers.[35]

Is there a relationship between charging structures and performance? The RiY and RiC are two measures that were discussed above for reporting charges. But they do not have any implications for whether it is better for the incidence of charges to be on contributions or on fund value. There is no reason why a fund could not have a simple fee based solely on contributions made. However, there is an important implication with a charging structure that is based solely on contributions: the total (compounded) charge (the take) as a proportion of the zero-load terminal fund value is independent of the realized return on investments. This is not the case if the charging structure is based on the fund value: the percentage take rises if the realized return exceeds the assumed or projected return (for example, 9 per cent) and falls if the realized return is below this. To illustrate, in the case of the 25-year plan discussed in Section 2.3, and either a fund-based charge of 1.7 per cent of the annual fund value or a contribution-based charge of 23.18 per cent of each contribution, the percentage take varies with the realized investment return as follows:

Realized return (%)	5	6	7	8	9	10	11	12	13
Fund-based charges	20.81	21.5	22.09	22.64	23.18	23.68	24.16	24.61	25.03
Contribution-based charges	23.18	23.18	23.18	23.18	23.18	23.18	23.18	23.18	23.18

If a plan has the bulk of its charges based on the fund value, this provides a strong statement about the plan provider's own perception of his ability to deliver investment performance in excess of the assumed or projected rate. It is this argument that appears to have persuaded the UK Government to have only fund-based charges for SPPs and for the Pensions Commission to recommend the same for the new system of Personal Accounts (with a target of 30 basis points per annum of assets under management).

Certainly a charging structure based on a single proportionate charge on fund value would be much easier for consumers to understand. More importantly, a single charge would eliminate the front-loading of current charging structures that does so much damage to the net returns of plan members with low persistency rates. In doing so, it provides better incentives for providers to ensure that the plans they sell meet the genuine needs of their clients: company takes increase considerably if plan members maintain their contribution records.

At the same time, however, a single proportionate charge based on fund value provides, at best, only weak incentives to deliver superior investment performance. While fund managers receive higher fee incomes if they generate higher fund values, earning greater returns usually involves taking on greater risk, the result of which could be very poor performance relative to other fund managers, and this would be damaging for reputations. Thus, with charges based on fund values, the additional return that could be expected from choosing an active investment strategy that differed substantially from that of the median fund manager is unlikely to compensate for the risk of ending up in the fourth quartile and the resulting loss of reputation. The outcome is herding of both investment behaviour and performance, not only around the median fund manager, but also around the index.

One way to provide appropriate incentives to those fund managers who believe that they can generate superior investment performance (although there is strong evidence that they will be unable to do so consistently over time) is to use performance-related investment management fees. In one example of this, the fee is determined as some proportion, f_1, of the difference between the fund's realized performance and some benchmark, $g^{\#}$ (possibly the regulator's 9 per cent), plus a fee, f_2, to cover the fund manager's overhead costs based on the absolute value of the fund (V_t):

$$\text{Performance-related fee in period } t = f_1(g_t - g^{\#})V_t + f_2V_t. \quad (6.19)$$

This would reward good ex post performance and penalize poor ex post performance, whatever promises about superior ex ante performance had been made by the fund: the fund would have to accept a reduced fee or even pay back the client if g_t was sufficiently below $g^{\#}$ (although the latter case generally involves credits against future fees rather than cash refunds).

Another possibility that is less extreme since it does not involve refunds is:

$$\text{Performance-related fee in period } t = f_i V_t, \quad (6.20)$$

where f_i is the fee if the fund manager's return is in the *ith* quartile. An example of (6.20) is the Newton Managed Fund:

Quartile rank	Up to £10m	Fund size £10–£50m	Above £50m
1st	0.94 per cent	0.59	0.04
2nd	0.79	0.44	0.03
Median	0.69	0.34	0.02
3rd	0.59	0.24	0.01
4th	0.44	0.09	0.01

Figure 6.8 presents the frequency distribution for this fee structure for a fund in the range £10–50m and a 25-year investment horizon, based on a monte carlo simulation with 1000 replications from a distribution of returns that is assumed to be normal with a nominal mean return of 9 per cent p.a. and standard deviation of 18 per cent.[36] The 90 per cent confidence interval for the fees lies between 0.22 and 0.45 per cent p.a., while there is a 25 per cent chance that the fee will exceed 0.37 per cent p.a. and a similar chance that it will be less than 0.31 per cent.

With front-loaded charging structures in the early years of a pension plan, the gap between high and low charges is, in the words of a former industry regulator, 'too great to be closed by superior performance. By year 10, over half of plan holders will have lapsed, and for them, charges will have been the key factor in their relative returns. Holders of high-charge plans who persist longer might be lucky enough to have performances that close charge gaps, but equally such gaps might be widened by poor performance'.[37]

The best way to reduce the probability of this occurring as well as providing the appropriate incentives for promoting the long-term commitment from both plan sponsors and members needed to deliver an adequate pension in retirement is to have charging structures that are simple, fully transparent, non-front-loaded and performance-related.

6.7.2 High Lapse Rates

The UK government is trying to deal with the problem of high lapse rates for its new system of Personal Accounts by using auto-enrolment, and there have also been some recent successes in the US with the 'save more tomorrow' pension plans introduced by Thaler and Benartzi (2004).

The government could also help to reduce lapse rates during the accumulation stage by making participation in second-pillar pension plans, such as PPPs, mandatory. There is a growing body of support for mandatory contributions into second pensions, including Field and Owen (1993), Borrie (1994), World Bank (1994), Dahrendorf (1995) and Anson (1996), as well

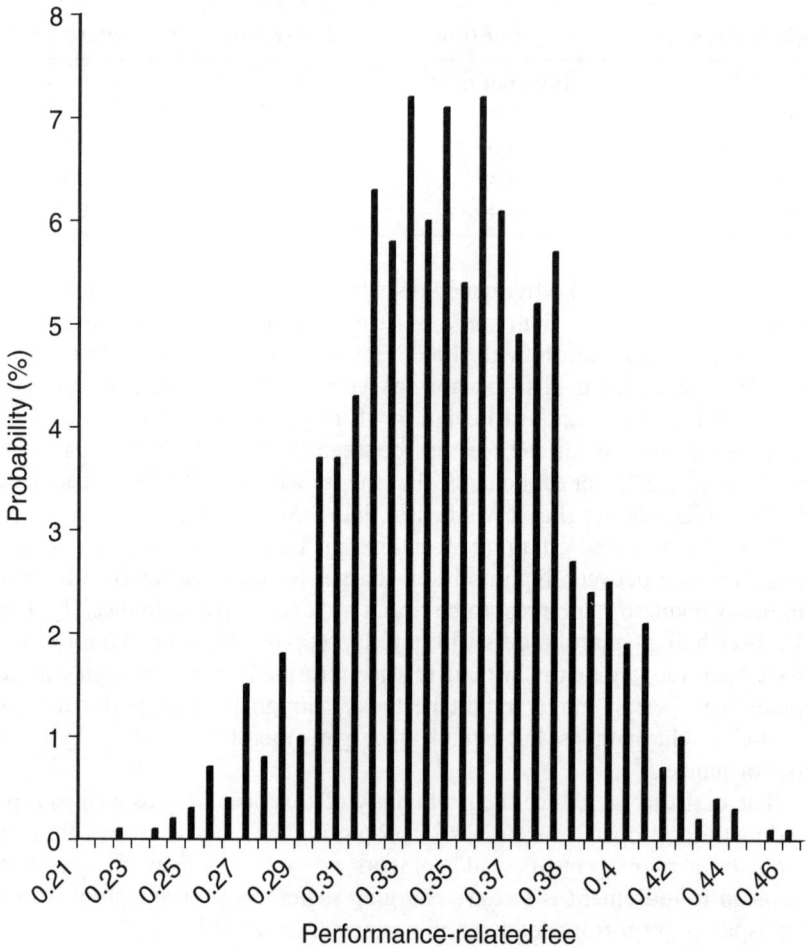

Note: The diagram shows the distribution of 1000 monte carlo simulations of performance-related fees (as an annual percentage of the fund value) in the Newton Managed Fund.

Figure 6.8 Frequency distribution of performance-related fees

as surveys of customers conducted by NatWest Bank and Coopers & Lybrand (reported in Field (1996, pp. 52–3)). Compulsory contributions are seen as one way of dealing with individual myopia and/or procrastination and the problem of moral hazard. The first issue arises because individuals either do not recognize the need and/or do not have the will power to make adequate provision for retirement when they are young: see Mitchell and

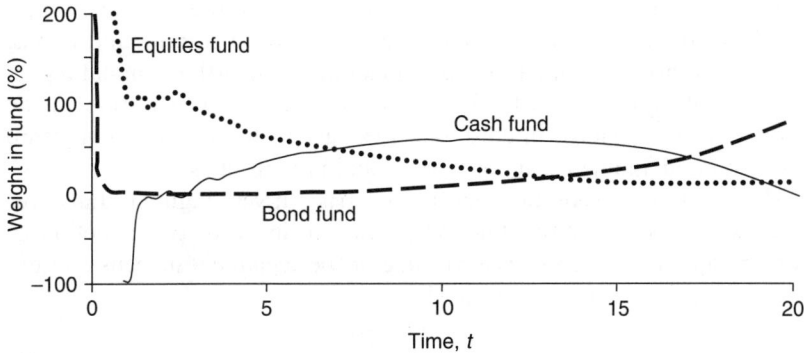

Source: Cairns et al. (2006, Fig. 5).

Figure 6.9   Stochastic life-styling

Utkus (2004). The latter problem arises when individuals deliberately avoid saving for retirement when they are young because they know the state will feel obliged not to let them live in dire poverty in retirement.

6.7.3   Investment Management and Annuitisation

The fund management industry has a poor track record of offering products that help PPP members hedge the risks that they are forced to assume. Yet there are strategies and instruments capable of doing this. One such strategy is 'stochastic life-styling' (see Cairns et al., 2006). This is an investment management strategy that hedges productivity risk and inflation risk during the accumulation stage and interest rate and annuity risk at the point of retirement. Three mutual funds are needed to implement the strategy: an equities fund, a bond fund and a T-bill or cash fund. Figure 6.9 depicts the optimal investment strategy for a plan member with $R_A = 6$ who starts his plan 20 years before retirement. The initial investment in the equities fund is very high, with an asset allocation well in excess of 100 per cent. The explanation for this is that a young plan member will be endowed with a large amount of human capital (the present value of expected future labour income which itself is risky owing to uncertainty concerning productivity growth over time), but will typically have a low amount of financial wealth. So, if they treat their human capital as an asset, young PPP members have very unbalanced and undiversified investment portfolios. In order to correct this, young members could use their pension plan to borrow cash and invest in financial assets, such as equities and bonds. The purpose of the equities fund is to hedge productivity shocks and to benefit from the equity risk premium. The purpose of the cash fund is first to finance the initial very high leveraged positions in equities and bonds, and then to hedge the inflation risk in labour income (the nominal return on cash will adjust to reflect inflationary expectations). The purpose of the bond fund is to hedge interest rate risk, given the inverse relationship between bond and hence annuity prices and interest rates.

The weight in the equities fund (q_{Et}) starts out very high, but falls over time as the accumulation stage progresses in line with the depletion of human capital and the increase in value of the accumulating pension fund (see Cairns et al., 2006, equation 25):

$$q_{Et} = \frac{V_t + PV_t}{R_A V_t}, \tag{6.21}$$

where PV_t is the present value of future contributions into the plan which, with a constant contribution rate, will be proportional to the present value of future labour income and hence human capital. Over time, PV_t will fall and V_t will (typically) rise and so q_{Et} falls over time. Towards the end of the accumulation stage, as annuity risk becomes a more important risk to hedge than inflation risk, the weight in the bond fund rises (q_{Bt}) and the weight in cash fund (q_{Ct}) falls:

$$q_{Bt} = \frac{(R_A - 1)(V_t + PV_t)e^{-K(T-t)}}{R_A V_t} \tag{6.22}$$

$$q_{Ct} = -\frac{PV_t}{V_t} + \frac{(R_A - 1)(V_t + PV_t)(1 - e^{-K(T-t)})}{R_A V_t}, \tag{6.23}$$

where T is the retirement date and K measures the speed of adjustment of interest rates when out of long-run equilibrium. Since both V_t and PV_t evolve stochastically over time, so will q_{Et}, q_{Bt} and q_{Ct}, hence the name of the strategy: 'stochastic lifestyling'. Note that the three funds can be index funds, that is, they do not need to be actively managed.

Annuity risk can be hedged in other ways. The simplest strategy is a planned programme of phased annuity purchases, using the principle of dollar cost averaging. This strategy could be used as a cheaper alternative to the lifestyle investment strategy mentioned above: rather than switching out of equities into bonds, the proceeds from selling the equities could be used to buy deferred annuities during the switchover period prior to retirement (see Horneff et al., 2006). A more sophisticated form of pre-retirement planning is protected annuity funds which employ derivative instruments. One example places a fraction (such as 95 per cent) of the funds on deposit and the rest in call options on bond futures contracts: if interest rates fall during the life of the option, the profit on the options will compensate for the reduced interest rate. Another example places a fraction of the funds in bonds and the rest in call options on an equity index, thereby gaining from any rise in the stock market over the life of the options.

The investment strategy during the decumulation phase can also be improved. Most PPP members in the UK purchase a level (that is, non-index-linked) annuity on their retirement date. This locks them into a bond-like investment for the remainder of their lives, which could be in excess of 20 years. Further, this 'investment' dies when they die, since it is not possible to bequeath an annuity when the annuitant dies.

Blake et al. (2003) considered some alternatives to the standard annuity that allows some investment flexibility. These investment-linked decumulation programmes come in two variations: (a) an income drawdown (or systematic withdrawal) variation, in which an income is drawn from the pension fund (which otherwise remains invested in higher return assets such as equities) with the residual fund paid as a bequest to the plan member's estate if he dies before age 75,[38] and (b) an annuity variation, in which the residual fund reverts to the insurer, in return for which the insurer agrees to pay a survival credit at the start of each year while the plan member is still alive:

- *Flexible income programme* with a life annuity purchased at age 75: each year an income is drawn from a managed fund equal to the annuitization value of the pension fund. If the fund falls in value, the income received has to fall in tandem, so there is some volatility to the annuity in contrast with a level annuity. But since the pension from a level annuity is based on the yield on government bonds, it is likely that the pension from an investment-linked programme such as this, based as it is on the return on equities, will generate a higher overall income, assuming the plan member lives long enough.
- *Flexible income programme with a deferred annuity* purchased at retirement age and payable at age 75: in this case the plan member purchases a deferred annuity at age 65 which will provide an income from age 75 equal to that which would be payable at that age from an immediate annuity bought at age 65. He invests the remaining monies at age 65 in a managed fund. He then draws an income from the fund on the same basis as the flexible income programme above, up to age 75 when the deferred annuity comes into payment. On death before age 75, the value of the deferred annuity policy is lost. It is cheaper to purchase at age 65 a deferred annuity that comes into payment at age 75 than to wait to purchase the annuity at age 75; this is because there is some chance that the purchaser will not live long enough to

receive the annuity payments and this is reflected in the deferred annuity price.

- *Unit-linked programme* with a life annuity purchased at age 75: in this case, the plan member uses his retirement fund to purchase a fixed number of units in a managed fund at age 65. The number of units received will depend on the forecasts for mortality made at age 65. Each year a number of units are sold and the plan member's income will change in line with changes in the price of these units. At age 75, assuming he lives that long, he uses the residual fund to purchase a life annuity. The outcome will be similar to that of the flexible income programme described above, and identical in the case where a survival credit is payable. In the US, they are known as variable annuities.[39]

- *Collared income programme* with a life annuity purchased at age 75: this programme is similar to the flexible income programme, but involves a smoothing out of investment returns. Instead of investing solely in a managed portfolio, the fund invests in a mixed portfolio of equities and put and call options with the aim of achieving significant protection against downside equity risk. For each unit of equity held, the portfolio is long one at-the-money put option and short one call option. The strike price of the call option is chosen so that the prices of the put and call options are equal. This means that the net cost of the resulting collar is zero. As a result, we have 100 per cent participation in equity returns subject to the cap and floor. This is one way of selling some of the upside potential to pay for downside protection. The resulting smoothing of investment returns is similar in some respects to a with-profits policy, although in the present case the smoothing method is much more explicit.

- *Floored income programme* with a life annuity purchased at age 75: like the collared income programme, this programme involves forgoing some upside potential to pay for downside protection. The plan member is guaranteed to get a minimum return of zero (that is, holds an implicit at-the-money put option), and pays for this by selling off a proportion of the equity performance above 0 per cent. He will get some proportion (say, k) of the rise in the value of equities, with the difference of $(1 - k)$ being used to 'pay for' the put. In effect, a fraction $(1 - k)$ of an at-the-money call option is sold to pay for the put option. This annual return structure can also be achieved in a more simple way by investing in cash plus k at-the-money call options. This programme is also sometimes known as a participating-equity or guaranteed-equity programme.

6.7.4 Government Amelioration of Market Failures

Greater innovation by the private sector can only go so far and where innovations have proved too expensive to manage they have been dropped.[40] The government could therefore do more to ameliorate market failures in the private provision of annuities which arise, in part, from aggregate risks that are difficult if not impossible for private insurance companies to hedge. Two key examples are inflation risk and longevity risk.

A number of proposals have been suggested recently to help private sector pension plan providers hedge inflation risk. For example, in order to help the private sector hedge against inflation risk more effectively, the Goode Report (1993, section 4.4.44) in the UK suggested that the government introduce a new type of bond, with income and capital linked to the retail price index, but with payment of income deferred for a period. Such bonds were given the name 'deferred income government securities' (DIGS). DIGS could be introduced with different starting and termination dates and would allow all deferred pensions to be indexed to prices. DIGS had not been introduced in the UK by 1997, although the introduction of the government bond (gilt) strips market in the same year could help UK insurance companies construct DIGS synthetically.

The introduction of 'limited price index bonds' would allow annuities to be partially indexed to inflation: annuitants could have higher starting pensions if they were to accept that the subsequent uprating of the pension would compensate for inflation only up to a stated limit (for example, 2.5 per cent p.a.).

The main causes of private market failure in annuity provision are the risks associated with adverse selection and longevity risk. Again, making participation in second-pillar pensions mandatory rather than voluntary would do much to remove the adverse selection bias in the demand for annuities. There are a number of ways in which the government could also help insurance companies hedge the risk associated with underestimating mortality improvements. It has been argued that the government should take some responsibility here since mortality improvements arise at least in part from public health campaigns and so on. The state could sell annuities directly to the public. It would therefore be bearing both the aggregate and the specific risks associated with mortality improvements. This is effectively what the state does when it provides state pensions.

Alternatively, the state could issue 'survivor' (or 'longevity') bonds, a suggestion made in Blake and Burrows (2001). These are bonds whose future coupon payments depend on the percentage of the population of retirement age on the issue date of each bond who are still alive on the date of each future coupon payment. For a bond issued in 2000, for instance, the coupon in 2010 will be directly proportional to the amount, on average, that an insurance company has to pay out as an annuity at that time. The insurance company which buys such a security bears no aggregate longevity risk and, as a consequence, cost loadings fall. The coupon payments fall over time, but continue in payment until the last members of the cohort have died. The insurance company would still retain the specific risk associated with the pool of annuitants that purchase its annuities (for example, it might explicitly market annuities to groups such as non-smokers who can be expected to experience lighter than average mortality), but this is likely to be a smaller and more forecastable risk than the risk associated with underestimating aggregate mortality improvements many years ahead.[41]

6.8 CONCLUSION

A well-designed pension plan is designed from back to front. Working backwards from the anticipated death date of the member, the plan should ascertain what size pension the member desires and then calculate the requisite fund size on the nominated retirement date. Depending on the member's attitude to risk and desire to make a bequest, the pension can be paid either in the form of a life annuity or using an income drawdown programme. Working backwards again and taking into account the length of the accumulation period and the plan member's risk-aversion parameter and salary profile, the plan will determine the optimal (stochastic lifestyling) investment strategy and the required net contributions. Finally, the plan determines the gross contributions needed to cover the plan provider's costs and profit.

There is little evidence that DC pension plans in the UK have been well-designed as a single integrated financial product. The key design failures are high charges and lapse rates, inappropriate investment strategies, no evidence of outperformance from active investment management, and poorly designed annuity and income drawdown programmes.[42] On top of this, those delivering key services have little incentive to treat a pension plan as a single integrated financial product with the long-term goal of securing a reasonable income replacement in retirement. Sales staff receive up-front commission from the initial contributions into the plan and so have no financial interest in ensuring the plan's long-term suitability to the member; investment managers take whatever net contributions are available and invest these the best that they can, but generally have no particular target fund level to achieve; and the annuity provider takes whatever fund size is available on the retirement date and offers the best annuity available on that particular day. Further, no one on the provider side has any particular incentive to minimize costs to the plan member or to set and then meet any particular performance targets.

The best way of delivering value in the pensions industry is to have charging structures that are simple, fully transparent, non-front-loaded and performance-related. Although it is possible for good investment performance to compensate for high charges, there are limits and we have shown that it is virtually impossible for superior investment performance to be delivered over the long investment horizon needed to build up a decent pension in retirement. It is difficult, therefore, to disagree with view of the Office of Fair Trading (1999b) that 'The best way [to run a simplified defined contribution pension plan] is to embrace passive fund management, thus requiring funds to compete in terms of their administration costs, not their spurious promises of future excess returns'.[43]

There are not many economic activities in which the provider of a service extracts up to 50 per cent of the value of the product in charges. But this is what happens with individual DC pensions in the UK. It is hard to argue that this represents good value for money and certainly institutional customers would not accept charges of this size. If something is not done to improve product design and to reduce costs, the very concept of DC pension plans will fall into disrepute. If that happens, where else can workers turn for retirement income security, given the gradual demise globally of state pay-as-you-go pension plans and occupational final-salary plans?

NOTES

1. The author is grateful to Solange Berstein for very useful comments on an earlier draft.
2. For further details about PPPs see Blake (2003).
3. This section draws on Blake and Board (2000).
4. Office of Fair Trading (1997, 1999a).
5. Slade (1999).
6. Financial Times Business Publications, London.
7. See Blake (1998).
8. Cash is the term that fund managers use as a short hand for low-risk assets such as Treasury bills.
9. The expected value of the fund T years from its inception is given by:

$$\bar{A}_T = C\frac{((1+r)^{T+1} - (1+\pi)^T(1+r))}{(r-\pi)},$$

where C is the value of the initial annual contribution into the fund, π is the expected annual real rate of increase in contributions and r is the expected annual real rate of return on the investments in the fund. The terminal fund risk (σ_{AT}) is given by the standard deviation of $\bar{A}_T$ which will be a complex function of the standard deviations of π and r and the covariance between them. Table 6.4 reports the terminal fund risk after 40 years ($\sigma_{A,40}$). See Blake (2003, ch.13) or Blake (2000, ch.14).

10. A typical final-salary plan in the UK has an accrual rate of $\frac{1}{60}$th and hence will generate a pension of two-thirds of final salary after 40 years of service.

11. The liabilities in a DB plan will be proportional to a term involving the product of the accrued benefit after 40 years of plan membership (two-thirds of final salary) and an annuity factor (*PA92*): $0.667 \times (1 + \pi)^{40} \times PA92$ (where π is the expected annual real growth rate in earnings). The annuity factor is the present value of one unit of pension payable for the life of the pensioner. In the UK, this will be based on the Institute of Actuaries' *PA92* mortality tables and its successors. For a 65-year-old male the annuity factor is 13.6, while for a 65-year-old female it is 16.5, reflecting her greater longevity.

12. Samuelson (1963, 1989, 1991). See also Blake et al. (2001).

13. See, e.g., Fabozzi and Konishi (1991), Blake (2003, ch.13) and Haberman and Sung (1994). Haberman and Sung (1994) suggest some alternatives to (6.17), namely that the term in C_t^2 is replaced by the squared deviation from planned contributions, $(C_t - \overline{C})^2$, or by the variance of contributions, $\mathrm{var}(C_t)$.

14. Standard dynamic programming problems are solved over the full investment horizon using backward solution techniques based on, for example, Bellman's optimality principle. Such problems can be reduced to a series of single-period optimization problems if the objective function is time-separable and if the state variables (in this case the asset returns) are time-independent processes.

15. The data were provided by Standard & Poor's Micropal.

16. However, as we shall see later on, it is highly unlikely that the same fund will find itself in the top quartile (or indeed the bottom quartile) for 40 years in a row.

17. Blake (2003).

18. The data set for this study was provided by the WM Company and covers the managed funds of occupational pension plans. However, given the highly concentrated nature of the UK fund management industry, very similar results can be expected for the managed funds of personal pension plans. Furthermore, very similar results have been found for the US; see Lakonishok et al. (1992).

19. Davis (1988) reports a survey of UK and US fund managers in which they acknowledge the existence of a herding effect. More recent studies from the US confirm the importance in the assessment of fund managers performance of their performance relative to a peer-group benchmark (see Brown, Harlow and Starks (1996), Chevalier and Ellison (1997)).

20. There are other features of UK pension fund performance worthy of note. First, there was some evidence of spillover effects in performance, but only between UK and international equities. In other words, the funds that performed well or badly in UK equities also performed well or badly in international equities. This suggests that some fund managers were good at identifying undervalued stocks in different markets. This result is somewhat surprising since the world's equity markets are much less highly integrated than the world's bond markets, yet there was no evidence of spillover effects in performance across bond markets. Secondly, there was evidence of a size effect in performance. Large funds tended to underperform smaller funds: 32 per cent of the quartile containing the largest funds were also in the quartile containing the worst performing funds, whereas only 15 per cent of the quartile containing the smallest funds were also in the quartile of worst performing funds. These results confirm the often-quoted view that 'size is the anchor of performance': because large pension funds are dominant players in the markets, this severely restricts their abilities to outperform the market.

21. *Pensions Management*, September 1998.

22. There is some recent evidence that 'star' fund managers do exist, but they are very few in number and it takes a long performance history to identify them, see Kosowski et al. (2006).

23. This effect is called survivorship bias or median drag.

24. Using US data, survivorship biases of up to 1.4 per cent per annum have been reported, see Malkiel (1995).

25. See Bodie (1990).

26. Association of British Insurers. More than half the world's life annuities are sold in the UK (300,000 in 2005, with premiums of £8bn: see HM Treasury (2006)).
27. Barclays Capital (2006).
28. MacDonald (1996).
29. William Burrows of William Burrows Annuities.
30. According to O'Brien et al. (2005), British males under-estimate their life expectancy by 4.62 years, while British females underestimate theirs by 5.95 years, compared with the estimates of the UK Government Actuary's Department.
31. Again very similar results have been found in the US, see Grinblatt and Titman (1992), Hendricks et al. (1993), Brown and Goetzmann (1995), Carhart (1997).
32. There is, however, some evidence that a small number of fund managers do have genuine and persistent skills (see Kosowski et al. (2006)).
33. These costs, typically for increased research and as salaries to skilled fund managers (so-called stars), will usually be passed on to the policy holders; see Berk and Green (2004).
34. The theoretical justification for this position was originally stated by Grossman and Stiglitz (1980) who found that an efficient equilibrium in financial markets is characterized as offering the same *net* returns to all investors, after allowing for differences in risk, research costs and transactions costs. This means that there is no incentive for any investor to change his or her investment strategy. This means that the *gross* return to investors who engage in research may be higher that the *gross* return of those who do not. However, the increased return must be exactly offset by the costs of this research; if it is greater there will be incentives for more people to engage in research, which will drive down the profits from such research; if it is less then investors will cease research, raising the gains to those who remain engaged in research.
35. Pensions Commission (2005).
36. We assume that the asset portfolio has the same mean return as the regulator's assumed return of 9 per cent p.a. Based on long-run returns reported in Barclays Capital (2006), such a portfolio would be invested 35 per cent in equities and 65 per cent in bonds and would have a standard deviation of about 18 per cent p.a.
37. Chapman (1998, p. 88).
38. In the UK, it is mandatory to purchase a life annuity with a DC plan by age 75 at the latest.
39. These were first issued in 1952 in the US by the TIAA-CREF, the Teachers Insurance and Annuity Association of America – College Retirement Equity Fund.
40. For example, although derivative-related annuities are offered (e.g. by AIG), some providers stopped selling them because of the management costs involved (e.g., Prudential), see Bulman (1999).
41. In March 2007, JPMorgan, in collaboration with Watson Wyatt and the Pensions Institute, released LifeMetrics, a toolkit for measuring and managing longevity risk. This comprises the LifeMetrics Index on current and historical mortality and longevity; the LifeMetrics Framework which consists of tools for measuring and managing longevity and mortality risk; and LifeMetrics Software for forecasting future mortality. The aim of LifeMetrics is to encourage the development of a capital market in longevity risk transference by providing the relevant benchmarks against which instruments such as longevity bonds and swaps can trade. For more details, see www.jpmorgan.com/lifemetrics.
42. There are other design failures in DC pension plans that are beyond the scope of this study, such as poor mapping between actions (e.g. implementing an investment strategy) and results (e.g. subsequent investment performance), poor feedback (e.g. about the result of actions) and poor fail safety (if the plan member does nothing, does this lead to a good or bad outcome?); see Norman (2002) for more on the principles of good design.
43. Office of Fair Trading (1999b, p. 2).

REFERENCES

Anson, Sir John (Chairman) (1996), *Pensions 2000 and Beyond*, Report of the Retirement Income Enquiry, London.

Barclays Capital (2006), *Equity-Gilt Study*, London: Barclays Capital.

Berk, J. and R. Green (2004), 'Mutual fund flows and performance in rational markets', *Journal of Political Economy*, **112**(6), 1269–95.

Blake, D. (1998), 'Pension schemes as options on pension fund assets: implications for pension fund management', *Insurance: Mathematics & Economics*, **23**(3), 263–86.

Blake, David (2003), *Pension Schemes and Pension Funds in the United Kingdom*, Oxford: Oxford University Press.

Blake, D. and J. Board (2000), 'Measuring value added in the pensions industry', *Geneva Papers on Risk and Insurance*, **25**, October, 539–67.

Blake, D. and W. Burrows (2001), 'Survivor bonds: helping to hedge mortality risk', *Journal of Risk and Insurance*, **68**(2), 339–48.

Blake, D. and A. Timmermann (1998), 'Mutual fund performance: evidence from the UK', *European Finance Review*, **2**(1), 57–77.

Blake, D., A. Cairns and K. Dowd (2001), 'Pensionmetrics: stochastic pension plan design and value-at-risk during the accumulation phase', *Insurance: Mathematics & Economics*, **29**(2), 187–215.

Blake, D., A. Cairns and K. Dowd (2003), 'PensionMetrics 2: stochastic pension plan design during the distribution phase', *Insurance: Mathematics & Economics*, **33**(1), 29–47.

Blake, D., B. Lehmann and A. Timmermann (1999), 'Asset allocation dynamics and pension fund performance', *Journal of Business*, **72**(4), 429–62.

Blake, D., B. Lehmann and A. Timmermann (2002), 'Performance clustering and incentives in the UK pension fund industry', *Journal of Asset Management*, **3**(2), 173–94.

Bodie, Z. (1990), 'Pensions as retirement income insurance', *Journal of Economic Literature*, **28**(1), 28–49.

Borrie, Sir Gordon (Chairman) (1994), *Social Justice – Strategies for National Renewal*, Report of the Commission for Social Justice, London: Vintage.

Brinson, G., L. Hood and G. Beebower (1986), 'Determinants of portfolio performance', *Financial Analysts Journal*, **42**(4), 39–48.

Brown, S.J. and W. Goetzmann (1995), 'Performance persistence', *Journal of Finance*, **50**(2), 679–98.

Brown, K.C., W.V. Harlow and L.T. Starks (1996), 'Of tournaments and temptations: an analysis of managerial incentives in the mutual fund industry', *Journal of Finance*, **51**(1), 85–110.

Bulman, W. (1999), 'What's the outlook for annuities?', *Pensions Management*, July.

Cairns, A., D. Blake and K. Dowd (2006), 'Stochastic lifestyling: optimal dynamic asset allocation for defined contribution pension plans', *Journal of Economic Dynamics & Control*, **30**(5), 843–77.

Campbell, J. and L. Viceira (2002), *Strategic Asset Allocation: Portfolio Choice for Long-term Investors*, Oxford: Oxford University Press.

CAPS (various), *General Reports*, Leeds: Combined Actuarial Performance Services.

Carhart, M. (1997), 'On persistence in mutual fund performance', *Journal of Finance*, **52**(1), 57–82.

Chapman, J. (1998), 'Pension plans made easy', *Money Management*, November, 88–91.

Chevalier, J. and G. Ellison (1997), 'Risk taking by mutual funds as a response to incentives', *Journal of Political Economy*, **105**(6), 1167–1200.

Dahrendorf, Lord Ralf (Chairman) (1995), *Wealth Creation and Social Cohesion in a Free Society*, Report of the Commission on Wealth Creation and Social Cohesion, London: Xenogamy.

Davis, E.P. (1988), *Financial Market Activity of Life Insurance Companies and Pension Funds*, Economic Paper No.21, Basle: Bank for International Settlements.

Fabozzi, Frank J. and A. Konishi (eds) (1991), *Asset-Liability Management*, Chicago: Probus.

Field, F. (1996), *How to pay for the future: building a stakeholders' welfare*, London: Institute of Community Studies.

Field, F. and M. Owen (1993), 'Private pensions for all: squaring the circle', Fabian Society Discussion Paper No. 16, London.

Finkelstein, A. and J. Poterba (2002), 'Selection effects in the United Kingdom annuities market', *Economic Journal*, **112**(476), 28–50.

Goode, Roy (1993), *Pension Law Reform: Report of the Pension Law Review Committee*, CM 2342-I, London: HMSO.

Grinblatt, M. and S. Titman (1992), 'The persistence of mutual fund performance', *Journal of Finance*, **47**(5), 1997–84.

Grossman, S.J. and J. Stiglitz (1980), 'On the impossibility of informationally efficient markets', *American Economic Review*, **70**(3), 393–408.

Haberman, S. and J.-H. Sung (1994), 'Dynamic approaches to pension funding', *Insurance: Mathematics & Economics*, **15**(2–3), 151–62.

Hendricks, D., J. Patel and R. Zeckhauser (1993), 'Hot hands in mutual funds: short-run persistence of relative performance', *Journal of Finance*, **48**(1), 93–130.

HM Treasury (2006), *The Annuities Market 2006*, London: HM Treasury.

Horneff, W., R. Maurer and M. Stamos (2006), 'Optimal gradual annuitization: quantifying the costs of switching to annuities', Working Paper, Goethe University, Frankfurt, April.

Kosowski, R., A. Timmermann, R. Wermers and H. White (2006), 'Can mutual fund "stars" really pick stocks? New evidence from a bootstrap analysis', *Journal of Finance*, **61**(6), 2551–95.

Lakonishok, J., A. Shleifer and R. Vishny (1992), 'The structure and performance of the money management industry', *Brookings Papers: Microeconomics*, 339–91.

Lunde, A., A. Timmermann and D. Blake (1999), 'The hazards of mutual fund underperformance: a cox regression analysis', *Journal of Empirical Finance*, **6**(2), 121–52.

MacDonald, Angus S. (1996), 'United Kingdom', in Angus S. MacDonald (ed.), *The Second Actuarial Study of Mortality in Europe*, Brussels: Groupe Consultatif des Associations D'Actuaires des Pays des Communautés Européennes.

Malkiel, B.G. (1995), 'Returns from investing in equity mutual funds 1971–1991', *Journal of Finance*, **50**(2), 540–72.

Mitchell, Olivia and Stephen Utkus (eds) (2004), *Pension Design and Structure: New Lessons from Behavioural Finance*, Oxford: Oxford University Press.

Norman, Donald A. (2002), *The Design of Everyday Things*, New York: Basic Books.

O'Brien, C., P. Fenn and S. Diacon (2005), 'How long do people expect to live? Results and implications', Centre for Risk and Insurance Studies, Nottingham University Business School, CRIS Research report 2005-1, April.

Office of Fair Trading (1997), *Consumer Detriment under Conditions of Imperfect Information*, Research Paper 11, London.

Office of Fair Trading (1999a), *Vulnerable Consumers and Financial Services*, Report 255, London.

Office of Fair Trading (1999b), *Response to the Treasury Consultation Document 'Helping to Deliver the Stakeholder Pension'*, March, London.

Pensions Commission (2005), *A New Pensions Settlement for the Twenty-First Century*, Norwich: The Stationery Office.

Personal Investment Authority (1998), *Fourth Survey of Persistency of Life and Pension Policies*, October, London.

Samuelson, P.A. (1963), 'Risk and uncertainty: a fallacy of large numbers', *Scientia*, **98**, 108–13.

Samuelson, P.A. (1989), *A Case at Last for Age-phased Reduction in Equity*, Proceedings of the National Academy of Sciences, Washington, DC.

Samuelson, Paul A. (1991), 'Long-run risk tolerance when equity returns are mean regressing: pseudoparadoxes and vindication of "businessman's risk"', in Brainard William, William Nordhaus and Harold Watts (eds), *Macroeconomics, Finance and Economic Policy: Essays in Honour of James Tobin*, Cambridge, MA: MIT Press.

Slade, P. (1999), 'Quote manipulation claims', *The Independent*, 30 January.

Thaler, R. and S. Benartzi (2004), 'Save more tomorrow: using behavioural economics to increase employee saving', *Journal of Political Economy*, **112**(1), S164–S187

Towers-Perrin (1998), *European Active Investment Management Charges*, August, London.

World Bank (1994), *Averting the Old-Age Crisis*, Oxford: Oxford University Press.

APPENDIX: THE DECOMPOSITION OF TOTAL RETURN

The decomposition of the total return on the portfolio is due to Brinson et al. (1986). Assume that there are M asset categories in the portfolio and define:

θ_{sjt} = strategic asset allocation in the jth asset class at time t,
θ_{ajt} = actual weight in the jth asset class at time t,
r_{sjt} = strategic return in the jth asset class at time t,
r_{ajt} = actual return in the jth asset class at time t.

As an arithmetic identity:

$$\sum_{j=1}^{M} \theta_{ajt} r_{ajt} = \sum_{j=1}^{M} \theta_{sjt} r_{sjt} + \sum_{j=1}^{M} \theta_{sjt}(r_{ajt} - r_{sjt}) + \sum_{j=1}^{M}(\theta_{ajt} - \theta_{sjt})r_{sjt}$$

$$+ \sum_{j=1}^{M}(\theta_{ajt} - \theta_{sjt})(r_{ajt} - r_{sjt})$$

or Total Return = Strategic Return + Return from Security Selection + Return from Market Timing + Residual Return. The strategic asset allocation is typically specified by the client in the light of an asset-liability modelling exercise. The strategic return is the return on an agreed benchmark, such as a market or peer-group index.

Discussion of 'It is all back to front: critical issues in the design of defined contribution pension plans'

Solange Berstein

Blake's interesting chapter puts forward solid arguments to back up his main idea: pension plans should be designed considering all links of the chain that go from the contributions to the pension payout. Moreover, every link should take into account what the purpose of a DC pension plan is: to provide an adequate pension in accordance with the contributions made throughout the life cycle. Throughout the chapter, Blake is able to depict a convincing argument showing that DC pension plans in the UK seem not to follow this rule, since each link looks as if it has been designed in isolation from the whole chain. The conclusions of the chapter are easily extrapolated to other DC pension systems, which both extends its relevance and increases the necessity to clarify some issues regarding the implementation of some of its recommendations. In the following, I will concentrate on the most relevant conclusions from the point of view of mandatory DC pension systems.

This chapter analyses six issues: charges, lapses, investment strategy, investment performance, fund annuitization and the incentives for managers. These all are, certainly, relevant aspects in the design of a pension system. In my comment I would like to add another three elements which I consider as important as the six considered by the author, especially from the viewpoint of a mandatory DC scheme, although they might not be less relevant for any DC system. These elements are income profile, regulation and financial literacy.

Why is income profile important in a DC scheme? It is important because the whole history of contributions of a worker has an impact on his/her final pension; even in some DB schemes the benefit formulas are being modified to incorporate elements which make benefits closer to contributions. Therefore, knowing what income profiles look like might be an important consideration for pension plan design. In fact, if our concern is replacement rates in terms of final salary, in a DC scheme early contributions are very important in determining the final pension. This implies that higher contribution rates might be required if income profiles are particularly steep.

Another element that is relevant is regulation, especially for mandatory systems which are heavily regulated. The reason for this heavy regulation has to do with information asymmetries and (implicit or explicit) guarantees (Berstein and Chumacero, 2006). It is not rare to hear in some discussions that pension funds should be regulated in a certain way because that would help the development of the capital market or other specific sectors. However, if we think of it as if it is stated in the chapter, that *the* purpose of pension fund plans should be to provide adequate pension benefits, the argument for establishing a regulation should not be founded on something else. It might be argued that the development of those specific sectors, because of general equilibrium considerations, also benefits pension funds, but then the argument should follow from that point. How regulation is designed could have an important impact on the benefits level and also on the volatility of those benefits.

A final issue which I would like to mention as an important element for pension plan design is financial literacy. This is in direct relation to how paternalistic the design should be. An excessive number of choices might imply that people are not able to make the right decision. Furthermore, the evidence shows that people might not even be able to make a decision at all. This implies that the design of the default option is crucial, because most participants would end up accepting that default (Weaver, 2005).

The chapter stresses the fact that all the six elements have to be seen in an integrated way and I would add these last three to that argument. As is mentioned in the chapter, there seems to be a temptation to separate the accumulation and decumulation phases in the case of DC pension schemes. In fact, sometimes there are totally different industries as providers and even different regulators and supervisors. Therefore, a special effort must be made to see the pension cycle as a unified package. This might be particularly important at the moment of retirement, where the annuitization risk has to be correctly managed and mitigated, which is one of the six elements mentioned by the author. The main argument that supports the fact that, in DC schemes, or at least in the UK, future retirees face an important interest rate risk is that there is a fixed date for annuitization. This is not necessarily the case in every DC scheme, as there are systems where it is possible for the individual to handle the risk of annuitization better. However, just being able to choose the annuitization date, by having the alternative of a drawdown for some period of time, might not be enough. In the case of Chile, where there is the possibility of having a programmed withdrawal and switching to an annuity when convenient for the individual, it must be said that annuities are 'sold' and not 'bought'. Therefore, the information provided is not necessarily the best, given that the sales agents receive a commission only if the retiree buys an annuity.

In the following I will comment on two other important elements mentioned by the author: charges and investment strategy. With respect to charges, after showing some interesting ways to measure their impact, in terms of the terminal value of the retirement account, Blake concludes that, owing to the strong arguments against a clear relationship between charges and performance, the best alternative to keep charges low is for the regulatory authority to cap charges and to allow penalty-free transfers between plans. Furthermore, he proposes that charging structures should be kept simple and fully transparent (to help consumers to understand), non-front loaded and performance-based. In this regard, it is fair to say that there is more agreement on how to implement a simple and transparent charge structure than with respect to the way to implement a performance-based charging structure, which in fact might be going in the opposite direction. Some recent papers have discussed the implications of performance-based charging schemes for portfolio managers (Carpenter, 2000; Basak et al., 2005), and some of the lessons point towards the need for a careful design in terms of considering potential side-effects, such as risk taking problems. Additionally, elements such as different investment horizons and risk appetite could potentially misalign the investment decisions of pension fund portfolio managers with respect to what would be desired by pension plan members. Therefore, even if there might be a benefit, this is uncertain, according to what the same author argues when he discusses investment performance, and it could imply important costs.

With respect to price caps, it has to be said that this is not easy to contrive and that there are some risks. It is difficult to set a price cap at the right level: if too high, there is somehow a validation of a high price and it might even constitute a focal point for collusion (Knittel and Stango, 2003). If too low, you might be getting the industry into financial trouble, which could lead to serious financial distress; or the quality of service could be critically affected, not only with respect to performance, but also as regards the other activities that are involved in the management of retirement accounts.

Portability of pension funds, or penalty-free transfers between plans, is also part of the author's recommendations in relation to charges. I think this is very important in achieving market discipline. I would say that, if we want prices to be as low as possible, we need competition to drive them down. Competition is only effective if there are low switching costs (Klemperer, 1995), otherwise there is important monopoly power of providers. In summary, simplicity in the fee structure and portability are crucial: first, to make it easy for the workers saving for retirement to figure out what is the effective price they are paying and, second, to make it possible for people to switch if they realize their provider is too expensive. In fact, in the case of Chile, there are only two types of fees, a fixed fee and a percentage over salary fee, this makes the price unique for every individual and no provider can claim to be the cheapest of all providers, because it would depend on the salary of the worker. This makes communication of this type of information extremely difficult. Given the lack of knowledge in the case of Chile,[1] it is mandatory for every pension fund manager to send, together with the pension statement to their clients, a sheet that has the computed individual fee for that person for each of the possible managers. Providing this information would be significantly easier if there was only one price.

In terms of investment strategies, Blake proposes to design investment strategies around some focal pension level which is to be determined from some preference specification (quadratic-mean-variance or some more general concave utility index) or some reasonable benchmark (such as a replacement ratio). Once the pension target has been determined, the remaining steps are just a matter of characterizing the investment strategy that delivers the desired pension level (that is, a problem of contingent claim replication). As an example, Blake recommends the adoption of the investment strategy that is the solution of a utility maximization problem having the particularity of considering a more suitable 'numeraire' (a replacement ratio), which implicitly takes into account the 'annuity risk', since the utility function has the annuity factor as one of its arguments. Alternatively, he suggests the use of deferred annuities and investment strategies involving derivatives as a way to immunize pension funds against interest rate risk. By and large, Blake's recommendations point in the right direction: the investment strategies of DC pension plans should be designed around a sensible pension target. What remains to be determined, though, is the target to be pursued, which is among the most relevant questions policy makers and regulators of DC pension systems around the world are trying to figure out. Indeed, the determination of such a target would allow the implementation of more sensible (pension) risk-based investment rules, better suited for long-term investors.

Investment strategies among Latin-American mandatory DC pension systems are subject to several of the features identified by the author. Herding is a recognized issue, and portfolio managers seem to be markedly risk-averse in the dimensions they are concerned about: underperforming their peers. Unfortunately, their concerns and those of the pension plan members sometimes diverge on important matters. Policy makers and regulators would like to have a better idea of what an investment strategy aimed at delivering an adequate pension should look like. This would certainly help better to align incentives between portfolio managers and pension plan members.

Overall, David Blake's chapter is an important contribution, and its observations should not pass unnoticed. Pension plans should be understood as an integrated financial product, with all elements involved in both the accumulation and disbursement phase blended together to deliver adequate retirement income. Still, many questions remain to be answered by the academic and policy making community. What should be the target with respect to pensions? How to deal with the heterogeneity among pension plan members? How to communicate information consistently? And, finally, how much freedom to choose should be given to individuals?

NOTE

1. According to the EPS 2002, a survey that represents all affiliates to the pension system, only 3 per cent said they knew how much they were charged and from those almost none gave the right figure when asked how much that was.

REFERENCES

Basak, S., A. Pavlova and A. Shapiro (2005), 'Offsetting the incentives: risk shifting and benefits of benchmarking in money management', Discussion Paper No. 5006, Centre for Economic Policy Research.
Berstein, S. and R. Chumacero (2006), 'Quantifying the costs of investment limits for Chilean pension funds', *Fiscal Studies*, **27**(1), 99–123.
Carpenter, J. (2000), 'Does option compensation increase managerial risk appetite?', *Journal of Finance*, **55**(5), 2311–31.
Klemperer, P. (1995), 'Competition when consumers have switching costs: an overview with applications to industrial organization, macroeconomics, and international trade', *Review of Economic Studies*, **62**(4), 515–39.
Knittel, C.R. and V. Stango (2003), 'Price ceilings as focal points for tacit collusion: evidence for credit cards', *American Economic Review*, **93**(5), 1703–29.
Weaver, R.K. (2005), 'Design and implementation issues in the Swedish individual pension accounts', Working Paper 2005-05, Center for Retirement Research.

7. Risk-based supervision of pension funds: a review of international experience and preliminary assessment of the first outcomes

Gregory Brunner, Richard Hinz and Roberto Rocha[1]

7.1 INTRODUCTION

Over the past several decades privately managed pensions have evolved from their origins as a supplemental form of deferred compensation to become an important, and in some cases central, element of social insurance systems. Their supervision has made a similar transition to meet the requirements of this new role, evolving from an initial emphasis on ensuring compliance with tax laws and labour contracts and relatively simple methods to limiting investment risk, towards a much more expansive approach designed to ensure proper management of all the risks associated with complex institutions relied on to provide secure sources of retirement income.

The wave of innovation and reforms in Latin America and Central and Eastern Europe beginning in the early 1980s transformed pension funds from primarily employer-sponsored defined benefit (DB) arrangements into more diverse forms including, most significantly, the emergence of special purpose financial intermediaries operating on a defined contribution (DC) basis. This largely removed the capacity to rely on employers to guarantee outcomes placing financial risks squarely on the shoulders of members. This transition shifted the nexus of supervision from controlling agency risks to managing systemic financial and portfolio risks. Initially the new supervision regimes were based on simple quantitative asset allocation limits with very proactive compliance enforcement. Bounding downside risk over short periods through investment controls was the primary concern. The risk–return efficiency or effective capital allocation were very secondary considerations.

By the beginning of the new millennium several factors combined to accelerate these changes in supervision methods. Private pension funds in a number of countries accumulated asset levels exceeding those of more traditional financial institutions, in some cases more than 100 per cent of GDP, leading to a commensurate increase in attention to their systemic importance. A 'perfect storm' of rapidly declining interest rates coincident with collapsing equity prices exposed the fragility of the loose funding requirements for the remaining DB schemes. Concerns about the capacity of the new DC plans to produce adequate levels of retirement income also focused attention on the efficacy of their design and operation. This led a number of countries to begin to adopt supervision systems based on various risk-based approaches that established new standards for the operation of pension funds and guided the conduct of their oversight activities.

The objective of this chapter is to review the experience in four of the pioneers in developing risk-based supervision for pension funds: Australia, Denmark, Mexico and the Netherlands. These countries each have large well-established pension systems that provide a useful initial review because they constitute a representative sample of the characteristics of pension systems worldwide, including occupational and open pension funds as well as both defined benefit and defined contribution arrangements. The chapter draws on individual country studies that form part of a joint project of the World Bank and the International Organisation of Pension Supervisors (IOPS), as well as discussions with pension supervisors and market participants in these countries. The reader is referred to the case studies for a more detailed analysis of individual countries.[2]

The chapter is structured as follows. The second section reviews the origins of risk-based supervision in banking and insurance, and the progress that has been achieved in developing further the risk-based approach under the Basel II and Solvency II agreements. The third section provides an overview of the pension systems of the four countries and the factors that have motivated the introduction of risk-based supervision in these countries. The fourth section – the core of the chapter – provides a more in-depth discussion of the main elements of risk-based supervision of pension funds in the four countries. This is followed by a very preliminary assessment of the impact of the new supervisory approach on the sectors, as well as some observations on the challenges that supervisors will face in the future. Finally, the sixth section concludes and draws some preliminary lessons for other countries.

7.2 CONCEPTUAL ORIGINS OF RISK-BASED SUPERVISION: BASEL AND SOLVENCY II

7.2.1 Risk-based Supervision in Banking and Insurance

The movement towards risk-based supervisory approaches can be traced to the development of early warning systems for banks. The earliest of these systems was the CAMEL system for risk rating adopted by the United States in the 1980s.[3] In 1988, the Basel Committee on Banking Supervision implemented the Capital Adequacy Accord (Basel I) which provided a risk-based framework for assessing the capital adequacy of banks to cover credit risks. The development of this framework was an important step on the path towards risk-based supervision. It sought to ensure an adequate level of capital in the banking system by applying weighting to credit exposures based on broad risk classifications.

During the 1990s a number of supervisors implemented risk assessment and early warning systems. In 1993, the Bank of Italy implemented an off-site monitoring system called PATROL; in 1997, the German Federal Supervisory Office introduced an early warning and monitoring system called BAKIS. In the same year the French Banking Commission introduced an off-site supervisory bank rating system called ORAP. In 1998, the Financial Service Authority in the United Kingdom introduced its RATE model, a comprehensive bank risk rating system, and the De Nederlandsche Bank (DNB) implemented a comprehensive system called RAST which has evolved into the FIRM Model applied to all financial entities regulated by DNB today.

In 1999, the Basel Committee began the process of replacing the Basel I Accord with a more up-to-date framework which requires banks to improve risk management and corporate governance in conjunction with improved supervision and transparency. The new framework, known as Basel II, is designed to encourage good risk management by tying regulatory capital requirements to the results of internal systems and processes, thus creating incentives for improvements in risk management. In addition to making the calculation of regulatory capital more risk-sensitive and recognizing the quality of internal risk management systems, the framework added two pillars to the model: the supervisory review process and the market discipline. The three pillars of the new model are shown in Table 7.1.

The Basel II framework provides banks with a choice between a standardized approach to calculating credit risk using specified risk factors and an internal ratings-based approach which is subject to explicit approval by the bank supervisor which would allow banks to use their internal ratings

Table 7.1   The three pillars of Basel II

Pillar 1 Minimum capital requirements	Pillar 2 Supervisory review process	Pillar 3 Market discipline
Risk-based capital rule reflecting: • Market risk • Credit risk • Operational risk	• Regulatory compliance • Reporting obligations leading to more transparency and accountability	• Meaningful disclosure

Note: The interest rate risk on the banking book (loans, deposits) is not included in pillar 1 of Basel II, but in pillar 2. However, it is included in pillar 1 of Solvency II.

systems for credit risk. It has been built through a process of extensive exploration by regulators of emerging industry practices in risk management and considerable testing and calibration.

The framework requires implementation of an effective and comprehensive risk management system. It is envisaged that banks will set up a proper organizational structure, policies, procedures and limits for credit, market and operational risk. Banks are also required to have an integrated approach to risk management that covers the risks in particular business segments as well as the bank as a whole.

The second pillar, supervisory review, allows supervisors to evaluate a bank's assessment of its own risks and assure themselves that the banks' processes are robust. Supervisors will have the opportunity to assess whether a bank understands its risk profile and is sufficiently capitalized against its risks. This pillar will encourage adoption of risk-focused internal audits, strengthened management information systems and the development of risk measurement and compliance units.

The third pillar – market discipline – ensures that the market is provided with sufficient information to allow it to undertake its own assessment of banks' risks. It is intended to strengthen incentives for improved risk management through greater transparency. This should allow market participants better to understand the risks inherent in each bank and ultimately to support well-managed banks at the expense of poorly managed banks.

The movement towards greater risk focus is also being reflected in the insurance industry. The International Association of Insurance Supervisors (IAIS) is currently working to develop a common international framework for assessing the solvency of insurers. At a regional level, work is under way in Europe on the Solvency II project which aims to adopt a risk-based approach to capital requirements for insurance companies, and to introduce qualitative requirements for senior management, risk management, model validation and internal controls. There will also be recognition of internal modelling in collaboration with the actuarial profession. Solvency II will involve a three-pillar approach similar to Basel II, introducing a supervisory review process and enhanced transparency.

The current solvency framework in Europe dating from the early 1970s defines capital requirements for insurers in terms of solvency margins typically based on simple rules applied to technical provisions or premiums. Under Solvency II the first pillar will define the resources that a company needs to be considered solvent. It will define two thresholds for capital. The Solvency Capital Requirement will set a threshold for supervisory action and a Minimum Capital Requirement will provide a basis for stronger action or even withdrawal of the company's licence to write new business. As with Basel II, the capital requirement can be calculated using either a simple standardized model or an internal model which has been approved by the supervisor. Pillar 2 will take into account qualitative measures of risk control focusing on risk management processes, individual risk capital assessment, and aspects of operational risk, including stress testing. Pillar 3 will address disclosure requirements incorporating more consistent international accounting standards. In many European countries which operate DB pension schemes or guarantee arrangements which involve technical reserving, the rules applying to insurance companies may also apply to pension entities.

Across the globe the trend is inexorably moving towards improved risk management based on the three key elements outlined in Figure 7.1. First, institutions themselves are focusing on improving their own risk management. They are developing risk management strategies and they are measuring and assessing risk in a more comprehensive manner. In many institutions this involves the creation of dedicated risk management units. They are implementing controls to ensure that risk management polices are followed and are ensuring that risk management information is presented to management and board in a meaningful fashion.

Secondly, supervisors are responding to this by building up their ability to assess risk. The basic tools of on-site and off-site supervision are taking on a risk focus, and specialist risk units are being created with expertise to tackle complex issues. Many regulators are encouraging improved risk management by implementing regulatory standards and providing guidance. Finally, more external parties are being encouraged to take a role in the risk assessment process, either through broadening the role of some traditional players such as auditors and actuaries, or through encouragement of greater scrutiny by outside parties through greater transparency of reporting.

The Basic Risk Management Architecture

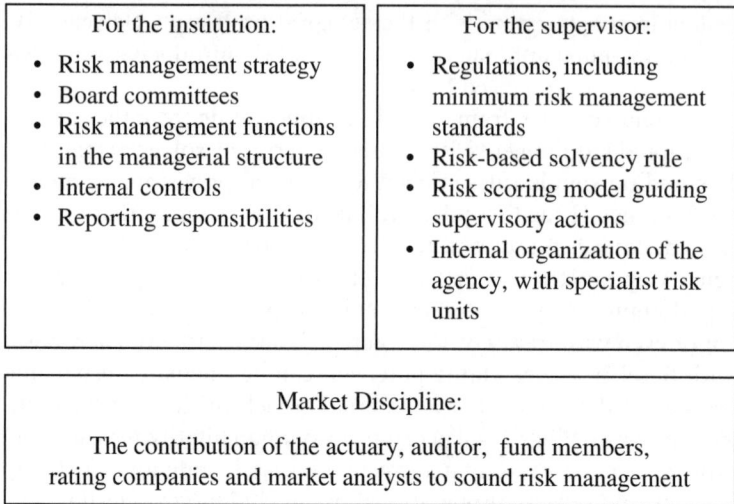

For the institution:	For the supervisor:
• Risk management strategy • Board committees • Risk management functions in the managerial structure • Internal controls • Reporting responsibilities	• Regulations, including minimum risk management standards • Risk-based solvency rule • Risk scoring model guiding supervisory actions • Internal organization of the agency, with specialist risk units

Market Discipline:
The contribution of the actuary, auditor, fund members, rating companies and market analysts to sound risk management

Figure 7.1   The basic risk management architecture

7.3   INTRODUCTION OF RISK-BASED SUPERVISION FOR PENSIONS

7.3.1   Overview of the Four Pension Systems

This section provides an overview of the private pension systems of the four countries examined to provide an understanding of the factors that motivated the introduction of risk-based supervision. Further background information on the pension systems of these countries is provided in the individual country papers.[4]

As shown in Table 7.2, all of the countries have mandatory or quasi-mandatory private pension systems. In Australia and Mexico, contributions to private pension plans are imposed by legislation. In the Netherlands and Denmark, contributions take place in the context of collective labour agreements. These are classified as quasi-mandatory, because most workers are covered by these agreements. The mandatory or quasi-mandatory nature of contributions results in high coverage rates, except for Mexico. The lower coverage ratio in Mexico, despite the legal obligation to contribute, is explained by the large share of the labour force in the informal sector and the lower number of active contributors relative to the total universe of pension fund members.[5]

Table 7.2 Main characteristics of the four private pension systems, December 2005

	Mandate	Coverage (% of labour force)	Assets (% GDP)	Number of funds	Legal structure of pension funds	Type of plan
Netherlands	Quasi-mandatory	90	120	700	Occupational	Mostly DB
Denmark	Quasi-mandatory	80	124	111	Occupational and open[1]	Mostly DC with absolute return guarantee (DB-like)
Australia	Mandatory	90	104	1 004	Occupational and open[2]	DC
Mexico	Mandatory	29	8	18	Open	DC with ceiling on downside risk (VaR)

Notes: (1) Denmark: 44 corporate funds, 30 industry-wide funds, 37 life insurance companies; (2) Australia: 681 corporate funds, 86 industry-wide funds, 194 retail funds, 43 public sector funds. The figures do not include small funds.

Sources: Hinz and Van Dam (2006), Andersen and Van Dam (2006), Thompson (2006), Bernstein and Chumacero (2006b), Rofman and Luchetti (2006).

The pension systems in these countries are very large, with assets exceeding 100 per cent of GDP in all cases, except for Mexico. The relatively small size of assets relative to GDP in the Mexican case is due to the lower coverage ratio and the fact that the Mexican system is much younger, having started operations only in 1998. However, the mandatory nature of contributions to individual accounts implies that the private pension system will continue growing at a fast rate and increase its share in the financial sector.

Three countries have a large number of funds, ranging from 111 in Denmark to 1000 in Australia, and these funds may operate more than one pension plan. Many of these are occupational funds structured as non-profit trusts or foundations that were originally created on a voluntary basis and have been operating for several decades. They include single funds and larger multi-employer or industry-wide funds. Australia and Denmark also have several for-profit commercial institutions managing pension funds, including life insurance companies in the Danish case.

Mexico has only 18 funds currently licensed. The difference in the number of funds is a result of the different origins and characteristics of the Mexican system. The Australian, Danish and Dutch systems have their roots in voluntary arrangements with employers. Most funds were initially established with liberal licensing/authorization rules designed to encourage participation and coverage. By contrast, the Mexican system was established as a mandatory system of open funds subject to a strict regulatory framework, including much stricter licensing rules.[6]

Dutch pension funds manage primarily DB plans (the Netherlands has been one the few countries that has successfully resisted the move towards DC plans). The Danish system is a DC system that offers benefit guarantees and operates on a risk-sharing (or profit-sharing) basis. The guarantees introduce a core liability and the risk of insolvency of the provider. Therefore the Danish system exhibits some of the characteristics of a defined-benefit system, although it operates with more flexible rules than pure defined-benefit systems and seems to be moving in the direction of DC plans with fewer guarantees.[7]

Australian pension funds manage primarily traditional DC plans with no formal guarantees. There are still some DB plans, but these are mostly restricted to public sector funds, and account for a small share of total assets. Australia best represents a pure defined contribution system.

Mexican funds, by contrast, manage their DC plans under a new regulatory framework that includes a limit on downside risk defined by a ceiling on the daily absolute Value at Risk (VaR). This is a significant departure from the set-up introduced in Chile and other countries in Latin America and Central Europe that relied on quantitative portfolio restrictions to manage risks. Most of these countries have introduced minimum relative return guarantees that intensify herding behaviour and lead pension funds to base their investment strategies on tracking errors or relative VaRs vis-à-vis the benchmark portfolio. Pension fund managers in these countries are more concerned with relative risk (the risk of deviating from the benchmark and facing a capital call to honour the relative return guarantee) than with absolute risk. The Mexican experiment is both innovative and controversial, and is being followed with interest in other countries.

7.3.2 Factors Motivating the Adoption of Risk-based Supervision in Pension Systems

Some of the factors that have motivated the introduction of risk-based supervision of pension funds are common to all the four countries, while others seem to be country-specific. Table 7.3 summarizes the motivating factors that have been identified in the individual country studies.

Table 7.3   Factors motivating the adoption of risk-based supervision

	Policy of reducing the risk of under-funding, insolvency of DB plans (or DC plans with guarantees) due to sudden and adverse price movements	Policy of limiting maximum loss to members of DC plans due to adverse movements in asset prices	Search for efficiency gains, especially from improve-ments in risk/return trade-off	Increasing complexity of financial instruments and markets	Effort to allocate efficiently scarce supervi-sory resources	Spillover from bank/ insurance supervision; change in approach after integration of agency
Netherlands	X			X	X	X
Denmark	X		X	X	X	X
Australia				X	X	X
Mexico		X	X	X	X	

Preventing underfunding of DB plans was a strong factor motivating the adoption of risk-based supervision in the Netherlands. Dutch funds enjoyed the equity boom in the 1990s and started taking contribution holidays when funding ratios reached levels considered as high. However, these funding ratios proved insufficient to absorb the adverse price movements in the early 2000s – the crash of the equity market combined with the drop in interest rates led several funds to become under-funded or only marginally funded. Regulators interpreted the outcome as indicating a weakness in the supervisory approach that was perceived as lacking sufficient foresight and concern for the risks facing the institutions.

The introduction of a more risk-based approach to supervision in Denmark was also motivated by a concern with the solvency of pension providers, but the surrounding conditions were different from those in the Netherlands. First, the new Danish 'traffic light' system (explained in more detail below) preceded the equity crash in the early 2000s. By the time equity prices collapsed and interest rates declined, the new system was already in place. Secondly, the new system was introduced as a quid pro quo for a more liberal investment regime in which the ceiling on equity invest-ments was raised to 70 per cent. Danish funds were allowed to make riskier investments provided that they held sufficient capital to absorb the risk. Thirdly, the Danish system operates on a risk-sharing basis, which means that the system has buffers that can absorb at least part of the adverse price movements. These differences imply that the first motivating factor was more important in the Netherlands than in Denmark. However, there was still concern about provider solvency in Denmark, justifying the inclusion of this factor.

Concern with adverse price movements was also one of the motivating factors in Mexico, although the Mexican system is a DC system where the investment risk is shifted to the individual and there is little risk of provider insolvency. The policy concern in Mexico was not the risk of provider insolvency, but the exposure of retiring workers to extreme downside losses and the extreme volatility of benefits across cohorts.[8] It is also interesting to note that, as in the Danish case, the adoption of a VaR ceiling in Mexico and the introduction of strict risk management rules were a quid pro quo for the introduction of a more liberal investment regime that allowed pension fund managers to make riskier investments and use derivatives.

The search for efficiency gains was also one of the main motivating factors in Denmark and Mexico. In both cases, the investment regime was liberalized and pension funds allowed to investment more in equity and other assets perceived as risky. In Mexico, pension funds were allowed to use derivatives, subject to certification by the supervisor. The relaxation of the investment regime was motivated by the perception that pension funds were constrained below the efficient investment frontier and that there was scope for longer-term improvements in the risk–return trade-off. The relaxation of investment rules was accompanied by other rules designed to strengthen risk management and constrain excessive risk taking.

The need to establish rules that enabled pension funds to take advantage of the increasing sophistication and complexity of financial instruments and markets was a motivating factor in all the four countries. This reflects a more general recognition by financial supervisors worldwide that it is no longer feasible to monitor all of the operations of financial institutions, and that a more effective approach entails ensuring that these institutions have sound risk management practices and internal controls.

In the Netherlands, Denmark and Australia, the adoption of risk-based supervision was also driven by the need to allocate scarce supervisory resources efficiently. Especially in Australia and the Netherlands, supervisors need to monitor a large number of institutions. A traditional, compliance-based supervision would be either too costly or ineffective in these cases. The risk-based approach allows supervisors to focus their scarce resources in the institutions exposed to greater risks and/or with weaker risk management capacity. This factor was less important in Mexico, where only 18 funds are allowed to operate.[9]

The integration of financial supervisory functions in one entity also seems to have been a motivating factor in the Netherlands, Denmark and Australia. The adoption of risk-based supervision in pensions seems to have been accelerated in the countries that integrated their agencies and adopted the same basic supervision approach to all financial institutions. There was in these cases an accelerated transfer of supervisory 'know-how' from banking and/or insurance supervision to pension supervision. Mexico was again the exception, as the supervisory agency (Consar) was a single entity when the new approach was adopted and has remained a single entity since then.

7.4 THE MAIN ELEMENTS OF RISK-BASED SUPERVISION FOR PENSIONS

7.4.1 Common Objectives and Elements of Design

As discussed earlier, one of the main objectives of risk-based supervision in banking and insurance is to ensure that institutions adopt sound risk management procedures and hold appropriate levels of capital. Regulators and policy makers are aware that many leading institutions have already adopted good risk management practices and some companies would already be able to meet the more demanding requirements of Basel II and Solvency II. These financial institutions recognize that sound risk management practices are in the interest of stakeholders and are rewarded by the market, as indicated by the growing consideration of the quality of internal risk management by rating companies.[10]

Pension supervisors face challenges that are in many aspects similar to those faced by bank and insurance supervisors. They recognize the need to evolve to an approach that emphasizes sound risk management by the supervised institutions, in order to strengthen financial stability and ensure more efficient outcomes for pensioners. They are also aware that several pension funds in their countries have already started adopting good risk management practices. The challenge that pension supervisors face is to ensure that all licensed institutions comply with minimum standards of risk management and hold appropriate levels of capital (in the systems where this is relevant).

In order to examine the way pension supervisors have addressed this challenge, it is useful to consider Figure 7.1 which identifies the three main groups of players involved in the overall architecture of risk management. The first group consists of the supervised institutions. The second group is the supervisory agency, and the third consists of other market participants that may have the capacity to influence the decisions and actions of pension funds. These include auditors, actuaries, fund members, rating companies and market analysts.

One of the main objectives of risk-based supervision is to ensure sound risk management at the institutional level. As indicated in the left-hand box of Figure 7.1, the capacity of the institution to identify, measure and manage all the relevant risks would be reflected in the presence of a sound internal architecture of risk management that includes a reasonable risk management strategy, evidence of board involvement in risk management, the existence of risk management functions performed by competent, independent and accountable professionals, and proper internal controls.

The question is what tools supervisors have to ensure these outcomes. As indicated in the right-hand box of Figure 7.1, the broad elements of the supervisory toolkit include the regulations issued by the supervisor, including direct regulations focused on the risk management architecture and risk management procedures, a risk-based capital rule (in the environments where this is relevant), and a risk-scoring model that guides supervisory strategies and procedures. In addition, the supervisory agency will organize itself, consistent with the requirements of these elements, by establishing some units focused on managing the relationships with the supervised entities and other technical units more specialized in the measurement and analysis of different type of risks.

Finally, the third group of relevant players includes those market participants who may contribute to market discipline and the adoption of sound risk management practices by the institutions. The role of some of these players depends on regulations issued by the supervisor as well. For example, the role of the auditor may be enhanced by expanding the scope of the audits to include an assessment of the effectiveness of risk management systems and internal controls, and imposing whistle-blowing obligations. The influence of fund members, rating companies and other market analysts may be strengthened by good accounting, auditing and disclosure rules issued by the supervisor.

It is possible to relate the main components identified in Figure 7.1 with the three pillars in the Basel II/Solvency II framework. The risk-based solvency rule constitutes the first pillar and is relevant in DB systems or DC systems which offer benefit guarantees. The second pillar represents the supervisory process. Figure 7.1 emphasizes risk-scoring models, because these models have become essential tools around which pension supervisors organize their off-site and on-site supervisory actions. The third pillar, market discipline, is directly represented by the third block in Figure 7.1. This pillar plays an essential role in the Basel II and Solvency II framework, but its relevance for pension supervision depends more closely on the particular type of system, as discussed below.

7.4.2 Overview of the Main Components of Pension Supervision in the Four Countries

As illustrated in Table 7.4, pension supervisors in the four countries have developed these tools to varying degrees, reflecting the different environments. In the Netherlands, Denmark and Australia, the institutions must comply with corporate governance rules that emphasize the role and responsibilities of the board and must also have a risk management plan or risk management guidelines, but do not have to adopt a specific architecture of risk management. By contrast, all Mexican pension funds have to adopt a very specific and detailed risk management architecture laid out in a specific regulation issued by the supervisor.

The different approach followed in Mexico reflects the particular characteristics of the Mexican system, including the much smaller number of relatively homogeneous institutions. It is possible to implement this type of regulation in a system with only 18 pension funds. It would be very difficult – and also questionable – to implement this type of regulation in a system with 1000 pension funds, including large and small funds with very different capacities. Supervisors could generate severe inefficiencies by imposing a one-size-fits-all type of regulation. Of course, the build-up of risk management capacity in the institutions is a supervisory objective in Australia, Denmark and the Netherlands, but supervisors try to achieve this objective through other means, such as the incentive effects associated with their risk scoring model or by imposing sanctions on institutions with weak capacity to manage risks.

Risk-based solvency rules are relevant in the Netherlands and Denmark, because of the nature of their systems. Dutch supervisors have recently implemented a detailed and formal risk-based solvency rule that addresses longevity, market, credit, currency and interest rate risks and that penalizes asset–liability mismatches. Denmark has adopted a model that can be classified as hybrid. The formal solvency rule is not risk-based, but is complemented by a standard stress test called the 'traffic light system' that entails a test of the resiliency of the institution to fluctuations in interest rates and asset prices. The Danish traffic light system shares some common elements with the new Dutch solvency rule but also has some important differences. It is not a formal solvency rule, as already noted, and is applied in the context of a risk-sharing model, which implies a lower risk of insolvency. Risk-based solvency rules are not relevant in DC systems such as Australia and Mexico, but Mexican regulators have

Table 7.4 Main components of risk-based supervision in the four countries

	Requirements for the internal risk management architecture	Risk-based solvency rule	Risk scoring model	Role of market discipline/disclosure	Organization of supervision agency
Netherlands	Internal review of Board's management of long-term risks Risk management plan in fund's business plan (Abtn)	Fully developed risk-based solvency rule	Fully developed and unified framework, considering quantitative and qualitative aspects Applied to all financial institutions with relevant adaptations	Low Possibly higher in some cases through single employer balance sheet	Integrated agency Specialized pension units and specialized ALM and legal units
Denmark	Board of Directors required to issue risk management guidelines	Hybrid rule: solvency margin and risk-based traffic light system	Partially developed	High	Integrated agency Specialized pension units and specialized risk units
Australia	Risk management strategy and plan required for licensing	No formal solvency rules for DC plans[1]	Fully developed and unified framework considering quantitative and qualitative aspects Applied to all financial institutions	Medium	Integrated agency Lead supervisors and risk/technical specialists

| | | | with relevant adaptations | Partially developed: elements of risk scoring for operational and financial risk | Medium/High | Single-purpose entity, with specialized operational and financial risk units |

| Mexico | Very specific and detailed architecture laid out in a regulation issued by the supervisor | No formal solvency rules for DC plans However, VaR ceilings to limit downside risk | | | | |

Note: [1] Australia imposes basic technical solvency requirements for the remaining DB funds; the size of solvency buffer is assessed as part of PAIRS.

adopted a ceiling on daily VaR that limits the exposure of DC fund members to downside risk.

Australia and the Netherlands have made substantial progress in building comprehensive risk scoring models that are applied to all financial institutions, with adaptations depending on the type of institution. In the Netherlands, solvency indicators are considered as inputs to the risk scoring model, providing a link between the risk-based capital position and the risk scores. It is also interesting to note that the Australian risk scoring model takes into consideration the institution's exposure to financial risks (and the capacity to manage these risks) in the risk scores, even though it is applied to DC plans where financial risks are shifted to the individual members. APRA (the Australian Prudential Regulation Authority) examines the adequacy of investment management processes, including the investment strategies, asset allocation, diversification, liquidity needs and performance measurement, monitoring and benchmarking. It looks not only for compliance with the broad investment rules but also at the way risk management compares to good industry practices. Denmark and Mexico have made only partial progress in this area. Both countries have developed elements of a risk scoring model to guide their supervisory actions, but have not yet developed full models.

Market discipline does not seem to play a very important role in the Netherlands, although the disclosure of the fund's solvency position and its implications for the sponsor may impose an element of discipline in single employer funds. Market discipline plays a more important role in Mexico and Denmark, where there is more scope for individuals or sponsors to change the provider, and supervisors in both countries ensure a high level of disclosure to facilitate comparisons and well-informed decisions.

Finally, all the supervisory agencies have reorganized themselves to conduct a type of supervision that requires more specialized skills. In Australia, Denmark and the Netherlands there are units focused on the relationship with the institutions and specialized units providing expert/technical support on different types of risks. The Mexican supervisory agency has a particular set-up that mirrors the internal risk management architecture imposed by regulation.

7.4.3 Regulatory Requirements for Risk Management Architecture

Table 7.5 provides more detail on the regulatory requirements for the internal risk management architecture. Australia, Denmark and the Netherlands impose some requirements on risk management as part of licensing or initial registration procedures. This includes the elaboration of a risk management plan or risk management guidelines. These requirements are not very detailed, with the supervisors allowing for differences, depending on the size of the institution. These countries do not seem to impose specific regulatory requirements on the internal risk management architecture, although Dutch funds must have an internal body reviewing long-term risk management, as well as independent risk management functions.

As mentioned before, Mexican supervisors have followed a different approach, issuing a direct regulation that specifies in detail all the elements of the internal risk management architecture. All pension funds must have two Board committees dedicated to risk management, one focused on operational risk and the other on financial risk. Each committee must have at least five members, of which three are Board members. At least one of the Board members must be independent. The other members are the Chief Executive Officer (CEO) and the Chief Risk Officer (CRO). The CRO heads an independent and central risk management unit (UAIR), addressing both operational and financial risks, and must report to the Board, the CEO and the supervisor. The regulation specifies in detail the duties and obligations of the CRO, including the interactions with other key executives such as the Chief Investment Officer. The regulation also requires the presence of a compliance officer ensuring observance of all the regulations.

It is difficult to make a comparison of the effectiveness of these two approaches, because Australian, Danish and Dutch supervisors may also induce institutions to adopt sound risk management practices through their risk scoring models. As explained in more detail below, risk scoring models measure the exposure of institutions to risk and their capacity to manage these risks. This capacity is assessed in some detail, entailing the assessment of the quality of very specific elements of risk management, procedures and control. Institutions which receive low scores are typically subject to more intensive supervision and pressed to remedy their deficiencies.

The Australian supervisory agency (APRA) introduced a guidance note on risk management to further explain the risk management requirements inserted into the legislation in the context of a comprehensive relicensing programme that has resulted in a sharp reduction in the number of institutions. APRA stresses that effective risk management is critical to the safety and soundness of the operations of the trustee. Its supervisors report that several institutions could not demonstrate their capacity to prepare or implement a coherent risk management plan during the relicensing process.

The Australian experience suggests that pension supervisors probably need to consider a combination of tools to ensure the introduction of sound risk management practices in all institutions, while also providing

Table 7.5 Regulatory requirements on the risk management architecture

	Risk management plan/strategy	Board committees for risk management	Minimum participation in Board committees	Centralized risk management function	Reporting obligations of chief risk officer (CRO)	Relationship of CRO with other functions	Compliance officer
Netherlands	Required to be included in the business plan submitted at time of licensing	Accountability body that inter alia reviews long-term risk management	No specific requirements	Must be independent of all other departments in the pension fund	No specific requirements	No specific requirements	No specific requirements
Denmark	Board of Directors required to issue risk management guidelines	No specific requirements	No specific requirements	No specific requirements	No specific requirements	No specific requirements	No specific requirements
Australia	Required for licensing Complexity and detail depend on fund's size	No specific requirements	No specific requirements	No specific requirements	No specific requirements	No specific requirements	No specific requirements
Mexico	Written policies and procedures for	Two Board committees for	Board committees must have at	Central risk management unit (UAIR)	To CEO, Board and supervisor	Specified in detail	Compliance officer required

| addressing operational and financial risk | operational and financial risks | least five members: three Board members, of which one independent, the CEO and the CRO | dealing with operational and financial risks and headed by chief risk officer (CRO) |

the necessary flexibility for institutions with different sizes. The Mexican approach can only be implemented in systems with fewer and larger pension funds. The Mexican approach merits consideration by countries with similar systems, although its effectiveness would need to be assessed in the coming years. One of the issues that would need to be examined is whether the approach works well across different institutions, including institutions which are part of financial conglomerates owned by parent companies abroad – a very common situation in systems like the Chilean and the Mexican.

7.4.4 Risk-based Solvency Standards

The main elements of the solvency requirements for the four countries are summarized in Table 7.6. The Netherlands has developed the most structured and formal of these solvency regimes. This system originated with a set of solvency standards first developed in 1997 that were subsequently refined and introduced with the new Pensions Act, effective on 1 January 2007. The Dutch system includes a minimum solvency margin and solvency buffers designed to minimize the risk of underfunding due to longevity improvements or fluctuations in interest rates and asset prices.

Liabilities (technical provisions) are measured with a mortality table that reflects predicted longevity improvements. The discount rate used is the market yield curve measured by the Euro swap curve. The interest rates used for discounting are only slightly higher than those in government bonds of equivalent duration, owing to the high credit standing of banks operating in the market and the high market liquidity. All pension funds must comply with a minimum solvency requirement equivalent to approximately 5 per cent of technical provisions. However, funds must also build additional solvency buffers whose magnitude depends on the degree of asset–liability mismatches, and that are designed to reduce the probability of underfunding to only 2.5 per cent on a one-year horizon. For example, funds that invest more in equity, or fixed income assets with shorter duration than the duration of liabilities, or foreign currency assets, must maintain stronger buffers.

In line with the approach followed in Basel II, pension funds may opt to comply with a standardized model or build their own internal models to compute their solvency requirements, although these models need to be approved by the supervisor. In the standardized model, the solvency buffers are calculated through a stress test based on six broad risk factors and a formula for aggregate risk that takes partially into account correlations across asset classes. The methodology implies that the typical Dutch fund will need to maintain a sizable buffer amounting to 30 per cent of technical

Table 7.6   Risk-based solvency requirements

Country	Measurement of liabilities (TPs)		Minimum solvency requirements	Solvency buffers
	Treatment of longevity risk	Discount factors		
Netherlands	Group-specific mortality table adjusted for predicted longevity improvements	Market yield curve measured by Euro swap curve	5% of technical provisions (from EU IORP Directive) Measured once a year using current market values Maximum period for correction of deviations: 3 years	Maximum probability of underfunding within one year measured with stress test: 2.5% Solvency buffers determined by risk factors specific to each asset class Example of risk factors include yearly decline in Equity: 25–35% (depends on type) Currency: 20% Real estate: 15% Maximum period for correction of deviations: 15 years
Denmark	Fund-specific mortality table approved by actuary and supervisor Traffic light stress test includes assessment of the impact of a 5% improvement in longevity	Market yield curve measured by Euro swap curve	Solvency margin defined by EU Life Directive: 4% of technical provision plus 0.3% of risk-bearing investments Measured every six months using current market values	Traffic light system is a stress test rather than part of the formal solvency rule, are taken into consideration in the supervisory assessment Test defines three zones: green, yellow and red Final outcome depends on whether entity remains solvent after test

Table 7.6 (continued)

Country	Measurement of liabilities (TPs)		Minimum solvency requirements	Solvency buffers
	Treatment of longevity risk	Discount factors		
			Period of correction from minimum required standards: one year	Example (yearly variations): Listed equity: red 12%, yellow 30% Interest rate (medium duration) Red +/– 0.85%; Yellow +/– 1.2%
Australia	No formal liabilities in DC plans	No formal liabilities in DC plans	No solvency requirements for DC plans	No solvency requirements for DC plans
Mexico	No formal liabilities in DC plans	No formal liabilities in DC plans	No formal solvency requirements, but value at risk (VaR) limit designed to limit downside risk for DC members Historic VaR calculated with rolling 550-day sample at 5% significance with different limits imposed on the two portfolios; price vector provided by two independent vendors Higher risk portfolio: 1% maximum daily loss Standard risk portfolio: 0.6% maximum daily loss	

provisions. To reduce the buffer, the fund will need to reduce the mismatch by, for example, shifting from equity to bonds or increasing the duration of the bond portfolio.

The Dutch approach provides an incentive for pension funds to build their own internal models, because a more refined methodology and more accurate parameters will probably reduce the size of the required solvency buffer. However, if pension funds decide to build their own models, this may prove challenging to the supervisor, who will have to assess each of these models.[11]

Although pension funds may be able to reduce their solvency requirements by building their own models, the Dutch risk-based solvency rule has still been criticized for being too costly and not taking into consideration the possibility that long-run risks are lower because of lower correlations of asset classes over time or mean reversion of equity returns.[12] Dutch regulators clearly preferred to adopt a conservative view, while introducing an element of flexibility by allowing a relatively long period of 15 years for compliance.

The Danish solvency requirements are slightly less specified but grounded on the same principles. As with the Netherlands, there is a minimum solvency margin based on the current valuation of liabilities that is supplemented by a stress test based on the composition of assets. The stress test places each fund into one of three 'traffic light' zones that indicate the current solvency position. It is distinguished from the Dutch approach because it does not explicitly link remedial measures to the status of the funds but rather seeks to maintain funds within a solvency corridor through signalling devices and market pressures. A solvency status is calculated for every institution twice a year and places each institution in one of three categories: a green light for those deemed within acceptable solvency status, a yellow light for those determined to be in danger of facing solvency problems and a red light for the institutions that face severe and immediate problems.

Rather than impose a single potential scenario of adverse market conditions, the Danish approach establishes two sets of parameters for each risk factor, which effectively imply a mild and a strong stress test. If a fund is put into theoretical insolvency by the mild test it is deemed to be in the red zone. In other words, funds in the red zone cannot withstand even a moderate adverse shift in asset prices. Those which remain theoretically solvent under the mild test but not the strong test are placed in the yellow zone. For example, a decline in equities of 30 per cent is posited for the red test and 12 per cent for the yellow. The factors are 8 per cent and 12 per cent, respectively, for real estate. Factors are also stipulated for varying duration of fixed income instruments, credit risk and others. Funds which remain theoretically solvent after the strong test are put in the green zone.

Frontiers in pension finance

Failure to meet the yellow scenario is treated as an early warning indicator. An institution that receives a yellow light is placed under intensified supervision. The primary goal of intensified supervision is to increase the risk awareness of the management of the pension institution. When an institution receives a red light, it may be subjected to more drastic intervention. The supervisor may order the institution concerned to take the measures necessary within a specified time limit if its financial position has deteriorated to such a degree that it puts the interests of policy holders and other affected parties at risk.

A red light does not necessary imply that the institution will immediately be subject to crisis management. The supervisor will normally require monthly reporting from the institution as well as a commitment that it will not increase its overall risk exposure. If the institution remains in a red light situation for a prolonged period a reduction in risk will be required although measures to reduce risks and/or risk exposures are not specified in detail. However, action plans prepared by the institution concerned must be submitted to the supervisor. The Danish Financial Supervisory Authority decides the maximum period for the restoration of the financial position, depending on the size of the shortfall and anticipated market developments. The DFSA is expected to monitor the performance of the operating plan and demand changes in the plan if the financial position of the institution suffers further deterioration. If the base capital of the pension institution is less than one-third of the solvency requirement or is less than the minimum capital requirement, the period for restoration of capital will be stated in months and will not normally exceed one year.

Australia, which has rapidly transitioned almost to an entirely DC-based system over the past decade, does not incorporate explicit solvency requirements on the risks of DC fund portfolios. However, the exposure to financial risks is captured in the risk scoring model, and the supervisor will check whether the institution has the capacity to manage these risks. If the institution proves to be unable to manage the risks associated with a more aggressive or complex portfolio it becomes subject to more intensive supervision.

Mexico has taken an entirely different approach to volatility risk. Within their DC system the relevant characteristic is the volatility of the value of member's accounts rather than asset–liability balance. While not strictly speaking a solvency measure in the traditional meaning, the parameters that Mexico requires their pension funds to remain within serve a similar purpose, to ensure the adequacy of the asset base and retain its fluctuations within a prescribed level. This may be viewed as implicitly assuming a liability (or minimum return) for the pension system.

The Mexican limitations are established in the form of a maximum permissible 'value at risk' or VaR which the funds are permitted to have.

Mexico now permits two types of portfolios (Siefores) within each of the pension companies (Afores). The standard portfolio established at the outset of the system's design is limited to a composition that is estimated through the methodology outlined below to be associated with a maximum loss in a day of less than 0.6 per cent of its value. The higher risk/return portfolio that was recently introduced into the system must maintain a VaR of less than 1.0 per cent.

The VaR is calculated by the supervisor on a daily basis, based on a rolling 500-day sample of the prices of all of the permissible assets. The price vector is provided by two independent price vendors, to ensure a common valuation methodology and comparability. The VaR is historic and calculated with a 5 per cent level of significance for each portfolio (the individual portfolios are reported to the supervisor through automated systems). If any of the funds drifts outside of the permissible limits the supervisor is able to intervene and provide specific instructions regarding the reallocation required to move back within the prescribed standard. This has not occurred yet, as the actual VaRs remain well below the ceilings.

7.4.5 Supervisory Risk Scoring Systems

All supervisors gain an understanding of the risk profile of pension funds through their normal supervision activities. Any basic supervision framework involves the collection of data from pension funds. This can be as basic as the collection of annual accounts but, more typically, will involve collection of data through a set of standard forms designed by the supervisor and submitted by the pension funds on a regular basis. Through the analysis of collected data supervisors will have a picture of the financial strength of the funds. This can be supplemented by the collection of additional information from on-site inspections and the market. This information can be combined for the computation of overall risk scores for each institution. The various risk scoring systems from the four countries reviewed are shown in Table 7.7.

Australia was the first of the four countries to introduce a fully developed scoring system with the development in 2002 of a structured framework for risk assessment in pension funds known as the Probability and Impact Rating System (PAIRS). The results of this structured methodology for ranking pension funds according to the relative threat of failure are then mapped into a supervisory response framework (SOARS). The model makes a distinction between larger funds which are subject to detailed assessment and smaller funds which are subject to a streamlined and more automated assessment. Additional focus is also given to funds which are DB.

Table 7.7 Risk scoring methods

	Type of risk scoring system	Aims of the model	Main elements of risk scoring system	Special features for pensions	Supervisory response framework
Netherlands (FIRM)	Comprehensive risk scoring model applied to all types of institutions covered by integrated supervision authority	Identify and measure all major risks and the capacity of the entity to manage them Determine supervisory response Induce build-up of internal risk management capacity	Definition of gross or inherent risks, as well as mitigating factors through risk controls Use of default scores and templates Combined probability and impact Single net risk score built up from common elements	Risk-based solvency standards (FTK) applied to pensions and insurance provides major inputs to the risk scoring model and is a supervisory tool on its own	Used for planning supervisory cycle, frequency and nature of interventions
Denmark	Set of early warning indicators, including the results of the traffic light stress test	Identify areas and institutions exposed to greater risks Determine supervisory response Induce build-up of internal risk management capacity	Risk scoring model is partly developed Relies relatively more on the results of the traffic light stress test	Traffic light is a stress test that complements the EU solvency margin requirements	Used for planning supervisory cycle, frequency and nature of interventions Yellow light triggers more intensified supervision Red light likely to trigger remedial action

Australia (PAIRS)	Comprehensive risk scoring model applied to all types of institutions covered by integrated supervision authority	Identify and measure all major risks and the capacity of the entity to manage them Determine supervisory response Induce build-up of internal risk management capacity	Definition of gross or inherent risks, as well as mitigating factors through risk controls Use of default scores and templates Combined probability and impact Single net risk score built up from common elements	Capital strength component excluded for DC funds	Risk scoring maps directly to supervisory response (SOARS)
Mexico	Set of early warning indicators Developing a risk scoring model		Under development Actual VaRs will be input to the model	VaR limit computed daily	If breach of VaR results in a loss, compensation must be paid

APRA applies the same broad supervisory model to superannuation funds as to banks and insurance companies. The analyst is asked to assess the significance of the risks and mitigating factors and to assess the extent to which each contributes to (for the inherent risk factors) or reduces (for the management and control areas) the overall risks of the fund. Weighted numerical assessments are combined into an overall score. This score is converted to a risk rating using a non-linear function to ensure that higher risk funds are given greater attention. After taking into account an impact rating based on fund size, the scores are converted into a supervisory attention index which maps into a 'supervisory stance' and action plan. In this way the rating directly defines how the supervisor will manage their relationship with the pension fund. Funds in the 'normal' category are subject to regular supervision activities. Those in the 'oversight' category receive more intense monitoring and more frequent contact. Funds rated for 'mandated improvement' are expected to develop and implement plans for improvement, while those rated 'restructure' require strong enforcement action. The framework imposes a stronger analytical discipline to a still largely judgmental process and provides an audit trail to analyse and explain supervisory decisions and actions. It allows APRA to allocate more resources to institutions whose failure would have a greater impact on the financial system.

In the Netherlands in 2005, the DNB introduced an integrated method for analysing risk for all financial institutions, known as the Financial Institutions Risk Analysis Method (FIRM) which replaced the earlier pension and insurance specific system known as MARS. As for Australia, supervision in the Netherlands is based on the ongoing process of information collection, consultations with the supervised entities and a structured approach to the assessment of risk and the manner in which those risks are managed. Under the FIRM model, the DNB takes into account the assessment of solvency outlined earlier and combines this with an evaluation of the pension entity, the risks to which it is exposed and the quality of the risk management procedures in place. As with Australia, the results of the risk assessment become the basis for decisions regarding the nature and intensity of supervisory action.

The FIRM model adopts a four-stage approach to building the risk assessment. In the first step a detailed profile of the pension fund is constructed. The second step identifies relevant management units and functions and assigns weights to these. Using this functional breakdown the third step evaluates gross risks and assigns a score to this assessment. In contrast to Australia, the Dutch system combines probability and impact into a single score within the system rather than assessing these separately, based on the view that the two elements are so closely related they should not be independently considered. The various types of risks identified in

Australia and the Netherlands are very similar. The additional focus in the Netherlands on technical insurance and mismatch risks reflects the primarily DB nature of the pension system.

The fourth step in the Netherlands seeks to obtain an insight into the quality of risk controls for each risk category to derive a final value that represents the net risks of the pension fund. The aggregation of risks is based on a mathematical algorithm which puts emphasis on high risks and poor controls. The reports which form part of the FIRM model form a basis for the planning of supervision activities. The frequency of on-site inspections is determined largely by the risk profile of the fund. During an on-site inspection, data are collected which allow the FIRM model to be updated and high risk areas which have been identified are examined closely.

Concurrent with the introduction of the VaR standards in 2002, the Mexican supervisory authority Consar has developed elements of a risk scoring model, in the form of early warning indicators for assessing operational and financial risks. The current methodology entails three risk factors (low, medium and high) and gives emphasis to irregularities detected during supervision activity. Reflecting the fact that Mexico operates a DC system, it is not surprising that the main weaknesses identified relate to internal controls and the collection of contributions. Supervision strategies are focused on the most critical areas identified by the early warning system. However, Consar is in the process of incorporating other elements of risk into the VaR, such as credit risk, and assessing how it can make greater use of the VaR results for risk scoring.

Denmark has also developed elements of a risk scoring model, in the form of an internal rating system with three internal quality scores covering organization, procedures and internal controls, as well as ratings on insurance risks, which mainly cover longevity risk exposure of the different institutions. The DFSA combines these internal score or early warning indicators with the traffic light results, to guide the intensity and scope of supervisory activity.

7.4.6 Market-based Discipline and Third Parties

The importance of market discipline in risk-based supervision depends fundamentally on the type of pension system, and the extent to which supervisors ensure disclosure and enhance the roles of third parties such as the external auditor. In general, the market discipline pillar is more relevant in open pension systems that allow selection of the provider. Even in these cases, however, the supervisor must ensure proper accounting, auditing and disclosure rules ensuring the access of fund members and market analysis to relevant and accurate information.

As shown in Table 7.8, all the four countries have adopted market valuation of balance sheets. While this is a standard feature of DC systems, such as the Australian and the Mexican, it has only recently been introduced in the Netherlands and Denmark. In all the countries external auditors need to verify the accuracy of financial statements. In Australia and Mexico, their role is expanded to include an assessment of the quality of risk management systems. In all four countries external auditors have 'whistle-blowing' obligations; that is, they need to report material problems to the supervisor.

Mexico imposes extensive disclosure requirements, including monthly disclosure of individual portfolios, returns, fees and VaRs. Denmark discloses annually a large number of performance and solvency indicators of individual providers, allowing for direct comparisons of performance. The Australian Securities and Investments Commission has detailed product disclosure requirements for funds which allow members to direct their investment strategies. However, disclosure requirements on fund performance remain comparatively less extensive in Australia, a somewhat surprising result considering that members have recently been allowed to switch across pension funds. The less demanding disclosure requirements in the Netherlands are expected, reflecting the closed nature of the Dutch system.

Overall, the market discipline pillar seems to play a more important role in Mexico and Denmark, followed by Australia and the Netherlands. Mexico would seem to meet all the requirements for a strong third pillar, although the benefit guarantee extended to older workers probably weakens market discipline (Bernstein and Chumacero, 2006b). The Danish system also assigns an important role to the third pillar, as indicated by the comprehensive disclosure requirements.

Australia has recently extended the scope of external audits to include an assessment of the quality of risk management systems. The extent to which external auditors can perform this task effectively is open to question, but the fact that regulations include this obligation reveals the intention to increase the importance of third party monitoring. Moreover, the recent decision to allow members to switch funds may increase pressure for more disclosure in the future. In the Netherlands, disclosure requirements are less extensive, although the obligation for single sponsors to reflect the situation of their funds in their balance sheets may introduce an important element of market discipline.

7.4.7 Internal Structure of the Supervision Agency

The supervisory agencies of the four countries include one which is responsible solely for supervising retirement savings (Mexico), two independent

Table 7.8   Role of market discipline, third parties, disclosure

	Accounting rules	Selected auditing rules		Disclosure requirements
		Scope of audit	Accountability	
Netherlands	Fair valuation of assets and liabilities	Financial statements	Whistle blowing obligations	Single employer funds included on balance sheet of sponsor
Denmark	Fair valuation of assets and liabilities	Financial statements	Whistle blowing obligations to supervisor authority for 'material' issues	Extensive disclosure of individual indicators of efficiency and solvency – key performance indicators – on supervisor's website
Australia	Net market value for assets	Financial statements and assessment of risk management systems	Whistle blowing obligations	Operating statement and statement of financial position for all funds
Mexico	Mark-to-market Regulated price vendors ensuring consistent portfolio valuation and comparability	Financial statements and assessment of risk management systems	Whistle blowing obligations	Extensive disclosure of individual investment policies, fees, returns, and VaRs

integrated supervisors (Australia and Denmark) and one where the central bank serves as an integrated financial supervisory authority (the Netherlands).

In Mexico, Consar was initially focused on collecting information and ensuring compliance with the rules and regulations, particularly the tight controls over investment. In the past few years it has undergone an internal reorganization to allow it to implement more effectively a risk-based approach to supervision. The main supervision activities have been separated into operational and financial areas under two separate vice-presidencies. Consar has been building up its technical capabilities to assess the impact of VaR models and enable assessment of the risk management practices within the pension fund managers.

The Danish FSA was established in its present form as an integrated financial sector regulator in 1988. Major segments of the financial industry are supervised in different divisions. The Life and Pensions Division is one of ten divisions responsible for supervision and regulatory techniques. Staff in this division takes part in off-site surveillance and on-site inspections. The Division was responsible for developing the traffic light stress test, in close collaboration with the Banking Division which had developed expertise in this area.

Within the Dutch Central Bank, supervision is organized around several operating directorates aligned with particular types of institution such as conglomerates, banks, insurance companies and pension funds. Each division is supported by a supervisory policy division with responsibilities across all types of institutions and by centres of expertise in specialist areas such as 'Asset-Liability Management'. The development of FIRM has involved representatives from all supervisory divisions but it is owned by a Division Director from one of the supervisory divisions. An expert team comprising representatives from all operational divisions is responsible for ensuring that the system is updated as required.

Within APRA, supervision follows a more integrated model in which staff can have responsibility for several types of financial institution. In their supervisory and analytical work, analysts responsible for routine supervision are supported by specialists in credit, market and operational risk and can draw on actuarial support. A separate group within the Policy and Research Division provides technical support for the PAIRS/SOARS model, and collects data on risk rating for regular reporting to management and the Executive Team within APRA.

7.5   PRELIMINARY ASSESSMENT OF THE IMPACT OF RBS

This section provides some initial observations that can be gleaned from the limited information available about the changes that are associated with the adoption of risk-based supervision. It is important to stress that any assessment must be seen as preliminary, because these new supervisory systems have been introduced very recently and are designed to control pension systems whose outcomes in relation to the ability to deliver retirement benefits for a typical member extend across many decades.

7.5.1 The Netherlands

The new Dutch supervisory paradigm is primarily directed to the resiliency of the solvency of DB pension plans. Although not formally imposed until very recently, both the FIRM scoring system and the solvency standards had similar antecedents in prior systems that were either announced or put into practice over the past four to five years, a period likely to be sufficient for underlying effects to begin to come to light. These risk-based approaches potentially impose significant costs, that may induce funds to change their strategic asset allocation, increase contribution rates, reduce benefits or implement a combination of all these solutions. They may also induce employers to stop sponsoring DB plans altogether and move towards less onerous DC plans.

Despite these increasing risks to plan sponsors, which in other countries such as the UK and US have resulted in a massive substitution of DC arrangements and some decline in coverage, neither of these can be observed in the Netherlands. The overall coverage rate remains above 90 per cent, one of the highest in the world, and the total number of members has remained essentially unchanged since 2004. Virtually all of these remain DB plans, with DC plan coverage showing an increase from 2.3 to 3.6 per cent of members between 2004 and 2006. This seeming resiliency of the DB system to regulatory encroachment must be considered in the context of a system founded in collectively bargained industry-wide arrangements that, at a minimum, are likely to be insulated from changes in form over the short term. The only possible effect that can be observed in the aggregate data is a decline in the number of funds from over 1000 in the late 1990s to 860 in 2004 and 798 in 2006. This reduction may reflect the higher costs imposed by the new system that make small funds less viable, but it may reflect other causes as well. In any case, another five years may be required to observe conclusively any effects of the new rules on coverage, plan selection and fund size.

What has happened more clearly in recent years is dramatic changes in the secondary aspects of pension scheme characteristics. While much of this is likely related to broader pressures of population aging, to some extent they may be interpreted as a partial process of hedging risk exposure in response to the new more stringent solvency measures. The proportion of Dutch pension funds that provide benefits based on final pay has declined from 54 per cent in 2002 just prior to the initial introduction of risk-based rules to about 10 per cent. A less marked increase in the incidence of conditional indexing of promised benefits to price levels has occurred, from 90 per cent in 2002 to an almost universal 98 per cent in 2006, although there was very little room for movement in this indicator.

As mentioned before, another area to observe the impact of the new supervisory system is in the investment patterns of funds. Two effects were generally posited in response to rules that impose high costs for asset–liability mismatches. These are a movement away from equities to fixed income and increases in the duration of fixed income portfolios. As shown in Table 7.9, the aggregate balance sheet information on pension funds does not appear to support the first of these expectations. The available evidence does, however, seem to indicate the second expected impact – the lengthening of the duration of the fixed income portfolios to better manage the mismatch exposure that is exacerbated with the volatility of the new market based discount rate. As shown in Figure 7.2, from the end of 2003 to the end of 2005, average duration increased by a year to more than six years with some funds moving to much higher durations.

It is possible that pension portfolios will become more conservative in the future, as pension funds build their internal models and reassess in more detail the impact of the new rules on their solvency position. At the same

Table 7.9   *Asset allocation of Dutch pension funds, 2001–2005 (% of total)*

	2001	2002	2003	2004	2005
Land and buildings	11	11	10	10	10
Investments, non-consolidated	1	1	1	1	0
Shares and other variable yield securities	42	35	40	40	42
Bonds and other fixed yield securities	36	41	39	40	40
Mortgage loans	3	4	3	3	2
Private loans	5	3	2	2	1
Deposits	0	0	0	0	1
Other investments	2	2	3	2	3
Liquid assets	1	2	2	2	2
Total (Euro millions)	460 777	427 297	481 811	542 112	624 881

Source: DNB data and authors' calculations.

Frequency (%)

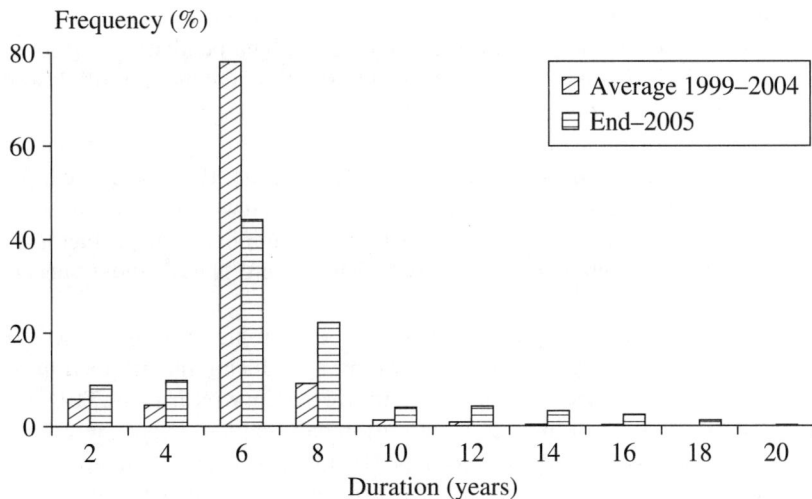

Source: Kakes and Broeders (2006).

Figure 7.2 Distribution of the duration of Dutch pension fund fixed-income investments

time, the absence of more pronounced shifts in strategic asset allocation could also be due to the long period of compliance. As mentioned before, pension funds are allowed 15 years to address shortfalls in the required solvency buffers. This relatively long period of compliance introduces a necessary element of flexibility, especially in view of the uncertainty regarding mean reversion of equity returns.[13]

7.5.2 Denmark

The introduction of the risk-based approach to supervision occurred just prior to the decline of interest rates and the drop in equity prices in 2000–2002, making it difficult to distinguish the effects of the introduction of the new system from external factors. Immediately after the introduction of the more risk-oriented rules, pension institutions suffered huge losses on their equity portfolios, while the present value of technical provisions increased dramatically. A very high proportion of contracts had been issued with guaranteed returns. Guaranteed rates were lowered by two-thirds in two stages over the 1990s, but pension institutions continued to be exposed to the residual high-rate contracts for both past and future contributions that could still be made under the terms of the previous contracts.

The mismatch between assets and liabilities was aggravated by the presence of large investments in mortgage bonds with embedded call options. As borrowers exercised their option to refinance their mortgages with lower interest rates, pension institutions did not experience an increase in the market value of their bond holdings. In this situation, a large number of institutions found themselves in the yellow light under the new traffic light system, while some were even in the red light. For a few companies the situation turned out to be so severe that they encountered real problems in fulfilling their solvency requirements and they were placed under special supervision by the authorities.

As shown in Table 7.10 and Figure 7.3, pension institutions reacted to the financial crisis and the new stress testing by reducing the proportion of equities following two years of substantially negative returns in 2001 and 2002. They also began to close the duration gap that had led to the deterioration of their solvency position by increasing investment in foreign bonds which offer longer durations. The institutions also began to engage in extensive hedging operations, mostly through the use of long-term interest rate swaps in the more liquid Euro market.[14] Although such policies ran the risk of 'locking-in the losses', it was generally accepted that under the new solvency standards pension institutions could not afford to suffer additional losses and further endanger their position.

The increased use of derivatives and the changes in strategic asset allocation significantly improved the position of pension funds in relation to unfavourable interest rate movements, as indicated in the simulations shown in Table 7.11. While, in 2001 and 2002, an interest rate fall of one percentage point produced a net loss of more than DKK 15 billion, the new portfolio structure had transformed a negative 100 basis point decline into

Table 7.10   Changes in the asset allocation of Danish life companies and pension funds (per cent)

	Domestic bonds	Foreign bonds	Domestic equities	Foreign equities	Investment trusts	Other assets
1998	54.4	1.3	13.4	12.3	1.9	16.7
1999	46.6	2.1	12.6	18.3	3.5	17.0
2000	44.7	4.8	11.3	18.5	4.6	16.1
2001	45.1	10.7	8.6	12.5	6.3	16.8
2002	53.0	13.6	4.6	6.9	6.2	15.7
2003	51.3	12.4	4.4	8.0	8.1	15.8
2004	43.2	14.6	4.6	8.3	12.3	17.1

Source: DFSA.

Asset composition in Danish pension companies 1999–2004

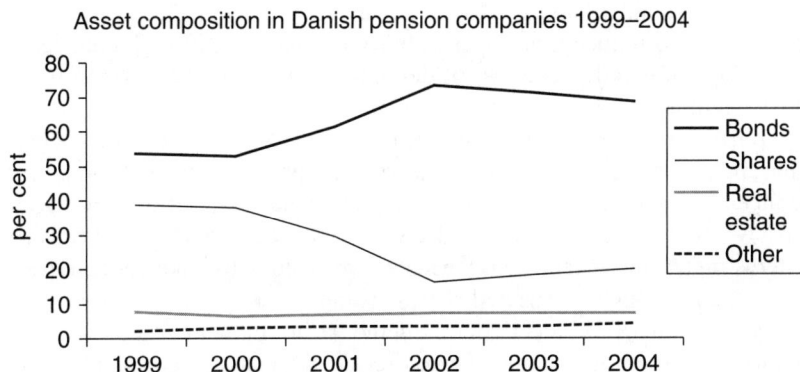

Source: Danish FSA, Market Development for Life-assurance Companies and Nation-wide Pension Funds.

Figure 7.3   Asset composition in Danish pension companies, 1999–2004

Table 7.11   Simulation results of change in interest rates

Year	Change	Liabilities DKK bn	Assets DKK bn	AL gains DKK bn	Derivatives DKK bn	Net gains DKK bn
2001	−1%	−65.0	49.4	−15.6		−15.6
2002	−1%	−66.6	26.7	−39.9	25.1	−14.8
2003	−1%	−52.0	40.2	−11.8	26.9	15.1
2004	−1%	−76.1	40.7	−35.4	43.8	8.4

Source: Ladekarl et al. (2006).

an estimated net gain of DKK 15 billion in 2003 and DKK 8 billion in 2004.

In addition to these changes in asset allocation, there were also other important changes in the rules for profit distribution (the Danish system is dominated by risk-sharing or profit-sharing policies, as mentioned before). Until recently, most institutions set the rate of profit distribution to clients one year ahead. This rate was an important competitive parameter among pension institutions. However, after 2002, many institutions introduced a variable rate of profit distribution that depends on investment performance during the year. This more flexible approach made it easier for institutions to meet their obligations, but, coupled with the substantial reduction in guaranteed rates of return, it created considerable uncertainty in the eyes of policy holders.

Overall, the introduction of risk-based supervision in Denmark has led institutions to reduce their asset–liability mismatches through changes in asset allocation and greater use of derivatives. One important consequence of these adjustments has been the decline in the expected rate of return on the portfolio and the decreased enthusiasm of providers to offer benefit guarantees. The greater use of derivatives has apparently helped companies reduce asset–liability mismatches at a reasonable cost, but does not seem to have been able to arrest a decline in the expected rate of return. Interestingly, new clients have been more willing to take more risk in exchange for a higher expected return, as indicated by the growth of unit-linked and other products that are offered without any guarantees or with reduced levels of guarantee. Therefore, the Danish system seems to be moving towards a more traditional DC system with fewer guarantees.

These trends seem to contradict the conclusion of other researchers, that the use of derivatives (especially long-term interest swaps) has allowed Danish companies to address the mismatches and also preserve returns.[15] On the contrary, the available evidence suggests that the new risk-based rules have induced pension funds to hold more conservative portfolios and lower guarantees, and that young members are favouring contracts that entail higher expected returns and more volatility. This is an area that should merit more research, as it would throw more light on the impact of risk-based supervision on portfolio strategies.

7.5.3   Australia

There are two main elements to changes in the risk-based supervisory framework in Australia which have had an impact on superannuation funds over the past few years. The first to be introduced was the PAIRS/SOARS framework. The second was the introduction of a comprehensive licensing framework for all superannuation funds.

The PAIRS/SOARS framework was intended to improve APRA's supervisory performance and not directly affect the industry. APRA assesses the timeliness and effectiveness of its intervention, by tracking the migration of institutions between the different supervisory stances. In the three years since the model was introduced the great majority of institutions in 'Mandated Improvement' or 'Restructure' at some point over this period have either improved or left the industry, with no entity failures. Of the 168 institutions that have been in these two stances, 57 have improved, 16 remain in their SOARS category, one has been downgraded and 94 have exited.[16] APRA does not publish these data separately for superannuation funds but has confirmed that around 100 have been superannuation funds. These figures suggest that these tools have made APRA more effective, but they have mainly helped industry by removing or remediating the weakest entities.

The second major change has been the introduction of superannuation licensing. At the beginning of the licensing transition period there were more than 1700 trustees operating. By the end of the licensing transition period, 307 trustee licences had been issued (with about twice as many registered funds). The trend towards industry consolidation had begun many years before APRA introduced licensing, but it has clearly hastened industry consolidation, including a trend towards corporate superannuation outsourcing. In order to be granted a licence, trustees had to demonstrate that they met the required minimum standards of risk and were well placed to provide beneficiaries with greater levels of safety and security for their superannuation accounts. New operating standards concerning fitness and propriety, risk management, adequacy of resources and outsourcing proved challenging to meet and many trustees have left the industry.

One of the reasons for reform of superannuation was to create a more professional industry where risk management standards, particularly for operational risk, were substantially improved. In its most recent annual report APRA notes that a regulated superannuation fund (excluding small funds) now manages, on average, over seven times the level of assets it managed five years ago, a period in which total superannuation assets have less than doubled. Superannuation funds have grown in terms of size, complexity and growing sophistication of risk management and the industry more closely resembles the other industries which APRA regulates.

Among those trustees that have exited have been some generally smaller entities with problematic investments involving highly undiversified portfolios (sometimes dominated by a handful of illiquid assets) and related party and employer-linked transactions. However, there has been little impact on broader investment strategies or any observable changes in the investment composition of the industry more generally.

APRA suggests that the implementation of PAIRS/SOARS has resulted in more consistent supervisory outcomes by allowing for a better calibration of APRA's reaction to supervisory issues across a large number of institutions and supervisors. The primary source of information for a PAIRS assessment is based on the findings from supervision activities. Any requirements placed on superannuation funds and recommendations for changes in behaviour or systems generally arise from these findings rather than from a particular PAIRS rating. However, while PAIRS does not mandate those changes on an institution per se it is very useful in calibrating the impact of these changes on the overall risk profile of a fund. Industry has indicated that improved consistency enhances its confidence in APRA's methods and procedures.

7.5.4 Mexico

As mentioned above, the search for efficiency gains and the concern with extreme portfolio losses were two important factors that motivated the adoption of risk-based supervision in Mexico. The relaxation of portfolio restrictions (including the permission to use derivatives) combined with stricter risk management requirements would lead to more efficient outcomes, and the exposure of individuals to downside risk would be contained by the VaR limit.

The impact of the regulatory changes is assessed by examining the resulting shifts in the efficient frontier and the actual changes in portfolio strategies. Consar[17] provides estimates of the efficient frontier for every year when the investment regime was liberalized. These estimates indicate that the frontier has been expanded quite substantially, especially in 2004, when there was another round of changes combined with the introduction of the VaR ceiling. Figure 7.4 illustrates the shift in the frontier resulting from the latest round of changes. The expansion of the frontier resulting from a relaxation of portfolio controls is expected and consistent with estimates for other countries, such as Chile.[18] However, the question is whether the expansion of the frontier has led to more efficient outcomes.

Pension fund managers have made use of the greater freedom to invest by moving away from very basic portfolios, and investing more in domestic and foreign equity, as well as foreign fixed income instruments. As shown in Table 7.12, the share of public sector bonds has declined from almost 100 per cent to 75 per cent more recently, and the share of higher yield, privately-issued domestic and foreign assets has increased commensurately. The average maturity and duration of the fixed-income portfolio has also increased significantly, as shown in Figure 7.5. These portfolio shifts are reflected in risk-return combinations that are higher and to the right, as shown in Figure 7.4. The average computed VaRs have increased, although they are still well below the ceiling, as shown in Figure 7.6.

The outcomes are positive overall, as there has been a diversification away from a very basic and low-return portfolio consisting primarily of government securities with short durations. There is no evidence of gains in the risk–return trade-off, strictly defined as a decrease in risk for the same return, or an increase in return for the same levels of risk. However, this is not surprising, as pension funds were basically investing in the risk-free portfolio. The right and upward movements in risk–return combinations and the increase in the average VaRs must be interpreted in this context. Even after these initial shifts, portfolios remain undiversified relative to pension funds in other countries, and VaRs remain well below the ceiling.

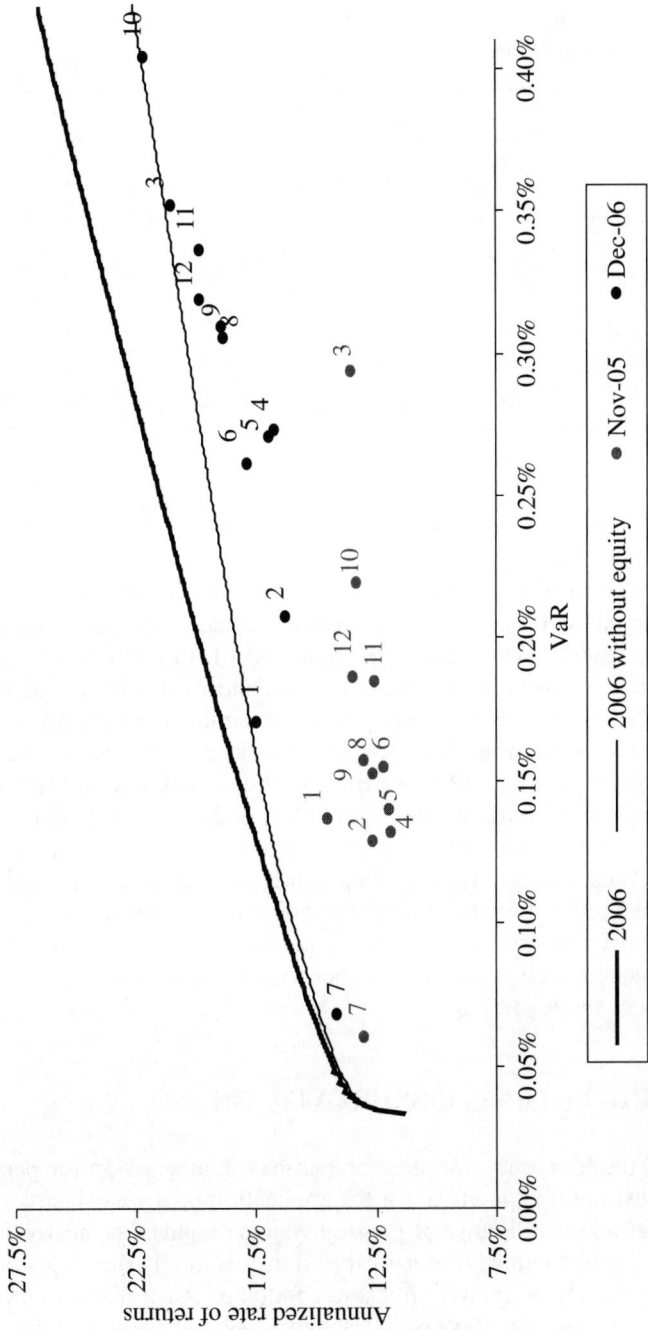

Figure 7.4 *Shifts in the efficient frontier and actual gains in risk–return trade-off*

Legend:
— 2006
— 2006 without equity
• Nov-05
• Dec-06

X-axis: VaR
Y-axis: Annualized rate of returns

Table 7.12   *Average composition of the aggressive pension portfolio in*
               Mexico (Siefores)

	2000	2001	2002	2003	2004	2005	2006
Government bonds	92.6	89.8	85.5	84.5	85.5	86.1	76.5
Corporate bonds	5.4	7.8	12.3	11.0	9.6	7.8	6.6
Financial institutions bonds	2.0	2.4	2.1	4.5	4.9	4.0	4.9
Domestic equity						0.5	2.0
Foreign assets						1.6	10.0
Fixed income						0.6	4.2
Equity						1.0	5.8
Total	100.0	100.0	100.0	100.0	100.0	100.0	100.0

Source: Consar.

It is simply too early to make an assessment of the impact of the new approach in Mexico.

It is difficult to assess how portfolio managers will build their strategies once the actual VaRs approach the limits. Mexican supervisors have the power to increase the VaR limits if they conclude that the current ones limit pension fund managers excessively. However, a more fundamental question is whether VaR limits are the best approach for influencing the investment policies of DC pension funds and achieving efficient outcomes in the long run. The application of VaRs for pension funds remains controversial, as there are well-known arguments against the adoption of a short run risk measure for institutional investors that should operate with a long time horizon.[19] Whereas the Mexican approach is innovative and attractive in many respects, including the objective of containing downside risk, assessing its effectiveness will require a longer period and comparisons with the outcomes generated by other approaches to risk-based supervision of DC plans, such as the Australian.

7.6   CONCLUDING OBSERVATIONS

Review of the four early adopters of risk-based supervision for pension systems illustrates the potential for the application of these principles and methods across the full range of pension system designs. The nearly exclusively DB system operated by not-for-profit institutions in the Netherlands, the traditional DC employer-sponsored funds in Australia, commercial pension institutions in Mexico and a hybrid system with guarantees in

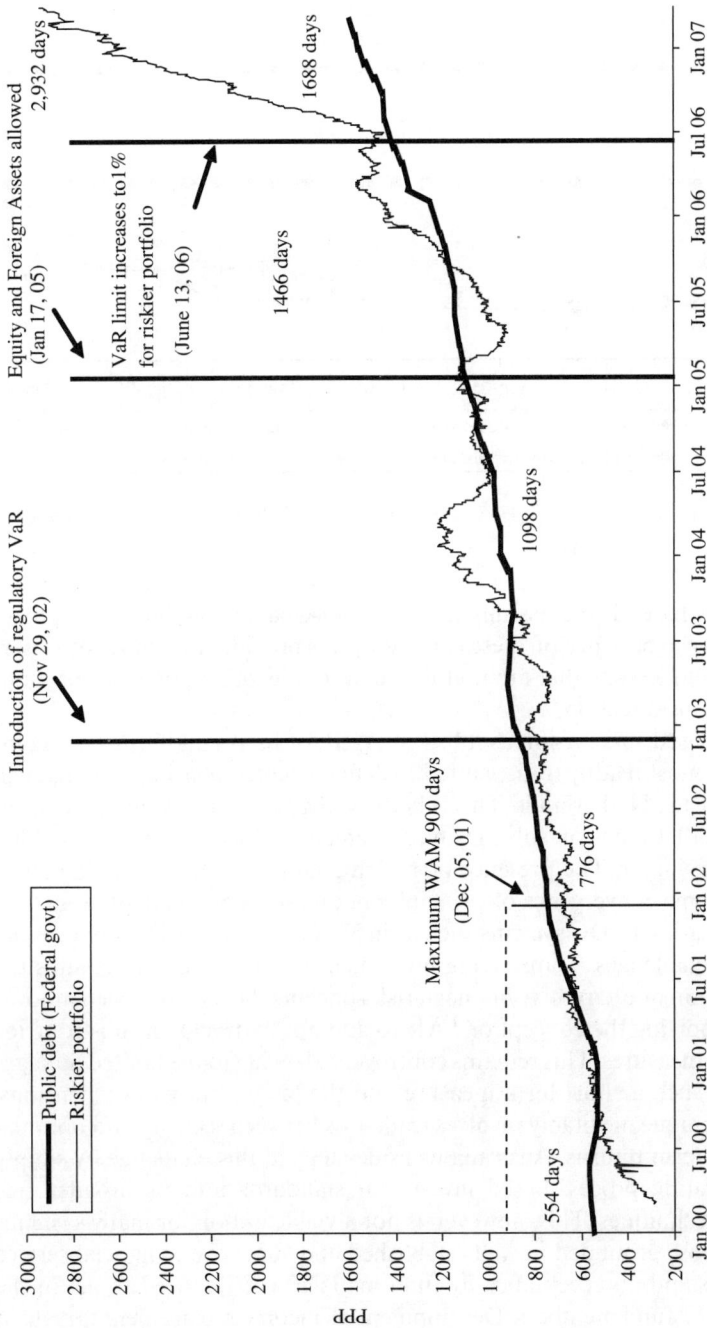

Figure 7.5   Maturity of the public debt stock and government securities in the riskier portfolio

207

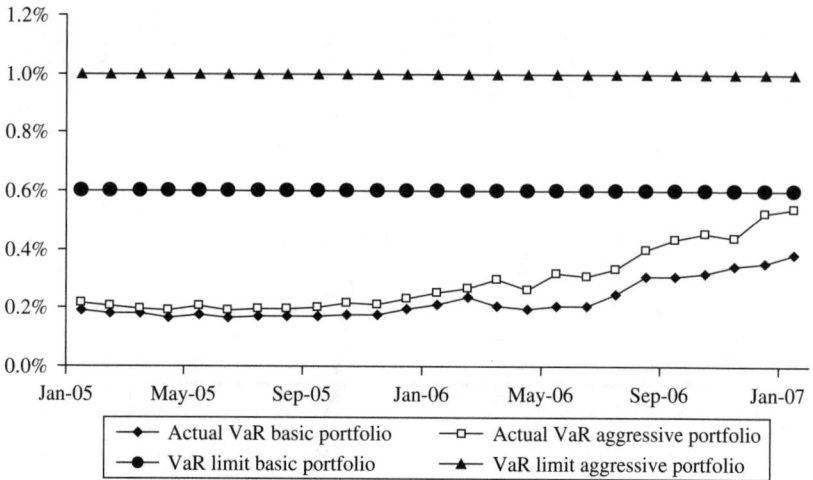

*Figure 7.6   Basic and aggressive portfolios: VaR limits and actual VaRs,
2005–2006*

Denmark have all successfully integrated risk-based standards and procedures. The experience of these early adopters provides a number of observations and lessons that are useful to consider as other countries begin to
move in this direction.

Risk-based supervision as it has emerged for banks and insurance companies is most readily transplanted to defined benefit pension systems such
as that of the Netherlands. This is because the types of risk and associated
methods that focus on solvency measurement and asset liability matching
are quite similar. The presence of return guarantees such as in Denmark
creates some convergence of principles but requires more adaptations.

Application to DC systems such as in Mexico and Australia imposes the
greatest challenges. Transferring investment risk to members requires the
formulation of alternative financial risk concepts. Mexico has been innovative in applying the concept of VAR to attempt to develop a substitute for
solvency measures. This remains controversial owing to the limited linkages
between such a short-term measure and the longer horizon of pensions.
This technique inevitably involves trade-offs between security and optimizing long-term returns. Australia has side-stepped this challenge by simply
incorporating process-based investment standards into its broader risk
scoring techniques. This, however, is not a viable option for many systems,
except those grounded in well established and supervised financial service
providers and an acceptance by fund managers of the need to act in the
interests of fund members. Development of income replacement targets to

which a fund member might aim, and scenarios based on contributions and investment returns, perhaps offers potential future enhancements to both of these approaches.

The usefulness of comprehensive risk scoring methods and fully articulated standards for risk architecture appear to offer considerable promise. There is a high potential for establishment of generic models that are applicable to a number of financial institutions which provide strong support for the integration of financial institution supervision. A relatively consistent approach to the design of risk scoring systems has emerged among the various countries, which will provide a useful template for others to follow. These appear to offer considerable potential for improving the quality of risk management. One of the key values of this approach is the capacity to limit the overall risk profile of pension funds in a manner that is readily adaptable to market innovations in comparison to the rigid standards that have characterized pension fund regulation in the past. Scoring systems also offer the promise of establishing sophisticated metrics to guide the allocation of supervisory resources and, through public disclosure, a strong basis to leverage market discipline.

There has been only limited progress to date, however, in utilizing enhanced disclosure and market competition to improve the efficiency and security of pension funds. Although very sophisticated risk scoring and evaluation techniques have been developed in three of the countries and are in the process of being implemented in Mexico, ratings are not disclosed to the market. Denmark remains at the vanguard of this process but limits this to only the summary solvency results rather than underlying analysis. The Netherlands limits disclosure of its risk management scores to the pension funds. Australia does not explicitly disclose to a fund its rating; however, funds will be aware of changes in supervisory stance which would accompany a rating change. This perhaps reflects a need for a continuing tension in adapting the tools derived from banking to the very different context of pensions. The shift in the 'culture' of supervision, from treating funds as voluntary occupational arrangements to true financial intermediaries that should be subject to the same transparency and market pressures as banks and mutual funds, remains a work in progress. Indeed, whereas supervisors rarely release a bank's rating for fear of causing a 'run' on weaker institutions, there may be scope for them to be more open in disclosing ratings for pension funds to encourage greater market discipline.

Evidence of the impact of risk-based methods is preliminary at best and it remains far too early in the process to draw any decisive conclusions. There is no indication of loss of pension coverage in any setting and other measurable effects have been largely at the margins. Funding ratios have improved but this likely would have occurred in any event thanks to the recovery of the asset markets coincident with the adoption of the new methods. Portfolios in the Netherlands and Denmark have become more conservative and exhibit indications of better duration matching and hedging of the risks in equities. The long-term costs of this in terms of returns remain to be seen. The Danish experience suggests that the increased visibility of risks associated with the new system has facilitated a transition to greater diversity of products in which new entrants are providing higher expected returns in exchange for lower guarantees while others move to lower returns and risks. This can be interpreted as movement towards a pure defined contribution system.

In Australia the introduction of the risk scoring in conjunction with stronger licensing standards has accentuated the existing strong trend away from DB plans and led to a consolidation in the industry as smaller funds have increasingly been absorbed by larger entities. This is likely due to a far broader set of factors with adoption of risk-based supervision hard to distinguish. In Mexico it is simply far too early to draw any conclusions because the system remains in a formative stage. The early evidence, however, provides promising indications of improvements in portfolio efficiency associated with the relaxation of asset allocation requirements in favour of risk-based measures. Thus far, this probably provides more compelling evidence of the political economy of adopting risk-based methods than the financial outcomes. The applicability of short-term VaR measures remains controversial.

A variety of difficult challenges will need to be addressed as these risk based systems evolve. Both the Dutch and Danish systems implicitly place little reliance on the traditional notion of mean reversion in equity markets by utilizing fixed parameters in their stress testing. If the historical pattern of returns persists, this will likely lead to excessive solvency buffers and perhaps price effects in the equity markets as pension funds' share of aggregate capital continues to increase. This issue is partially addressed through the 15-year adjustment periods for failure to meet solvency requirements and the ability of funds in the Netherlands to propose their own stress-testing methodology. The balance that is achieved between short-term solvency protection and flexibility in the system will be instructive. Likewise the capacity of the supervisor to effectively evaluate individual internal solvency models will provide useful lessons for others contemplating similar elements to achieve efficiency through flexibility.

There are related issues in the mechanics of the methods. For practical (and likely political reasons) the solvency standards that are in use are based on retrospective measures of asset class volatility. This has the potential to create price distortions and unduly limit innovation and the emergence of new instruments, and may not accurately reflect the nature of some potential investment categories. For practical purposes, the mark to market pricing requirements of these standards effectively limit pension funds to assets with observable prices. The trade-off between gains from the transparency of market discipline arising from such standards will have to be very carefully considered in relation to the longer-term constraint on risk–return efficiency of overall portfolios. This limits pension funds' capacity to pursue the illiquidity premiums available in some types of investments that are often perceived as advantageous to pension funds because of their relatively minimal liquidity requirements.

Three more general challenges are also important in considering the utility of risk-based approaches. Most fundamental is the applicability of the risk standards to the inherent nature of pension funds. Thus far these have no direct linkage to a fully articulated concept of retirement income adequacy. There is no empirical basis for the 1 per cent daily VaR in Mexico that considers how much return and volatility over the multiple decade investment time horizon of the typical participant is appropriate. The 97.5 probability standard in the Dutch FTK does not have any direct founda-tion in the capacity of pension funds to remain solvent over the long term, a criticism that was well voiced during the consultation period. Similarly, to the extent these are based on a perceived 'average' member of the fund, they may be poorly aligned with the diverse requirements of members with widely varying time horizons and/or differing risk appetites. In this respect, risk parameters would have to be calibrated to multiple portfolios or the varying financial circumstances of funds sponsors which may so compli-cate matters that the transparency and capacity to administer the system are lost.

A second general problem is that the solvency standards are potentially pro-cyclical in nature. Funds holding more volatile assets will have incen-tives to sell these when faced with market fluctuations. If pension funds are sufficiently large, these can become potentially self-reinforcing cycles that exacerbate instability and ultimately limit the potential diversification and therefore risk management capacity of the funds.

Finally, the political economy of the risk-based supervision of pension funds remains untested. By their very nature these approaches presume that some level of risk is appropriate for pension funds and seek to calibrate their parameters to this standard level. None have yet to weather the kind of 'perfect storm' of nearly simultaneous asset meltdowns and interest rate collapse or contagion effects that were associated with their introduction. It remains to be seen whether politicians will be able to sustain reasonable risks when the real losses to members' accounts are incurred or will retreat into the mode of absolute security at any cost when faced with angry pensioners marching in the streets. In principle even a probability as low as 2.5 per cent will occur within the period in which an individual is involved with the pension system.

Despite these challenges, risk-based supervision methods are likely to continue to gain acceptance. They provide a forward-looking paradigm around which to organize supervision that offers the promise of reduced risk of insolvency of DB funds, potential efficiency gains in the investment process and flexibility that will permit innovation in pension fund management and investment practices without requiring extensive annual revision of pension laws. However, as in all such matters, there is likely to be no free lunch. Risk-based solvency standards may lead to more conservative portfolios in DB funds and constrain DC funds to a presumed average risk tolerance, sacrificing some potential return in both cases. Increased ability to use derivatives resulting from these models may to some extent mitigate these outcomes, but this is not applicable to all countries. All of the approaches will impose new pressures on supervisors and require increased sophistication from all parties. The further development of these systems will be closely monitored and undoubtedly provide many more useful lessons as others consider how to proceed down this path.

NOTES

1. This chapter is part of a broader project on risk-based supervision coordinated jointly by the World Bank and the IOPS. The authors are grateful to Constantinos Stephanou, David Madero, Dirk Broeders, Dimitri Vittas, Heinz Rudolph, Laura Ard, Luiz Mario Hernandez Acevedo and Peter Skjodt, for useful inputs and comments on an earlier draft.
2. Bernstein and Chumacero (2006b), Hinz and Van Dam (2006), Anderson and Van Dam (2006), Thompson (2006).
3. Sahajwala and Van den Bergh (2000) provide a study of a number of supervisory risk assessment systems under development in various G10 countries.
4. See note 2.
5. The total number of individual accounts amounts to 84 per cent of the labour force, but a large share of pension fund members move in and out of informality and do not contribute on a regular basis. This phenomenon is common in Latin America and other emerging countries (Rofman and Luchetti, 2006).
6. It is interesting to note, in this regard, that Australian regulators have recently implemented a comprehensive re-licensing programme based on much stricter licensing criteria that has reduced significantly the number of funds.
7. Dutch funds can opt for an unconditional or a conditional benefit indexation rule. The latter rule introduces an element of risk sharing, but the Dutch system basically remains a traditional defined benefit system.
8. It is possible that the introduction of the VaR ceiling was also motivated by the existence of government guarantees, especially the guarantee that workers with accrued rights in the former PAYG system will not receive a pension lower than the one they would have received (Bernstein and Chumacero, 2006b).

9. Mexican supervisors also make use of early warning indicators to guide supervisory actions, but this motivating factor was clearly more important in the other countries, where a much larger number of funds are allowed to operate.
10. Standard and Poors and Moody's have developed their own methodologies for rating the quality of the internal risk management of insurance companies and take the results into consideration in the elaboration of the final ratings. See, for example, Ingram (2006).
11. The implementation of Basel II will impose similar challenges for bank supervisors.
12. Jorion (2003) provides a review of the debate on mean reversion and empirical tests. See also Bodie (1995), Campbell and Viceira (2002, 2004) and Campbell et al. (2003).
13. See note 12.
14. The response of pension institutions to the financial turmoil and the growing use of derivatives are analysed in some detail in Ladekarl et al. (2006).
15. Boeri et al. (2006).
16. APRA Annual Report 2006.
17. The authors are grateful to the staff of Consar for providing the calculations for use in this chapter.
18. Bernstein and Chumacero (2006a).
19. Barberis (2000), Campbell, Chan and Viceira (2003), Campbell and Viceira (2002, 2004) discuss optimal portfolio strategies with short and long time horizons. Dowd and Blake (2006) present a critical view of VaRs as a risk indicator.

REFERENCES

Andersen, E. and R. Van Dam (2006), 'Risk-based supervision of pension funds in denmark', unpublished manuscript, The World Bank, Washington, DC.

Barberis, N. (2000), 'Investing for the long run when returns are predictable', *The Journal of Finance*, **55**(1), 225–64.

Bernstein, S. and R. Chumacero (2006a), 'Quantifying the costs of investment limits for Chilwan pension funds', *Fiscal Studies*, **27**(1), 99–123.

Bernstein, S. and R. Chumacero (2006b), 'Risk-based supervision of pension funds in Mexico', unpublished manuscript, The World Bank, Washington, DC.

Bodie, Z. (1995), 'On the Risk of Stocks in the Long Run', *Financial Analysts Journal*, **51**(3), 18–22.

Boeri, T., L. Bovenberg, B. Coeuré and A. Roberts (2006), *Dealing with the New Giants: Rethinking the Role of Pension Funds*, Geneva Reports on the World Economy No. 8, London: centre for Economic Policy Research.

Campbell, John Y. and Luis M. Viceira (2002), *Strategic Asset Allocation. Portfolio Choice for Long-Term Investors*, Oxford: Oxford University Press.

Campbell, J.Y. and L.M. Viceira (2004), 'The term structure of the risk–return tradeoff', manuscript, Harvard University.

Campbell, J.Y., Y.L. Chan and L.M. Viceira (2003), 'A multivariate model of strategic asset allocation', *Journal of Financial Economics*, **67**(1), 41–80.

Dowd, K. and D. Blake (2006), 'After VaR: The theory, estimation, and insurance applications of quantile-based risk measures', Discussion Paper PI-0603 (June), The Pensions Institute, London, UK.

Hinz, R. and R. van Dam (2006), 'Risk-based supervision of pension funds in the Netherlands', unpublished manuscript, The World Bank, Washington, DC.

Ingram, D. (2006), 'Enterprise risk management: insurance ratings', Standard and Poor's.

Jorion, P. (2003), 'The long-term risks of global stock markets', Financial Management Association.

Kakes, J. I. and D. W. G. A. Broeders (2006), 'The sustainability of the Dutch pension system', De Nederlandsche Bank, *Occasional Studies*, 4(6)

Laderkarl, T., R. Laderkarl, E. Andersen and D.Vittas (2007), 'The Use of Derivative to Hedge Imbedded Options: The Case of Pension Institutions in Denmark', World Bank Policy Research Paper 4159, March, The World Bank, Washington, DC.

Rofman, R. and L. Luchetti (2006), 'Pension Systems in Latin America: Concepts and Measurements of Coverage', Social Protection Discussion Paper 0616, World Bank, Washington, DC.

Thompson, G. (2006), 'Risk-based supervision of pension funds in Australia', unpublished manuscript, The World Bank, Washington, DC.

Discussion of 'Risk-based supervision of pension funds'

Coen N. Teulings

The chapter by Brunner, Hinz and Rocha gives a nice overview of the organization of supervision of pension funds in four countries, the Netherlands, Denmark, Australia and Mexico. The four countries differ considerably in the maturity and coverage of the system – and hence, in the assets as percentage of GDP – the number of funds to be supervised, and, finally, the nature of the pension contract. In some contracts, participation is mandatory, at the level either of a firm or of an entire industry. In other contracts, participation is voluntary. The first two countries (the Netherlands and Denmark) are more of the defined benefit (DB) type, while the latter two are more of the defined contribution (DC) type. The latter difference has important implications for the type of supervision that is needed. In an ideal type of DB system, liabilities are fixed, and hence the main task of supervisors is to monitor whether the fund has sufficient assets to serve these liabilities. In an ideal type of DC system, the payout to the retirees is flexible, depending on the value of the available assets. By definition, the value of assets always suffices to serve liabilities under this system. Hence, supervision should focus on the communication with the participants, that is, whether the promised degree of risk taking corresponds to the actual behaviour of the pension fund and on the corporate governance of the fund. Although the distinction between DB and DC is not clear-cut in practice, some of the differences in the structure of supervision can be seen in the description of the actual systems in the four countries discussed in the chapter.

The chapter copes well with the complexities in the details of the supervision system. Large-scale pension funds are a relatively new phenomenon, so it is not surprising that the optimal structure of supervision has not been fully worked out yet. The chapter describes some stages in the evolution of the supervision system. In particular, the 'perfect storm' of rapidly declining interest rates and falling equity prices in 2000–2002 showed the fragility of the existing supervision framework. The revision of the supervision since then has to a large extent been modelled along the lines of the revision

of the supervision on the banking and the insurance industry, the Basel II
and Solvency II agreements. It remains to be seen if this is the right analogy.
In particular, the notion of using the maximum probability of the reserve
ratio being below a threshold might be adequate for insurance companies
and banks, which must be able to serve their liabilities at any point in time.
For pension funds, with long-run obligations and assets, such a short-run
criterion does not seem to be adequate. Though this criterion has played a
useful role in the Netherlands in coping with the recovery from the 'perfect
storm', it had undesirable side-effects, in particular from a cyclical point of
view. Further research into criteria with a clear underpinning in economic
theory that therefore can be expected to suit better the specific needs of this
industry remains a priority. Such a criterion should allow for a balanced
assignment of risk, both between generations and within the lifetime of
each generation.

The chapter sketches three roles for the market mechanism in the organization of the supervision. First, markets can provide ratings and other
evaluations of the quality of the assets, the investment policy and the corporate governance of the fund. Competition among trade marks might
enhance the quality and cost-effectiveness of these rating activities. Secondly,
markets can provide prices of assets, contributing to the transparency of
the fund's performance and thereby to the governance of the fund. The
recent popularity of investing in private equity and hedge funds reveals a
fundamental trade-off here. On the one hand, the transaction cost of a
public capital market may turn private equity into a more profitable investment, but, on the other hand, the availability of public valuations of the
assets might offset the advantage of a higher return on investment. Thirdly,
markets may allow for competition between pension funds, enhancing the
efficiency of the fund's administrative operation and the performance of its
asset managers. From a Dutch perspective, where mandatory participation
is the rule, this final role of markets will not be easy to realize. Pension contracts imply both intra- and intergenerational solidarity, which imposes
constraints on the feasibility competition between 'pension delivery organizations' (PDOs). Adverse selection would destabilize a free market. It is an
interesting exercise to work out a scheme of compensation payments to
offset the implicit subsidies between various groups of participants in a
fund, to allow competition between funds. A simpler alternative might
be to revise the contract to limit cross-subsidization between groups. It
remains to be seen whether mandatory participation will be abolished in the
foreseeable future in the Netherlands.

The chapter touches upon the role of the sponsor at some places. In my
view, a radical solution is the best option in this case: a complete elimin-
ation of this role. In many current funds, the sponsor provides an often

vaguely specified guarantee of future claims of participants on the fund. This can be seen as a put option of the fund (or its participants) on the sponsor. The IFRS/IAS accounting standards require the sponsor to list the value of this option explicitly as a liability on its balance sheet, which requires market valuation. This is equivalent to a further completion of financial markets, so that this guarantee becomes a tradable asset. As soon as this step is taken, it is no longer evident that holding a put option on the sponsor is optimal, neither for the fund, nor for the sponsor. Enron and similar affairs reveal that it is decent policy for a fund to diversify its claims. Similarly, it is unclear why the sponsor should write such an option. Others might be in a better position to do so. Hence, from a risk-sharing point of view, abolishing any formal role of the sponsor is the best solution.

8. The ideal pension-delivery organization: theory and practice

Keith P. Ambachtsheer

8.1 INTRODUCTION

The publication of Harry Markowitz's celebrated article (1952) 'Portfolio Selection' marked a major milestone in the evolution of investment theory. For the first time, the concepts of return, risk, diversification, an efficient investment frontier and investor risk tolerance were all brought together, and logically integrated into a procedure for selecting 'optimal' investment portfolios. Over the course of the following 20 years, various versions of Markowitz's portfolio theory, further shaped by others such as Richard Brealey, William Sharpe and Jack Treynor, began to be applied by investment institutions. Then, in the early 1970s, Fisher Black, Robert Merton and Myron Scholes expanded investment theory dramatically by showing how the principle of arbitrage-free valuation could be applied to pricing options. Their discovery sparked the birth of a new wave of practical risk management techniques applicable to banking, insurance and pension balance sheets. The discoveries of portfolio theory and option valuation theory would both garner Nobel prizes in the 1990s.[1]

Fate would have the present author enter the world of institutional investing in 1969, thus providing a now almost 40-year window to observe, and write about the evolution of institutional investment practices over this period. Perhaps not surprisingly, one's perspective does not stay constant over such a long period of time. In my case, it has shifted from the narrow perspective of studying the application of the new investment theories in practice to the broader perspective of studying the conditions under which financial institutions create measurable value for their clients/beneficiaries. Such a broader perspective requires more than just an understanding of investment theory and its application. It also requires an understanding of organization theory and its application. We have come to understand that the willingness and ability of a financial institution to create value for its clients/beneficiaries depends on three factors: (1) the degree of alignment of financial interests between an organization's owners/managers and its clients/beneficiaries, (2) the quality of organization governance and design, and (3) scale economies. These three factors are examined in greater detail below.

8.2   TOWARDS AN INSTITUTIONAL THEORY OF DELIVERING PENSIONS: THE AGENCY FACTOR

Classical economic theory had little to say about how savings are transformed into investments, and how the resulting accumulations of wealth should be managed. Under the assumption of perfect markets, the demand for, and supply of, financial intermediation services logically leads to the determination of volume, pricing and market structure.[2] Two publications in the 1930s marked the beginning of a process towards building a more realistic, operationally useful institutional theory of financial intermediation. Both made the point that the alignment of interests between agents and principals is an important element in organization value-creation.

1. *The Modern Corporation and Private Property* by Adolf Berle and Gardiner Means (1933) asserted that the efficiencies predicted by classical economic theory will not necessarily come to pass in organization structures where the decision-makers are agents rather than principals. Unless prevented by a strong oversight discipline acting in the best interests of the principals, 'rent-seeking' agents could and would make decisions to further their own interest, rather than those of the principals.
2. *The General Theory of Employment, Interest, and Money* by John Maynard Keynes (1936) also made important observations about 'real world' savings-to-investments conversion processes in its famous Chapter 12 ('The state of long-term expectation'). Keynes keenly observed that, in their role as agents, investment committees often prefer 'to fail conventionally rather than succeed unconventionally'. He also observed that institutional fund management seemed to be akin to beauty contests where the goal is to predict which stocks average opinion will think most beautiful six months from now, rather than invest in new, wealth-creating business ventures.

Thus through these two publications, Berle, Means and Keynes resolutely placed the agency cat among the principal pigeons. Thirty-five years later, George Akerlof (1970) would introduce an additional element in the construction of a realistic institutional theory of financial intermediation.

3. *The Market for Lemons: Quality, Uncertainty, and the Market Mechanism* asks why the prices of new cars plummet once they are driven out of the showroom. Akerlof's answer is informational asymmetry between the owner of the (now used) car and any future buyer. The sellers of used cars know if their vehicles are lemons. Potential buyers do not. Used-car pricing reflects this reality. What if used-car buyers are not aware of the informational asymmetry between them and used-car sellers? Then the asymmetry would not be reflected in used-car prices, and buyers would pay too much for too little. Generalizing, this is the predicted outcome in any market where the sellers know more about what they are selling than buyers know about what they are buying. The market for investment management services is a classic example of such a market.[3]

Six years after Akerlof, Peter Drucker (1976) would place the principal–agent and informational asymmetry problems in a pensions-retirement savings setting.

4. *The Unseen Revolution: How Pension Fund Socialism Came to America* expressed Drucker's worry that the emerging pension delivery organizations of the 1970s might lack the 'legitimacy' required to become credible owners of the means of production. Why? Because corporate pension plans would not necessarily be run as pure arm's-length, single-purpose pension agencies. With corporate managers in charge of investment policy, there was no guarantee that their decisions would not at least in part be motivated to further corporate interests, rather than those of its workers. Similarly, in industry-wide and public sector pension plans, there was no guarantee that investment decisions would not at least in part be motivated to further the interests of labour leaders and politicians, rather than those of union members and public servants. Quite apart from these principal–agent concerns, Drucker also worried about the legitimacy of the investment processes themselves, wondering whether pension trustees had the necessary skills and experience to distinguish between genuine value-creating investment strategies, and the 'beauty contest' strategies that Keynes alluded to 40 years earlier.

By expressing a worry about requisite pension trustee skills and experience quite apart from his principal–agent concerns, Drucker identified the other value-creating factor that we go on to address in further detail below.

8.3   TOWARDS AN INSTITUTIONAL THEORY OF DELIVERING PENSIONS: THE GOVERNANCE FACTOR

While there is now a burgeoning literature on corporate governance, this is not yet the case with pension fund governance. Here is a short list of pension fund governance-related publications that we are aware of.

1. *Fortune and Folly: The Wealth and Power of Institutional Investing* (1992) caused a stir when its authors, anthropologists John Conley and William O'Barr, described behaviour at nine major USA pension funds based on two years of observation. They concluded that the aim of pension fund governance appeared to be focused more on responsibility deflection, blame management and fostering cozy relations with services suppliers, than on good governance and creating value for fund stakeholders.

2. *Excellence in Pension Fund Management: What is It?* (1995) by Ambachtsheer, Boice, Ezra, and McLaughlin describes the results of a survey of 50 senior North American pension fund executives. Asked to estimate the 'excellence shortfall' in their organizations, the median response was a material 66 basis points per annum in lost return. Asked to identify the sources of excellence shortfall, the three causes mentioned most frequently were poor decision processes, inadequate resources and lack of focus or mission clarity.

3. *Improving Pension Fund Performance* (1998) by Ambachtsheer, Capelle and Scheibelhut found some correlation between pension fund governance quality and pension fund performance, and identified a number of factors statistically associated with fund performance. The study, based on a survey of 80 senior North American and European pension fund executives, found the quality of fund oversight to be generally problematical, requiring corrective action. A recent update of this survey (2006) found that pension fund oversight continues to be generally weak. Resulting problems include a lack of delegation clarity between boards of trustees and managements of pension delivery organizations, board micro-management, and non-competitive compensation policies. Some of the results of this new survey are discussed further below.[4]

4. *Pension Fund Trustee Competence: Decision-Making in Problems Relevant to Investment Practice* (2006) by Clark, Caerlewy-Smith and Marshall studied the problem-solving capabilities of pension fund trustees in the UK and found these capabilities 'surprisingly heterogeneous', with potentially significant implications for pension fund governance.

All four of these studies confirm that the concern about the quality of pension fund governance that Drucker expressed 30 years ago was not misplaced.

8.4 TOWARDS AN INSTITUTIONAL THEORY OF DELIVERING PENSIONS: AN INTEGRATIVE HYPOTHESIS

Recently, Ambachtsheer (2005) offered a more formal version of a normative theory of optimal financial intermediation that integrates Markovitz's portfolio theory elements with the organization theory elements discussed above. This more holistic theory, dubbed 'Integrative Investment Theory' (IIT), posits that client/beneficiary value creation is driven by five factors: agency issues (A), governance quality (G), risk specification (R), investment beliefs (IB) and financial engineering (FE):

$$\text{Client/Beneficiary Value-Creation} = F\{A, G, R, IB, FE\}.$$

Specifically, IIT hypothesizes that pension delivery organizations that (a) deal effectively with agency issues (A), (b) practise good governance (G), (c) properly specify and manage relevant client/beneficiary risks (R), (d) possess realistic, research-based investment beliefs (IB), and (e) implement chosen investment policies effectively (FE), will create more client/beneficiary value than pension delivery organizations that do not have these five characteristics.

Arguably, among these five factors, A and G are primary in the sense that they create the context for getting the remaining three factors right. In other words, without a proper alignment of interests and good governance, it will be difficult to get R, IB and FE right. This is a testable hypothesis, as will be shown below. We assess the importance of the A factor by comparing the results of similar investment mandates carried out by large samples of Canadian and USA pension funds and mutual funds. Our hypothesis is that pension funds have a better alignment of interests between management and pension fund clients/beneficiaries than mutual funds do, and that, hence, pension funds will produce more value than mutual funds. We assess the importance of the G factor by comparing the investment results of a large sample of European, North American and Pacific Rim pension funds with high governance scores to those with low governance scores. Our hypothesis is that funds with high scores will produce more value than those with low scores.

8.5   TESTING THE AGENCY HYPOTHESIS

A recent study commissioned by the Rotman International Centre for Pension Management (ICPM) at the University of Toronto tested the agency hypothesis. The study, titled 'Economies of Scale, Lack of Skill, or Misalignment of Interest? A Study of Pension and Mutual Fund Performance', by Bauer, Frehen, Lum and Otten was first presented at an ICPM Workshop in October 2006, and can be accessed through the ICPM website. The mutual fund data came from the Globefund.com (for Canadian funds) and the CRSP (for USA funds) databases. The pension fund data came from the databases of the global benchmarking firm CEM Benchmarking Inc. CEM has return and expense data for Canadian and USA defined benefit (DB) pension funds starting in 1992, and for USA defined contribution (DC) pension funds starting in 1997.[5]

A key metric in the study was Net Value Added (NVA), which is calculated in two steps. A fund's gross return minus the return on the relevant market benchmark over the same period is defined as a fund's Gross Value Added (GVA) over that period. GVA minus the fund's total expense ratio (TER) over the same period is defined as a fund's NVA over that period. Table 8.1 below reports the average GVAs, TERs and NVAs for the domestic equity components of large samples of Canadian and USA mutual funds and pension funds. Each analysis was performed using the maximum available data for the specified time period.

Thus the Canadian DB92 NVA averages are based on annual observations beginning in 1992 and ending in 2004. The Canadian mutual fund (MF) data start in 1996, hence the Canadian DB96 NVA average is also calculated to provide a more direct comparison with Canadian MF96 NVA average. The USA DB NVA averages are based on the 1992–2004 period, thus there are USA DB92 and USA MF92 calculations. The USA DC NVA averages are based on the 1997–2004 period, leading to USA DC97 and USA MF97 calculations. Other metrics in the tables are the number of annual fund observations (N) on which each of the calculated averages is based, the standard deviations (SD) are metrics indicating the degree of dispersion around the calculated NVA averages, and the t-statistics are measures of statistical significance of the calculated NVA averages, with values greater than $+2$ or less than -2, indicating strong statistical significance.

We summarize the key study findings summarized in Table 8.1 as follows:

1.   The average Canadian pension fund participant received positive value from domestic equity investments, both over the 1992–2004 (DB92 NVA $=+0.76$ per cent) and 1996–2004 (DB96 NVA $=+1.23$ per cent)

Table 8.1 Canadian and US mutual fund and pension fund average domestic equity NVAs and related statistics

	N	GVA	TER	NVA	SD	T-Stat
CDN DB92	968	+ 1.01%	0.25%	+ 0.76%	1.88%	+ 5.70
CDN DB96	636	+ 1.47%	0.25%	+ 1.23%	1.92%	+ 8.05
CDN MF96	2 781	+ 0.15%	2.75%	− 2.60%	4.95%	−15.19
US DB92	1 699	+ 0.20%	0.32%	− 0.12%	1.67%	− 1.53
US MF92	23 395	− 1.59%	1.19%	− 2.78%	5.48%	−33.27
US DC97	510	+ 0.18%	0.62%	− 0.44%	1.35%	− 4.58
US MF97	18 782	− 1.33%	1.20%	− 2.53%	5.49%	−28.12

periods. This included the deduction of an average 0.25 per cent per annum for incurred investment expenses. In contrast, the average participant in Canadian domestic equity mutual funds over the 1996–2004 period gave up considerable value (MF96 NVA = −2.60 per cent). This loss was entirely due to the average 2.75 per cent per annum in incurred investment expenses. Any incurred sales charges would make the value loss even more severe.

2. The average USA pension fund participant received marginally below market-equivalent performance from domestic equity investments, both over the 1992–2004 (DB92 NVA = −0.12 per cent) and the 1997–2004 (DC97 NVA = −0.44 per cent) periods. This included the deduction of an average 0.32 per cent for incurred investment expenses in the DB case, and 0.62 per cent for all expenses (for example, including administration) in the DC case. In contrast, the average participants in USA domestic equity mutual funds over the 1992–2004 and 1997–2004 periods gave up considerable value (MF92 NVA = −2.78 per cent, MF97 NVA = −2.53 per cent). Part of this loss was due to the incurred investment expenses. An even greater part was due to the average USA domestic equity mutual fund underperforming its benchmark on a GVA basis (that is, before expenses). Any incurred sales charges would make the value loss even more severe.

Are there explanations for these findings?

8.6   POSSIBLE EXPLANATIONS FOR THE FINDINGS

Why would North American mutual fund investors subject themselves to material wealth losses relative to implementing the same basic investment policy through North American pension funds? Or equivalently, why would North American mutual fund investors pay materially higher average fees (even before including sales charges) for the same investment service available to North American pension fund participants, and which produced inferior investment results even before the far greater fees? A number of possible answers come to mind.

1. *Pension fund expenses are understated*: this is in fact the case for the DB results. However, even if additional costs related to such functions as oversight, custody fees and other administrative costs were added to the DB fund domestic equity investment expenses, the total expense ratios might rise by 0.15 per cent.[6] A 0.15 per cent reduction in the calculated average pension fund NVAs in no way affects the study's basic findings.

2. *The results are not comparable because of style and risk differences*: the study tested for this possibility and found no significant style or risk differences between the pension and mutual fund samples.

3. *Only 40 per cent of North American workers have access to pension fund management*: this is in fact the case. With only 40 per cent of the workforces covered by an occupational pension plan, the other 60 per cent has to fend for itself. However, this fact by itself cannot explain why North American investors in domestic equity mutual funds pay more (even before sales charges) for an inferior product. For example, exposure to domestic equities could be acquired by buying and holding exchange-traded funds (ETFs) for a small fraction of the fees North American investors pay to mutual funds.[7]

4. *Mutual funds are sold, not bought*: the market for investment management services is highly asymmetric, with the buyers of these services knowing far less about what they are buying than the sellers know about what they are selling. Information economics predicts that in such a market buyers will pay too much for too little. Research results from the field of behavioural finance support this conclusion. This research shows people to be generally unsophisticated, inconsistent, hesitant and even irrational regarding financial matters, which creates the opportunity for the for-profit financial services industry to step in proactively and sell their products and services at too-high prices.[8] The veracity of this third explanation is supported by the findings of a recent survey of 1865 Canadian mutual fund investors. When asked why they had bought mutual funds, 85 per cent said they were persuaded by 'someone who provided me with advice and guidance'.[9] We conclude it is the combination of informational asymmetry and behavioural dysfunction on the part of the customers, and opportunistic acuity on the part of the suppliers, that best explains the findings summarized in Table 8.1.

Indeed the consequences of this toxic combination of generally naïve mutual fund buyers and smart mutual fund sellers are even worse than the numbers in Table 8.1 suggest. A USA mutual fund study based on 1985–2004 data published in Jack Bogle's book 'The Battle for the Soul of Capitalism' (2005) found that the average USA equity mutual fund underperformed the market by the same 2.8 per cent that we reported in Table 8.1. However, individual investors underperformed the average experience of the mutual funds they invested in by a further average 3.3 per cent per annum. Why? Because many mutual fund investors switch from fund to fund in search of better performance, thus falling into the naïve investor 'buy high, sell low' behaviour predicted by the behavioural finance literature, and in the process generating further unrewarded sales and trans-action expenses. When the separate effects of the average mutual fund underperformance and individual investor underperformance are com-bined, the total average performance shortfall adds up to a catastrophic 6.1 per cent per annum.

8.7   TESTING THE GOVERNANCE HYPOTHESIS

Another recent study commissioned by ICPM tested the governance hypothesis. The study titled 'Pension fund governance today: strengths, weaknesses and opportunities for improvement', by Ambachtsheer, Capelle and Lum, was also first presented at the October 2006 ICPM Workshop, and can also be accessed through the ICPM website. To gather information on pension fund governance, the researchers designed a survey to be answered by a pre-selected group of senior pension fund executives with titles such as Chief Executive, Chief Investment Officer, Executive Director, VP-Pensions and so on. The common factor among these pension executives was that their funds had supplied return, cost and risk-related data to CEM Benchmarking Inc., an organization that measures the cost-effectiveness of pension fund organizations around the globe. Completed surveys from 88 pension executives were received. For 81 of these 88 respondents, we also had complete sets of fund data ending in 2004. The aggregate assets of these 81 funds amounted to $1.4 trillion dollars at the end of 2004. Table 8.2 provides additional information on the characteris-tics of these 81 funds. Note that the sample represents a good mix of funds by both geographical and sponsor-type criteria.

The survey itself consisted of two parts. One part asked the pension fund executives to assign a rank from six to one to each of 45 statements related to various aspects of the oversight, management and operations areas of their own pension fund. Each statement was phrased so that, the higher the assigned ranking, the more favourable the senior executive's view was of that particular element or activity of fund oversight, management or oper-ations. For the 81 completed surveys received for which there were also fund performance data available from CEM Benchmarking Inc., the 45 rankings were averaged to create a single 'CEO Score'. The other part of the survey asked two open-ended questions, one about the key oversight challenges the executives see facing their boards of governors today, and the other about the key management challenges they see themselves facing today.

In this chapter, we focus on the study tests for a statistical relationship between the 'CEO Scores' representing proxies of organization governance quality as perceived by its own CEO, and investment performance as

Table 8.2   Characteristics of the responding pension funds to the 2005 survey

Region	% (EW)*	% (DW)**
Australia / New Zealand	4%	1%
Canada	41%	13%
Europe	11%	32%
United States	44%	54%
Sponsor type	% (EW)*	% (DW)**
Corporate	38%	14%
Public Sector	41%	66%
Other	21%	20%
Size	Median	Mean
Billions $USD	$3.7Bn	$17.9 Bn

Notes: * Equal-weighted, ** dollar-weighted.

measured CEM. There are two sets of 'CEO Scores' and fund performance metrics. The 45 statements were originally composed in 1997, and ranked by 80 pension fund executives of funds for which there were also CEM fund performance data at that time.[10] These same 45 statements were used again in the 2005 survey. As already noted, this time 81 responses were received from fund executives whose funds also had investment performance data in the CEM database.

8.8   GOVERNANCE QUALITY AND ORGANIZATION PERFORMANCE

Imagine two pension funds, each with a board of governors. The board of Fund 1 has been carefully selected, based on a template that sets out optimal board composition in terms of the relevant collective skill/experience set, positive behavioural characteristics and an unconflicted passion for the well-being of the pension fund organization and its stakeholders. The board of Fund 2 was randomly selected out of the telephone book. Which of these two boards do you think would get higher oversight rankings for such important tasks as CEO selection and evaluation, clear delegation of authority to management, monitoring of outcomes versus goals, and self-evaluation of board effectiveness? Which of these two funds will likely generate better organization performance over the long term? Surely we would all agree that the logical answers are Board 1 and Fund 1, and that we would be able to 'prove' our hypothesis if we had perfect metrics representing governance quality and perfect metrics representing organizational performance.

What if we only had imperfect quality and performance metrics? Would we still find a positive statistical association between governance quality and organizational performance? This is the question the study addressed. The 'CEO Scores' were used as proxies for fund governance quality. With means of 4.8 (1997) and 4.9 (2005) and standard deviations of 0.6 (1997) and 0.7 (2005), these metrics likely overstate true governance quality and understate the true variance in that quality.[11] Nevertheless, there likely is still some information content in the relative values of the 'CEO Scores'.

As fund performance proxies, the study used the Net Value-Added (NVA) metric supplied by CEM Benchmarking Inc. that has already been defined above. The NVAs used in the NVA/CEO Score analyses reported below are all annualized, based on four years of continuous experience. The mean annual NVA in the CEM database is 0.2 per cent with a sample standard deviation of 3.0 per cent. This is based on all 3513 annual NVAs in the database contributed by 666 different pension funds over the period covering 1992–2004. While this dataset does not suffer from the same degree of mean and variance biases as we noted is likely the case with the subjective Pension CEO Scores, all key CEM data are supplied by the participating pension funds, including operating costs and policy asset mix benchmarks. So some level of 'noise' is likely introduced in calculating the NVA performance metrics. Further, in theory, the NVAs should be assigned risk-related 'haircuts'. However, consensus on how to best do this has yet to be reached. As a result of these shortcomings, the NVA metrics are also less than perfect.[12]

8.9   PENSION CEO SCORES MEET NVA METRICS

So what happens when the imperfect Pension CEO Scores meet the imperfect NVA metrics? In other words, does the positive relationship between the Pension CEO Scores and the NVAs that we would surely find with perfect data come through with our less-than-perfect data? Figure 8.1 tells the tale. The short answer is that, yes, even with imperfect data, the outline of a generally positive statistical relationship between governance and performance emerges. With the 1997 Pension CEO Scores, the NVA-CEO coefficient hits + 0.4 twice, first for the four-year NVA performance period ending in 1997, and then again for the four-year NVA performance period ending in 1999. With the 2005 Scores, the NVA-CEO coefficient hits + 0.8 for the four-year NVA performance period ending in 2003, before falling back to + 0.4 for the four-year NVA performance period ending in 2004.

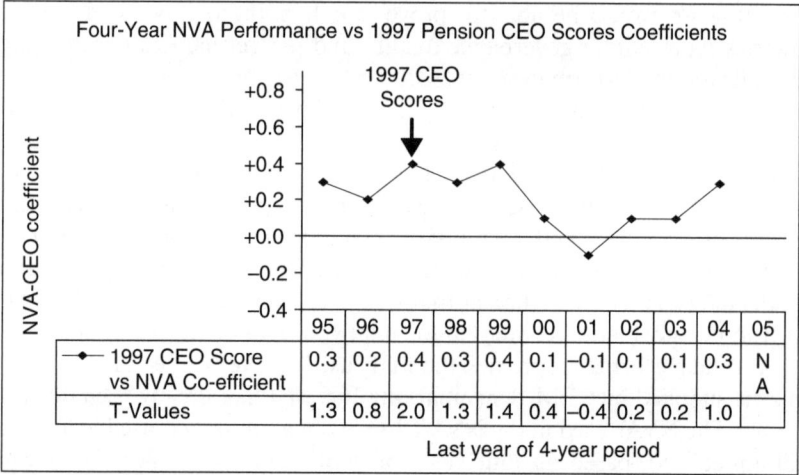

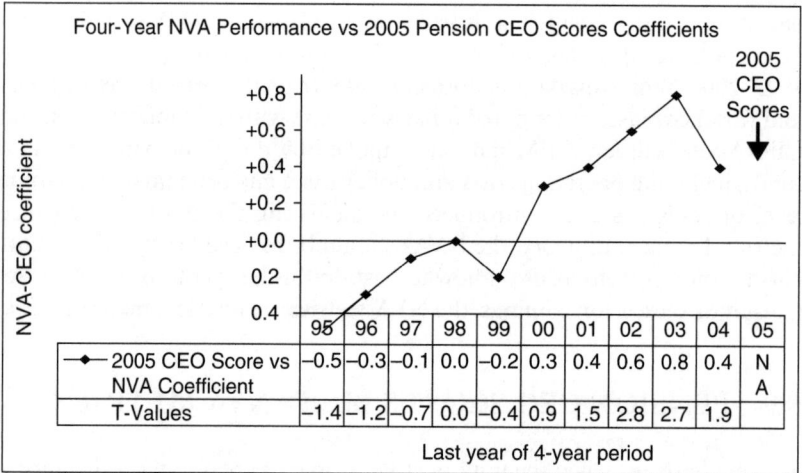

*Figure 8.1   Pension fund governance and performance: are they
              statistically related?*

What intuitive meaning can we give to the time patterns of these NVA-CEO coefficients? The study indicates that the Pension CEO Score range was effectively from three to six. Multiplying this three-point 'poor–good' gap by an NVA-CEO coefficient of + 0.4 leads to a four-year NVA gap of 1.2 per cent per annum. A coefficient of + 0.8 doubles the four-year NVA gap to 2.4 per cent per annum. The implication is that the 'poor–good' governance gap, as assessed by pension fund CEOs (or equivalents) themselves, has been 'worth' as much as 1–2 per cent of additional return per annum, as measured by CEM. In our view, these statistical findings likely understate the real 'value-added' potential of truly high-performance pension fund governance and management.[13]

8.10   FURTHER INSIGHTS

Today, the 1997 Pension CEO Scores permit the calculation of NVA versus Pension CEO Score experience well after 1997. Note that the statistical significance of the NVA-CEO coefficients based on the 1997 Scores peaks at the four-year NVA performance period ending in 1997 (that is, at a t-value of 2.0), and generally declines after that. In contrast, given the availability of NVA data since 1992, the 2005 Scores permit the study of experience well before 2005. Note that the NVA-CEO coefficients based on 2005 Scores are statistically insignificant in the earlier four-year NVA performance periods, and attain statistical significance only when they get closer to 2005, the year the survey was completed. One possible explanation for these patterns is that the quality of pension fund governance has not been stable over this extended timeframe. There is some statistical support for this hypothesis. For the subset of 28 funds for which there were both 1997 and 2005 Pension CEO Scores, the correlation coefficient between the two data sets was positive, but a fairly low 0.5. This is not entirely surprising. Excellence in governance requires high capability consistently applied. To achieve this over extended periods of time is a high hurdle.

The statistical tests described in the study use all of the four-year NVA data available for the funds in the CEM database for which there were also Pension CEO Scores. So in this sense the study results do not suffer from 'data mining' problems. Stated differently, while the authors indicate that by playing with various subsets of the total database produced some additional statistical results that looked interesting, they did not publish them. They felt that any specifically selected subset results, no matter how interesting, could simply represent noise rather than signal. Having said that, they made one exception. One of the cost categories in the CEM database is 'Oversight/Management Costs', which captures fund costs allocated to the internal governance, management and control functions.

A reasonable hypothesis is that funds with higher Pension CEO Scores would invest more in these functions than funds with low scores. So, statistically, we should find a positive relationship between Oversight/ Management Costs (OMC) and Pension CEO Scores, after adjusting for fund size. The OMC-CEO coefficient was in fact 1.4 (t-value 3.0). So again, taking the Pension CEO Score range to be from three to six, the implication is that high-scoring funds spend an average four basis points (that is, 3 × 1.4) more per annum on the internal governance, management and control functions than low-scoring funds. This is an additional $4 million per year for a $10 billion fund. Clearly, the CEOs and boards of governors of the high-scoring funds are allocating greater resources to the OMC function, suggesting that the CEO scores are not random numbers, but are positively associated with governance quality.

8.11   THE AGENCY AND GOVERNANCE FACTORS: FINANCIAL IMPLICATIONS

To appreciate fully the impact and consequences of the findings of the agency and governance studies, consider a worker earning a constant $50 000 per annum over a 40-year working life. A sum of $10 000 per annum is saved for retirement. Assume a passive stock/bond market-based life-cycle investment policy earns a pre-expense 3 per cent real rate of return over the 40-year period. At the end of the 40-year period, a 20-year annuity is bought with an embedded interest rate of 1.5 per cent. Table 8.3 sets out the annual pension this worker will receive with net (that is, after-expense) returns of (a) 4 per cent, (b) 2.6 per cent, (c) 1.5 per cent and (d) −2 per cent.

Why these four net return examples? The combined findings of the agency and governance studies suggest that, relative to a 3 per cent market-based passive return, a net 4 per cent return realization is realistic for an interests-aligned, well-governed pension fund. At a 2.4 per cent return, the pension fund would simply be generating the market-based return less expenses. The studies suggest that a 1.5 per cent to −2 per cent is a realistic experience range for most mutual fund investors. At 1.5 per cent, the mutual fund investor experiences market-like gross returns, relatively low expenses, and assumes the investor does not engage in the kind of 'buy high, sell low' activity that Bogle describes in his book. At the other end of the range, the −2 per cent case assumes expense ratios at the high end of the range, as well as active engagement in the further wealth-reducing behaviours by individual mutual fund investors described by Bogle.

Table 8.3 indicates that, under realistic assumptions, the typical mutual fund investor faces a minimum pension reduction of 22 per cent (that is, from $41 000 per year to $32 000 per year) relative to the typical pension fund participant (that is, with a mutual fund net return of 1.5 per cent, and a pension fund net return of 2.6 per cent). That pension reduction grows to 72 per cent if we push the mutual fund participant net return down to −2 per cent, and the pension fund return up to 4 per cent (the pension

Table 8.3   The impact of differing net returns experiences on pension adequacy

	Net Realized Return			
	4%	2.6%	1.5%	−2%
Annual savings (over 40 years)	$10 000	$10 000	$10 000	$10 000
Final savings (after 40 years)	$988 000	$707 000	$551 000	$272 000
Annual pension payment	$57 000	$41 000	$32 000	$16 000
Working income replacement rate	114%	82%	64%	32%

reduction now is from $57 000 to $16 000 per year). This measures the pension shortfall between a participant in an interest-aligned, well-governed pension fund and the participant in high-expense mutual funds who also engages in adverse 'buy high–sell low' trading activity over time.

8.12   THE IDEAL PENSION DELIVERY ORGANIZATION: FROM THEORY TO PRACTICE

Integrative Investment Theory posits that agency and governance factors are important drivers of client/beneficiary value creation in pension delivery organizations. The analyses described in this chapter offer empirical support for this proposition. Specifically, the research findings suggest organizations with aligned interests that are also well-governed can potentially deliver workers more than twice the pension per dollar of retirement savings, relative to organizations that have agency conflicts and/or are poorly governed. What are the practical implications of these findings? Five come to mind.

1. *Broad workforce participation in occupational pension plans managed by pension delivery organizations with aligned interests that are also well-governed has significant welfare-enhancement potential*: this was also the conclusion of the UK's Turner Commission on pension reform, which recommended enroling the entire non-covered part of the UK workforce into such arrangements. The government has indicated that it will act on the Turner recommendations, with the details yet to be resolved.[14]

2. *'Aligned interests' mean legal structures in which the financial interests of the clients/beneficiaries are not in conflict with those of other potential stakeholder groups*: an obvious example of such an 'in conflict' group is the owners/managers of 'for-profit' mutual fund management companies. It is in the financial interest of such groups to exploit the informational asymmetry between their customers and themselves. Empirical findings cited in this chapter suggest the 'for-profit' mutual fund industry is successfully exploiting this asymmetry.

3. *'Good governance' means an organization design that flows logically from a clear organization mission, to effective oversight and executive functions, to a series of efficient operational functions required to achieve the organization mission*: the ICPM-commissioned pension fund governance research project cited earlier in this chapter found that the oversight function in pension-delivery organizations continues to be generally weak to this day. This is the case because the selection processes for members of boards of trustees continue to be flawed, and board self-evaluation-of-effectiveness processes continue to be weak to non-existent. These weaknesses in turn have organizational consequences. They include difficulties in sorting out the competing financial interests of various stakeholder groups in DB plans, lack of delegation clarity between board and executive responsibilities, board micro-management rather than a strategic oversight focus, and non-competitive compensation policies in pension funds.[15]

4. *'Good governance' also means understanding the importance of scale in the delivering pension investment and administration services*: insufficient scale leads to high unit costs as well as an inability to attract the human resources required to run the investment and administration 'businesses'. In this case, 'good governance' means understanding these realities, and merging the too-small pension fund with one that does have sufficient scale. Research by CEM Benchmarking Inc. throws an interesting light on the importance of the scale factor. Pooling all of the single-year total fund Net Value Added (NVA) data collected over the 1991–2005 period, and regressing the NVAs against log 10 of the funds' dollar values in the relevant year, produced a regression coefficient of 0.28 ($t = 4.3$). The fund dollar values in the CEM database range from a low of $100 million to a high of $250 billion. This implies a low–high size-related NVA differential in the CEM database approaching 1 per cent per annum. More detailed analysis shows this material large-fund return advantage to be partially a straight unit cost advantage, and partially a more-innovative-strategies advantage (that is, greater, and more successful, use of alternative strategies such as emerging markets,

private equities and hedge funds). Analyses using CEM's pension benefit administration database suggest similar scale benefits accrue on that side of pension delivery organizations.

5. *Government policies can foster both the 'aligned interests' and 'good governance' dimensions of pension-delivery organizations*: governments should ensure that pension-delivery organizations are not handicapped in any way in serving their clients/beneficiaries. Governments should also ensure that pension-delivery organizations meet objective organization performance/effectiveness standards. For example, CEM has developed metrics that could be used as proxies to set minimum organization performance/effectiveness standards in both the investment and administration 'businesses'.[16]

There is one opinion we sometimes hear that these findings do *not* support. It is sometimes argued that the benefits of interest-aligned, well-governed pension-delivery organizations attach themselves only to DB plans, and not DC plans. This study shows this opinion to be a non-sequitur. An interest-aligned, well-governed pension-delivery organization can deliver any pension formula more effectively than an organization without such characteristics. While we hold strong views that the optimal pension formula is in fact neither DB nor DC, that is a topic for another day.[17]

NOTES

1. Markowitz, Sharpe and Miller won the 1990 Nobel Prize in Economics for their contributions to the development of investment and capital markets theory. Merton and Scholes (Black died in 1995) won the 1997 Prize for developing a new method to value options and derivatives.
2. Merton and Bodie (2004) develop an overarching theory of financial system design by bringing together three related theories of finance: neoclassical, behavioural and institutional. The focus of the institutional theory dimension is to deal with market frictions and agency problems. However, their paper stops short of prescribing optimal governance practices and organization structure.
3. Akerlof won the 2001 Nobel Prize in Economics for the development of pricing theory in markets with asymmetric information.
4. See Ambachtsheer et al. (1998, 2006).
5. Globefund.com is a provider of Canadian mutual fund data. The Centre for Research in Security Prices (CRSP) database covers all USA mutual funds from 1962 to the present, and includes such fund-specific information as expense ratios, fund flows, investment style, etc. CEM Benchmarking Inc. is a Toronto-based firm founded in 1991, which focuses on benchmarking both the investment and benefit administration sides of pension delivery organizations in Europe, North America, and the Pacific Rim. See www.cembenchmarking.com for more information.
6. Governance and other overhead costs estimate based on statistics provided by CEM Benchmarking Inc.

7. For example, ETF fees based on the S&P500 are as low as 0.07 per cent.
8. See Mitchell and Utkus (2004) for a history of, and key research findings in the behavioural finance field related to pension system design.
9. See 2006 Pollara survey posted in the website of the Investment Funds Institute of Canada www.ific.ca.
10. See Ambachtsheer et al. (1998).
11. Recall the rating range was from 6 to 1. So the means of 4.8 in 1997 and 4.9 in 2005 suggest a bias towards assigning relatively high scores to the 45 statements. This is common practice in these types of surveys. See Ambachtsheer et al. (2006) for a more detailed discussion of the rating distributions.
12. See Ambachtsheer (2007), Chapters 32 and 33 for a more detailed discussion of possible approaches to risk-adjusting returns.
13. We know of a few individual funds that have generated excess returns of 3 per cent per annum or better over extended periods of time. While we believe these results to be due to excellent governance practices, it is impossible to 'prove' this statistically. For example, even purely random processes will produce a few excellent performance records if the samples are large enough.
14. See Ambachtsheer (2007), Chapter 43 for more detail.
15. See Ambachtsheer et al. (2006) for more detail on the strengths and weaknesses of current pension fund governance practices.
16. CEM benchmarks the cost effectiveness of both the investment and benefit administration 'businesses' using standardized metrics. Regulations could require that the boards of trustees of pension delivery organizations establish minimum cost-effectiveness standards for both of the 'businesses' they are overseeing.
17. See, for example, the preface and introduction to Ambachtsheer (2007).

REFERENCES

Akerlof, G. (1970), 'The market for lemons: quality, uncertainty, and the market mechanism', *Quarterly Journal of Economics*, **84**(3), 488–500.

Ambachtsheer, K. (2005), 'Beyond portfolio theory: the next frontier', *Financial Analysts Journal*, **61**(1), 29–33.

Ambachtsheer, K. (2007), *Pension Revolution: A Solution to the Pensions Crisis*, New York: John Wiley & Sons.

Ambachtsheer, K., R. Capelle and H. Lum (2006), 'Pension fund governance today: strengths, weaknesses, and opportunities for improvement', Working Paper, www.rotman.utoronto.ca/icpm.

Ambachtsheer, K., R. Capelle and T. Scheibelhut (1998), 'Improving pension fund performance', *Financial Analysts Journal*, **54**(6), 15–21.

Ambachtsheer, K., C. Boice, D. Ezra and J. McLaughlin (1995), 'Excellence shortfall in pension fund management: anatomy of a problem', Working Paper, cited in 'Pension Fund Excellence'.

Bauer, R., R. Frehen, H. Lum and R. Otten (2006), 'Economies of scale, lack of skill, or misalignment of interest? A study of pension and mutual fund performance', Working Paper, www.rotman.utoronto.ca/icpm. A more recent version of the paper (2007) is titled 'The Performance of USA Mutual Funds: New Insights into the Agency Costs Debate'.

Berle, Adolf and Gardiner Means (1933), *The Modern Corporation and Private Property*, Harcourt, Brace, New York: Macmillan Co.

Bogle, John C. (2005), *The Battle for the Soul of Capitalism*, New Haven, Conn.: Yale University Press.

Clark, G.L., E. Caerlewy-Smith and J.C. Marshall (2006), 'Pension fund trustee competence: decision-making in problems relevant to investment practice', *Journal of Pension Economics and Finance*, **5**(1), 91–110.

Drucker, Peter F. (1976), *The Unseen Revolution – How Pension Fund Socialism Came to America*, New York: Harper & Row.

Keynes, John Maynard (1936), *The General Theory of Employment, Interest, and Money*, New York: Harcourt, Brace.

Markowitz, H. (1952), 'Portfolio Selection', *Journal of Finance*, **7**(1), 77–91.

Merton, R.C. and Z. Bodie (2004), 'Design of financial systems: towards a synthesis of function and structure', Working Paper, Harvard Business School.

Mitchell, Olivia and Stephen Utkus (2004), *Pension Design and Structure*, Oxford: Oxford University Press.

Discussion of 'The ideal pension delivery organization: theory and practice'

Ambrogio Rinaldi

Ambachtsheer refers to his Integrative Investment Theory (IIT), that puts together different parts of economics in order to obtain a comprehensive (holistic) theory of optimal pension delivery: in particular, portfolio theory is integrated with principal/agent and governance factors. Against the background of IIT theory, Ambachtsheer takes stock of two recent empirical studies in order to show that these two factors – the degree of alignment of 'principals' (pension fund members) and 'agents' (pension fund trustees and/or managers) and the quality of pension fund governance – can both be statistically associated with the creation of value for pension fund members. He then concludes that the two factors are indeed important for the optimal pension delivery, and draws several practical implications of his findings.

In my discussion, I concentrate on Ambachtsheer's conclusions, and I find it useful to employ the Italian system of private pensions as a 'laboratory' in which to test their general relevance. I argue that not only the structures of each pension delivery organization (the focus of Ambachtsheer's chapter), but also the degree of contestability of the market for private pensions is an important element that should be considered in the optimal design of pension delivery. I also argue that the Italian system of private pensions (as recently reformed and made contestable) should receive attention as an interesting compromise between 'paternalistic' systems mainly based on occupational DB schemes, and systems based on DC individual accounts offered directly to individuals by many competing financial providers.

What are the essential elements of the Italian system of private pensions, as established in the 1990s and then reformed again recently, with full effect from July 2007, that I want to put forward in relation to Ambachtsheer's conclusions?

1. For all employed workers that entered the workforce starting from 1995, only DC plans are admitted.

2. Starting from July 2007, all employed workers in the private sector (12 million) are automatically enroled in their 'natural' pension fund, with a contribution rate of about 7 per cent of gross salary (a sum so far kept by employers as a book reserve item in order to finance the severance pay (so-called TFR) to be paid to workers at termination of employment). However, the individual may explicitly refuse the payment of the TFR into the pension fund system, and consequently maintain the previous regime, that provides for a low but safe rate of revaluation of the TFR).

3. A central role is reserved for industry-wide, stand-alone contractual pension funds (CPFs), that in most cases are the 'natural' pension funds where workers will be automatically enroled on a no-objection basis and that are going to receive the TFR-originated contributions. The CPFs are non-profit entities run by workers and employers on a parity basis, in favour of which industry-wide national labour contracts usually provide for additional contributions (typically 1 to 2 per cent) to be paid by the employer, conditioned to a matching contribution of the worker. These CPFs are obliged to appoint external managers for the management of their assets.

4. The system is open to competition between the CPFs and the so-called 'open' pension funds (OPFs), collective investment vehicles with annuities attached, set and run for a profit by financial institutions. Competition is favoured by a high degree of transparency and comparability between the plans, and is set to work through a carefully designed system of choices that can be exercised at collective and/or individual level:

    • by collective agreement at company level, the workers may opt out as a group from the industry-wide pension fund into an OPF: in this case both the TFR-originated and the employers' contributions are fully portable;

    • members may individually opt out from the occupational scheme (that may be either a CPF or the OPF collectively selected at company level) and select their own preferred OPF, or also a so-called 'PIP', a personal insurance policy available at individual level and designed to comply with the pension regulation and thus qualify for the fiscal benefits. However, in this case members have a right to carry with them only the TFR-originated, not the employers', contribution.

5. For all workers that stay silent, the default investment option is set to be a guaranteed sub-fund, that is offered by every CPF and OPF open to group membership; the pension fund cannot bear the risk connected with the guarantee and therefore has to purchase it for a fee from the asset manager or a third party.

How consistent is the Italian private pension system with Ambachtsheer's ideas? In principle, the typical Italian CPFs are good candidates as Ambachtsheer's optimal pension delivery organizations: they are large-scale (being industry-wide and the natural destination for automatic enrolment) and with aligned interests (being stand-alone and with workers that appoint half of the governing board). On the other hand, OPFs and PIPs are in principle prone to interests misalignment and high costs.

I want to argue that, in order to draw conclusions about the optimal pension delivery organization, it is essential to analyse explicitly not only the design of each pension entity, but also the competitive structure of the market for pension delivery as a whole. This is an element that is largely missing in Ambachtsheer's analysis. However, all the factors that he emphasizes as important (interest alignment, governance, scale) are indeed the crucial ones, also when one considers the competitive dynamics.

In this perspective, the analysis of the Italian market is instructive. On the one side, the position of the 'incumbents', the industry-wide CPFs, have been made contestable, as workers can opt out as a group and (although possibly at the cost of missing the employers' contributions) as individuals, and go for OPFs or PIPs. As a result, CPFs are stimulated to practise good governance, effective management and appropriate oversight of outsourced functions (such as asset management, that Italian CPFs are obliged to outsource). Even if they are not directly in competition one with the other, they are all exposed to a similar degree of competition, as in a system of communicating vessels.

On the other side, the fact that industry-wide CPFs are the natural destination for most workers puts pressure on financial companies offering OPFs and PIPs, forcing them to ease the interest misalignment with respect to their clients. In particular, it may be anticipated that in most cases group opt-outs from CPFs will occur only after a careful selection of available options (typically, trade unions will take care of members' interests), thus favouring competitive price-setting behaviour for OPFs. Interestingly, it may be argued that the search activity performed in the market segment for group membership is likely to produce positive externalities for individuals as well, as OPFs typically host both group and individual membership, and also PIPs are indirectly put under pressure, although they compete directly only in the market for personal pension plans.

I find it interesting to focus on a specific point that Ambachtsheer makes on personal pension plans and, in general, on retail investment vehicles. He notes that costs of these products are unduly high, and explains this fact with the misalignment of interests that characterizes these products: in particular, he notes that there are conflicts of interest and information asymmetries between pension and mutual fund managers/sellers and their customers.

While I do share Ambachtsheer's view in general, for the sake of precision I note that the reference to the concept of conflicts of interest may be misleading in this case. In fact, there are two possible sources of interest misalignment: 'contrasts of interest' and 'conflicts of interest'. A *contrast of interest* describes the situation in which a seller and a buyer are expected to be opposite anyway: the interest of the seller is for a high price, and is in obvious contrast with the interest of the buyer for a low price: it should be considered fully compatible with the proper functioning of markets.[1] On the other hand, a *conflict of interest* describes the situation of an agent delegated by a principal to a certain activity, that bears an interest in running that activity that is not aligned with the interest of the principal. The agency issues stressed by Ambachtsheer are strictly connected only to conflicts of interest and not to contrasts of interest.

In the market for retail pension products, contrasts of interest (and not necessarily conflicts of interest)[2] are standard between pension providers and customers, but, as suggested above they should not be seen per se as a potential source of market failures, and should not be expected to produce unduly high costs, where market forces and competitive price setting are in place. In contrast, information asymmetries, also stressed by Ambachtsheer,[3] are indeed to be considered a true and widespread source of market failures in the market for retail pension products. They are generated on the supply side through product design prone to opacity and hidden costs, and are amplified on the demand side by the lack of financial literacy of potential and current members.

In conclusion, I find that, although with some qualifications, Ambachtsheer's recommendations for optimal pension delivery are robust, and incidentally useful to rationalize and support important features of the Italian private pension system, such as the central role set for industry-wide CPFs. Interestingly, the analysis of the Italian example suggests that it is useful to complement Ambachsheer's approach to the design of single pension organizations with the analysis of the structure of the market and its contestability. In this framework, the experience in the coming years of the functioning of the Italian market for pension provision will be instructive.

NOTES

1. In this regard, remember the famous quotation from Adam Smith: 'It is not from the benevolence of the butcher, the brewer, or the baker, that we expect our dinner, but from their regard to their own interest'.
2. Conflicts of interest may and do in fact occur, but in more subtle ways. In particular, the high cost of a specific pension plan may arise from costs linked to activities that the agent (the pension provider) is supposed to run in sole interests of the principal (the pension

plan member): for example, the selection of an expensive investment vehicle (as a mutual fund) in which to invest the pension plan money, possibly with part of the cost that goes in favour of the agent itself, or excessive trading, with the trading commissions that at least in part are transferred back to the agent.

3. Let me note that the reference he makes to the famous 1970 paper by Akerlof could be better qualified. In that paper information asymmetries result in disappearance from the market of quality items in favour of low-quality ones, and not in unduly high costs.

9. Pension guarantees, capital adequacy and international risk sharing

Zvi Bodie

9.1 INTRODUCTION

Around the world today there are striking differences in the structure of pension systems. The roles played by families, employers, trade unions, financial intermediaries, community organizations, affiliation groups and governmental agencies vary tremendously. Yet, despite these differences, in almost every industrialized society people regard some minimum level of old-age income as necessary, and therefore make coverage mandatory. Contributions to the mandatory system are generally regarded as a tax, and government is expected either to provide or to guarantee those benefits as part of the social safety net. On top of this mandatory level is a layer of occupational pension benefits designed to replace one's earnings from employment after a specified normal retirement age. There are large cross-country differences with regard to the systems for insuring these occupational pensions.

In the US, only about half of the working population is covered by any type of occupational pension plan. Currently less than half of those covered have plans of the defined-benefit type, and the benefits are explicitly guaranteed (up to specified limits) through a federal government corporation called the Pension Benefit Guaranty Corporation (PBGC). In the case of single-employer defined-benefit plans, the sponsoring firm must make up any shortfall between the liabilities and the assets of the plan. Pension benefit obligations are an explicit liability of the firm sponsoring the plan.[1] Thus the firm is the primary guarantor of pension benefits, and the PBGC is insurer of last resort.

In the US, the UK and several other countries, there is a major shift away from defined benefit plans and towards defined contribution plans, in which individuals have the ability to choose but bear all of the investment risk. But participants in these plans rarely have the knowledge or the time to manage their own accounts. Therefore, over the past few years, asset management firms and other financial institutions have been offering target-date retirement funds and managed investment accounts. In the US, the government has recently approved them as default options for 401k defined contribution plans. In my opinion, it is essential that, as a condition for such approval, they carry a guarantee of some minimum level of income, wealth or rate of return provided by the asset management firm.

Perhaps the most basic rule of the marketplace is *caveat emptor* – buyer beware. This warning recognizes the fundamental asymmetry that normally exists between buyers and sellers. It is because of this asymmetry that many consumer products cannot be successfully marketed without a money-back guarantee. These products require the consumer to trust the producer. Nothing inspires trust as immediately or effectively as a credible money-back guarantee. Retirement investment products sold to consumers should offer such guarantees too.

There are at least three reasons to require that a guarantee should be a default option for consumer-oriented retirement investments.

1. It greatly reduces the moral hazard problem in the provision of such products, and therefore results in lower marketing and distribution costs for society.
2. It makes it far more transparent to consumers what they are buying, and therefore reduces the need for costly financial 'education' which has not proved effective in the past.
3. Many consumers mistakenly think there is almost no risk in the long-run performance of the stock market. Making consumers aware that there is such risk, and that it can only be avoided at a cost, increases consumer and societal welfare.

In Germany, this consumer protection approach extends to defined contribution pension plans. As a matter of law, every German DC plan must guarantee participants that they can at least get back the nominal value of their contributions. I am in favour of a less extreme form of consumer protection – that sellers of retirement investment products must make available to their customers such a guarantee as the default option. Customers would have the right to opt out of the guarantee, but this would require an explicit action on their part.

In the Netherlands, almost the entire working population is covered by occupational pension plans. These plans are mandatory, yet there is no *explicit* guarantee programme for them. Employers are legally responsible for making contributions to pension plans, but underfunded pension promises are not a legal liability of the employer or of the government.

However, prudential regulation of pension funds in the Netherlands has always been quite strict, and has been made even more strict in the recent past.

A common objection to having government provide guarantees is that, once people have them, the discipline of the market is lost. There are limits, however, to relying on market discipline in the case of pensions. Perhaps the most important of those limits is imposed by the problem of *time inconsistency*. The essence of time inconsistency is that, despite a commitment that is optimal *ex ante*, it is sometimes optimal ex post to renege. Everyone knows that, since government makes the rules, it can change them too. The government, therefore, is caught in a *paradox of power*. For market discipline to work, the government must bind itself convincingly not to bail out institutions that get into trouble. But the government is too powerful not to intervene.

The evidence for the existence of implicit government guarantees is clearest in the case of deposit insurance. In countries facing widespread bank defaults, the government almost always bails out depositors, even when there is no explicit deposit insurance. Surely, in a democratic country like the Netherlands, the same principle would apply to occupational pensions, especially since they are mandatory.

The chapter is organized as follows. Section 2 lays out the principles for the management of a system of pension guarantees. Section 3 explores the relationship between pension asset-liability mismatch risk and capital adequacy using option pricing theory as the analytical framework. Section 4 draws some lessons from the mistakes made by the US Government in managing its Pension Benefit Guarantee Corporation. Finally, Section 5 concludes with some suggestions for public policy.

9.2   PRINCIPLES FOR MANAGING PENSION GUARANTEES[2]

Regardless of whether it is run by a private-sector organization or a government agency, there are certain principles that must be followed if a system of guarantees is to remain viable. Functionally, guarantees are insurance policies that oblige the guarantor to make the promised payment if the insured pension fund fails to do so. The economic loss to the guarantor is equal to the difference between the promised payment and the price received from the sale of the assets that are available from the fund as collateral for this obligation. This difference is called the 'shortfall'. All assets of the fund that the guarantor has recourse to seize will be called 'collateral' assets, even if they are not formally pledged and segregated. For the guarantee activity to be sustainable without recourse to subsidies from other sources, premiums charged for the guarantees must be large enough to cover both actuarial loss experience and operating costs.

The basic methods that any guarantor (whether private-sector or government) has to manage its business on a sound basis are as follows:

- *Funding restrictions:* set standards for the full funding of promised benefits (that is, 'capital adequacy' and act swiftly to limit losses when these funding standards are violated (that is, avoid 'forbearance').
- *Matching restrictions:* require the insured entity to hedge its insured liabilities by matching the market-risk exposure of its assets to its insured liabilities.
- *Pricing:* set a premium schedule for the guarantee commensurate with the guarantor's exposure to the risk of a shortfall.
- *Transparency:* require disclosure of information about the insured institution's assets and liabilities in a format that is relevant to evaluating the guarantor's exposure to shortfall risk.

The methods substitute for each other in varying degrees, hence there is room for trade-offs among them. With all methods, the guarantor must monitor the market values of the insured liabilities and the assets securing them on a regular basis. The length of time permitted for making up a funding deficit is a key parameter to be set in determining the optimal trade-off among methods.

For example, let us set the premium equal to the cost of a single guarantee. For simplicity, assume that there are no operating costs. If the value of collateral assets, V, exceeds the promised payments, B, the guarantor keeps the premium and pays nothing. But if the value of assets is less than the promised payments, the guarantor must pay the difference, $B - V$. The guarantor's maximum profit is equal to the premium plus interest earned from investing the premium prior to payment of losses or expiration of the guarantee. This maximum profit is diminished by the shortfall or loss experience from issuer defaults. The guarantor's profit function is thus given by:

$$P(1+r) - \max[0, B - V]$$

where P is the premium and r is the interest rate.

The guarantor bears the full downside risk of the collateral assets. It does not, however, participate in the upside gains that an owner of those assets would receive. Because of this asymmetry, the guarantor's expected loss is an increasing function of the volatility (that is, standard deviation) of the difference between the promised payment B and the asset value V. Therefore, to sustain themselves as viable economic entities without cross-subsidies from other insured institutions or from taxpayer funds, the guarantor must charge a premium that is directly related to the magnitude of the potential shortfall. This magnitude depends directly on the length of time permitted to make up a funding deficit.

If a funding shortfall must be made up immediately, as is the case with margin loans made by brokerage firms and margin requirements of organized futures exchanges, then the guarantor can charge a premium that is relatively small. It need only cover the costs of monitoring the system, but typically pension funds are allowed relatively long periods in which to make up a funding shortfall.

9.3 MISMATCH RISK AND CAPITAL ADEQUACY IN THE LIGHT OF OPTION THEORY

In this section we consider the trade-off between capital adequacy and matching restrictions using option pricing theory as our analytical framework. The tighter the matching restrictions, the smaller the amount of buffer capital required to maintain the integrity of the pension promise. Many in the investment industry hold the view that a stock portfolio is an effective hedge against the pension liability when the investment horizon is long-term. However, using option pricing theory it becomes evident that the cost of insuring a pension liability collateralized with equities actually *increases* with the length of time required to make up a funding deficit.[3]

Assume a defined-benefit plan sponsor is faced with the obligation to pay a fixed amount as a pension benefit T years from now, and it will not have to make up any funding deficits until then. It fully funds its obligation by contributing to the pension fund an amount equal to the present value of the promised benefit. It can invest in an *immunized* default-free bond portfolio maturing in T years earning a certain risk-free rate of interest. If instead the sponsor invests in a stock portfolio then there is a risk of a shortfall at time T.

The basis for the proposition that stocks are less risky in the long run appears to be the observation that, the longer the time horizon, the smaller the *probability* of a shortfall. If the ex ante mean rate of return on stocks exceeds the risk-free rate of interest, it is indeed true that the probability of a shortfall declines with the length of the investment time horizon. For example, suppose the rate of return on stocks is log-normally distributed with a risk premium of 8 per cent per year and an annualized standard deviation of 20 per cent. With a time horizon of only one year, the probability of a shortfall is 34 per cent, whereas at 20 years that probability is only 4 per cent.

But the probability of a shortfall is a flawed measure of risk because it ignores how large the potential shortfall might be. It is easy to see this point if we assume that stock returns follow a simple 'random walk'. In any one-year period, assume the rate of return on stocks can take only one of two values, either +20 per cent or −20 per cent, independent of its past history. Consider the worst possible outcome for time horizons of increasing length. For a one-year horizon one can lose 20 per cent of the initial investment, for a two-year period 36 per cent, and for a 20-year period as much as 99 per cent. Using the probability of a shortfall as the measure of risk, no distinction is made between a loss of 20 per cent or a loss of 99 per cent.[4]

If it were true that stocks are less risky in the long run, then the cost of insuring against earning less than the risk-free rate of interest should decline as the maturity of the pension obligation increases. But the opposite is true. To see this, define the cost of shortfall insurance, P, as the additional amount of money one has to add at the investment starting date to ensure that at the maturity date the pension portfolio will have a value at least as great as it would have earning the risk-free interest rate. Thus, for each dollar insured against a shortfall, the total amount actually invested at the starting date is $1 + P$.

To find P, we use modern option pricing methodology.[5] Insurance against shortfall risk is effectively a *put* option. The put is of the European type (i.e. it can only be exercised at the expiration date), and it expires in T years. The put's exercise price is the insured value of the portfolio. If at the expiration date T years from now the portfolio's value exceeds its insured value, then the put expires worthless. If, however, there is a shortfall, then the put's payoff is equal to the shortfall.

Because we are insuring a pension obligation that grows at the risk-free interest rate, the exercise price of the put equals the price of the underlying stock portfolio compounded at the risk-free T-year interest rate.[6] Therefore the *put-call parity theorem* tells us that the price of the put equals the price of the corresponding call.[7]

To show that the value of the put increases with T, we could use any option pricing model based on the condition that the financial markets do not allow anyone to earn risk-free arbitrage profits. Because it is so compact and so widely used in practice, we will use the Black–Scholes formula. In our special case, the formula reduces to a relatively simple form. Moreover, with no loss of generality, we can express the price of the put as a fraction of the price of the stock:

$$\frac{P}{S} = N(d_1) - N(d_2)$$

$$d_1 = \frac{\sigma\sqrt{T}}{2}$$

$$d_2 = \frac{-\sigma\sqrt{T}}{2},$$

where:

S = price of the stock,
T = time to expiration of the option in years,
σ = standard deviation of the annualized continuously compounded rate of return on the stock,
$N(d)$ = the probability that a random draw from a standard normal distribution is less than d.

Note that P/S is independent of the risk-free interest rate; it depends only on σ and T. Table 9.1 and Figure 9.1 show the result of applying the formula to compute P/S assuming the annualized standard deviation of stock returns is 20 per cent. The cost of the insurance rises with T, the term of the insurance. For a one-year term, the cost is 8 per cent of the investment. For a 10-year term, it is 25 per cent, and for a 50-year term it is 52 per cent. As the term grows without limit, the cost of the insurance approaches 100 per cent of the investment.[8]

Some economists and other observers of the stock market have claimed that stock returns do not follow a random walk in the long run. Rather, they argue, the behaviour of stock returns is best characterized as a mean-reverting process. It is mean reversion in stock returns, some say, that is the reason stocks are less risky for investors with a long time horizon.

Figure 9.1 is valid for mean-reverting processes too. The reason is that arbitrage-based option pricing models, such as the Black–Scholes or binomial models, are valid regardless of the process for the mean. They are based on the law of one price and the condition of no-arbitrage profits. Investors who disagree about the mean rate of return on stocks, but agree about the variance, will therefore agree about the option price.

For the relation depicted in Figure 9.1 to be invalid, mean reversion is not enough. Stock prices would have to behave just like the price of a

Table 9.1   Cost of shortfall insurance as a function of time horizon

Length of time horizon in years	Cost of insurance as percentage of investment
0	0
1	7.98
5	17.72
10	24.84

Notes: The table was derived using the Black–Scholes formula with $\sigma = 0.2$ per year; the cost of the insurance is independent of the risk-free rate.

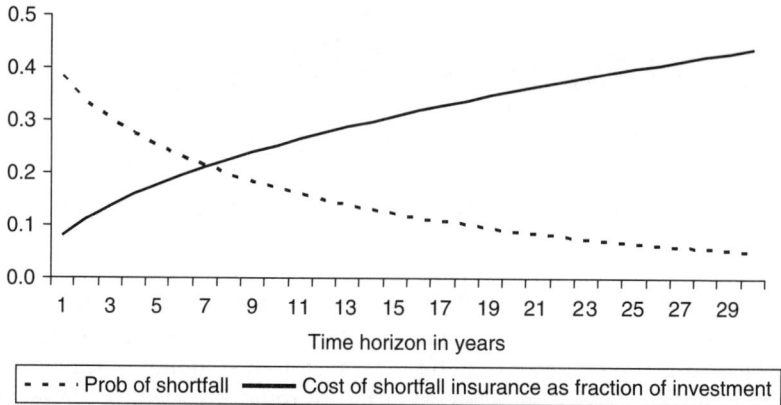

Figure 9.1   Probability of a shortfall and cost of insurance as a function of time

T-period zero-coupon bond that converges towards the bond's face value as the horizon date approaches. In other words, stocks would have to be indistinguishable from the risk-free asset for a T-period horizon.

The policy parameters that a guarantor can in principle control are (1) the required funding ratio, (2) the speed with which a pension fund must make up for a shortfall below the required funding ratio, (3) the required degree of matching between the pension liabilities and the assets backing them, and (4) the premium charged for the insurance. Table 9.1 and Figure 9.1 are relevant to assessing the relationship among these parameters.

T is the time interval permitted to make up a funding shortfall. For a given T and asset-liability mismatch, the cost of the guarantee P represents the minimum required buffer. Thus, the shorter the time interval and the better the match, the lower the required buffer. If the pension sponsor invests the pension assets in common stocks or other types of equity securities rather than in fixed-income securities that immunize the guaranteed benefits, then the exposure of the government to a potential shortfall is increased. The required funding ratio must therefore be increased.

For the guarantee system to be viable, volatility need not be reduced to zero, but it does have to be known (or at least bounded) and not subject to significant unilateral change by the insured pension plan. If the insured pension-plan sponsor can unilaterally change the composition of the asset portfolio, then the government faces a problem of moral hazard since some sponsors will have an incentive not to fund their plans adequately and increase the risk of their assets.

9.4   THE EXPERIENCE OF THE PBGC

The PBGC insures the pension benefits of Americans covered by private defined-benefit pension plans. Since defined-benefit plans in the US are backed by the corporations that sponsor them, the PBGC is actually a reinsurer. If the pension assets are insufficient to cover the pension liabilities, it is up to the corporate plan sponsor to make up the shortfall. It is only when the corporate sponsor goes bankrupt with insufficient assets to pay the benefits promised to employees that the PBGC takes it over and makes up the shortfall. There is a cap on the PBGC-insured benefit, so that highly compensated employees of firms that go bankrupt do not typically get full benefits. By law, the PBGC is supposed to finance all of its operations from three sources: (1) the premiums it collects from companies that still sponsor defined-benefit plans, (2) the assets it recovers from terminated underfunded plans, and (3) the interest, dividends and capital gains it earns on its accumulated reserves.

The current system overcharges sponsors of healthy plans in order to subsidize the ailing ones, but, in the US, employers are not required to offer any kind of occupational pension plan, and companies that do sponsor plans can choose a defined-contribution design rather than the traditional defined-benefit plan. In recent years, virtually all new pension plans have been DC plans, and many sponsors of DB plans have switched to the DC plan design. For the PBGC, this creates a problem of *adverse selection*. Well-funded plans have an incentive to terminate their defined benefit plans to avoid being 'taxed' through high actuarially unfair premiums to bail out underfunded plans of financially weak sponsors. The result is that only sick and undercharged firms will be left in the insurance pool. Thus we have a classic case of the Law of Unintended Consequences: insurance designed to strengthen the traditional pension system winds up accelerating its demise.

As a result of a combination of falling interest rates and falling stock prices during the period 2000 to 2003, many defined benefit pension plans went from being well-funded to underfunded. As a result of a wave of bankruptcies of steel companies and airlines with severely underfunded pension plans, the PBGC found itself facing a massive cumulative deficit.

In 2006, the US Government enacted the Pension Protection Act to address these problems.[9] It raised premiums, tightened funding rules and improved the measurement and reporting of corporate pension liabilities, but it did nothing to take account of the asset–liability mismatch in setting PBGC premiums or to restrict the exposure of the PBGC by requiring closer matching of pension assets to liabilities. Indeed, the Pension Protection Act does not even recognize that there is a mismatch problem.

The experience of the PBGC suggests that it can be difficult – perhaps impossible – for the US government to manage its system of pension guarantees by adjusting the price it charges to properly reflect the risk posed by a mismatch between pension assets and liabilities or by requiring closer matching of assets to liabilities. The only alternative left is to require a larger buffer of risk capital for plan sponsors that expose the guarantor to greater mismatch risk.

Corporate plan sponsors in the US and the UK have begun to recognize that mismatch risk in their defined benefit pension plans is destructive of shareholder value. They are gradually adopting strategies known as 'liability-driven investing' (LDI). In practice, these strategies are implemented through the use of a swaps overlay. A swap contract consists of two parties exchanging (or 'swapping') a series of payments at specified intervals (say, every six months) over a specified period of time (say, 10 years). The payments are based upon an agreed principal amount (called the 'notional' amount), and there is no immediate payment of money between the parties. Thus the swap contract itself provides no new funds to either party.

Around the world today banks and investment companies use swaps extensively to manage their exposures to currency, interest-rate, credit-default and equity-market risks and to lower their transaction costs. Pension funds have so far made relatively little use of swaps.[10] The advantage of the swap contract is that it is non-invasive. Company pension plans can continue to hold their equity portfolios, but eliminate the mismatch with their liabilities with a debt-for-equity swap. Consider a company with large pension liabilities, which are fixed in nominal terms and have long durations. The company could enter a swap that exchanged returns on a stock market index for a fixed interest rate. If the company (or its designated fund managers) is particularly good at managing the equity portfolio, the swap will allow the firm to retain that value added. In this way, it could eliminate the market risk of the portfolio but retain the value-adding risk of the superior fund-management performance. There is no shortage of potential counterparties for such a transaction; any professional investor seeking to increase its exposure to equity returns would be interested.

When the PBGC was created in 1974, it was argued that no private insurer could provide the kind of shortfall-risk insurance required by beneficiaries of private defined-benefit plans. If that was ever true, it certainly is no longer true today. In the 1980s, a whole new industry devoted to offering such risk-management products developed in the United States and has become a large global business. In this new financial environment it is enough for the government to provide the basic hedging instruments necessary for private-sector firms to fashion financial products to match the market exposures of pension plans.

9.5 POLICY RECOMMENDATIONS

I conclude with some recommendations for public policy:

1. To maintain a reliable pension safety net the government must require and enforce accurate and transparent reporting of the market value of liabilities and the assets backing them.
2. When retirement income is provided through individual investment accounts, it is essential that they carry a guarantee of a minimum level of income, wealth or rate of return provided by the firm managing the assets.
3. Careful attention must be paid to the degree of matching between the liabilities and the assets backing them. The greater the mismatch risk, the greater the required buffer and the more quickly a funding shortfall must be eliminated.
4. Government can help by providing default-free 'building block' securities to serve as hedges and to facilitate correct pricing of guarantees.
5. International risk sharing by means of swap contracts and similar market innovations can help to reinforce the pension safety net by providing a much wider and deeper global pool of risk capital to back pension promises.

NOTES

1. This is different from the situation in the Netherlands, where single-employer pension benefits are a liability of the pension trust rather than the sponsoring corporation. Corporations that sponsor pension plans in the Netherlands have therefore objected to accounting standards requiring them to recognize underfunded pension obligations in their balance sheets.
2. This section of the paper is based on Merton and Bodie (1992).
3. For a more complete development of the material in this section, see Bodie (1995).
4. Using expected shortfall as the measure of risk does not solve the problem. See Treussard (2005).
5. The reference here is to the option-pricing theory originally developed by Black and Scholes (1973), and Merton (1973). There is an extensive literature on using option-pricing models to estimate the value of financial guarantees. For a comprehensive list of references, see Merton and Bodie (1992).
6. Another way to state this is that the exercise price of the put equals the forward price of the underlying stock.
7. The put-call parity theorem for European options says that:

$$P + S = C + E\,e^{-rT},$$

   where P is the price of the put, S is the price of the underlying stock, C is the price of the corresponding call, E is the exercise price, and r is the risk-free interest rate. In our case: $E = Se^{rT}$. By substituting into the put-call parity relation we get $P = C$.
8. Note that P is *not* equal to the expected value of the shortfall. However, if risk-neutral probabilities are substituted for actual probabilities, then one arrives at P.

9. The Pension Protection Act of 2006, http://www.whitehouse.gov/news/releases/2006/08/20060817.html.
10. See Bodie and Merton (2002).

REFERENCES

Bodie, Z. (1995), 'On the risk of stocks in the long run', *Financial Analysts Journal*, **51**(3), 18–22.
Bodie, Z. and R.C. Merton, (2002), 'International pension swaps', *Journal of Pension Economics and Finance*, **1**(1), 77–83.
Merton, R.C. and Z. Bodie (1992), 'On the management of financial guarantees', *Financial Management*, **21**(4), 87–109.
Treussard, J. (2005), 'On the validity of risk measures over time', Boston University Working Paper.

Discussion of 'Pension guarantees, capital adequacy and international risk sharing'

Kees Koedijk

This chapter deals with a number of important issues regarding the sustainability of pension systems. It proposes to make these pension guarantees more explicit by applying contingent claims analysis. In addition it also describes how guarantees can be implemented more efficiently by using financial market instruments.

In many countries a shift from defined benefit to defined contribution is taking place. As a result risks are shifted towards the plan's participants. From the behavioural finance literature we know that individuals are only partly rational in making decisions regarding their pension wealth (Cronqvist and Thaler, 2004; Mitchell and Utkus, 2004). In addition, competition among pension product providers, both nationally and internationally, is likely to increase in the near future. As a result individuals will be faced with even more choices. Note that pensions are a typical 'experience good'; the consequences of choices can be evaluated only over a long term. Consequently, the reputation of pension product providers becomes crucial. Following a survey study, Van Dalen and Henkens (2006) report that the confidence in pension funds and insurers has increased in the Netherlands between 2004 and 2006. At the same time the confidence in the government has decreased. Koedijk, Slager and van Dalen (2007) suggest that a reason for this result might be that the goals and intentions of pension funds and insurers are perceived to be much more transparent than those of the government.

Pension guarantees provide the necessary framework in which consumers can be protected from making the wrong pension decisions, even though these guarantees may (partially) impair the discipline of the market. In order to set up a system of guarantees, Bodie proposes four requirements.

1. Setting standards for full funding, including prompt action when funding standards are violated; in the Dutch context this is included in the Financial Assessment Framework.

2. Set restrictions on matching the liabilities with the assets, which could be done by requiring that pension funds perform an assets and liabilities management (ALM) study.
3. Disclose information on a plan's assets and liabilities such that the guarantor's exposure to shortfall risk can be measured.
4. Set a premium that covers the guarantor's exposure to shortfall risk.

The chapter focuses mainly on determining the premium for shortfall risk. The guarantee can be interpreted as a contingent claim; if the assets fall below the level of the promised payments the guarantor has to pay this funding difference, otherwise no payments are allowed. The important insight that can be gained from this set-up is that it provides a way to calculate the fair value of the premium that the guarantor should obtain for providing the guarantee. The familiar Black–Scholes framework can be applied to calculate this premium. Note that the contingent claims analysis presented in the chapter just scratches the surface of much broader applications of these methods to evaluate pension fund performance. See Kocken (2006) for a comprehensive overview. For example, indexation policies could be viewed as contingent claims as well. Many pension plans have the option to (partially) index the liabilities to consumer price developments. The chapter is completely silent about this, but when providing guarantees to consumers indexation is crucial. As real liabilities cannot be directly replicated with traded financial market instruments, the valuation of these options has to be done in an incomplete market; see De Jong (2005).

In the case of the guarantor being a corporate sponsor, the impact of the associated pension plan's financial health directly influences the balance sheet of the sponsor as a result of the latest accounting standards. As Jin, Merton and Bodie (2006) show, this might have a substantial impact on the cost of capital. In the current chapter Bodie notes that corporate pension plans in the US and the UK are more and more following liability-driven investment (LDI) strategies to match the assets with the liabilities. Swap contracts can be used to implement these strategies. The market for swap contracts is large and, as a result, it is quite easy to manage specific investment risks. However, an important dimension Bodie misses in the chapter is that swap contracts are subject to credit risks. Given the probably large size of the notional value in a typical pension swap contract, the impact of a counterparty default could be disastrous for both the plan and its sponsor, if this credit risk is not recognized and managed well.

In summary, this chapter addresses some important issues regarding the sustainability of pension systems. The policy recommendations at the end of the chapter are very relevant to securing consumer protection in pension systems all around the world. However, as discussed above, the analysis is incomplete and should be extended in a number of interesting and much-needed dimensions.

REFERENCES

Black, F. and M. Scholes (1973), 'The pricing of options and corporate liabilities', *Journal of Political Economy*, **81**, 637–659.

Cronqvist, H. and R. Thaler (2004), 'Design choices in privatized social security systems: learning from the Swedish experience', *American Economic Review*, **94**(2), 424–8.

De Jong, F. (2005), 'Valuation of pension liabilities in incomplete markets', Netspar Discussion paper, no. 2005-024.

Jin, L., R.C. Merton and Z. Bodie (2006), 'Do a firm's equity returns reflect the risk of its pension plan?', *Journal of Financial Economics*, **81**, 1–26.

Kocken, Th. (2006), 'Curious contracts: pension fund redesign for the future', S-Hertogenbosch: Tutein Nolthenius.

Koedijk, K., A. Slager and H. van Dalen (2007), 'Blinde vlekken van de denkers and doeners in de pensioensector', unpublished manauscript, in Dutch.

Merton, R. C. (1973), 'Rational theory of option pricing', *Bell Journal of Economics and Management Science*, **4**, 141–183.

Mitchell, Olivia S. and Stephen P. Utkus (2004), *Pension Design and Structure – New Lessons from Behavioral Finance*, Oxford: Oxford University Press.

Van Dalen, H. and K. Henkens (2006), 'Vertrouwen in pensioenfondsen: wie kennis vermeerdert' (in Dutch), *Economisch Statistische Berichten*, **91**, 616–618, in Dutch.

10. Frontiers in pension finance and reform: institutional innovation in the Netherlands[1]

Lans Bovenberg

10.1 INTRODUCTION

All over the world retirement systems are under severe pressure. In continental European countries, large pay-as-you-go schemes are vulnerable to aging. Occupational defined-benefit plans in which companies guarantee pension benefits are being phased out in the Anglo-Saxon world. The retreat of governments and companies as sponsors of pension systems calls for institutional innovation in pension insurance.

This chapter argues that stand-alone collective pension schemes in which participants share risk among themselves are an attractive third way between the extensive public pay-as-you-go (PAYG) schemes of continental Europe and the individual pension plans that are increasingly replacing defined-benefit plans in the Anglo-Saxon countries. Whereas the large pay-as-you-go systems are not sustainable in light of the demographic trends, individual pension plans suffer from financial illiteracy and associated marketing and other transaction costs.

The Dutch pension system contains strong elements that may be appealing to other countries as well. As the first pillar of the pension system, the public pay-as-you-go system focuses on poverty alleviation by offering a flat benefit. To maintain standard of living in retirement, the second, occupational, pillar supplements these minimum retirement benefits. This is accomplished through compulsory participation of workers in occupational pension schemes at a sectoral or company level (for the larger firms). Finally, individuals can voluntarily add to their occupational pensions through personal pension plans in the third pension pillar. This chapter maintains that Dutch occupational pension funds can evolve into stand-alone pension schemes that fit the needs of employees in a dynamic, innovative economy.

The rest of this chapter is structured as follows. Section 2 describes the challenges faced by the elaborate pay-as-you-go systems in continental

Europe and the occupational defined-benefit plans in the Anglo-Saxon countries. It argues that continental European countries should focus their public retirement systems on poverty alleviation by gradually reducing public benefits for those earning higher incomes. At the same time, occupational defined-benefit pension plans in the Anglo-Saxon countries, which offer guaranteed pensions, have become too expensive, while their pension promises often end up being empty. These plans should thus be phased out, as is indeed happening.

With governments and companies retreating as sponsors of old-age insurance, Section 3 discusses the need for institutional innovation to help individuals in financial planning over the life cycle. Individual pension plans suffer from transaction costs as households typically lack the basic financial knowledge and computational ability to implement complex financial plans. Collective stand-alone pension schemes that assist individuals in accessing financial markets and exploiting the potential of complex financial instruments appear to be an attractive vehicle to offer old-age pension insurance. To illustrate the potential of stand-alone collective pension schemes, Section 4 turns to the case of Dutch sectoral pension funds, which have been evolving in the direction of stand-alone pension funds. This section describes several further reforms that are needed to enhance the sustainability of these stand-alone pension schemes in view of various trends, such as aging and increased mobility of workers on transitional labour markets.

10.2   RETIREMENT SYSTEMS UNDER STRESS

10.2.1   Pay-as-you-go Pensions

Pay-as-you-go systems are vulnerable to low fertility rates

Pay-as-you-go schemes in continental European countries are especially vulnerable to lower fertility because they rely on human capital of the young to finance the pensions of older generations. As generations invest less in the human capital of the next generations by reducing fertility, they should invest more in financial capital. In other words, lower fertility calls for gradually shifting from pay-as-you-go financing to funded pension schemes (see Sinn, 2000).

The need for increased saving as fertility declines is closely related to the so-called 'intergenerational contract'. This implicit agreement between generations demands that each generation invests in the human capital of the next and is taken care of at the end of its life by the generations in which it has invested. Hence, each generation cares twice – once for the previous and once for the next generations – and is taken care of twice, as a child and in old age. This contract used to be implemented on a family level. In modern societies, with shrinking family size and an increasing number of families without children, it is increasingly socialized. On a macro level, however, it is still valid. If generations invest less in human capital of children, they ought to invest more in financial capital in order to maintain their standard of living in old age.

Focus pay-as-you-go systems on poverty alleviation

Most continental European countries, including Germany, France and Italy, have integrated the two main functions of pensions – poverty alleviation and old-age insurance – into a single comprehensive public pension system. These countries should consider focusing the public scheme on poverty alleviation by gradually reducing earnings-related PAYG benefits for those earning higher incomes.[2] This would yield a better balanced portfolio between funded and PAYG schemes, as workers with middle- and higher incomes substitute private, funded pensions for public PAYG benefits (see Table 10.1). Individuals would thus better diversify political and market risks.

The public scheme dealing with poverty alleviation is explicitly redistributive and should be financed from general tax revenues. Reliance on broad-based taxes paid by the entire population (rather than on payroll taxes) shifts the tax burden away from workers to those outside the labour force, including the retired. Including retirement benefits in the base of the progressive income tax would allow the tax system to continue to play an effective role in intra- and intergenerational risk sharing. In this way, the tax system can pool risks and shift these risks to those who can bear them best.

Table 10.1   Pension systems in various countries

| | Netherlands | Germany | France | Italy | Spain | Switzerland | UK | US |
			% of total retirement benefits					
PAYG public pensions	50	85	79	74	92	42	65	45
Occupational pensions	40	5	6	1	4	32	25	13
Personal pensions	10	10	15	25	4	26	10	42

Source: Börsch-Supan (2004).

Reducing PAYG benefits for, and increasing the tax payments by, the more affluent elderly is consistent with the trend towards a more heterogeneous older population. When PAYG schemes were established, the Second World War had impoverished the older generation. Since poverty was thus concentrated among the elderly, poverty alleviation called for transfers from the younger to the older generation. At present, in contrast, age is generally no longer a good indicator of poverty, as many elderly have accumulated substantial financial wealth and more risks have shifted to the beginning of the life cycle. Hence, information on age should increasingly be supplemented by other information (in particular, on incomes and family status) to identify those most in need of income support.

The currently retired generation has not been able to anticipate lower public PAYG benefits. Moreover, this generation cannot adjust easily because it has already depreciated its human capital. Accordingly, a strong case can be made for changing the rules of the game (that is, reducing PAYG benefits and increasing taxes on the elderly) only gradually.[3] Extensive grandfathering provisions protecting those who are currently old are expensive, however, and would eliminate benefits in terms of enhanced fiscal sustainability. Indeed, grandfathering implies that younger generations have to pay not only for their own private benefits but also for the public benefits of the currently old. The government thus faces a trade-off between flexibility and stability. To enhance confidence and trust in a stable social contract while at the same time facilitating timely adjustments, governments should announce as early as possible any prospective changes in the social contract. This would allow the large baby-boom generations to anticipate reduced public transfers in retirement by starting to build up more funded pensions.

10.2.2 Occupational Defined-benefit Systems

Occupational defined-benefit pensions are on the way out
Occupational defined-benefit plans in which companies guarantee fixed pension benefits by absorbing all financial market and demographic risks are on their way out. Several developments have led to the demise of defined-benefit plans. First of all, aging of the members[4] of the funds has expanded the obligations of the funds compared to the premium base (see Figure 10.1). This implies that unanticipated shocks in financial markets and longevity require larger changes in pension contributions in order to shield pension rights from these shocks. Guaranteed pension obligations have thus become more expensive, in that they result in more volatility in payments for the contributors. More generally, in an aging world economy that thrives on entrepreneurship and in which human capital becomes

increasingly scarce, the capacity for absorbing financial risk declines while the demand for risk taking increases. Whereas safe returns thus decline, rewards for risk taking increase. In any case, with the financial and actuarial risks of pension obligations starting to dominate those of their core business, companies no longer want to underwrite the risks of their pension funds. As an example, General Motors' pension liabilities are roughly equal to its market capitalization, at $12 billion. Indeed, rather than becoming an insurer outfit, a company such as GM wants to focus on its core business.

Another reason why defined-benefit plans with a company guarantee are going out of business is an increasingly competitive and dynamic world economy. More intense competition implies that companies exhibit shorter life spans and enjoy smaller rents with which they can guarantee defined-benefit pensions. In a dynamic economy, constant innovation results in substantial creative destruction. Firms can thus offer less security to their employees. Indeed, defined-benefit promises more and more often end up being empty. Workers become residual risk bearers because companies often are in trouble at the same time that the pension fund is experiencing financial distress. The probability that a firm

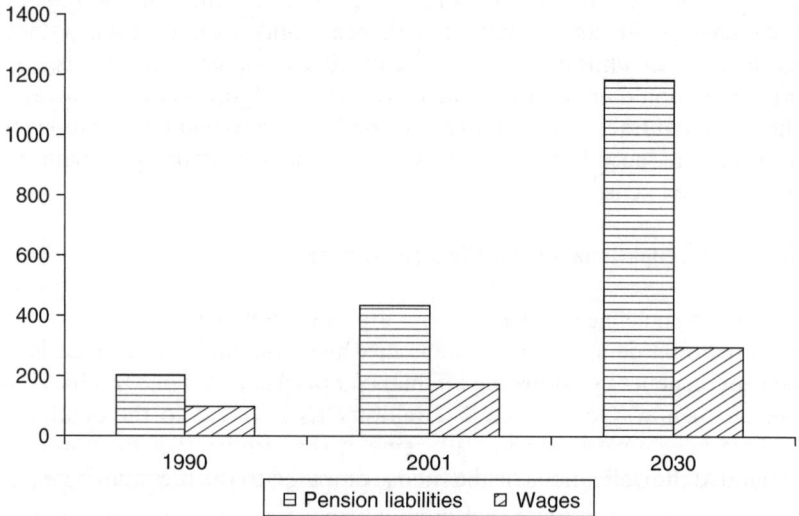

Source: CPB Document 67, the Hague,
www.cpb.nl/nl/pub/cpbreeksen/document/67/doc67.pdf.

Figure 10.1   Liabilities and premium base of Dutch pension funds, 1990–2030

will experience periods of financial stress during the long horizon of the pension funding is substantial, especially in sectors facing intense international competition. The increased bankruptcy risk of sponsoring companies in a dynamic, more competitive economy implies that workers with defined-benefit claims are saddled with the substantial credit risk of the company for which they work. Hence, the workers are exposed to the risk of losing not only their job but also part of their pension if the company they work for cannot stand the competition. They tie their fate to the firm as regards not only their human capital but also their pension rights.

New accounting rules (FRS 17/IAS 19/FAS 87) provide another stimulus for companies to get out of the pension insurance business. These new accounting regulations disclose pension risks assumed by companies, thereby enhancing transparency. Moreover, solvency regulations force pension funds to mark their obligations to market. This enhances market discipline and facilitates better risk management. Most importantly, it enhances transparency by revealing the substantial costs of defined-benefit obligations. Indeed, ad hoc actuarial rules for discounting pension obligations have in the past led to mispricing of pension guarantees.

The demise of defined-benefit plans can be welcomed
The demise of occupational defined-benefit pension plans can be welcomed for several reasons. First of all, to better diversify risks (credit risks, in particular), workers should invest their pension saving in the capital market rather than in the firm for which they work. Another reason why the decline of occupational defined-benefit schemes may be a blessing rather than a curse is that occupational defined-benefit plans often tend to suffer from conflicts of interest between the shareholders of the firm and the members of the pension fund. Among other things, it is often not quite clear to whom the surplus in the fund belongs and whose interest the fund should serve: the interests of the workers or the interests of the employer. Indeed, by changing its investment portfolio, the fund can redistribute resources between the various stakeholders of the fund. To illustrate, just like the other holders of corporate debt, the members of the fund have in fact written a put option to the shareholders of the firm. By encouraging the fund to invest more in risky assets, firms that face substantial bankruptcy risk can increase the value of this put option for the shareholders of the firm at the expense of the other stakeholders of the pension fund (see, for example, Kocken, 2006). In this way, the shareholders of the firm, who enjoy limited liability, can reap the upside of the returns on the assets in the pension fund but shift the risks of the downside to the members of the pension fund.

10.3 A THIRD WAY: COLLECTIVE STAND-ALONE PENSION FUNDS

10.3.1 Institutional Innovation called for

While old institutions are crumbling rapidly because governments and companies are withdrawing from their roles as risk sponsors, it will take considerable time to set up new retirement institutions. In the absence of new pension institutions that are better adapted to the modern knowledge economy in which we live, individuals will have a very hard time planning for their retirement.

Households typically lack the basic financial knowledge and computational ability to implement complex financial planning over the life cycle (see Lusardi and Mitchell, 2006; Van Rooij, Lusardi and Alessie, 2006). In addition to individuals, markets are also imperfect. For example, annuity markets in many countries are poorly developed as a result of not only the financial illiteracy of households, but also adverse selection due to heterogeneous longevity risk (see Finkelstein and Poterba, 2004). In addition, the distribution of individual pension plans involves high marketing and management costs and, as evidenced by recent episodes in the UK, a substantial risk of misselling.

10.3.2 Stand-alone Collective Pension Plans as a Third Way

Now that private and public sponsors are reducing risks on their balance sheets, collective pension plans based on capital funding offer an appealing third way between the purely individual DC plans in the Anglo-Saxon countries and the collective pay-as-you-go systems in the continental European countries. These collective pension plans allow individuals with scarce cognitive abilities to delegate complex saving and investment decisions to professionals. The latter assist individuals in properly exploiting their long-run investment horizon and in gaining access to complex investment strategies provided by modern financial markets. Mandatory participation combats adverse selection in annuity markets and reduces marketing and other transaction costs. Moreover, more sophisticated life-cycle investment by pension funds on behalf of long-term investors stabilizes financial markets and facilitates macroeconomic stability. Finally, these collective schemes can create risk-sharing contracts between generations that are not (yet) available in financial markets. To illustrate, they in effect offer deferred wage-indexed annuities, which are not yet traded on financial markets.

These pension funds stand alone in the sense that they lack a risk-absorbing sponsor in the form of the government or corporations. Pension funds thus face a hard budget constraint so that the members of the fund become the explicit risk bearers: they have to either share risks among themselves or shift risks to others by trading financial instruments on capital markets. An important advantage of stand-alone pension funds is that the ownership of the assets lies unambiguously with the members. Companies no longer have a claim on a possible surplus in the pension fund and are thus no longer tempted to increase the risk profile of their pension fund in order to maximize the return on the company's equity at the expense of the members' fiduciary interest.

10.4 STAND-ALONE PENSION FUNDS: INSTITUTIONAL INNOVATIONS

As the second pillar of the Dutch pension system, Dutch sectoral pension schemes have been evolving in the direction of stand-alone pension funds. This section describes this evolution and discusses the major remaining challenges facing the Dutch pension funds. Indeed, several developments call for further reforms in the way occupational pension funds operate. Maintaining the virtues of the Dutch pension system in a rapidly changing environment requires the timely response of occupational pension schemes and their stakeholders to these trends. Responding sooner rather than later will allow pension reforms to be implemented gradually rather than suddenly. This helps to maintain confidence in stable, credible long-term commitments.

10.4.1 Complete Contracts on Risk Sharing

Explicit agreements about how members share risks are becoming more important, for several reasons. First, being the residual risk bearers in pension plans, members should be informed about what risks they face so that they can take this into account in their own financial planning. Secondly, risks increase as pension funds become mature and members age (see subsection 10.2.2). The way these risks will be shared is thus increasingly important for the members. Thirdly, information and communication technology helps to define individual property rights without giving rise to excessive transaction costs.

Making explicit agreements about how risks are shared before the shocks actually materialize (that is, implementing state-contingent rules) also prevents costly political conflicts when the shocks hit.[5] These risk-sharing rules thus alleviate political risks and pension-related anxiety among workers. Moreover, sharing risks ex ante allows for contracts that are advantageous for all parties (that is, giving up resources in one contingency is traded with receiving resources in another contingency). After the shock (that is, ex post, when the contingency that actually materializes is known), in contrast, one of the parties has to give up resources. Insurance then becomes redistribution. Finally, explicit risk sharing on the basis of complete contracts avoids litigation, which is often the result of ambiguous, incomplete risk-sharing agreements, and which generates additional transaction costs.

In the Netherlands, pension funds have strived to make risk-sharing contracts more complete. Several large pension funds now employ policy ladders: rules that state explicitly how both the extent of indexation of pension rights and a possible recovery premium (levied on top of the cost-based premiums for the newly accumulated pension benefits) vary with the funding ratio. These policy ladders can be viewed as more complete contracts compared to the previous rather incomplete ones, which allowed for a great deal of discretion by the governing board. Indeed, in the past, funds would make only rather ambiguous statements that pension rights would be indexed as long as the financial position of the fund would allow it.

Further improvements are possible in making the policy ladder more complete, so that property rights on the assets are more clearly defined. To illustrate, the current policy ladders tend to be silent on what happens in case the funding rate (assets as a percentage of the nominal liabilities) falls below 105 per cent or rises above the level that is necessary to finance fully indexed pensions. Hence, it is still not clear who owns the so-called buffers (the capital in excess of the nominal liabilities).[6] Indeed, these buffers may help to raise the pensions of, especially, the younger members above the nominal obligations. However, depending on the decisions of governing board, these buffers may also be saved for the benefit of future generations or be used to cut premiums. The policy ladders are also incomplete in the sense that they do not specify investment decisions. By changing investment decisions, governing boards can redistribute resources among the various stakeholders of the fund, depending on the various options that are written by the stakeholders of the fund (see Hoevenaars and Ponds, 2006). Finally, policy ladders are at present no more than guidelines for the governing board. Since they have no legal status, they do not offer the same protection as legal property rights do.

10.4.2 Smaller Role of Recovery Premiums in Risk Sharing

Intergenerational risk sharing
Pension funds allow generations to share financial and human capital risk. In particular, by linking pension benefits to wages of workers, they allow retirees to share in the wage risks of workers. Moreover, in traditional final-pay schemes, young workers share in financial market risks faced by the

older members through so-called 'recovery premiums'. In the case of an adverse financial shock, for example, pension premiums are raised so as to contain the decline in pension benefits paid out to retirees, to protect the pension rights of the workers, and to reduce the resulting funding deficit. In a defined-benefit scheme with wage-indexed retirement benefits that carries mismatch risk because of investments in risk-bearing assets, the active participants (the workers who pay premiums into the fund) in effect borrow from the older, retired members by issuing non-tradable wage-indexed bonds to these older members, and use the funds to invest in the risk-bearing assets. In fact, the risky pension contributions produced by the mismatch risk allow the young to transform their human capital into an asset with exposure to financial risks (see Beetsma and Bovenberg, 2006).

Borrowing to buy risk-bearing assets

Indeed, the first-best asset allocation in simple models of life-cycle investment implies that one should borrow at the beginning of one's career and invest the proceeds in the stock market to acquire sufficient exposure to the equity market. Adverse selection and moral hazard, however, typically preclude borrowing against future labour income. In the absence of slavery, financial institutions cannot use human capital as a collateral to ensure that the loan is paid back. Compulsory participation in collective pension schemes can alleviate the adverse selection and moral hazard problems faced by financial intermediaries when young workers borrow against their human capital in order to gain the optimal exposure to priced equity risk. In effect, mandatory participation helps to secure the human capital of the younger generation as collateral, thereby limiting bankruptcy risk and thus relaxing the credit constraints faced by young generations. The welfare gains of being able to avoid the borrowing constraints completely have been estimated at around 3 per cent of certainty equivalent consumption during the life cycle (see Bovenberg et al., 2007).

In the past, borrowing-constrained young workers were willing to provide pension guarantees at low costs because their borrowing constraints prevented them from taking advantage of the risk premiums offered on capital markets. The workers offered the pension insurance at less than market price: they did not charge the equity premium for the risk they bore in the form of fluctuating recovery premiums.[7] Pension funds could therefore offer guaranteed pensions while at the same time benefiting from the equity-risk premium.

Going short before entering the workforce

In principle, one can share current shocks not only between currently living generations but also with generations that are not yet participating in the pension scheme when the shocks actually materialize. The pension fund actually buys risk-bearing assets on behalf of future generations by, in effect, borrowing from older generations. From an ex ante point of view, this internal trade is actually welfare improving. The reason is that financial shocks are shared even more broadly, namely not only with the currently participating generations but also with future generations (see Teulings and de Vries, 2006). Just like current young generations, the future generations were offering the pension insurance implicit in bonds they issued to older generations at less than the market price. Current generations thus benefited from the welfare gains generated by this risk taking of future generations.

Rising costs of recovery premiums as implicit taxes
Reliance on fluctuating recovery pension premiums to implement intergenerational risk is increasingly costly, however, in terms of adverse demand- and supply-side effects. This is especially so because the aging of the members of pension schemes demands greater changes in contributions to contain fluctuations in pension benefits because pension obligations expand compared to the premium base (see Figure 10.1 and subsection 10.2.2). Hence, the costs of volatile premiums are increasingly being recognized.

On the demand side
Fluctuating recovery pension premiums are likely to affect the demand side of the economy in a pro-cyclical fashion. In particular, in a recession, risk premiums tend to be high, while risk-free interest rates are typically low. High risk premiums reduce the value of risk-bearing assets (including equity). Moreover, with mark-to-market valuation, low interest rates imply that the value of the guaranteed liabilities is substantial, at least as long as the pension schemes have not hedged the interest rate risk through derivatives.[8] With the low funding rates that result for the low value of assets and the high value of liabilities, pension funds have to raise premiums in a recession, which hurts the cash flow of workers and exacerbates the recession. This 'pensions accelerator' mechanism is thus comparable to the 'financial accelerator' arising from worsening credit conditions (Bernanke and Gertler, 1989).

The supply side
Regarding the supply side, the fluctuating pension contributions distort the labour market. Indeed, higher pension contributions aimed at correcting funding deficits actually act as an implicit tax on labour. Workers will try to avoid paying this tax by working in the informal sector or moving to another sector. Indeed, with increasingly mobile labour in a transitional

labour market, employers may have to pay compensating wage differentials to attract workers to their sector if these workers are forced to pay off funding deficits of the sectoral pension scheme through recovery premiums. Workers can thus shift the burden of the implicit tax to others, such as consumers in non-tradable sectors or to shareholders in tradable sectors facing intense international competition. Firms thus bear the risks of the fund, even though they do not pay the statutory premiums. Indeed, underfunding can in effect be viewed as debt overhang that will depress economic activity in the sector (or firm) concerned.

Also political considerations yield the discontinuity principle
If active workers face substantial recovery premiums to correct the funding problems of pension schemes, they may vote with not only their feet (by seeking employment elsewhere or reducing labour supply) but also their voice. In particular, they may encourage the pension scheme to default on the implicit pension obligations to older workers and retirees: for example, by no longer indexing their pensions to inflation. By exacerbating competition on labour, capital and commodity markets, political economy considerations make current members vulnerable to large negative buffers. In other words, a pension contract that generates substantial debts for young and future generations may not be time-consistent, and thus may be neither credible nor sustainable.

This is why regulators adopt the so-called 'discontinuity principle': a pension scheme should be able to comply with its obligations also if, starting today, no new generations would be willing to enter the scheme. Recognizing that pension schemes cannot easily secure the human capital of future generations, this discontinuity principle limits the scope for risk sharing among non-overlapping generations. Pension schemes thus face a tension between, on the one hand, the discipline of capital funding and, on the other hand, the flexibility to allow risk sharing across non-overlapping generations.

As an alternative to pension funds, families and governments can share risks across non-overlapping generations. Governments implement this risk sharing through public debt policy, pay-as-you-go financed pensions, or publicly financed education. By issuing long-dated longevity bonds, for example, governments could allow present generations to share longevity risks with yet unborn generations (see also subsection 10.4.5). Compared to pension funds, the government is often in a better position to redistribute across individuals and to share macroeconomic risks across non-overlapping generations. The reason is that governments are endowed with tax power over a large pool of people: the nation as a whole. Collective pension schemes, in contrast, wield less effective tax power, even if workers in a sector are forced to participate in a sectoral scheme. This is because labour-market mobility within a country is growing and is greater than labour mobility between countries. The main drawback from intergenerational risk sharing through the public budget is that governments suffer from more political risks than pension funds do. Society thus faces a fundamental trade-off between facilitating intergenerational risk sharing, on the one hand, and containing political risks, on the other.

10.4.3   Restructuring Liabilities of Pension Funds

Limits of liability-driven investment

Some pension schemes contain the fluctuations in recovery premiums by restructuring portfolios to match the guarantees in defined-benefit pension plans, the so-called 'liability-driven investment'. Extensive liability-driven investment aimed at matching risk-free pension promises may endanger macroeconomic and financial stability and growth. As long-term safe interest rates are driven down by the demand of pension funds for bonds, guaranteed pension promises become ever more expensive, thereby requiring even more pension saving. This process may set in motion a deflationary spiral. At the same time, the supply of risk-taking capital may dry up, thereby harming innovation and growth. Moreover, additional demand for fixed-income assets may undermine fiscal discipline and widen global financial imbalances by simulating private borrowing.

A shortcoming of liability-driven investment with secure pension liabilities is that young individuals fail to take advantage of the risk premium of equities; buying guarantees is indeed quite expensive in terms of lost expected returns. By shifting financial risks to other parts of the financial system, pension funds cannot act as a stable long-term investor on behalf of participants and members with a long-run investment horizon.

Defined-benefit pension schemes should therefore restructure their liabilities rather than simply restructuring their assets to better match the existing liabilities. Collective pension schemes should thus think hard about determining the optimal liability structure from the point of view of the members, now that sponsors and participants are less willing or able to guarantee benefits at low implicit prices. As a direct consequence, the price for guaranteed retirement benefits has increased. It has thus become more attractive to have more risky pension rights, which suggests the possibility of a liability swap away from secure claims to equity-type claims. Members can thus continue to take advantage of the price of risk, which tends to increase as a consequence of aging (see subsection 10.2.2). The pension fund therefore does not have to shed all risk to capital markets, but can absorb this risk through more flexible liabilities.

Dutch pension funds

The largest Dutch pension schemes have moved away from final-pay schemes to career-average schemes with conditional indexation of nominal pension rights. Pension schemes have thus made the indexation of not only the pension rights of the already retired members but also the pension rights of the active members conditional on the financial performance of the pension fund. Younger workers share in financial market risk through not only recovery pension premiums but also their pension rights. As a result of these reforms, the active working population absorbs more risks in terms of their pension rights than in terms of recovery premiums. In the case of a negative financial shock, for example, workers face not only higher pension contributions but also a lower real value of their pension rights. Hence, more risks are borne in terms of pension capital rather than human capital. Instead of younger workers, the older workers, who have accumulated most pension rights, are thus most exposed to current financial market risks.

Optimal risk sharing through pension rights

The current risk-sharing arrangements in the Dutch pension funds can be improved further. Efficient risk sharing implies that an adverse shock causes consumption of all agents to decline by the same percentage.[9] Risks are thus shared as broadly as possible. With permanent income determining consumption, everybody's wealth should thus decline by the same percentage after a negative shock. Efficient risk sharing is important because it allows an economy to take more risks without endangering macroeconomic stability. This boosts innovation and economic growth through entrepreneurship and experimentation.

The most important components of the aggregate wealth of individuals are pension wealth, housing wealth and human wealth (that is, the discounted value of future labour income). For younger workers, human wealth is the most important wealth component. For older members, in contrast, pension rights account for most of individual wealth. In fact, retirees have (almost) completely depreciated their human capital. Hence, in order to achieve the same relative change in overall wealth for all cohorts (as required by optimal risk sharing), the pension wealth of young cohorts should fluctuate more than that of older generations if a shock hits the pension funds. By adapting pension rights in this way, one can shift financial and demographic risks to younger generations without having to rely on the recovery premium instrument.[10] Whereas pension rights for younger generations are relatively uncertain (the system resembles a defined-contribution system), pension rights are less risky for the elderly. As individuals grow older, they thus transform their defined-contribution claims into defined-benefit claims.

Young agents bear risks through pension rights rather than volatile labour taxes

Having younger workers share in financial market risk through their pension rights rather than recovery pension premiums yields smaller adverse effects on supply and demand sides of the economy. As regards the supply side, intergenerational risk sharing does not distort labour incentives if pension rights rather than recovery pension contributions fluctuate with macro financial market and longevity risks. Intuitively, members cannot escape the ex post transfers to retirees by working less or by moving to another sector (including the informal sector). Debt overhang is excluded, as liabilities move together with assets. Funding deficits are thus excluded, so that workers are no longer taxed on their work effort. Indeed, members (those who have accumulated pension rights) rather than participants (those who pay contributions) are the residual risk bearers of the fund.

Also demand effects of pension risks are reduced. In particular, adverse financial shocks are not directly transmitted into the cash flow of workers. Rather, they are transferred into the 'paper' pension rights of (especially) young workers. In this way, the pension fund exploits the long 'recovery horizon' of these workers; these workers feature a long period during which they can undo negative effects on pension wealth by paying a somewhat higher contribution financed by lower consumption (see subsection 10.4.7) or by higher work effort (see subsection 10.4.6).

Long recovery horizon benefits macroeconomic stability

Exploiting the long horizon of young workers to buffer shocks enhances macroeconomic stabilization. Indeed, the marginal saving propensity out of pension wealth is smallest for young households exhibiting long horizons and substantial human capital. In particular, it reduces the tension between facilitating macroeconomic stabilization and enforcing the discipline of markets, which tend to be cyclical. In particular, by letting the pension obligations to young workers fluctuate more with interest rates and risk premiums (and thus taking advantage of the long recovery horizon of young workers), we limit the pro-cyclical effects of the discipline of mark-to-market valuation. Young members should in fact be stable long-term investors who are in the best position to absorb financial-market volatility.

To contain pro-cyclical effects further, accumulated new pension rights may be relatively small in recessions (when interest rates tend to be low and pension rights are thus relatively expensive) and large in booms in order to avoid pro-cyclical variations in saving rates that would otherwise arise (that is, raising pension saving if interest rates fall, and decreasing savings if interest rates rise).

Hard and soft obligations of pension funds

This hybrid system of both defined-contribution and defined-benefit elements can be viewed as a pension fund that has on the liability side of its balance sheet both *soft* equity claims (or *junior* claims) and *hard* debt claims (or *senior* claims). The active members who are not yet retired, and especially the young members who still have substantial human capital, hold most of the *soft* claims and are thus the actual residual risk bearers of the fund. Workers therefore are important owners of equity and the associated control rights. They thus control an important part of the economy's capital stock, albeit in a different way than Marx anticipated. The retired generations own more secure claims in the form of debt.[11] The young agents are in fact the owners of an insurance company that protects older members against old-age risks if the pension fund has not matched the guaranteed pension rights of the older generations on the capital market. In this way, young agents can go short and increase the exposure of their claims to risk. The claims on this insurance outfit are not traded on capital markets, but are assigned to agents depending on the nature of their work effort on the labour market.

Dutch pension funds already make a distinction between hard and soft claims. However, they grant the wrong hard guarantees to the wrong people. In particular, the hard rights (the guarantees) are defined in *nominal* rather than *real* terms. Hence, the Dutch pension system (and the pension rights of young agents with a longer investment horizon in particular) is vulnerable to inflation now that pension funds are tempted to match these nominal obligations with nominal assets.[12] Moreover, these hard rights are granted to all members, irrespective of their characteristics (such as age[13]). The solvency rules in the Dutch risk-based supervisory framework focus, in fact, on the hard rather than the soft pension rights, which typically involve the ambition of the pension funds to index pension rights to prices or even wages. Hence capital funding does not necessarily extend also to soft pension rights.

If the older generations were to hold most of the debt claims in accordance with the requirements for optimal intergenerational risk sharing, the duration of the debt-like obligations of the pension funds would fall. This would relieve some of the current pressure on the returns at the long end of the market for fixed income securities. Hence, rather than adding high duration fixed-income assets to meet the duration of their fixed-income promises, pension funds may want to reconsider the fixed-income promises to young members. Internal and external supervision should ensure solvency so that members who hold secure claims (mainly the old) are protected against bankruptcy. This supervision should thus ensure that the bond-like promises issued by the young members of the fund to the older members are in fact credible; the put option that the debt holders have actually written to the shareholders should not have to be exercised.

Optimal life-cycle investment
Individuals transforming their defined-contribution claims into defined-benefit claims as they grow older is consistent with optimal investment behaviour over the life cycle (see Bodie, Merton and Samuelson, 1992). Young agents invest more in risk-bearing assets because most of their wealth consists of less risky human capital.[14] As agents grow older, they move more into secure assets, which preferably are also protected against inflation (see Teulings and de Vries, 2006).

These arguments for diverging investment behaviour of young and old become even stronger with habit formation.[15] In that case, the young have more time to adjust their habits and thus should be able to take on more risk than the old. In any case, downward protection of the standard of living of the elderly, who have depreciated their human capital, thus goes together with more risky DC-type pensions for the young, who can exploit their human capital to buffer risks. This gives the young more upward potential so as to keep their pension costs within bounds. A hybrid system of both defined-contribution and defined-benefit elements thus emerges, involving risk sharing between young and old members.

Compared with an occupational pension scheme in which the sponsoring firm absorbs the risks, the young members take over the risk-bearing role of the sponsor (or the shareholders of the sponsoring firm) in a stand-alone pension scheme. Whereas younger members lose guarantees, they should be compensated by more upward potential. In other words, young workers may lose pension rights if the stock market turns bad, but in return accumulate more additional rights if financial markets perform well. This two-sided 'solidarity' of the young protecting the old in bad times and the young gaining more in good times serves the legitimacy of the pension system.[16]

10.4.4   Less Back-loading of the Accumulation of Benefits

Many pension plans are back-loaded. This means that most workers accumulate most of their pension rights at the end of their working career. In particular, the young pay the same price for a deferred annuity even though the money they contribute will be paid out later and thus can yield a higher overall return. This lack of market pricing implicit in the uniform pricing of deferred annuities implies that the young are taxed on their working effort, while the old are subsidized.

The back-loading of benefit accumulation belongs to an era in which a breadwinner worked his entire life in a full-time job at a single employer who took care of the pension risks for the employee. Back-loading starts to result in inequitable outcomes, however, in a transitional, more flexible labour market in which workers experience voluntary periods of (partial) time-outs from work or become self-employed during certain phases of their life course.[17] Lack of market pricing implicit in the uniform pricing of deferred annuities complicates free choice and free competition, and results in all kinds of distortions. To illustrate, it discourages people from becoming an entrepreneur later in life or from moving abroad. More generally, it inhibits the portability of pension rights if people engage in various transitions in the labour market.

Another reason why the back-loading of benefit accumulation becomes less attractive involves a shift of risk bearing. Sponsors (such as employers) are increasingly shifting pension risks to workers. To contain risks for elderly members, young workers have to absorb more risks (see subsection 10.4.3). To reward these younger workers for taking over the risk-bearing role of sponsors, they should (in expectation) collect more pension rights for the pension premium paid.[18]

The back-loading of benefit accumulation creates political risk for older workers by making the system vulnerable to individual systems (in other countries or other sectors, including self-employment) in which young workers can buy pension rights for the monetary value of their contributions (after the deduction of transaction costs). Indeed, the pension rights that middle-aged workers anticipate accumulating in the remaining working period (after subtracting the premiums that these workers will pay during the rest of their lives) are not backed by financial assets, but rather rely on the promise of young workers (or employers) to supplement the money put in by middle-aged workers. Burdening intergenerational risk sharing with predictable redistribution makes the pension system less robust: the pension scheme faces a larger discontinuity risk. In particular, younger agents may leave the system if they are confronted with substantial recovery premiums. Indeed, the implicit pay-as-you-go (PAYG) financing implicit in the back-loading of the financing of benefits makes the pension scheme less well funded (and thus more vulnerable to political risks) than appears from the official funding rate.[19]

Addressing the back-loading of benefit accumulation, and thus marking pension premiums to market (in the sense that the premium paid corresponds to the value of the additional pension rights accumulated), is difficult because it creates the familiar transitional burden of moving from PAYG to full funding. Possible solutions include using collective buffers or asking sponsors who want to get rid of the risk to pay a one-time fee for transferring these risks to their younger workers. In any case, a long transition

period will allow pension schemes gradually to implement two-sided solidarity between the young and the old.[20]

In order to contain distortions in transitional labour markets, our proposals in this subsection (reducing the back-loading of benefits) and the
previous one (absorbing shocks in terms of pension rights rather than
recovery premiums) in fact lead to marking to market the additional
pension rights that workers accumulate by paying contributions: workers
get back the monetary value of their contributions in the market value of
their pension rights. In this way, pension contributions become part of the
labour reward rather than being a tax or subsidy on work.[21] Additional
pension rights are priced actuarially fairly: they do not add to or subtract
from the wealth of the other stakeholders in the pension scheme.

10.4.5   Sharing Longevity Risk

Funded schemes are vulnerable to longevity risk
A longer life expectancy raises the length of the inactive period that needs
to be financed. Hence, increased longevity puts financial stress on not only
pay-as-you-go schemes but also funded pension schemes. In fact, if retirement ages do not adjust to higher life expectancy, funded pension schemes
are particularly vulnerable. The reason for this is that the longer life spent
in retirement calls for more financial saving, which depresses the return on
capital. This is bad news for funded pension schemes. Moreover, if commodities and services are not perfectly tradable, shifts in the real exchange
rate and real wages imply that the return on pension saving declines, even
in a small open economy that is perfectly integrated in world financial
markets. Intuitively, as the older, inactive generations become larger in
number compared with the active working generation, a tight labour
market raises real wages, thereby depressing the real value of the capital
that the older generations have accumulated.

Aging societies should not only raise financial saving through more
funded pension schemes but also increase investment in human capital so
as to protect long-run labour supply: aging challenges not only fiscal
budgets but also risk taking and labour supply. It thus calls for more accumulation, better maintenance and more intense use of human capital in
addition to fiscal discipline and additional private saving. Indeed, human
capital allows households to buffer more risks.

Internal trade of longevity risk
To prevent this stress on funded pension systems, longer life expectancy for
cohorts younger than 65 years of age must go together with a higher retirement age (or lower annual benefits) for the cohorts concerned if lower

mortality is associated with lower morbidity and thus more human capital. If these shocks materialize only at older ages at which the cohort has already depreciated its human capital, younger cohorts (who exhibit a longer horizon and more flexibility to adapt) should optimally share a larger part of these risks. A collective pension scheme can implement this particular way of sharing risks between generations. In particular, the pension fund can promise an annuity to retirees while at the same time making the pension rights of the active members conditional on the capital that remains available after meeting these obligations to the retirees. The pension fund then, in fact, issues longevity bonds on behalf of the active members to the retired members. In this way, pension funds actually create new non-tradable assets that are not yet available on financial markets.[22] Pension governance and pension supervision should ensure that these contracts between generations not only are beneficial ex ante but also can be enforced ex post (that is, after financial and human capital risks have materialized). Immediate and thus continuous adjustment of pension rights to developments in capital and labour markets can help in this respect.

Longevity bonds and indexing retirement age to longevity
In addition to stimulating financial innovation, liquid markets for longevity-indexed bonds would help to establish objective market prices for longevity risk. This would assist regulators and help pension funds in setting the terms of trade for internal risk trading between generations. Moreover, longevity bonds would allow members of a pension fund to trade, not only with other members in the same fund, but also with capital-market participants more generally. Indeed, there is a strong theoretical case for developing macro-markets for such contingent securities (see Shiller, 2003).

In theory, governments can be providers of longevity bonds, as they are in a good position to shift this risk onto future and younger generations. These generations may be able to absorb these risks best through a longer working life associated with more human-capital investment. Governments, however, already bear substantial longevity risk on their balance sheets through public pay-as-you-go systems. Indeed, governments are able to issue longevity bonds on behalf of younger and future generations only if they reduce their exposure to longevity risk by linking the age at which these generations first receive their public pension to life expectancy.

Also tax benefits for pension saving can be linked to life expectancy.[23] The rule of automatically linking public pensions and tax privileges to life expectancy avoids the political costs of discretionary decisions to limit eligibility to public pensions and tax benefits if longevity increases further. Agreeing on a risk-sharing rule ex ante also reduces the political risks associated with collective discretionary decision-making. Moreover, it allows individuals and firms to adapt gradually to a longer working life by better maintaining human capital and adjusting the organization of work. An increase in spending on disability pensions and unemployment benefits is thereby avoided.

Higher retirement age crucial for more investment in human capital
A higher effective retirement age when longevity increases is crucial, for several reasons. First of all, it maintains the return on funded pension systems by raising labour supply and thus containing the potential rise in the capital–labour ratio. It also raises the return on human capital by lengthening the horizon for investments in human capital. Moreover, longer and deeper involvement in paid employment allows people to exploit their longer life to reconcile the two ambitions of, first, investing in the next generation as a parent and, secondly, pursuing a fulfilling career in paid work in which one keeps learning and applying new technologies. A longer active working life facilitates greater flexibility in employment patterns over the course of life for men and women alike by loosening the link between age and career progression. This reduces career pressure at the biologically determined time when parents care for young children, thereby promoting gender equality, fertility and child development. Parents of young children can continue to invest in the human capital of their children without having to depreciate their own human capital. Rearing children thus becomes less costly in terms of depreciated human capital of the parents. In this way, countries escape a vicious circle of early retirement and lower fertility in which politically stronger older generations favour generous passive spending on pensions and healthcare at the expense of investments in the human capital of younger generations.

10.4.6   Labour-market Flexibility

Labour-market flexibility boosts risk taking and innovation
More flexible labour markets complement a longer and more flexible work life. Together with better maintained human capital, they allow the speed and extent of phased retirement to act as a buffer for absorbing aggregate financial market and aggregate longevity risks. In an actuarially neutral pension system, working one year longer (and thus receiving annuities one year later) tends to raise the annual pension by about 7 per cent. The speed and timing of retirement is thus a powerful instrument for absorbing risks.

Flexible labour market institutions should also enable parents of young children to easily enter, re-enter and remain in the labour market. With workers able to absorb risk, pension funds can continue to supply risk-bearing capital, thereby boosting innovation and growth. We thus prevent the vicious circle of a risk-shedding scenario in which inflexible labour markets make workers unwilling to bear risk, and pension funds invest mainly in low-risk government bonds, thereby crowding out productive investments (see Boeri et al., 2006).

More flexible labour markets for elderly workers
Allowing the speed and time of retirement to act as an instrument to buffer risk requires adjusting the implicit labour contract according to which workers are underpaid when young and overpaid later on. Indeed, increasing the retirement age at which the employer lays off the employee must not put undue strain on the employer. Employees should thus accept more wage flexibility over the life course (payment according to labour productivity: mark-to-market reward for labour) and internal flexibility in working practices (so as to protect their labour productivity at higher ages).

With a more flexible labour market for elderly workers, older workers bear less risk because they are less dependent on their firm surviving. The differences narrow between the *insiders* who are lucky enough to work for a surviving firm and the *outsiders* whose firms have not survived. Moreover, golden chains no longer tie older workers to their employer. This facilitates entrepreneurship and a more efficient allocation of labour. Indeed, workers can more easily transfer between different states in the labour market (such as entrepreneurship, full-time employment, part-time work, part-time retirement and so on).

Younger workers
More generally, more flexible labour markets with new, flexible career patterns should allow young households to bear more risks by allowing these households to vary their labour effort, depending on the shocks they have experienced throughout their lifetime. This requires European labour markets to become more inclusive so that workers do not have to be continuously full-time employed in order to enjoy a successful career.

New roles for employers
In such a transitional labour market, the role of employers thus shifts from a risk-bearing sponsor to, first, a facilitator of investments in human capital; secondly, an insurer of that human capital by protecting it; thirdly, the creator of flexible work arrangements that allow elderly workers to adjust the speed and time of retirement to the pension rights; and fourthly, the creator of flexible career path and workplaces that allow young parents to invest in the human capital of their children without having to depreciate their own human capital. Employers should attune work to the needs

of employees who want to remain employable in the face of substantial family obligations and rapid innovation (and thus creative destruction).

Homogeneous insurance pools
Employers may also assist in creating collective pools for old-age and other human capital insurances (such as disability and unemployment insurances) for their workers. By thus keeping the costs of these insurances under control, they improve their position on the labour market and reduce their wage costs. An important factor in determining the type of insurances and the optimal investments of the pension scheme is the type of human capital of the workers and the associated risks and possibilities to absorb risks by adjusting labour supply. This suggests that the pools should be homogeneous in terms of human capital. Moreover, the retirement plans should be closely integrated with human resource management (HRM) of the employers.

10.4.7   Increased Flexibility in Financial Planning

Optimal risk sharing requires flexible premiums
Flexibility in premium rates allows agents to bear more risks and thus to benefit more from the rewards to risk taking. Indeed, after an expected shock, it is optimal to adjust consumption levels during the rest of one's lifetime. In effect, this involves spreading the risks over the longest possible recovery period.[24] Consequently, if agents feature the same preferences with constant relative risk aversion, optimal risk sharing demands that everybody's consumption declines with the same percentage after a negative shock (over the remaining life time). This implies that the change in premium for the workers should be (as a percentage of the wage) equal to the relative fall in pension benefits paid to the retirees.[25]

Rigid premiums reduce welfare and risk taking
If the contribution rate is fixed a priori and does not respond to shocks, the part of wealth that is dedicated to pre-retirement consumption does not contribute to risk sharing. Indeed, consumption during the working life does not react to wealth shocks at all. Only the part of wealth that is dedicated to post-retirement consumption is exposed to stock-market shocks, which implies suboptimal risk exposure. Under plausible parameter values, the welfare loss (in terms of the level of certainty equivalent consumption during the entire adult life) of this individual defined-contribution plan is 6.1 per cent relative to the optimal risk sharing in which individual premiums can respond to shocks (see Table 10.2). Simulations also show that the increased ability to adjust consumption during the working life allows

Table 10.2   The welfare effects of various pension schemes (per cent)

	First best	DC	DB	No risk taking
Welfare loss compared to first best	0	6.1	5.2	9.1
Average percentage of assets invested in stocks	45	25	29	0
Optimal contribution level	—	19	—	21
Optimal benefit level	—	—	72	79

Notes: Computations are derived on the basis of the model of Teulings and de Vries (2006) and the model parameters are as follows: riskless interest rate 2 per cent, equity premium: 4 per cent, volatility of stock returns: 20 per cent, parameter of risk aversion: 5, rate of time preference: 2 per cent, duration of working period: 40 years, duration of retired period: 20 years.

for more risk taking. In particular, in a steady state, a pension scheme that optimally adjusts premiums and benefits to shocks can invest 45 per cent of its financial wealth in risk-bearing assets. In a pension scheme that fixes the premium at an optimal level of 19 per cent of wage income, in contrast, this portfolio share is cut almost by half, to 25 per cent.[26]

Individual-specific premiums
In order to contain the effects of shocks on pension benefits, pension schemes may thus levy individual-specific pension contributions, depending on the shocks that a specific individual has experienced throughout his or her lifetime. The pension scheme may thus have a substantial exposure to risk without making the pension benefits substantially more risky. The pension scheme may thus ask for a voluntary, individual increase in the premium after an agent has suffered several adverse shocks. Alternatively, it may set such an increase in the premium as a default. In that case, an individual can then always opt out of this premium increase. Giving the individual the option to pay supplementary premiums on top of the base premium requires these supplementary premiums to be close to actuarially fair. Indeed, this is another reason for marking-to-market the additional pension rights that are being accumulated by paying more contributions (see subsection 10.4.4).

Tailor-made policies and their costs
Allowing members to opt out of their default portfolio choice can further refine the system. Moreover, in setting the default portfolio, one can take into account other characteristics of members besides age, such as the

nature of human capital, the income level, the flexibility of retirement choices implied by the flexibility of the labour market for the elderly, and owner-occupied housing and its financing. To illustrate, agents with particularly risky human capital that is strongly correlated with financial market risks should invest less in risk-bearing assets (see Viceira, 2001). The same holds true for workers that are liquidity-constrained, face substantial idiosyncratic human capital risk, exhibit habit formation and do not exhibit much flexibility in their retirement choices and thus cannot use the speed and timing of retirement to absorb risks (see Bodie, Merton and Samuelson, 1992; Gollier, 2005). These individual financial planning solutions tend to become more important now that individual life cycles have become more heterogeneous and ICT allows for more tailor-made products. At the same time, the costs of more tailor-made features in collective schemes should be traded off against the associated additional transaction costs and the potential for adverse selection.

Pension funds as financial planners
Pension funds can become financial intermediaries that help individuals with their financial planning over the life cycle. In particular, they can advise workers in accumulating and insuring human and financial capital over the life cycle. This may give rise to competition issues, however, as the provider of collective retirement products has market power on the markets for individual products, like supplementary pensions, additional disability insurance, healthcare and other insurances, mortgages and so on. Public regulation may thus be necessary. For example, a digital infrastructure may have to be set up to facilitate the exchange of standardized financial information between various suppliers of financial services. The suppliers of collective retirement plans thus lose their monopoly on the information about the pension rights of an individual. Indeed, individuals themselves rather than the suppliers of financial services should be the owners of their own digital financial planning register. This creates the potential for more competition in the market for financial services, even though an individual is forced to participate in the collective pension plan of the sector in which he or she works. As regards the mandatory level of saving, competition on the wholesale rather than on the retail level is preferred. Hence, whereas participants and members have little freedom of choice, there is substantial competition on the wholesale level for asset management and other services (for example, on administration and IT).

Financial education
Pension funds can also offer financial education. Advice and education about financial and career planning is an important investment in the

human capital of workers, a service that can be especially appreciated by young workers. More freedom of choice will result in greater responsibility for one's choices – and people should be prepared for that. Better financial education would also allow an increasing fraction of the workforce to use individual pension plans in diversifying their pension portfolios.

Freedom of choice also clearly has its limits, however. In particular, mandatory collective pools for old-age and other insurances for those with similar types of human capital and associated risks reduce transaction costs and adverse selection. The associated insurance schemes should set sensible defaults for those workers who do not have the expertise or time to choose themselves.

10.4.8 Improved Pension Governance

Although restricting individual choice protects financially illiterate individuals with scarce cognitive abilities from making mistakes in complex intertemporal financial decisions under uncertainty, it does give rise to agency issues and problems associated with collective decision making. Governance arrangements should thus address principal–agent issues that arise if unsophisticated consumers delegate complex financial decisions to professionals. Members should have confidence that the trustees take delegated decisions in the interests of the members so that a certain lack of individual choice remains legitimate. In this connection, the non-profit character of pension funds organized as trusts can bolster the confidence of the participants and members that pension funds act in their interests. Indeed, the members themselves are the shareholders of the pension funds, which prevents a conflict of interest between policyholders and shareholders.

Making risk-sharing contracts more complete and limiting discretionary decision making can alleviate governance problems. Contracts will, however, always remain incomplete: for example, in specifying investment decisions over a long period. With incomplete contracts, governance rights should depend on residual risk taking. An important challenge is to adjust the governance structure to the newly emerging risk-sharing contracts in which members bear risks in stand-alone pension funds mainly in terms of their pension rights rather than in terms of recovery premiums. Rather than those who pay the premium (employers and/or employees as participants), the members of a pension fund (those who have pension rights) should have their interests represented in the governing board.[27] If members are residual risk bearers but social partners have a large say in the governing board, then social partners may be tempted to put pressure on the fund to set the price for new pension rights (that is, the pension contributions) below the market value for these additional rights. The current members then actually pay the associated implicit subsidy on the additional pension rights for participants.

Another challenge is to ensure that management of the funds is conducted in a professional manner. Pension fund trustees and supervisory bodies are not always well equipped to understand complex investment principles and regulations, and to monitor their fund managers adequately. Outside professionals can help in this respect. This calls for a two-tier governance structure for pension funds with, first, a supervisory board or board of trustees representing the interests of members and, second, a professional executive board to deal with the funds' daily operations. The board of trustees should be appointed by a meeting of members.

10.5   CONCLUSIONS

Several developments affect the future of old-age insurance. Most of these trends – aging, maturing pension funds, a knowledge economy that thrives on human capital and entrepreneurship, a more flexible labour market in which explicit and implicit taxes become more distortionary – yield two main implications. First, human capital will become scarcer compared to financial capital. Secondly (and relatedly), the capacity for absorbing financial risk will decline while the demand for risk taking increases. Whereas safe returns thus decline, risk premiums and rewards for investments in human capital increase. Two things therefore become more expensive: security and writing off human capital.

The key challenges for institutional innovation that are produced by these trends are as follows: first, to arrive at new, transparent risk-sharing arrangements; secondly, to stimulate the maintenance of human capital and the flexibility of the labour market so that human capital is exploited better and can more effectively serve as a buffer for absorbing risk; and, third, to better diversify the human capital and financial capital of workers so that emancipated workers become less dependent on the firm for which they work. Endowed with sufficient human and financial capital, adaptable individuals are empowered to embrace the non-verifiable, idiosyncratic risks associated with creative destruction in a dynamic competitive world economy. Making workers less dependent on their employer requires more employable workers through more general human capital, portability of pension rights and less back-loading of pension benefits (see subsection 10.4.4), and a shift from defined-benefit pension systems relying on sponsors to stand-alone pension schemes based on risk sharing through capital markets and intergenerational risk sharing (see subsection 10.3). Indeed, the two main new securities of workers are, first of all, their employability and the associated capability to adjust to shocks in labour and financial markets and, secondly, collective stand-alone pension funds with secure individual property rights and adequate defaults that help agents exploit modern capital markets to diversify their investments and engage in efficient financial planning during the life cycle.

While old institutions are crumbling rapidly because governments and companies are withdrawing from their roles as risk sponsors, considerable time will be needed to set up new retirement institutions. In the absence of new pension institutions that are better adapted to the modern knowledge economy in which we live, individuals will have a very hard time planning for their retirement. Indeed, more and more evidence emerges around the world suggesting that households by themselves cannot implement complex financial planning and must delegate these decisions to institutions.

Dutch pension funds have been evolving in the direction of stand-alone pension funds as an attractive third way between the extensive public pay-as-you-go schemes of continental Europe and the individual pension plans that are increasingly replacing defined-benefit plans in the Anglo-Saxon countries. Among other things, Dutch pension funds are striving to make the pension deal more explicit. Moreover, more risks are shifted toward the active working population, as the indexation of their rights is made conditional on the performance of the fund. In this way, more risk is absorbed in terms of accumulated pension rights rather than contributions. Finally, the introduction of individual life-course saving accounts allows workers to implement tailor-made solutions based on individual choice.

In the years to come, further gradual reforms will be required to make Dutch collective pension schemes sustainable in view of aging, a more transitional labour market, and more heterogeneous tastes and needs. In particular, contracts on risk sharing must be made more complete to define more clearly individual property rights; liabilities should be restructured so that young workers bear more risks in terms of their pension rights rather than recovery premiums; back-loading of benefit accumulation should be reduced; the retirement age should be linked to longevity while the labour-market for elderly workers becomes more flexible; individual-specific supplements should be integrated with collective savings; and pension governance should become more professional and adjusted to new risk-sharing contracts in which members rather than participants and employers are the residual risk bearers. Responding sooner rather than later will allow pension reforms to be implemented gradually rather than suddenly. Confidence in stable, credible long-term commitments will thus be maintained, thereby allowing the Dutch pension sector to keep its leading position in the world of pensions.

NOTES

1. The author would like to thank Roel Mehlkopf for valuable research assistance. He also received helpful comments on an earlier draft at the DNB-Netspar-IOPS conference on 'Frontiers in Pension Finance and Reform' in Amsterdam, March 22–23, 2007 and is particularly indebted to Ross Jones, who acted as a formal discussant during the conference.
2. A flat public pension may be preferred to means-tested public pensions because means-tested benefits may be stigmatizing. These latter benefits may also discourage saving. Finally, they may undercut the political support of the middle class for public pensions: targeted programmes for the poor may result in poor benefits.
3. Relative PAYG benefits can be reduced gradually by indexing benefits to prices rather than wages.
4. A *member* of a fund has pension claims on the fund. A *participant* in a scheme pays contributions, thereby accumulating pension rights.
5. In designing state-contingent rules, pension funds face a trade-off between commitment and flexibility. On the one hand, pension funds may want to create clarify ex ante how risks are shared, for the reasons described in the main text. On the other hand, funds may want to be left with some discretionary powers so that they can respond to unforeseen contingencies. This latter flexibility implicit in incomplete contracts requires, however, that participants trust the governing board to act in the fiduciary interests of the participants. This requires professional governance (see subsection 10.4.8 below).
6. The word *buffer* is in fact a misnomer. A positive buffer suggests that the fund owns assets in excess of its obligations, while it in fact signals merely that assets exceed the *nominal* obligations. The buffer thus includes the capital that is needed to index pensions for inflation. Hence, the pension fund may not have sufficient capital to cover all of its obligations (including the conditional obligation to index the benefits), even though the buffer is positive.
7. For constrained households that cannot freely access capital markets, the market value of assets can deviate from the shadow value as measured by marginal utility values. In particular, households that cannot borrow to acquire the optimal exposure to equity risk attach a larger shadow value to equity than the value on financial markets.
8. By protecting pension funds against low interest rates in an economic downturn, these derivatives may thus enhance macroeconomic stability, depending on how the ultimate risk bearers (to which these derivatives shift the risk) respond to the capital losses they incur.
9. This assumes that all agents feature the same constant relative risk aversion and that utility is time-separable and separable in consumption of commodities and leisure. More generally, optimal risk sharing implies that everybody's marginal utility changes with the same percentage after a shock hits. See Bohn (2005).
10. This assumes that pension wealth does not become negative to produce the required relative change in overall wealth. For young households, this may happen if shocks are adverse in the beginning of their working life. To prevent this happening, these households should buy call options to get the optimal exposure to stock market risk. If these instruments are not available, recovery premiums may be used to expose these households to equity risk, even though these premiums distort the labour market.
11. The retired generations may still find it optimal to have some exposure to stock market and longevity risk. Koijen, Nijman and Werker (2006) find that, with plausible parameter values, retired agents should hold 20 per cent of their pension wealth in equity. In fact, in the simplest model with homogeneous and constant relative risk aversion and no mean reversion of stock returns, all generations hold the same share of overall wealth in equity (see Bovenberg et al., 2007). Most of the equity is held by younger workers because they feature the longest remaining lifetime and are thus wealthiest.
12. For maturities of over 35 years, inflation risk is persistent and thus substantial over a long time horizon. Campbell and Viceira (2005) report that the annualized standard deviation of real returns on nominal bonds is as large as 8 per cent and exceeds that of stocks.

13. The ratio of soft to hard pension rights, however, is especially large for young partici-
    pants because of the long duration of their soft indexation claim in the fund.
14. A complication is that optimal investment behaviour may demand that young workers
    invest more than 100 per cent of their pension rights in equity. To allow young workers
    to acquire the optimal exposure to equity risk without running the risk of ending up with
    negative wealth, the pension fund can invest in call options on behalf of these workers.
    Alternatively, the pension fund may not match the obligations to older generations and
    thereby shift the mismatch risk to younger generations. If these risks erode the entire
    pension wealth of the younger generations, some limited recovery premiums on these
    generations may be necessary, even though these premiums distort the labour market
    (see subsection 10.4.2).
15. Loss-aversion preferences also strengthen these arguments (see Bernatzi and Thaler,
    1995). If agents exhibit loss aversion, the costs of risky investments rise less rapidly than
    the benefits of doing so (see Bovenberg et al., 2007). Hence, hard guarantees are rather
    expensive for young agents in view of their long time horizon. For older, loss-averse
    agents with shorter horizons, risk-bearing assets are less attractive.
16. Note that the risk trading between various participants can be based on objective
    market prices only if the underlying instruments are in fact traded on financial markets.
    To the extent that these instruments are not traded (as in the case for wage-indexed
    bonds or longevity bonds), the internal prices are subjective and may depend on the
    preferences, features and bargaining power of the trading partners. To the extent that
    participants do not have direct access to financial markets, shadow prices may differ
    from market prices. To illustrate, by allowing young workers with no collateral to
    borrow against their human capital so that these workers can invest in the stock market,
    the fund may be able to expropriate part of the premium on equity. The reason is that
    borrowing-constrained young workers require a reward for risk taking below the market
    price. See also footnote 8.
17. The transition from a final-pay to a career-average system (see subsection 10.4.3) implies
    increased back-loading. Under the final-pay system, the rights accumulated in the begin-
    ning of the career could become valuable if one experienced substantial wage increases
    during one's career. This is no longer the case under the career-average system.
18. The reforms proposed in subsection 10.4.3 and this subsection are also related in another
    way. In particular, young workers can absorb more risks in their pension rights if they
    accumulate more pension rights as a result of less back-loading.
19. This is another reason why the word *buffer* is a misnomer. In particular, the funding rate
    underestimates the implicit obligations to middle-aged workers who have in effect paid
    premiums in advance without having received the equivalent market value in pension
    claims. These workers expect to receive a subsidy from younger workers in the second
    half of their working life. In other words, they have an implicit claim on the pension fund
    that is not taken into account when computing the funding rate. Boeijen et al. (2006) esti-
    mate that the implicit obligation of PGGM (the Dutch healthcare sector pension fund)
    due to back-loading of benefit accumulation is in the order of 15 per cent of PGGM's
    current nominal obligations.
20. Another alternative is to extend the tax on youngsters and the subsidy on old workers
    from employees also to the self-employed. This alleviates the drawbacks of back-loading
    for domestic labour mobility. These explicit age-specific transfers could gradually be
    phased out as older workers get a stronger labour-market position.
21. The pension premium in the first, public pillar, in contrast, involves a tax element since
    the first pillar is aimed at fighting old-age poverty through intra- and intergenerational
    redistribution. Even if contributions are actuarially fair, they may still act like a tax if
    liquidity-constrained workers are forced to participate in pension saving.
22. If pension funds differ in their age composition, swaps between older and younger
    pension funds can in theory further facilitate this risk sharing. Alternatively, pension
    funds with many retirees may insure the longevity risk with insurance companies. In this
    way, the shareholders of the insurance company rather than the younger participants of
    the pension fund absorb the longevity risk. Moreover, insurance companies with many

life insurance products may be the most natural partner for this trade because these companies are short rather than long on longevity risk.

23. In fact, one can argue that all ages that are used to measure old age should be linked to longevity. In other words, one should measure old age from the end rather than the beginning of life.

24. The principle of smoothing shocks over the entire lifetime has other implications. With volatile, mean-reverting interest rates, for example, one should adjust the pension rights that are accumulated each year to the level of the interest rate. In this way, one avoids high pension premiums if additional pension rights are expensive owing to low interest rates. This also benefits macroeconomic stability, as aggregate saving does not rise in an economic downturn with low interest rates.

25. With habit formation, exploiting the long recovery horizon of the young becomes more important. Adjustment of short-run consumption levels then becomes more costly, so that most of the adjustment is postponed until habits have had time to adjust.

26. A defined-benefit scheme involves a welfare loss of 5.1 per cent with a portfolio share of 29 per cent in equity and an optimal fixed benefit level of 72 per cent of annual wage income. If the pension fund does not take risks at all, the welfare costs are 9.1 per cent (in terms of certainty equivalent consumption) compared with the 'first best', while the contribution level is fixed at 21 per cent.

27. Employers, however, are still stakeholders in the pension fund to which their workers belong. In particular, a well-functioning pension fund implies low insurance costs for the workers. This enhances the position of the employer on the labour market, thereby reducing wage costs.

REFERENCES

Beetsma, R.M.W.J. and A.L. Bovenberg (2006), 'Pension systems, intergenerational risk sharing and inflation', Netspar Discussion Paper, No. 2006-D020.

Bernanke, B. and M. Gertler (1989), 'Agency costs, net worth, and business fluctuations', *American Economic Review*, **79**(1), 14–31.

Bernatzi, S. and R. Thaler (1995), 'Myopic loss aversion and the equity premium puzzle', *Quarterly Journal of Economics*, **110**(1), 73–92.

Bodie, Z., R.C. Merton and W.F. Samuelson (1992), 'Labor supply flexibility and portfolio choice in a life-cycle model', *Journal of Economic Dynamics and Control*, **16**(3–4), 427–49.

Boeri, Tito, Lans Bovenberg, Benoît Coeuré and Andrew Roberts (2006), 'Dealing with the new giants: rethinking the role of pension funds', *Geneva Reports on the World Economy, CEPR and International Center for Monetary and Banking Studies*.

Bohn, Henning (2005), 'Who bears what risk? An intergenerational perspective', in David Blitzstein, Olivia S. Mitchell and Stephen P. Utkus (eds), *Restructuring Retirement Risks*, Oxford: Oxford University Press.

Börsch-Supan, A. (2004), 'Mind the gap: the effectiveness of incentives to boost retirement saving in Europe', *Mannheim Research Institute for the Economics of Aging*, Discussion Paper no. 52-04.

Bovenberg, A.L., R.S.J. Koijen, T.E. Nijman and C.N. Teulings (2007), 'Saving and investing over the life cycle and the role of collective pension funds', Netspar Panel Paper 1.

Campbell, J.Y. and L.M. Viceira (2005), 'The term structure of the risk–return trade-off', *Financial Analysts Journal*, **61**(1), 34–44.

Finkelstein, A. and J. Poterba (2004), 'Adverse selection in insurance markets: policyholder evidence from the United Kingdom annuity market', *Journal of Political Economy*, **112**(1), 183–208.

Gollier, C. (2005), 'Optimal portfolio management for individual pension plans', *CESifo Working Paper Series*, No. 1394.

Hoevenaars, R. and E. Ponds (2006), 'Valuation of intergenerational transfers in funded collective pension schemes', Netspar Discussion Paper, no. 2006-D019.

Kocken, Theo (2006), *Curious Contracts*, Uitgeverij, s-Hertogenbosch: Tutein Nolthenius (UTN Publishers).

Koijen, R.S.J., T.E. Nijman and B.J.M. Werker (2006), 'Optimal portfolio choice with annuitization', Netspar Discussion paper, no. 2006-D013.

Lusardi, A. and O.S. Mitchell (2006), 'Financial literacy and planning: implication for retirement wellbeing', *Dartmouth College and University of Pennsylvania*, January.

Rooij, M. van, A. Lusardi and R. Alessie (2006), 'Financial literacy and stock market participation', De Nederlandsche Bank, mimeo.

Shiller, R. (2003), *Macro markets: creating institutions for managing society's largest risks*, New York: Clarendon Press.

Sinn, H.W. (2000), 'Why a funded pension system is useful and why it is not useful', *International Tax and Public Finance*, **7**(4–5), 389–410.

Teulings, C.N. and C.G. de Vries (2006), 'Generational accounting, solidarity, and pension losses', *De Economist*, **154**(1), 63–83.

Viceira, L.M. (2001), 'Optimal portfolio choice for long-horizon investors with nontradable labor income', *Journal of Finance*, **56**(1), 433–70.

Discussion of 'Frontiers in pension finance and reform: institutional innovation in the Netherlands'

Ross Jones

Professor Bovenberg's comprehensive paper outlines the major problems facing pension systems and explores how collective pension schemes can optimally share financial and demographic market risks across generations where, it is argued, neither traditional defined benefit arrangements nor defined contribution funds can provide viable solutions.

Interestingly, Professor Bovenberg argues that the demise of defined benefits schemes can be welcomed. First, in investing their pension savings elsewhere, employees would be able to diversify better the credit risk they currently face in having their pension savings tied to their place of employment.[1] Secondly, the conflict of interest between shareholders and employees that may occur in relation to the ownership of a pension funds' surplus would disappear, along with the temptation to adopt a high-risk investment strategy to generate high returns and build up of surplus. It is difficult to reconcile this argument as the converse would hold true; employers would need to contribute more if the strategy failed and led to a funding deficit.

However, it may not be the case that the demise of DB schemes is desirable and inevitable. It would seem possible to establish and maintain sound defined benefit schemes that do not have the negative elements Professor Bovenberg describes. Firstly, in many jurisdictions, rules exist to ensure that pension funds are not invested in the firm in which the employee works. Secondly, rigorously applied funding and solvency rules further protect members from fall-out of employer failure. Thirdly, many of the conflict of interest issues between firm shareholders and pension fund members such as to whom any surplus in the fund belongs can and should be covered by an effective trust deed.

The chapter suggests that there is an incentive on the part of shareholders of the firm to gamble the assets of the pension fund because they can reap the upside of the returns while shifting the potential downside to members of the pension fund. Again, this outcome should not be possible if the governance of the pension fund requires the trustees of the fund to act in the interest of fund members rather than the employer.

The chapter does not see defined contribution funds as the best alternative to the traditional defined benefit schemes, citing lack of individual financial literacy and expertise, informational asymmetries and the inability to pool longevity risk as negative features of account-based arrangements.

Professor Bovenberg proposes a redesign of sectoral collective pension funds to achieve stand-alone institutions based on capital funding as a middle road between individual account based defined contribution funds and traditional defined benefit funds. However, he does not rely on the more usual hybrid DB–DC model that employs two principal solvency management tools, variations to contributions and indexation of all accrued liabilities. It seems that the model relies principally on variation to indexation rights of contributing members to control the funding position of pensioner members. As I understand the proposition, the funds would be basically defined contribution in nature, with pre-retirement rights accumulating from contributions and investment returns and hence relatively uncertain (particularly in relation to indexation rights). However, once the end pension benefit becomes payable it becomes less risky (as in a defined benefit situation). The pension benefit will be protected from financial shocks and longevity risk by the corpus of the whole fund. This protection will be achieved, not by additional contributions (or premiums) called for after a shock or on the basis of periodic actuarial review, but by the younger members of the fund having their pension rights adjusted downwards. The trade-off for this reduction in rights in bad times would be that these contributing members would accumulate increased rights if financial markets perform well.

The proposal appears attractive at first glance for the young contributing members who have time to build up their entitlements, and for those already retired with a pension benefit protected going forward. However, it appears to leave open the very real possibility of a 'double whammy' negative outcome for those close to retirement at the time of a financial shock – not only would this cohort be obliged to forgo entitlements to protect those already retired but when they get to retirement their benefit will be lower forever. The proposal would need to build in some form of a years-to-retirement scale in the adjustment of entitlements.

An essential ingredient in a design such as that proposed in the chapter is that there should be a clear understanding by all involved of how risks are to be shared in certain circumstances *before the event*, and Professor Bovenberg places strong emphasis on this point.

I have some difficulty with the way in which the proposal would work in a practical sense. The benefits gained when the individual reaches retirement are guaranteed. However, a contributor's accruing pension benefits before retirement age appear to fluctuate, for a number of reasons. These include the investment performance of each contributor's account in the plan and the overall obligations which the fund has to the current group of retired members. Therefore current contributors' pension rights appear to be the balancing item to maintain the overall solvency of the fund.

Given the high-level nature of this part of the chapter, I am not sure how these rights are accrued and varied according to the fluctuating experience of the fund over time, nor how such variations would be consistent with the objective of providing certainty before the event. I am also a little uncertain as to what an industry sector covers in the context of the chapter. It would seem that the number of industry sectors (and hence the number of plan participants) would be an important consideration in optimizing the ratio of retired members to contributing members, a relevant factor in the model.

The chapter argues that a government-run fund with similar characteristics would be subject to political risk, but suggests that the political risk of the proposed long-run intergenerational mandatory industry schemes is minor. I would think that any system which is authorized to mandate contributions and which promises security of a pension at retirement will also lead to government having no choice but to pick up the obligations if things go wrong. Consequently, I do not see the political risk of such a proposal being minor.

NOTE

1. If a fund is in deficit at the time of collapse of the employer–sponsor, the shortfall will be greater to the extent that fund assets were invested in the employer–sponsor.

11. Population aging, financial markets and monetary policy

Lucas Papademos

11.1 INTRODUCTION

The magnitude of the demographic changes unfolding in Europe poses substantial challenges for policy makers in virtually all areas and at both micro and macro levels. While this contribution cannot address all pertinent issues, it will focus on the key implications of population aging for the conduct of monetary policy and the development and functioning of financial markets. However, even this more focused subject requires the examination and assessment of an extensive set of potential effects and pertinent policy issues.

11.2 POPULATION AGING AND MONETARY POLICY: AN OVERVIEW

Population aging may have implications for monetary policy as a consequence of its possible effects on the economic and financial environment within which monetary policy is conducted. It can affect key features and the functioning of the real economy, as well as the structure and development of financial markets. More specifically, population aging can have a significant effect on the following:

a. long-term economic growth, by influencing the economy's potential growth rate and the equilibrium real rate of interest;
b. the dynamics of aggregate demand and the monetary policy transmission mechanism, by influencing the intertemporal allocation of saving and consumption, as well as the determination of asset prices and portfolio diversification;
c. the structure of financial markets and the role of different financial institutions in the intermediation process;

d. public finances, by the increasing expenditure related to public pension systems, most of which are based on the pay-as-you-go principle, and to public health and long-term care systems; and

e. international capital flows, to the extent that the pace of the aging process and the evolution of available investment opportunities differ significantly across countries.

Thus the potential impact of population aging on the structure and functioning of the economy and on the conduct of monetary policy could be substantial and far-reaching. At the same time, this impact is very gradual, fairly complex and highly uncertain. It is likely to become visible not within years, but rather over decades. The 'glacial' nature of these effects – to use a term coined by Charles Bean[1] – makes it difficult to link the long-term implications of population aging for the economy directly to the decisions taken by a central bank over a medium-term horizon. Moreover, the ultimate impact of population aging is conditional on the response of public authorities, the financial markets and the economic agents themselves.

In my presentation, I will examine in greater detail some of the potential effects of population aging on key macroeconomic variables and the monetary policy transmission mechanism and assess the implications of such effects for the conduct of monetary policy. I will also give an indication of the expected order of magnitude of some of these effects, while always keeping in mind the uncertainty and the conditionality surrounding any empirical estimates and the associated policy conclusions.

11.3   THE POTENTIAL IMPACT OF POPULATION AGING ON LONG-TERM GROWTH AND THE EQUILIBRIUM REAL INTEREST RATE

Let me first consider the implications of demographic change for two variables which are of particular relevance for policy-making, namely the economy's potential growth rate and the equilibrium 'risk-free' real interest rate. To explain why we should expect that exogenous demographic factors will, over time, exert considerable 'pressure' on key endogenous variables such as the potential growth rate and the equilibrium interest rate, I will point to three stylized demographic developments for the euro area derived from recent projections.[2] First, we are witnessing a marked slowdown in the growth rate of the working age population in Europe. In fact, from 2010, the working age population is expected to shrink. Secondly, life expectancy at birth is predicted to increase further in the future, rising from the current level of 78 years to around 83 years in 2050. Thirdly, the combination of these two developments (the reduced inflows into the labour force and the increased life expectancy) will result, ceteris paribus, in a steady increase in the old-age dependency ratio (which will rise from 26 per cent in 2006 to around 55 per cent in 2050). These developments will, indeed, result in significant changes to the macroeconomic landscape.

The effects of the expected demographic change on potential output growth over the long term cannot be predicted with precision. However, the direction of the impact is fairly clear (from first principles) and an initial estimate of its likely magnitude can be obtained if we assume that other determinants of potential growth remain unchanged. Let me illustrate this by reviewing a number of findings from a recently completed study by ECB colleagues, which is based on a comprehensive growth accounting framework. Real GDP growth can be decomposed into three determining factors: the rates of change of labour productivity, labour utilization and the working age population.[3] To generate concrete forward-looking scenarios, the study takes as a benchmark the average growth rates of these variables over the period 1995–2005. If we combine, in a first scenario, the projected likely evolution of working age population growth in the coming decades with the benchmark values for the growth rates of labour productivity and labour utilization, we find that potential output growth gradually declines, falling by nearly 1 percentage point by the year 2050.

Of course, it can – and, indeed, should – be argued that the trend growth rates of labour productivity and labour utilization are not going to remain unchanged, and that there is substantial scope for improvement in these two variables, which can be fostered through structural reforms. That said, to imagine that increases in the growth rates of labour productivity and labour utilization could entirely offset the negative contribution to potential growth by the projected decline in the working age population requires a high degree of optimism. To understand what this means in numerical terms, consider the following: in order to maintain potential output growth until 2050 at the current level of around 2 per cent, average labour productivity growth in the euro area would, ceteris paribus, have almost to double by the year 2030 from the benchmark value of 1 per cent to a level close to that recorded in the United States in the period 1995–2005, which was around 1.8 per cent. And such a significant average annual improvement in productivity would have to be achieved by an aging society, meaning that enhancing economic dynamism and innovation would represent a formidable challenge. Alternatively, if labour productivity growth were to remain at the benchmark value of 1 per cent, labour utilization growth would have to increase substantially from its benchmark value of 0.8 per cent by 2050. Although further significant improvements in labour utilization are certainly possible and desirable, there are natural limits which would be reached well before 2050 under such an (admittedly ambitious) scenario.[4]

Forward-looking growth projection exercises of this type are insightful and thought-provoking. However, I should stress that they do not capture adequately all general equilibrium interactions between the factors of production. In this respect, it is important to look at the interactions between these factors not only in the context of a closed economy, but also from an open economy perspective; that is, by examining the possible interactions between the euro area economy and the rest of the world. To illustrate this, let me review and assess some findings on the likely future path of the risk-free equilibrium interest rate, following a two-step approach which first focuses on a closed economy and then considers the issue in an open economy context.

Theoretical analyses of the likely impact of population aging on the real interest rate are often based on overlapping generations models, which have the advantage of being able to capture the effects of demographic changes and their impact on life-cycle savings in a concrete and transparent way. In the context of a closed economy, these models typically predict that over the next 25–50 years the expected demographic trend will result in a reduction of 50–100 basis points in the real interest rate.[5] This is a relatively broad range, which reflects the different assumptions made in the various studies regarding the likely effects that the slowdown in population growth and the increase in life expectancy will have on the capital–labour ratio and the saving rate, on the one hand, and on the potential shift toward funded pension systems, on the other hand.

Let me briefly elaborate on these consequences. First, a slowdown in working age population growth implies, all other things equal, that labour becomes scarcer than capital. This calls for a change in factor prices, as fewer people need to be 'equipped' with capital, and leads to an increase in the capital–labour ratio, resulting in a decrease in the real interest rate.[6] Secondly, an increase in life expectancy can reasonably be expected to increase the incentive to save, and this, ceteris paribus, also places downward pressure on the real interest rate. Thus the fact that different assumptions are made concerning the size of the likely impact of these two demographic trends on the real interest rate explains the wide range of predictions as regards the magnitude of that decline. Moreover, alternative hypotheses about the features and the design of future pension systems has significant implications for the predicted effects. The likely decline in the real interest rate will be larger in scenarios which assume, ceteris paribus, that reforms will result in a substantial shift towards funded pension systems, which will make the motive for additional savings particularly

strong. On the other hand, scenarios based on the assumption of an increase in the effective retirement age imply that the effects on the interest rate are mitigated because the profile of savings is less steep over the life cycle.

These type of models suggests that the long end of the yield curve could also experience a decline as a result of expectations of lower short-term interest rates in the future that are priced in the yields of long-term bonds. The magnitude of that impact will depend on the size of the expected decline in the equilibrium short-term real interest rate and on the extent to which financial markets form expectations about the effects of other factors and possible future policies which could moderate or even offset a decline in the equilibrium real rate stemming from the aging process. There is no clear-cut evidence as regards the magnitude of this impact, which can be presumed, at present, to be small and surrounded by a substantial degree of uncertainty.

This reasoning on the likely effects of aging on the equilibrium interest rate requires further qualification if one considers the issue from an open economy perspective. Demographic developments are not identical across major regions of the world. Two features are especially relevant in this respect. First, within the group of OECD countries, the effects of the aging process in Europe and, in particular, Japan are mitigated by a more benign aging outlook for the United States. Secondly, in most emerging market economies the phenomenon we refer to as 'aging' will not become an issue until some time in the future. These features should, in principle, mitigate the downward pressure on the real interest rate in Europe. In particular, open economy models suggest that capital should be flowing from developed economies (which have older populations and richer capital endowments, and where investment opportunities are relatively limited) to emerging market economies (where the population is younger, capital is scarcer and investment opportunities are relatively more abundant).

So much for the theory. What evidence is available from the world economy? It appears that capital is not exactly moving in the expected direction: we are currently observing a 'savings glut', which is originating mainly in Asia.[7] There are of course a number of factors that explain why this is the case. However, when we examine the demographic patterns, we find that some important emerging market economies, notably China, are not only growing very rapidly, but are also aging relatively rapidly, while their public pension systems are very inadequate or even non-existent. From this point of view, the pattern of international capital flows observed over the past few years could be partly explained by demographic developments, although specific exchange rate and trade policies have certainly affected these flows. Looking forward, while there is substantial scope for increased international factor mobility, I share the view that factor price differentials between the euro area and the rest of the world will not be entirely arbitraged away, either because of political barriers (which can restrict, in particular, the mobility of labour) or because of market-based risk concerns (which can impose limits on international capital flows across countries and regions). In conclusion, open economy considerations tend to mitigate, but do not entirely eliminate, the downward pressure of the aging process on the real interest rate discussed earlier.

The potential implications of aging for the economy's long-term growth and the equilibrium real interest rate that I have examined so far will of course affect the environment within which monetary policy operates. One important issue for policy makers is whether these effects, which imply gradual, but fundamental, changes to key aspects of the economy, will require any substantive change to the monetary policy strategy. I will address this issue with regard to the two key features of the ECB's policy strategy: its objective and analytical framework.

It is self-evident that the primary objective of the ECB's monetary policy to maintain price stability should not be affected by population aging. Indeed, I would argue that the pre-eminence of price stability as a policy goal of the central bank would be reinforced in an aging society because there is a greater need to ensure that the value of a growing proportion of wealth invested in nominal assets whose return is not likely to be indexed to inflation is not eroded by inflation.

Another issue that has been raised is whether the expected increase in the old-age dependency ratio and the wealth-to-income ratio might strengthen the case for the central bank to 'lean against the wind' in the face of asset price misalignments, because the welfare losses from boom-and-bust cycles in asset prices would presumably be larger in an aging society. If so, would this effectively imply a broadening of the central bank's objective? This is clearly not the case. However, this argument underscores the usefulness of the ECB's analytical framework, in which the results of the economic analysis, which focuses on identifying risks to price stability over the short to medium term, are cross-checked with the signals derived from the monetary analysis, which seeks to identify risks to price stability from a medium to longer-term perspective. This analytical framework allows the ECB to detect early warning signals about emerging asset price misalignments. More generally, it is also crucial that we continue to monitor and analyse carefully the way in which demographic forces, associated financial market developments and pertinent reforms could affect the monetary transmission mechanism over time, and in particular impact of aging on the functioning of financial markets. This is the subject on which I will now focus.

11.4 POPULATION AGING AND FINANCIAL MARKETS

In an aging society the relative importance of young and old people, in terms of size of those groups, changes in favour of the latter. Financial markets are affected by this shift, because these two groups of people have different saving and investment preferences and different financing needs. Consequently, they can be expected to make different use of financial markets and instruments. In economic theory, the well-known life-cycle hypothesis of saving suggests that individuals seek to smooth out consumption relative to their income over their lifetime. This implies that people accumulate savings during their working life and acquire assets so that, after they have retired, they can sell them, and thus dissave, in order to fund consumption. Moreover, older people can be expected to become more risk-averse as the time horizon of their investment shortens. These considerations raise three pertinent questions:

a. First, is the life-cycle hypothesis of saving supported by the empirical evidence in the euro area?
b. Secondly, if so, how would the implied changes in the aggregate saving pattern affect asset prices (such as bond, equity and real estate prices) in the context of an aging society?
c. Thirdly, what kind of changes to the financial intermediation process could we expect as a result of the differing financial requirements of a 'greyer' population?

With regard to the first question, a look at the evidence from households in the euro area shows that people do not actually seem to behave as postulated by the simple, stylized life-cycle hypothesis: in a number of euro area countries, old people tend to be net savers and even spend significantly less than working households.[8] That said, if we consider a more general specification of the life-cycle hypothesis, which takes into account the bequest motive, the existence of public social security systems and the fact that people live out of their pension after retirement, the implications of the generalized life-cycle theory are consistent with the facts. Pensions are, after all, equivalent to annuities stemming from rights accrued in the past, and in that sense, they are a form of wealth.[9] However, if the benefits of public pension systems were to be significantly reduced, people's behaviour might change, as they would have more of an incentive to increase their private savings during their working years in order to use them when they retire.

The life-cycle hypothesis of saving implies that an economy with an aging population will be characterized by a relatively high wealth-to-income ratio. A greater reliance on private savings and accumulation of wealth, following a pension reform, in order to sustain a certain consumption level and a longer life expectancy after retirement, would reinforce the effect of wealth on consumption. Therefore, the transmission of the effects of monetary policy on aggregate output and the price level via the wealth channel can be expected to become progressively more powerful as the baby-boom generation approaches retirement. The increasing significance of this channel will be gradual and its magnitude can only be ascertained empirically. At the same time, the bank-lending channel may become relatively less significant, as it tends to reflect the demand for credit by agents that are younger and with a lower level of wealth.

11.4.1   The Potential Impact of Aging on Asset Prices

To what extent and in what way do the increased saving of a diminishing group of younger people, and the greater dissaving of a growing group of pensioners influence asset prices? Two aspects are relevant and deserve particular attention in this respect: (a) whether, and to what extent, retired people can actually sell or mobilize the assets accumulated during their working years to finance their consumption during old age; and (b) whether, and to what extent, the inflow of a significant amount of funds into the pension fund industry will affect the prices of particular financial instruments, notably long-term bonds.

Are the assets accumulated by people of working age actually tradable after those people retire? This is a highly pertinent question, as the largest share of households' wealth in the euro area – around 60 per cent – is real estate. Of course, we should keep in mind that, in most cases, houses are often used to live in, which in turn makes the households' consumption pattern less dependent on the 'monetary value' of residential investment. Nevertheless, some recent studies suggest that investment risk in residential real estate is likely to increase over the coming 30 years as a consequence of population aging in the EU.[10] As a result of increased regional and cross-border movements of people, regional discrepancies in the real estate markets are correspondingly growing, among urban centres, rural areas and coastal areas. Against this background, large price swings cannot be ruled out in the longer term, in the event that a large number of retirees would like to sell their real estate property in a certain region.

But a potential mismatch of this type between buyers and sellers of assets in a domestic market could be mitigated by foreign investors, provided that the relevant assets were in fact internationally tradable. More generally, the more assets are internationally tradable, the smaller the impact of aging on asset prices will be, since demographic patterns and the age structures of populations differ across countries. Incidentally, it should be noted that there has been much attention to the possible impact of aging on the portfolio reallocations between bonds and stocks and very little on the related consequences for property prices.[11]

The second aspect I would like to address with regard to the impact of aging on asset prices concerns the way in which pension funds and institutional investors allocate the growing inflow of funds within their financial portfolios. Given the size of the funds under management, even small changes in the way they invest their portfolio and manage their liabilities could potentially have a significant impact on the price of assets in the financial markets. In particular, the price of long-term bonds, which determines the level of long-term interest rates, may increase because the potential demand for long-term bonds by institutional investors – and pension funds in particular – may be significantly higher than the outstanding supply of such bonds. This proposition has been broadly confirmed by recent analyses.

That said, the possible impact on bond prices of this excess demand for long-term bonds remains very hard to disentangle quantitatively from other factors.[12] Up until now, there is very limited empirical evidence that changes in institutional investors' asset allocation have exerted a significant impact on bond yields. However, in some cases – notably in the United Kingdom – there are some indications that long-term yields have declined partly as a consequence of regulatory developments which have affected the portfolio allocation of institutional investors.[13] In the short to medium run, it is difficult to foresee a sizable increase in the supply of long-term bonds. Over a longer horizon, however, governments, international institutions and other highly-rated entities could increase the issuance of long-term bonds. The net impact on long-term yields of these factors would be expected to become greater in the future, as the effects of regulatory policy reforms unfold in other countries and the importance of institutional investors increases. Moreover, this impact might be augmented by the additional and more general downward pressure on the long end of the yield curve stemming from the possible general decline in interest rates owing to population aging.

11.4.2 Aging and the Financial Intermediation Process

Let me now turn to some of the consequences of population aging for the financial intermediation process and the structure of financial systems more generally. We are already observing important changes in the role and functioning of the retirement savings industry. Confronted with population aging, governments are finding it increasingly difficult to maintain the entitlements of the existing public pension schemes. Many governments are moving in the direction of reducing benefits relative to contributions to public pension schemes, reducing the ratio of the post-retirement income to the net pre-retirement income. Faced with these changes or prospects, individuals will be increasingly supporting their old-age consumption via alternative pension plans. Thus it can be expected that a larger proportion of household savings will be placed in privately funded pension schemes and life insurance policies.[14] Accordingly, over the coming decades, a significant increase can be expected in the value of assets managed by the retirement savings industry, particularly in countries where this industry is less developed and there are underfunded public pension systems with defined benefits. The Netherlands is an exceptional case among the euro area countries in this respect, since in this country the pension fund industry is of a significant size.

As key financial intermediaries, banks will, of course, also be very much affected by population aging. What are the likely effects? Given the long-term nature of the effects of population aging and the wide range of possible counterbalancing forces, the answer to this question is highly tentative and should not be interpreted as a prediction. Demographic changes – through their impact on GDP and population growth rates – may result in a downward pressure on banks' intermediation ratios and to reduced demand for consumer credit and mortgages, lowering interest income. Banks will face incentives to move away from activities linked to liquidity and duration transformation and to increase revenue and value added per customer, for example by cross-selling non-bank financial products and focusing on services with higher added value. At the same time, banks face increased competition from other intermediaries and they might partly respond by offering new products tailored to 'senior citizens', for instance consumer loans, in order to finance increasing health and long-term personal care costs, and reverse mortgages, aimed at extracting value from real estate. Banks will also respond by searching for new markets. Such prospects are likely to foster the formation of large financial groups and the strengthening of cooperation between banks, insurance companies and mutual funds.

The blurring of boundaries between segments of the financial sectors (banks and other intermediaries) also has a number of regulatory implications because of the potential increase in cross-sector contagion. A number of regulatory policy reforms have been launched recently or are forthcoming in the pension and insurance sectors, partly triggered by the problems of underfunding in defined-benefit pension plans which emerged in recent years as a result of demographic changes.

11.5   IMPLICATIONS FOR CENTRAL BANK POLICY

What are the consequences of these developments for central bank policy? A first consequence is an increasing need to monitor carefully possible changes in the transmission of the effects of monetary policy particularly through the wealth channel, but also through the bank channel, in the light of the increasing importance of funded pension systems and private savings arrangements. As I indicated earlier, portfolio reallocations on the part of institutional investors could, at times, exert downward pressure on long-term yields that is not directly related to macroeconomic fundamentals or other structural factors. This, in turn, may lead to 'excessive' borrowing by the private sector and to temporary distortions in the allocation of resources. Another important policy issue is related to the increasing use by pension funds and insurance companies of novel, sophisticated and complex financial instruments to transfer risks on their portfolios to other market participants. Although this risk transfer entails benefits, it tends to complicate the assessment, by central banks and bank supervisors, of the outlook for financial stability, since it is becoming more difficult to keep track of the way the risks are actually distributed and the extent to which those ultimately bearing the risks are actually capable of doing so in situations of stress. How to address these financial stability concerns effectively is an important policy issue for central banks.

At the same time, taking into account the current and anticipated need for instruments capable of managing interest-rate, inflation and longevity risks, and possible demand–supply imbalances in financial markets other than the long-term bond market, policy makers have an important role in promoting the development and the efficient functioning of financial markets for the pooling and the transfer of risks. This task may also involve a more active role for government debt management offices which may promote the issuance of long-dated and inflation-linked bonds while taking decisions related to the management of the debt maturity of such bonds.

Lastly, I would also like to point to another issue from the perspective of the individual. The amount of risk borne by individual households depends on the design of pension schemes. Households' wealth is becoming more exposed to financial markets, and retirement income is subject to greater investment risk than before. This underscores the importance of fostering efforts to increase financial literacy among households, which – as survey evidence suggests – is limited, and it seems to be overestimated by the individuals themselves.[15]

11.6   CONCLUDING REMARKS

I have examined a fairly long list of issues pertaining to the potential effects of population aging on the real economy and the financial markets, and the possible implications of such effects for the conduct of monetary policy and the performance of other central bank tasks. I will not attempt to summarize the specific conclusions which have emerged from this examination. I would like, however, to stress a few general points.

Firstly, population aging could have implications for the monetary policy as a consequence of its possible effects both on the economy's aggregate supply and demand, and on the channels and dynamics of the monetary transmission mechanism, as also determined by the evolving structure of financial markets and the role of financial intermediaries. The aging process can affect both the long-term equilibrium values of key macroeconomic variables and important factors determining the dynamic response of the economy to shocks and policy actions.

Secondly, over an extended period of time, the cumulative effects of population aging could be significant and far-reaching, but the materialization of these effects is very gradual and their magnitude is surrounded by a high degree of uncertainty. Moreover, policy action (notably reforms in labour and product markets and in pension and health care systems) and the economic agents' responses to the expected demographic change and to the implementation of reforms will determine the ultimate impact of population aging on the real economy and financial markets.

Thirdly, another general conclusion is that the potential effects of population aging on the European economy should be mitigated as a result of the globalization of financial markets and the fact that demographic developments are not identical across major regions of the world.

Fourthly, with regard to the implications of population aging for the conduct of monetary policy, three points should be made:

- The effects of population aging on the real economy and the financial markets do not require any changes to the central bank's monetary policy strategy.
- The ECB's policy objective remains unaffected and, indeed, the primacy of price stability would be reinforced in an aging society to ensure that the value of a growing proportion of wealth invested in nominal assets whose return is not indexed to inflation is not eroded by inflation. It has been argued that the expected increase in the old-age dependency ratio and the wealth-to-income ratio could strengthen the case for 'leaning against asset price misalignments', as the welfare losses from boom-and-bust cycles in asset prices would

presumably be larger in an aging society. Such an argument does not imply the adoption of an additional policy objective, but rather underscores the usefulness of the ECB's strategy and analytical framework, which can help provide early warning signals about emerging asset–price misalignments.

- It is essential to monitor and analyse carefully the way in which demographic forces, associated financial market developments and pertinent reforms could affect the monetary transmission mechanism over time, as this will have implications for the conduct of monetary policy. More theoretical and empirical research is needed in order to enhance our understanding of these effects, to estimate their quantitative significance and to facilitate their monitoring.

My final point is more general but not less relevant for the conduct of monetary policy in an aging economy. There is an urgent need to continue to implement the appropriate reforms in labour and product markets as well as in pension and healthcare systems so as to counteract possible adverse effects of population aging on Europe's future growth and prosperity. Even though these effects will start to emerge over the next few decades, the reforms should be implemented sooner rather than later, because it will take a certain period of time before they achieve their full impact and because the political support for these reforms may diminish as the majority of voters approach the retirement age. Such reforms would also facilitate the conduct and enhance its effectiveness in preserving price stability and thus sustaining economic growth.

NOTES

1. See C. Bean (2004).
2. See A. Maddaloni, A. Musso, P. Rother, M. Ward-Warmedinger and T. Westermann (2006).
3. See A. Maddaloni et al. (2006).
4. However, it is worth emphasizing that the required improvements are smaller if one conducts the thought experiment of keeping the trend growth of output *per capita* in line with the benchmark values. That variable is also arguably more relevant from a welfare perspective.
5. For further details on the reasoning in this and the next paragraph, see, among others, D. Miles (1999), N. Batini, T. Callen and W. McKibbin (2006), P. Antolin, F. Gonand, C. de la Maisonneuve, J. Oliveira and K.Y. Yoo (2005), A. Börsch-Supan, A. Ludwig and J. K. Winter (2004), A. Börsch-Supan, F. Heiss, A. Ludwig and J. Winter (2004), E. Canton, C. van Ewijk and P.J.G. Tang (2003), A. De Serres, C. Giorno, P. Richardson, D. Turner and A. Vourc'h (1998), E. Kara and L.v. Thadden (2006), D. Krueger and A. Ludwig (2007).
6. The impact can be ambiguous, but most studies agree that capital will fall by less than labour and that, consequently, the capital–labour ratio, the crucial determinant of the interest rate in neoclassical growth models, will increase.

7.   See Ben S. Bernanke (2005).
8.   Incidentally, I would like to stress the need for more accurate and comparable data on household finance and consumption, especially in the euro area. The Eurosystem is currently evaluating the possibility of conducting a household finance and consumption survey in the euro area, and a network of experts has already been established in order to prepare a full proposal for such a survey.
9.   See, for example, A. Börsch-Supan and J.K. Winter (2001).
10. See chapter 2 in the ECB report *EU banking structures*, October 2006.
11. There is an extensive literature on the impact of demographic changes on stock prices. See, for example, J.M. Poterba (2004). For an empirical analysis of the impact in stock markets around the world, see A. Ang and A. Maddaloni (2005).
12. For an overview of pertinent studies, see the BIS report, 'Institutional investors, global savings and asset allocation', prepared by a working group established by the Committee on the Global Financial System, December 2006, page 24.
13. See I. Alexopoulou, F. Drudi and J. Scheithauer (2006).
14. For developments in the euro area, see ECB (2006a).
15. See 'Caveat investor', in *The Economist*, 12 January 2006.

REFERENCES

Alexopoulou, I., F. Drudi and J. Scheithauer (2006), 'What accounts for the low level of the term premium?', background paper for the BIS report *Institutional investors, global savings and asset allocation*, December.
Ang, A. and A. Maddaloni (2005), 'Do demographic changes affect risk premiums? Evidence from international data', *Journal of Business*, **78**(1), 341–79.
Antolin, P., F. Gonand, C. de la Maisonneuve, J. Oliveira and K.Y. Yoo (2005), 'The impact of aging on demand, factor markets and growth', OECD Economics Department Working Paper No. 420.
Batini, N., T. Callen and W. McKibbin (2006), 'The global impact of demographic change', IMF Working Paper No. 06/9.
Bean, C. (2004), 'Global demographic change: some implications for central banks', Overview Panel, Federal Reserve Bank of Kansas City Annual Symposium, Jackson Hole, Wyoming.
Bernanke, B.S. (2005), 'The global savings glut and the U.S. current account deficit', remarks at the Homer Jones Lecture, St Louis, Missouri, April.
Börsch-Supan, A. and J.K. Winter (2001), 'Population aging, savings behaviour and capital markets', NBER Working Paper No. 8561.
Börsch-Supan, A., A. Ludwig and J.K. Winter (2004), 'Aging, pension reform, and capital flows: a multi-country simulation model', University of Mannheim Discussion Paper No. 04-61.
Börsch-Supan, A., F. Heiss, A. Ludwig and J.K. Winter (2004), 'Pension reform, capital markets and the rate of return', *German Economic Review*, **4**(2), 151–81.
Canton, E., C. van Ewijk and P.J.G. Tang (2003), 'Population aging and international capital flows', European Network of Economic Policy Research Institutes, Occasional Paper No. 4.
De Serres, A., C. Giorno, P. Richardson, D. Turner and A. Vourc'h (1998), 'The macroeconomic implications of aging in a global context', OECD Economics Department Working Paper No. 193.
ECB (2006a), 'Demographic change in the euro area: projections and consequences', Monthly Bulletin, October.

ECB (2006b), 'The impact of aging on EU banks', EU banking structures, October.

Economist, The (2006), 'Caveat investor', 12 January.

Kara, E. and L.v. Thadden (2006), 'Monetary policy aspects of demographic changes', European Central Bank, mimeo.

Krueger, D. and A. Ludwig (2007), 'On the consequences of demographic change for rates of return to capital, and the distribution of wealth and welfare', *Journal of Monetary Economics*, **54**(1), 49–87.

Maddaloni, A., A. Musso, P. Rother, M. Ward-Warmedinger and T. Westermann (2006), 'Macroeconomic implications of demographic developments in the euro area', ECB Occasional Paper Series, No. 51, August.

Miles, D. (1999), 'Modelling the impact of demographic change upon the economy', *Economic Journal*, **109**(452), 1–36.

Poterba, J.M. (2004), 'Population aging and financial markets', paper presented at the conference *Global Demographic Change: Economic Impacts and Policy Challenges* organised by the Federal Reserve Bank of Kansas, Jackson Hole.

Panel discussions The importance of transparency and governance

Dirk Witteveen

Since we started exploring the frontiers in pension finance and pension reform, an astonishing number of scientific innovations and policy considerations have been put forward. One immediate conclusion is that a common understanding is arising in the pensions world on the techniques we should use – I am thinking about fair value accounting and the basic assumptions underlying investment strategies with respect to the trade-offs between risk and return. In this respect, Jeremy Gold and Raimond Maurer et al. show us how they are using these techniques to explore new ways of enterprise risk management and pension scheme funding.

However, another conclusion is that there are still open questions regarding pension plan design and the supervision of pension funds. Should we think of pensions in terms of investment or insurance, as Zvi Bodie claims? How do we strike the right balance between market powers, in which Jon Exley sees great virtue, and paternalistic interference by regulators? How to deal with cost issues and information asymmetries? David Blake makes these issues very concrete by presenting all the practical problems that surround the design of pension contracts. In this way we are getting closer to the right answers, but as Axel Börsch-Supan et al. argue, we are not even sure what the optimal age composition is of any workforce (including, for instance, that of the authors contributing to this volume).

The novel insights of this conference predominantly lie in the sphere of potential solutions. These can be found in different fields. Gregory Brunner et al. give an analysis of the way regulators around the world are reorganizing their supervisory approach to become more risk-based and thus more effective. Keith Ambachtsheer focuses on the question how value can be added by optimizing the design of pension delivery organizations. The virtues of economic science in general, and more specifically of government interference in the form of imposed guarantees and issuance of inflation linked bonds, are explained by Zvi Bodie. Finally, Lans Bovenberg puts the discussion in a broader perspective by elaborating on optimal pension plan design from a normative point of view. Finally, Lucas Papademos urged the need for appropriate labour market and product market reform.

With all these ideas in mind, we come to a panel discussion about the future direction of pension reform. Let us try to take stock of the key issues that will increase the potential for pension funds, governments and regulators to improve the efficiency and resilience of pension systems.

Looking forward, in my view, three topics stand out. First, transparency is vital to promote optimal pension planning. Indeed, the key objective of pension systems is to ensure that sufficient real resources are available at retirement. This is not self-evident. To start with, pay-as-you-go systems are highly exposed to the consequences of an aging society. With fewer workers relative to dependants, each worker's output will have to support a greater number of retired people. Given this growing imbalance, there is a welcome shift towards funded pension systems. Nowadays, these are usually designed as defined contribution schemes, which place substantial responsibilities and uncertainties on the shoulders of individual households. But, even in funded defined benefit pension schemes, beneficiaries bear significant risks. The 'perfect storm' over the period 2000 to 2002 highlighted the vulnerability of funded systems to adverse developments in financial markets. As a result, many companies have chosen to withdraw from bearing the residual risk of their defined benefit pension plans. In short, uncertainties in pension benefits have increased one way or the other. It is important for households to take this uncertainty into account when it comes to their own financial planning. As a consequence, there is a need for improving transparency through more timely and easy-to-understand customer information. Solange Berstein notes in this respect that simplicity goes hand-in-hand with effectiveness. It is quite a challenge to come up with a good format for customer information, as financial illiteracy is a global phenomenon. Or, as David Blake would phrase this, 50 per cent of the population does not know what 50 per cent means.

Secondly, also in my role as a director of a combined central bank and financial supervisor, we have to consider that adjustments to the pension system feed through into the overall economy. The level of pension contributions affects purchasing power and competitiveness, while macroeconomic developments influence the financial position of pension funds. These transmission channels also work the other way around. By way of example, when I announced on 12 September 2005 that the introduction of the new Dutch financial assessment framework for pension funds would be postponed by one year, long-term euro interest rates instantaneously increased by several basis points worldwide. That is what a supervisor in a small country can bring about. The largest pension fund in the world, the

Government Pension Investment Fund of Japan, with over $1 trillion of assets, currently has to operate under strict investment restrictions. What would happen to Japanese and global financial markets if this fund was given the freedom of investment policy of ABP and CalPERS overnight? In the pension debate, the macro dimension is often subordinated. Over the long term, however, broad-based policy choices must be made in which, at times, micro prudential interests are weighed against macroeconomic ones. One major constraint in all these respects is that a pension system is sustainable only if it has the continuous trust of the pension scheme members. The governance structure of pension funds is crucial in sustaining this.

Thirdly, there is growing agreement that traditional actuarial techniques are mispricing true pension costs and risks. If you discount a future pension liability at 6 per cent while market interest rates are 4 per cent, you clearly underestimate the true cost. Fair value reporting gives a market-consistent snapshot of the current financial condition of a pension fund. In this respect, mark-to-market valuation, in combination with risk-based solvency requirements, has already been fully implemented by Dutch law as the new financial yardstick for pension funds.

But fair value accounting is only one element in a balanced assessment, as pension issues require long-term continuity analyses as well. Since we are not in the business of fortune telling, we have to strengthen the analytical tools that help map out what the future of our pension systems may look like (especially through stochastic analyses). These should cover not only the probable but also the less probable (but not impossible) scenarios. Further theoretical progress is essential for that. And sometimes the reverse question should also be posed. If a certain approach does well in practice, how does it make sense in theory?

In sum, in the pension domain, practical and intellectual challenges abound.

The future direction of pension reform?

John Ashcroft

There are many directions in which pension reform will go and these will vary considerably from country to country. But the big trend we are seeing across most of the world is the recognition that purely voluntary pension saving is not a reliable solution to the aging of populations and people's growing expectations of a decent income in retirement. If the main public policy reason for pension saving is to reduce the ultimate burden on the taxpayer, it is essential that participation ratios are high among lower earners regardless of individual inertia, if not preference. If, as Jon Exley has argued, the most robust argument for employer-sponsored pensions is to tackle the free-rider problem, then they should be aimed at potential free-riders.

The response to these concerns has been the establishment of mandatory or quasi-mandatory pension systems that differ substantially from most longer established systems. Commonly, employees have to join one of a relatively small number of DC pension schemes which are licensed and fairly heavily regulated with a view to delivering a target level of benefits at retirement. These arrangements tend only to extend to the formal employment sector, leaving public policy makers with tricky issues relating to the informal sector – a further challenge for future pensions reform.

Much of the running in this development so far has been made in countries with less developed private pension systems which have needed to achieve an extensive level of private pension saving from a low base because they cannot afford universal state-funded provision at the level to which their citizens aspire. To a varying extent they also wish to replace unfunded state provision by market mechanisms. So we have seen interesting developments in Latin America, for example Chile and Mexico, East Asia, for example China, Hong Kong and Korea, and across much of Eastern Europe as well as Turkey.

There are fewer examples of mandatory or quasi-mandatory provision in the more developed world, and these have followed very different routes. The best known examples are Sweden and Australia, although the Dutch model could be seen as quasi-mandatory in those industries which require participation in a pension scheme. Reference has also been made at this conference to the planned introduction in the UK of a quasi-mandatory system (Personal Accounts) from 2012 (similar in many features to recent developments in New Zealand). As in the Netherlands, individuals will be able to opt out of the scheme, but employers will not be able to opt out of providing some kind of pension. Italy is also considering proposals for a mandatory system. It will be interesting to see how many more OECD countries go the same way.

While most of these models are defined contribution and hence put investment risks on the membership, there is also a public policy driver towards achieving adequate replacement rates in retirement. Reconciling these imperatives will be a challenge for governments and their regulators and supervisors. It is hard to see how mandatory DC provision can avoid being underpinned by some form of regulation to secure minimum rates of return.

These models may be very country-specific in their design but they are not necessarily inconsistent with the other key trend, the increasing globalization of labour and financial services markets. The large international players in financial services will be looking to participate in mandatory schemes which have the huge attraction of a relatively captive market, and in some cases may be able to compete with them. This could result in expectations of higher standards of governance, transparency and efficiency, which supervisors will need to act upon. There will be increasing pressure for a move towards risk-based regulation and supervision that replaces detailed rule-books with common principles applied consistently and fairly regardless of country of origin. The OECD principles of pensions regulation should provide a useful starting point for such a move.

With the continuing expansion in and complexity of private pensions, regulators and, in particular, supervisors, will be looking for risk-based approaches that improve efficiency and effectiveness. A regime that involves on-site inspection of every pension provider every year against a rigid check-list come what may is already hard to justify: when many of the providers' activities are based in other countries it may become impracticable.

The EU has already shown its commitment to breaking down barriers to facilitate cross-border provision. Its adoption, for instance, of the 'prudent person' principle for investment regulation provides a good example of replacing rules with principles. But I believe there is a role for pension supervisors to play by developing risk-based approaches. IOPS has made a start in drawing together experience in an attempt to distil some common principles. In particular, we have seen that the approach to regulating and supervising mandatory and voluntary pension systems is still somewhat different, but the IOPS/World Bank research into risk-based supervision shows that a risk-based approach can enable convergence. What is also clear, however, is that local circumstances do necessitate different supervisory responses and that flexibility of interpretation will be essential.

So, in summary, I think the major developments in pension reform will be (a) the continuing growth in mandatory and quasi-mandatory provision, usually DC but not necessarily pure DC; and (b) the move from rules to principles-based regulation and supervision, enabling common approaches to risk to be handled in a way that fits local circumstances but without impeding the development of global markets.

The supervision of pension funds in Europe

Henrik Bjerre-Nielsen

All European occupational pension funds should be covered by prudential regulation equivalent to Solvency II. I will deliver this message from three perspectives. The first is as recently retired Chair of the Committee of European Insurance and Occupational Pensions Supervisors (CEIOPS).

Pension contracts are a subset of financial contracts and hence share some common characteristics, including agency costs, which may be caused by either asymmetric information or asymmetric bargaining powers. Asymmetric information may provide the agent with the potential for risk shifting on credit-sensitive contracts and asymmetric bargaining powers may provide the agent with incomplete contracts, which he may use to serve his own interests.

Regulation and supervision of financial firms should mitigate agency costs and hence add value to financial contracts. Pension contracts are less subject to European regulation than most other types of financial contracts. They are mostly covered by national social or labour law or considered to be in the domain of the social partners. The exceptions are when pension contracts involve commitments from financial firms or from occupational pension funds with beneficiaries in several countries.

European prudential regulation and supervision of banking and securities firms has recently been substantially modernized by the implementation of Basel II rules. In a few years the same will apply for insurers as a result of Solvency II. It will include market-consistent valuation of assets and liabilities and risk-sensitive financial strength requirements. At this stage no decision has been taken as to whether and to what extent occupational pension funds should be covered by prudential regulation and supervision equivalent to Solvency II: that is, with regard to protection against risk shifting. However, that is probably not sustainable if European governments want to use occupational pension funds to meet the challenge of providing pensions to Europe's aging populations. Pension beneficiaries are likely to demand the same protection against agency costs as customers of other financial firms. Hence all occupational pension funds should be covered by prudential regulation and supervision equivalent to Solvency II.

Stricter prudential regulation and supervision will lead to lower options to default and hence lower market values of the shares issued by the firms, which are ultimately liable for financing the pension benefits. Major problems may therefore turn up in European countries where the true values of pension benefits may be far lower than their notional values owing to high values of the options to default of the issuers of these pension promises. However, transition periods may be extended and hence transition problems lowered by the creation of mandatory guarantee schemes in relevant countries.

The second perspective is from my position as Director General of the Danish FSA which is responsible for regulating and supervising all Danish financial firms. In Denmark we already have prudential regulation and supervision of insurers as well as occupational pension funds based on market-consistent valuation of assets and liabilities and risk-sensitive financial strength requirements: probably not as advanced as I hope that Solvency II will turn out to be – but not bad either.

My final perspective is as former economic adviser to the Danish Trade Union Movement. 25 years ago, only one-third of the Danish labour market was covered by occupational pension schemes. Today more than 80 per cent is covered by such schemes. Contribution rates are generally above 10 per cent – up from zero for a majority of workers. As an economic advisor to the Danish Trade Union Movement I was one of the very first supporters of that vision. I have spent a fair amount of my professional career being involved in setting up the system as part of the collective bargaining process. In my view the only reason why we were able to persuade workers and their representatives to defer wages is that we designed a system which gave them the necessary confidence that pension beneficiaries would get value for their money. One of the requirements in this respect was that occupational pension funds should be subject to proper regulation and supervision. In today's world, that includes prudential regulation and supervision equivalent to Solvency II.

Challenges for pension policies

Lans Bovenberg

Long-established institutions for insuring old-age risks are crumbling because governments and companies are stepping back from their roles as risk sponsors. These developments call for institutional innovation: how do we provide protection against old-age risks for people lacking the ability to implement complex financial planning over their life cycle?

This challenge of institutional innovation must be undertaken in an environment in which the costs of old-age insurance have become more transparent and are increasing due to low interest rates, increased longevity, substantial longevity risks, and rising healthcare and wage costs. These phenomena in part originate in aging and the associated scarcity of human capital. Aging also raises the price of old-age security by eroding the basis for absorbing risks, namely human capital.

Collective pools

I envision the following priorities for pension design in the coming decades: first of all, the creation of the appropriate mandatory collective pools for old-age and other insurances of human capital for individuals who feature similar types of human capital. These collective pools would reduce trans-action costs, combat adverse selection and set sensible defaults for workers.

Efficient risk sharing

Secondly, now that governments and companies are lowering the risk of their balance sheets by shifting these risks to pension funds, these latter funds should be more explicit about the allocation of risks and thus care-fully consider the optimal liability structure from the point of view of the beneficiaries. In this connection, the current Dutch system of nominal guarantees for all pension participants is clearly not optimal. First of all, it focuses on *nominal* rather than *real* guarantees, while retirees are inter-ested in the purchasing power of their pensions. Secondly, it provides these guarantees for everybody, irrespective of individual features such as age that determine an individual's capacity to bear financial-market risk. The

Dutch risk-based supervisory framework should accommodate a more sensible definition and distribution of pension liabilities.

Integrate individual and collective plans

Thirdly, regulation should reduce rather than increase the barriers between collective occupational plans and individual personal pension plans. Consumers want integrated advice and information about their financial planning. To illustrate, they want the flexibility to pay additional contributions voluntarily in case of adverse shocks. More generally, I anticipate and welcome financial innovation in the integration of pensions with, first, other insurances involving human capital or old age (such as disability insurance and healthcare insurance) and, secondly, the financing of owner-occupied housing.

To address possible competition issues between the providers of occupational and individual financial products, the financial sector should create a digital infrastructure to facilitate the exchange of standardized financial information between various financial institutions.

Professional governance

Fourthly, the governance of pension funds should reflect residual risk bearing now that employers are increasingly withdrawing as risk bearers. Hence, rather than only those who pay the premium (that is, employers and/or employees as participants), also the beneficiaries of a pension fund (that is, those who have pension rights) should have their interests represented in the governing board.

Another challenge is to ensure that management of the funds is conducted in a professional manner. Pension fund trustees and supervisory bodies are at present not always well equipped to understand complex investment principles and regulations, and to monitor their fund managers adequately. Financial experts should be in charge of pension funds and should be monitored by a professional supervisory board.

Issue indexed and longevity bonds

Fifth, the government could help pension funds and other financial institutions in pricing and trading risks by issuing longevity bonds in addition to wage- or price-indexed bonds with rather long maturities. This would allow financial institutions to hedge better not only longevity but also inflation and interest-rate risks in real annuities, now that corporations are no longer willing to absorb these risks.

A problem with the government issuing longevity bonds, however, is that the government itself is quite vulnerable to higher longevity through its own public pension obligations. If the government would reduce its exposure to longevity risks by linking the retirement age in public pensions to longevity, it would become a much more natural issuer of longevity bonds. This provides another argument in favour of an automatic link between longevity and the retirement age. Private pension plans could also implement such a link. In this way, they would face smaller longevity risks and would need longevity bonds mainly to reinsure their obligations to retired participants. Indeed, funded pension plans are just as vulnerable to longevity as public pay-as-you-go schemes are.

Retirement age as buffer and flexible labour market

Sixth, and related to this, the speed and time of retirement should act as another instrument for buffering risk. This requires adjusting the implicit labour contract according to which workers are underpaid when young and overpaid later on. Indeed, increasing the retirement age at which the employer lays off the employee must not put undue strain on the employer. Another advantage of this is that golden chains no longer tie older employees to their employer. This facilitates entrepreneurship and makes older workers less dependent on their job surviving.

Portability of human capital and pension rights

This brings me to the seventh priority: portability of pension rights. Making the worker less dependent on his or her employer is the next phase in the emancipation of the worker. This calls for less back-loading of pension rights in occupational pension plans, more attention to general employability and stand-alone pension funds in which beneficiaries do not bear the credit risk of the firm for which they work.

Conclusion

The greatest challenges for pension policies reside in labour – rather than financial markets – namely, longer and deeper involvement in paid employment. Indeed, aging calls not only for more fiscal discipline and additional private saving but, especially, for more accumulation, better maintenance and more intensive use of human capital and entrepreneurship.

Index

ABO (accumulated benefit obligation)
62
accounting 193, 195, 310
accounting rules 217, 263
accumulated benefit obligation (ABO)
62
actuarial cost method 63, 65
actuarial deficit 110, 111
actuarial loss 246–7
actuarial surplus 110, 111
actuarial techniques 310
adverse selection bias
  and defined contribution (DC)
    pension plans 132, 133, 151, 251
  and labour productivity in an aging
    society 94, 98
  and stand-alone collective pension
    plans 264, 267
age
  and civil servant pensions in Hesse,
    Germany 58–9, 60
  and cognitive abilities and
    intelligence 86, 87
  composition of labour force 83, 84
  deficit hypothesis 88
  and experience 85–6, 89–91, 92, 94,
    97
  and labour productivity 85, 97, 98
  see also labour productivity in an
    aging society
  and physical fitness 86, 97
  see also aging society
agency factors, in institutional theory
  219–20
agency factors in pension delivery
  'aligned interests' 234, 235, 240, 263
  and governance quality, financial
    implications 232–3
  hypothesis testing 223–7
  and ideal delivery 233–5
  in integrative investment theory
    (IIT) 222

and stand-alone collective pension
  plans 265
aging society
  and defined benefit (DB) pension
    plans 261–2
  and PAYG (pay-as-you-go) pension
    systems 3, 261, 309
  and stand-alone collective pension
    plans 268
  see also age; labour productivity in
    an aging society; longevity risk;
    longevity risk sharing; mortality
    rates; older workers; population
    aging in Europe; retirees
Akerlof, George 219–20
'aligned interests' 234, 235, 240–241,
  263
ALM (asset liability management) 82,
  178, 196
Almeida, H. 30, 40
Ambachtsheer, Keith P. 221, 222,
  227–8
annuitization, in defined contribution
  (DC) pension plan design 131–40,
  147–50, 161–2
annuity providers
  competition 239, 255, 282, 302, 317
  problem-solving in providing defined
    contribution (DC) pension
    plans 139–40
  problems in providing defined
    contribution (DC) pension
    plans 131–8
annuity rates, and risks in defined
  contribution (DC) pension plans
  132, 147, 148, 161, 163
APRA (Australian Prudential
  Regulation Authority) 180, 181,
  192, 196, 202–3
Asia 297
assembly lines, labour productivity 86,
  88–94, 97